THE FAMINE CAMPAIGN IN
SOUTHERN INDIA

THE FAMINE CAMPAIGN IN SOUTHERN INDIA

MADRAS and BOMBAY PRESIDENCIES
and PROVINCE of MYSORE

1876-1878

By

WILLIAM DIGBY

Vol. II

Published by

Gyan Publishing House
5, Ansari Road
Daryaganj, New Delhi-110002
Phone: 011-47034999, 9811692060
E-mail: books@gyanbooks.com

Distribution Network
gyanbooks.com
India, USA, Canada, UK, Australia, France

ISBN : 978-81-212-9800-1 (Set)
978-81-212-9798-1 (PB)
First Published, 1878

2nd Impression 2023

Printed at: Gyan Press, Delhi.

THE FAMINE CAMPAIGN IN SOUTHERN INDIA (Vol. II)
Author: WILLIAM DIGBY

Mr. C. A. Ainslie.   Mr. F. Howlandson.   Mr. Wm. Digby, *Hon. Sec.*   Col. Weldon.   Mr. W. W. Mussie.   Mr. R. G. Orr.
Very Rev. J. Colgan.   Mr. G. Thornhill, C.S.I.   Sir W. Robinson, K.C.S.I., *Chairman.*   Mr. G. A. Ballard.   Rev. J. M. Strachan, M.D.

MEMBERS OF THE EXECUTIVE COMMITTEE, INDIAN FAMINE RELIEF FUND.

THE

FAMINE CAMPAIGN IN SOUTHERN INDIA

(MADRAS AND BOMBAY PRESIDENCIES AND PROVINCE OF MYSORE)

1876-1878

BY

WILLIAM DIGBY

HONORARY SECRETARY INDIAN FAMINE RELIEF FUND

IN TWO VOLUMES

VOL. II.

1878

CONTENTS

OF

THE SECOND VOLUME.

———◆◆———

PRIVATE CHARITY.

CHAPTER I.

HINDUISM AND CHARITY.

PAGE

Charitable nature of Hindus—Comparison between English and Indian
pauperism—Will India need a poor law?—Problem of support of
pauper life in the East—Professional beggars—Native charity
being indiscriminate, much utterly wasteful—The Hindu family
system—Christianity and pauperism—Would the Christianism of
India render poor law inevitable?—Reasons for a belief in the
affirmative—How this may be avoided—English Church systems
unsuitable for India—Two courses open to the Indian Government
—Panaceas against famine 1-9

CHAPTER II.

INDIA HELPING HERSELF.

General effort prior to appeal to England—I. *Bombay*—Effort at Sho-
lapur—Normal poverty—Labour at the Morarjee Goculdass Mills
—Public meeting at a Parsee Baronet's house—Mode of relief
through selling grain without profit—Formation of the Deccan and
Khandeish committee—Meetings at Ahmednuggur and Poona—
Speech by Lord Mark Ker—The Sarvajanik Sabha—The Bombay
cattle saving fund — Mr. Morarjee Goculdass an Indian of the
right sort—First establishment in Sholapur of day nurseries—
Infantile dignity and independence—A comparison by a Native
Journal—A good Sunday's work—Inside a day nursery; food
distribution in the evening—Scenes on the roadside—Pilgrimage
over at eleven P.M.—Aid to distressed agriculturists—The Sarva-

PAGE

janik Sabha's distributing agencies—The Bombay anna fund—
The Maharaja Scindia's bounty—The Hon. Mr. Gibbs's depreciation
of private charity (11-26)—II. *Madras*—Private efforts in Madras
city in October–December, 1876—Generosity of doubtful value,
food being inferior—The town relief placed under police administration—Efforts in the large towns of the Presidency—Scheme of
the President of the Municipal Commission—Assisting Gosha
females—Voluntary taxation of rice traders at Cuddapah—Desire
to commit suicide without offending the Deity or the Rev. J.
Davies Thomas—Government moiety to private subscriptions—
Instructions to native officials by Mr. Pennington—Relief in a fitful
fashion (16-34)—III. *Mysore*—Private and Government operations
proceeding side by side 10-34

CHAPTER III.

THE APPEAL TO ENGLAND.

Meeting of the directors of the Monegar Choultry—Great suffering
among the high caste poor reported—Question referred to Government, and by Government passed on to Municipal Commission—
Subscriptions to be sought from the public—Mistake in agency employed—A desultory discussion—Fulfilling one's duty to the poor
—Formation of eight divisional committees—Proposal for an
appeal to England negatived—Prosecution of the idea by mover—
Resolution for submission to committee—Obstacles interposed—
Meeting held—Reasons urged for appealing to England—Requisition
to the Sheriff of Madras—Resolutions passed—Telegram to *The
Times*—Nomination of executive committee and other officials—
Draft appeal by the Bishop of Madras—The movement in England
hangs for want of a start—Meeting of executive committee—
Urgent appeal sent to Lord Mayor of London and several provincial
mayors—Initiation of the movement by Sir Thomas White—The
first 'cash' contribution—Subscriptions from the Royal family,
'Old Indians,' and others—Appointment of Mansion House committee—Response to the appeal in India—The good example of
Baroda—Deliberations of general committee as to objects of relief—
Definition of objects—Attempt to form local committees in the
Mofussil—Stoppage of proposed meeting in Calcutta—Misapprehen-
sions of Government of India—Indignation and excitement in
Madras—Act XVI. of 1877—An Act against humanitarian practice—The Viceroy's arrival at Madras—A conversation on the
railway platform—Lord Lytton and private charity—Defiant
attitude and messages of the executive committee—'Action of
Supreme Government unaccountable'—The question of private
charity forced upon the Viceroy and the Duke—Message to Lord
Mayor of London—The *Gazette of India Extraordinary*: collection
of private subscriptions—Unsatisfactory correspondence—Aid to
Bombay and Mysore—Appointment of delegates to distressed

PAGE
districts—Good work of relief committees—Usefulness of Sessions
Judges—Proportionate allotment of funds—Task of organisation
complete—Prompt distribution advocated—Prospects of the season
—Donation of 10,000 rs. from the Viceroy 35–83

CHAPTER IV.

THE COLLECTING COMMITTEES : THE MANSION HOUSE.

Simple procedure of the Mansion House committee—Telegrams from
Madras committee to London—Sympathy of subscribers—Letter
from Miss Florence Nightingale—Appeal to United Kingdom of
Mansion House committee—Sources of supply—Incidents of generosity—' Isn't the famine over yet, Auntie ? I think it is '—Money
received at the rate of 10,000l. per day—' A splendid instance of
national sympathy '—Letter from the Governor of Madras—Stoppage of subscriptions on November 5—Cordiality between collecting and disbursing committees 84–96

LANCASHIRE.

Eager response to appeal from Lancashire—Broadness of sympathy
—Letter from Mr. Steinthal—Practical views regarding prevention
of famines—Amount contributed—The Bolton and Blackburn
contributions—Letter from the Bishop of Manchester—A good
example by the employés of the Rhodes Printing Works—Suggestions from Blackburn 96–99

SCOTLAND.

Great interest in Edinburgh—Energetic efforts of Lord Napier and
Ettrick, and Dr. George Smith—Public meetings—Formation of
committee—Review of work done, with description of means used
—Amounts contributed by private charity in previous famines—
Glasgow and Greenock contributions 99–105

THE COLONIES.

Movement in Australia—Meetings at Sydney, Melbourne, Adelaide,
and elsewhere—Contribution per head of population—Great generosity of the Australian people—Incidents in collection in South
Australia—Largest individual donation from Victoria—Other
colonies contributing—Donation of 51l. from the Norfolk Islanders 105–109

CONTRIBUTIONS IN INDIA.

Donations from Native Princes—Regimental contributions . . 109

PRINCIPAL SUBSCRIPTIONS RECEIVED IN LONDON.

PAGE

Donations from the Royal family, wealthy Companies, &c.—Subscriptions from towns in Great Britain—The Colonies—Church and Chapel collections over 100*l*. 110-119

CHAPTER V.

THE DISTRIBUTING COMMITTEES: INCIDENTS IN THE WORK OF RELIEF.

Record of labours of local committees very voluminous—Mode of distribution adopted in Tripature and Uttengerry taluks--Copy of instructions to relief agents prepared by the Dindigul committee—Testimony of the Government of India to the good work done by the various committees—Nature of relief afforded : in Dindigul, in Coimbatore, taluk by taluk—Extortion by village officials discovered and checked in Trichinopoly--Interesting reports from relief agents in Kalastri—Decayed gentry in Tanjore—Distribution in Mysore—A page from a delegate's note book (F. Rowlandson)—Scenes by the wayside (Rev. J. Herrick)—Extreme wretchedness (F. Rowlandson)—A day's work by an honorary secretary (Rev. J. E. Clough)—Difficulties in distribution (Rev. E. Lewis)-- Taluk triumvirates (W.H. Glenny)—An audacious suggestion (F. Rowlandson)—Suffering among classes beyond the scope of Government operations (Dr. Cornish)—Horrors of the famine (W. Yorke)—Female nakedness (F. Rowlandson)—Insect pests in the fields—The patience of the people (E. Forster Webster)—Disappointments; gratitude (Rev. J. E. Clough)—Gratitude (Rev. T. P. Adolphus)—Extortion by village officials (W. H. Glenny)—Dislike to relief camps (F. Rowlandson)—The goodness of the poor towards each other (Dr. Cornish)—Practical Help (W. A. Howe)—Personal investigation of relief lists (J. Lee Warner)—The inadequacy of funds (1. W. Yorke, 2. J. Lee Warner)—A lively sense of gratitude (Dr. Cornish)—Absurd scenes (W. H. Glenny)—Unselfish children (F. Rowlandson)—A selfish reason (F. Rowlandson)—Typical cases of distress (Rev. J. M. Strachan)---Real charity by the taluk triumvirate (W. H. Glenny)—Evil of indiscriminate charity (W. H. Glenny)—Scene in a relief camp (Rev. J. H. Strachan)—From drought to deluge (J. Lee Warner) 120-164

THE 1-lb RATION.

CHAPTER I.

THE QUANTITY OF FOOD NECESSARY TO SUPPORT LIFE.

PAGE

Different opinions as to quantity necessary—The Behar experience
of 1873–4—The Duke of Argyll favouring the larger estimate—
Bombay arrangement of Professional and Civil Agency rates —
Madras Board of Revenue estimate—1½ lbs. of grain and a moiety
for condiments prescribed—Madras Government raise minimum to
1½ lbs. plus moiety—Argument by Mr. Price in favour of high
allowance of 2 lbs. per diem—Sir Richard Temple's proposal to
reduce the ration—Objections of the Madras Government—Adoption of the rate as an experiment 165–174

CHAPTER II.

THE CONFLICT BETWEEN THE DELEGATE AND DR. CORNISH.

Great outcry against the 1-lb. ration—*Protest by Dr. Cornish*—Statement of enquiries made in past years in India—Physiological
needs of the adult human body—Effect of insufficient food—Result of insufficient nutriment not immediately apparent—Difficulty
of recovering the starving—*Sir Richard Temple's reply*—The argument for economy pressed—Abstract scientific theories of little
use, as Indian populations have existed though neglecting them—
The practical question stated—The ration declared to be equal to
the work done on it—The ration intended for an individual, not
to be shared with non-workers—Preconceived physiological
theories derided—*Sir Richard Temple's further reply*—Result of
examining the 'Madras Manual of Hygiene'—Experience of soldiers alleged to favour reduced ration—Also the ration of the
British soldier in troop-ships—Dr. Cornish's motives com-
mended—*The Sanitary Commissioner's rejoinder*—Complaint in Dr.
Cornish's covering letter—The two courses before the Sanitary
Commissioner—The Delegate of 1877 contrasted with the Delegate
of 1873–4—Inconsistency proved—European experience not fully
trusted to—Indian enquiries available—Protest against experiments
on large bodies of people on works—Sudden changes and fluctuations in the *personnel* of gangs—Sunday wage and sustenance
for non-workers granted—The anticipated saving by new scheme
not probable—Results of careful experiment—Weighings indicate
much wasting—The scientific argument tested—General experience an unsafe guide—The dietary of native soldiers on
foreign service a mistake—Terrible sickness in the Burmese
wars—Mistake in the 'Madras Manual of Hygiene'—Half rations
and the result—Actual facts furnished by the famine—Effect of
privation on the people—Death-rate in Madras and other camps—

PAGE

Mortality in famine districts—Mortality in municipalities—Registered deaths—Two points of view: the health officials the commanding officers—*Short reply of Sir Richard Temple*—Aid to non-workers and the Sunday wage always contemplated—Sir Richard satisfied from personal investigation the reduced ration was sufficient—Seeing is believing—Distinction between people employed on works and in camps—If the ration proved insufficient Sir Richard ready to remove it—'Last words' by Dr. Cornish 175–210

CHAPTER III.

EVIDENCE *PRO ET CON* AS TO THE SUFFICIENCY OF THE RATION.

Consideration by the Madras authorities of the working of the reduced ration—Decision deferred for further enquiry and investigation—Orders for special care to be taken of people who were failing in condition—Discretion allowed to responsible officers—Reports on the ration; 1. W. H. Glenny; 2. Dr. Cornish; 3. Surgeon-Major Ross; 4. W. B. Oldham; 5. W. H. Glenny; 6. J. H. Master; 7. C. Raghava Rao; 8. Murugesem Mudaliyar; 9. Dr. Cornish; 10. Surgeon W. G. King; 11. F. J. Price; 12. R. S. Benson; 13. E. V. Beeby; 14. J. D. Gribble; 15. R. W. Barlow; 16. Dr. Cornish—A Bombay Journalist's opinion—*Surgeon-Major Townsend's Report*—History of the rations adopted in Madras—Question not to be decided on physiological grounds—Want of accurate information in India—Inspection of labourers on works at Adoni, Bellary, Cuddapah, and Vellore—Conclusion come to that the wage should not be raised—*Surgeon-Major Lyon's Memorandum*—Diet tables and food analyses—*Dr. Cornish's reply to Mr. Lyon*—Relation between weight and capacity for assimilating food—'Yond' Cassius has a lean and hungry look;'—Incorrect issues raised—Dietary difficulties in Madras jails—Condition of people subjected to slow starvation—Subsistence scale of diet perilously low—Public opinion opposed to continuance of low ration—Order of Madras Government raising the ration—*Evidence in favour of reduced ration*—Testimony of Bombay Officers; 1. R. E. Candy; 2. T. S. Hamilton; 3. A. F. Woodburn; 4. A. B. Fforde; 5. Apaji Raogi; 6. E. P. Robertson—Conclusion of Bombay Government that Professional and Civil Agency rates safe and sufficient. 211–246

CHAPTER IV.

THE QUESTION STILL TO BE SETTLED.

The two opinions held about sufficiency of 1-lb. ration—The question yet to be decided—Experience of the Poor Fund committee at

PAGE

Belgaum—A good day's work for a good day's wage—A parallel
with England—Sufficient wage from an economic point of view—
Sir Bartle Frere on the effects of privation on individuals—Famine
policy tested by proportion of deaths 247-252

APPENDIX A.

Contribution to *Times of India* on the result of an experiment with
reduced ration in Bombay prisons 253-256

APPENDIX B.

Correspondence between Dr. Cornish and Sir R. Christison on the
sufficiency of the Temple wage and ration 256-260

THE RAILWAYS.

Quantity of grain imported by sea—Conveyance to the distressed
districts—The Railways proved the saviour of Southern India—
Arrangements made for special traffic—The late Chairman of the
London and North Western Railway—His Grace's control of the
traffic—Dissatisfaction of the mercantile community—Statement
of the mercantile case—Increased price of grain owing to defective arrangements—What was expected in August 1877 of the
railways—Quantities of grain carried—Illustrative tabular returns—Railway extension an important feature in the famine
policy of the future 261-272

'FREE' TRADE IN FAMINE TIMES.

Government unable to profitably compete with private trade—Its
duty confined to making a good road, keeping an honest policeman, and finding the people means of purchasing . . . 273-278

RELIEF CAMPS.

A district's management of its famine problem—Coimbatore taken
as example—Preparations at the end of 1876—Road repairs and
sanitary improvement — Efforts of private charity at an early
stage—Closed camps; their drawbacks—Pressure upon Government officers—Practice adopted for relief purposes generally—
Luxuries preferred to necessaries—Relief camp imprisonment—

PAGE

The object and aims of a relief camp (as described in Mr. Elliott's
Famine Code)—Only cooked food given—Working of a camp—
Duties of officers in charge—*Narrative of Camp Mismanagement
by a Non-Official Gentleman*—A typical camp under native control—Bad feeding arrangements—A caste dispute—A day in
camp bad for the caste people but good for the remainder—Sham
applicants for relief—A village official caught pilfering—Loot of
provisions not given out—Cheating with corpses — European
supervision necessary in all camps — Quantity of food for sick
subject of much discussion—*Report of two Surgeons-General (Drs.
Gordon and G. Smith)*—A higher ration recommended—The
terrible mortality in camps—Evidence furnished by camps in (1)
Madras, (2) Salem, (3) North Arcot, (4) Cuddapah, (5) Bellary,
(6) Nellore, (7) Chingleput, (8) Kurnool—Nature of diseases in
camp—Chronic starvation a very deadly disease—A ludicrous
incident—Tables showing mortality in camps   .   .   . 279–316

VILLAGE RELIEF AND VILLAGE AGENCY.

The village relief system in Madras in August 1877—Variety and
intricacy of means to defraud—The fear of officials exhibited by
villagers—The inevitable consequence of trusting village officers—
Mr. R. Davidson on fraud and the impossibility of checking it—
The Board of Revenue anticipating fraud—Difficulty of proving
extortion—The money dole in villages—Close examination of
the subject by the Viceroy and his advisers—Some of the means
(sixteen) employed to defraud Government—Circumstances under
which the money dole can be fairly given—Principles of village
relief   317–329

MISCELLANEOUS.

(1) EMIGRATION.

Emigration as a panacea—Suggestion of the Marquis of Salisbury
and Sir Julius Vogel—Emigration ineffectual—British Burma as
a land of relief for Madras—Correspondence between the Burma
authorities, the Government of India, and the Madras Government—Failure of the Burma scheme—Emigration to Ceylon—
Principles on which it is carried out in normal times—Mr. Lee
Warner on emigration in 1877—The Ceylon Government wishing
emigration to be stopped—Reply of the Madras Government   331–350

(2) WEAVERS.

PAGE

How Indian famines affect artisans—Consideration of position of
weavers—Grants made by Government from time to time—Letter
from Mr. Sesbiah Sastri on and to Trichinopoly weavers—Wise
charitable relief in Krishna district (Rev. A. D. Rowe)—Sir
Richard Temple and the weavers 350–357

(3) SEED GRAIN.

Advances made by the Board of Revenue—Correspondence between
Government and the Board—Suggestion of Sir William Robinson—Letters and telegrams from collectors—Advances made by
the Board of Revenue—Grants from charitable funds . . 357–368

(4) PRICKLY-PEAR AS FOOD FOR CATTLE.

Suggestion by a Bellary firm—Letter of the Board of Revenue—
Experiments—Conclusions arrived at—Experiment in Mysore 368–375

MORTALITY ARISING FROM THE FAMINE.

NOTE ON THE BOMBAY TEST CENSUS.

By Col. Merriman, R.E.

Census taken on January 19, 1878—Nine Collectorates affected—Purpose of the Census—Results of the Census—Death-rate in 1872 377–384

APPENDIX TO COLONEL MERRIMAN'S NOTE.

Death-rate for the whole Presidency—Recorded death-rate during 1877
—Migration rates—Conclusions come to by the Bombay Government 384–388

MADRAS.

Partial census taken on March 15, 1878—Results—Remarks upon the
results of the partial census—*Times* Correspondent's summary—
Subject still *sub judice* 388–394

APPENDICES.

A.

PAGE

INSTRUCTIONS TO SIR RICHARD TEMPLE, BART., G.C.S.I., AS
FAMINE DELEGATE 397–405

B.

MINUTE OF AUGUST 12 BY H.E. THE VICEROY . . 405–422

C.

RULES OF THE NEW SYSTEM IN MADRAS . . . 422–431

D.

THE INDIAN FAMINE RELIEF FUND RECEIPTS AND EXPENDI-
TURE 432–435
MEMBERS OF THE MANSION HOUSE COMMITTEE . . . 436

E.

SOUTHERN INDIA'S GRATITUDE 437–471

F.

DAY NURSERIES 471–473

G.

WILD PLANTS AND VEGETABLES USED FOR FOOD.

1. Memorandum by Dr. Cornish; 2. List of Plants used in
Madras Presidency (Dr. Shortt); 3. Wild Herbs used in the
Kaladgi District, Bombay, during the Famine (J. M. Camp-
bell, B.C.S., and Dr. Wellington Gray) 474–480

H.

GOVERNMENT RELIEF OPERATIONS IN THE DISTRICT OF CUD-
DAPAH FROM FEBRUARY TO JUNE 1877 . . . 490–491

I.

STATEMENT OF PRICES OF FOOD GRAINS DURING THE FAMINE
1876–77 . . . . *To face* 492

ILLUSTRATIONS IN VOL. II.

MEMBERS OF THE EXECUTIVE COMMITTEE OF FAMINE
  RELIEF FUND . . . . *Frontispiece*

MAP SHOWING THE OPERATIONS OF THE FAMINE RELIEF
  FUND . . . . *To face p.* 77

FORSAKEN ! (By permission of the Proprietors of *The Graphic*) „ 119

FAMINE RELIEF CAMP, MONEGAR CHOULTRY, MADRAS (lithograph) · „ 294

INDIAN FAMINE.

PRIVATE CHARITY.

CHAPTER I.

HINDUISM AND CHARITY.

FROM a Hindu point of view the exercise of private charity in time of distress is a duty incumbent upon everyone who has the means wherewith to help his brother. In normal times there are no people on the face of the earth more given to charity than the Hindus. Proof of this is found in the fact that whilst every nation in Europe has had to devise some system of Poor Law administration whereby to relieve its necessitous poor, no approach to anything of the kind has been found necessary in India. In the years 1876 to 1878 the Indian Government will have expended on famine relief the sum of 11,000,000*l.*, that Government having rule over 250 millions of people. In England alone, during the same period, 21,000,000*l.* will have been spent on Poor Law administration, for less than one million of persons per annum. It is a question of practical politics whether, in supplanting Indian civilisation and religion by European modes of life and government, and by the inculcation of Christianity, something similar to the Poor Law of England will not have to be adopted in India. The question is now, or is likely soon to be, one of practical politics, and nowhere in this work could such a question be more fittingly considered than on the threshold of an exhibition of private charity and practical benevolence unexampled in Indian history.

The problem of support of the poor is a less difficult question to deal with in the East than in the West. In Oriental lands the means of supporting life are peculiarly easy. Little food, few clothes, and the minimum of fuel are required. Two classes of poor exist, one which earns a comfortable livelihood by begging—a religious or professional class ; the other, a criminal class, which supports a miserable existence by pilfering, and which forms one of the sections of the population of the jails. In ordinary years full provision for these classes is made, and professional beggars obtain a comfortable livelihood. These beggars are a feature of Indian life with which all who know anything of India must be familiar. Charity being enjoined by religion, the beggars make use of the arts of religion in obtaining support. Should relief be refused they call down the bitterest curses upon the heads of those who refuse, until ' for their much asking' they get what they desire. The blot which this causes upon Indian social life is manifest. Relief operations are not a matter of system but of individual caprice, and, consequently, abuses are many. A discriminate form of charity in the shape of work-houses, with strict avoidance of all out-door relief, would be an advantage, and would tend to reduce the evil which now exists. To accomplish this satisfactorily, however, one thing is needful which, in the present state of native society, it is hopeless to expect. Effort and trouble would be required from the more well-to-do natives themselves ; co-operation would be necessary from the donors of relief. Now, much native charity may be utterly wasteful, and the merciful tendencies of human nature perverted chiefly because of the false system, or no system, on which it is conducted. All indiscriminate almsgiving is an aggravation of the evil. The house-to-house contributions which are levied by the professional beggars, and, generally, are cheerfully given, if contributed to a common fund, and its distribution supervised by a native committee having a due sense of the trustworthiness demanded of dispensers of alms, would be an improvement on the present system. Relief in ordinary times, and when poverty is not increased, as it is in times of famine by exceptional circumstances, might then be confined to the utterly destitute and helpless. Industrial occupations might also be found for the blind and the lame : basket-making, stone-breaking, and the like. Industrial manufacture by the blind forms an interesting feature of their support in Great Britain. In the Coimbatore municipality, in the Presidency of Madras, this system is carried out, and the indigent poor have work provided for them. The difficulty is ever assuming larger dimensions, and will need close and anxious attention ere long.

But it is not with regard to the religious mendicant and professional beggars merely that the bright and praiseworthy aspects of Hindoo charity are exhibited. It is towards those of kindred, however far remote, that the most real charity is shown. The Hindu family system is such that all affection is limited to those of one's own kin and concentrated there. The family benefits, the nation suffers. Such qualities as patriotism, earnest care for the public good, and similar practices are impossible whilst the family is all and in all, and the community a matter of slight concern. Few national characteristics, whether in Eastern or Western countries, have worthier aspects for admiration than this family system so far as it goes ; the way in which generations are bound together and the kindliest feelings of kinship are fostered is worthy of all praise. But the system has many defects : it represses individuality, cramps personal effort, and is suited only for a backward state of civilisation. The population of India in bygone times was kept down by frequent wars and periodical famines, which fact accounts for the country not being over-populated by a system such as that described. Lord Macaulay, Mr. Grant Duff, and others believe that the English tongue will become the *lingua franca* of India; others as firmly believe that Christianity is destined to supersede all forms of religion now in India. Assuredly when the English tongue alone is spoken, and the Christian religion is generally professed, the difficult problems which are characteristic of European countries will be encountered in India.

'It is not a little startling to think,' said one member of the General Committee of the Monegar Choultry, Madras, to another, during an enforced pause in the business meeting held in July 1877, 'that if India becomes Christianised, if all the people become converted to what the missionaries teach, a Poor Law will be a necessary consequence.'

'That is startling,' was the reply, ' but why should such a result necessarily follow ?'

'Reasoning by analogy,' responded the first speaker, 'such must be the case. In all the Christian countries of Europe the poor are supported by the State. In India they are supported by the people themselves—their relatives generally, or, if they are religious mendicants or professional beggars, by those of their own religion. The Hindoo religion inculcates the utmost benevolence, and, as a consequence, that is done voluntarily here which elsewhere, in Christian countries for instance, is done by the Government.'

' Yes ; the family system in this land leads to much generosity, and to the support of many poor relatives by those who earn only trifling wages.   I know one member of this Committee, present in the meeting at this moment, who himself has been providing food for thirty-five people daily since the famine began.'

The conversation was broken off at this point, but the issues involved are of such great importance that they may not unfittingly form a theme for consideration. There can be little doubt that a Poor Law would be one of the results of India becoming Christianised.   The statement may to some be so startling that it will be asked, ' Why harbour such an idea for a moment? What necessary connection is there between Christianity and paupers supported by the State ?'   Much more than appears at first sight.   Christianity in the concrete will not allow of people dying for want of food ; Christians individually do not feel the claims of their religion so strongly as Hindus do the faith they profess; consequently, whilst one religion inculcates as powerfully as the other the paramount necessity for the exhibition of charity, the duty imposed on the individual is less felt by one body of worshippers than the other.   In Christian countries the State has to support those who, very frequently, should be maintained by their relatives and friends or by others akin to them who have means enough and to spare.   Professor Monier Williams, in a description published in *The Times* newspaper of his visit to Southern India, says he was particularly struck with the fact that the people of India were never ashamed of their religion. There is a good deal more in this than at first strikes the eye, for, on the contrary, an Englishman is very shamefaced—once in a while, perhaps, from purest humility, feeling that he is standing on the threshold of great mysteries—as regards his belief, and, consequently, is careless, through ignorance, of what claims the religion he professes has upon the display of active benevolence.

There are many who believe that India cannot be politically and socially regenerated without a change of faith—that change being from belief in the Hindu triad and the Muslim Prophet to trust in Jehovah and Jesus Christ. To the argument used it may be objected, if, as a consequence of a change of religion, pauperism and the evils of State aid to pauperism are to follow, will not the attendant ills outweigh the presumed advantages, and the last state of the continent be worse than the first? Not necessarily. The fear that State pauperism would be one consequence of the Christianising of India is born of a particular fact, which may cease to be of any importance if those who are engaged in missionary work become more anxious for the people's good to whom they minister than for denominational success. It is because an Oriental religion arrayed in an Occidental garment, fashioned after the mode of thought which dominates free and independent people, is being urged upon those whose idiosyncrasies are unfitted for the reception of it that there is occasion for fear lest what is unsuitable should be imposed upon an alien people. Many of those engaged in the work of changing the religion of the people of India are proceeding upon what seems to be altogether a wrong principle. The one peculiar fact connected with the religious truth revealed in the Bible is that, whilst the externals of worship may vary with the idiosyncrasies of race and the exigencies of climate, the essence, the faith, and the principles underlying these externals are admirably adapted for every individual of all the diverse peoples of the globe. This, however, seems to be overlooked by some engaged in evangelistic work amongst Hindus proper. A fatal desire seems to dominate the minds of many to introduce to India, where they would palpably be out of place, the externals they were accustomed to in Great Britain, and which were highly successful there because they were the outcome of the peculiarities, wishes, and desires of the English people. Those who are making the greatest mistake in this respect are the members of the High Church—the Ritualistic—party of the Anglican communion. Any one acquainted with the current history of India will not need telling of the evidence in support of this statement which has been forthcoming during the past few years. There are those who have raised the cry of the necessity for 'corporate' action on the part of the Church, and, for the sake of a mechanical unity, would impose upon that weak bantling, the Native Church, a round of ceremonies, a multiplicity of observances, altogether out of harmony with the normal state of things in India. No room is to be left for freedom of action, for the play of individual thought and effort ; Indian idiosyncrasies are to be overborne by, and merged in, a ritual and observances altogether foreign, which sit upon the worshippers like an ill-made garment.

It would be a calamity indescribable if Christianity were to bring to India the English Poor Law, and yet it seems clear that this is one sure and certain result of Anglican Christianity transplanted *en bloc*. Would it not be possible to maintain in the Hindu and other systems that which is indisputably good, and run through the existing channels pure streams instead of polluted ones? The Hindu family system has in it much of good, but it cannot continue in the presence of English Christianity. The system would be unsuited to Anglo-Saxon practice, but it does not follow that it is out of place in the body politic of another people. The benevolence strongly inculcated by the Sastras and other sacred works, though disfigured oftentimes by the feeding, as an act of merit, of lazy people who ought to be made to work—in this respect sharing the evils of official benevolence in England—has yet in it so much of good that surely Christianity could embrace these things while undermining the faiths of which they now form a part. Where the Indian system fails in the matter of true charity is that it has no power of expansion : it does very well for everyday ordinary family distress, but cannot cope with a great national disaster, in the spirit in which calamities are met by the various Indian (Christian) Governments. When, in the time of a native Government, a famine came, the people perished ; now, when a similar disaster is experienced, the people are saved, so far as may be. In exalting the individual over the family, Christianity and the progress which is the outcome of its fundamental principles, has made this farther reach possible. None other than a Christian people has yet done what was accomplished in India in 1876–78. Almost numberless instances of famine having unchecked sway are related in Indian history ; not many years ago Persia showed how supine and inert her authorities could be in the presence of preventible distress ; whilst simultaneously with the Indian famine being faced, fought, and conquered, China has confessed her inability to cope with wide-spread suffering, such suffering being caused through failure of food-supplies.

The outlook on the continent of India, in its impoverished soil unscientifically cultivated, is so gloomy that, whether through forms of English Christianity or by other means, the country seems to be approaching a chronic state of pauperism. During three years, more than eleven millions sterling were spent upon feeding the people.

The Indian Government have two courses before them: (1) doing nothing, and a Poor Law will be necessary in a generation ; (2) exerting themselves to improve agriculture, to ensure that the land shall be properly cultivated, and the idea of a Poor Law may be put off for several generations, for there is untold wealth a few inches beneath the surface of the soil if an improved plough is used to turn it up. That is, pauperism may be staved off if the authorities are wise and active, wise to prevent a yoke being put upon the people's neck which they are unable to bear, and active to devise such means as shall increase the food-producing qualities of the soil. Christianity may do much to help forward a better time, and may, if unwisely taught, do equally much to hinder real improvement.

The most pressing reform—though it is not recognised as such—before the Governments of India is the enlargement and improvement of the village system. Instead, as in past years, of unwise and deeply regrettable legislation, weakening village communes, which has characterised administration in all parts of the land, the utmost efforts ought to be made to add to their efficiency, from the munsif (the headman) to the scavenger. With an organisation such as exists, strengthened and improved, the machinery of government is comparatively easy, and, from an administrative point of view, no modification of a European Poor Law will be needed to help in feeding the poor. With better village government, better village statistics, and general widening of knowledge, agriculture could be improved, manufacturing industries introduced, and famine become as impossible in India as it is France.

CHAPTER II.

INDIA HELPING HERSELF.

CONSIDERING the proclivities of the people of India, it was only natural when, in 1876, distress became severe that private charity should be, apparently, more prompt than Government in providing food for the famishing. The same sights were characteristic of the chief cities in each of the Presidencies and the province affected. In Bombay the benevolent were early on the alert, and, throughout the whole period of distress, did exceedingly good service ; in Madras rich Hindus spent large sums in feeding many destitute and wandering people, but in the chief city their generosity was checked by Government, but not entirely stopped : in the mofussil,[1] scattered efforts were made by small committees, assisted by Government, but the efforts were few and fitful ; in Mysore, private efforts were exceedingly prompt and did efficient service. Soon, however, in Mysore, the means of the public came to an end, but non-official agency was still made use of, although Government funds were mainly expended, until a large portion of the munificent contributions from Great Britain and her colonies were placed to the credit of the Mysore Relief Fund. It may be as well, perhaps, in regard to private relief to follow the same system that has been adopted in regard to Government relief operations, and deal with the efforts of the Presidencies and provinces singly, according to their merit.

[1] The ' mofussil,' *i.e.* the country districts as distinguished from the Presidency town.

I.—BOMBAY.

In Sholapur the scarcity and distress consequent thereupon, first showed itself ; and it was in Sholapur that the most strenuous efforts were made by private liberality to mitigate suffering. At the best of times the people live from hand to mouth, and are exceedingly poor. The following anecdote is significant of the normal poverty of this the chief town of the district. When the Morarjee Goculdass mills were started in 1874, at a time in which there were no signs and no fears of a famine, the people went in hundreds praying to be employed even at an anna a day. Not many were wanted at the moment, still employment was found for some three hundred, at the fairer wage of an anna-and-half per diem, to level ground. All through the cold weather they slept outside on the bare ground close to their work, for fear strangers would come in overnight and take their work from them in the morning.[1]

A public meeting was held in the dwelling-house of Sir Jamsetjee Jeejeebhoy, Bart., at Bombay, in October, 1876, over which the baronet presided. Its object was to concert measures for the distribution of the money which had been raised for the relief of the poor by the efforts mainly, of Mr. Morarjee Goculdass. The desire of the public to share in relieving distress was heartily welcomed, and a letter was read at the meeting from Mr. Grant, collector of Sholapur, in which that gentleman showed the great good that would be done to the poor generally not employed on Government works, by rice being purchased in Bombay, forwarded to the distressed districts, and sold at cost price.[2]

[1] *Times of India*, October 16, 1876.

[2] Mr. Grant, in his letter to Mr. Morarjee Goculdass, thus describes the

Much practical discussion followed, and before the meeting came to an end, the Deccan and Khandeish Relief Committee was formed, and for many months was found most useful in mitigation of distress. With the exception of Dr. Blaney, the working committee was formed exclusively of Indian gentlemen, but subsequently other Europeans joined it.

Meetings followed in various parts of the Pre-

proposal :—' In order to assist both classes there are three courses open to us. The first is to provide employment in the form of relief works for those that are able to work, and this the Government are doing, and will no doubt continue to do. The next is to supply large quantities of grain from other parts of the Presidency where jowaree is plentiful and cheap for those that are in a condition to pay for it, and the last is to distribute in charity grain to those that are unable to work, and to others maintenance from any other source. With regard to relief works, everything must of course be left with the Government. In the city of Sholapur especially, and elsewhere, there are numbers of persons at the present time that can afford to purchase grain for themselves, and to subsist on their own means, provided they can get grain at a moderate price, but the Marwarees and others who have possession of all the grain in the district are holding back, and will not part with it except at such exorbitant rates that the people cannot afford to purchase it. To assist this class of persons, I would suggest that a sum of money should be raised in Bombay, as an advance or loan, for the purchase of grain in the bazaars or elsewhere. All grain thus provided might be sold for ready-money, with which fresh supplies might be obtained from time to time as required, the cost of carriage being provided for in reckoning the selling price. The original amount would thus remain intact, and be returned to the subscribers when no longer required. In order to provide for those that are entirely destitute, I cannot suggest anything but to raise a subscription for the purchase of grain for distribution in charity. At the present time I am causing jowaree to be sold at Sholapur by private arrangement at 8, 8½, or 8¾ seers for the rupee, by importing partly from the districts and partly from Jubbulpore and Oomrawuttee. If I had not done so, the price of grain would have risen to 5 or 6 seers per rupee, or even higher, as it did before we commenced operation. With the assistance you have so kindly offered, and by taking immediate measures in the manner suggested, I believe we can continue to sell not less than 8½ or 9 seers for some time longer. The poor classes in the district subsist entirely on jowaree, and therefore I have not thought it necessary to refer to other kinds of grain, or to the necessity of procuring them. If you can provide an immediate supply of jowaree, and forward it to Sholapur, you will confer an inestimable benefit upon thousands, and I will undertake the distribution, and also the recovering of the value of it, including cost of carriage.'

sidency, in quick succession. One was held at Shola-pur, and it was decided that a local fund should be raised. Another meeting was held at Ahmednuggur to consider what steps could be there taken.[1] A Mar-warce merchant had placed 25,000 rs. at the disposal of the Government for the purchase of grain, to be sold at prime cost.

At Poona a great meeting was held in the Council Hall, under the presidency of General Lord Mark Kerr, then commanding the Poona district. In opening the proceedings, Lord Mark Kerr said that he was pleased to see such a great meeting of classes and all races. The object for which they had met was a great one. This year, 1876, was to see proclaimed the Queen as the Empress of India; and he hoped that large sums of money would be collected, in order that great works could be carried out to inaugurate the event, and so enable the year to be remembered, not only on account of the proclamation, but also on account of the great works. They ought to begin at once and construct aqueducts, canals, reservoirs, and tanks throughout the country. Although the Almighty gave them an abun-dant rainfall, he had also given them forethought and intellect to use that abundance prudently and carefully. A famine had, however, come, and it now rested to see how much could be done to relieve it by means of such works. Mr. Norman, the collector of Poona, explained

[1] Of this meeting a gentleman present says:—

'It is worthy of note that such a gathering has never before assembled here for such a purpose. The wealthy Marwarees who were invariably con-spicuous by their absence on such occasions, were to be seen there. From this it was apparent that most of the people of this place evince great sympathy for the distress of their fellow-creatures, and showed great willingness to contribute, to the best of their power, for the relief of the distressed. One of the speakers suggested that grain-dealers who had hoarded extensive stocks of grain should take compassion upon the people and give grain in charity at this critical juncture.'

that the money subscribed would be devoted to the purchase of grain to be brought down to Poona, which would be distributed to the old and feeble who were distressed, but he hoped that work would be found either in the camp or the city for those able to work; and that such labour would be paid for partly in grain and partly in money. Some money should also be distributed to the larger towns in the collectorate, in which committees should also be formed and subscriptions raised. It must be remembered, continued the collector, that the famine was only just commencing, and they must yet look forward to six months of increasing scarcity. To meet that he hoped that a monthly subscription would be given, as well as a donation fund formed. His Excellency the Governor of Bombay favoured the movement, and sent a liberal donation, while altogether 9,000 rs. were subscribed in the room.

The Sarvajanik Sabha was also prompt to do much useful work in the way of voluntarily relieving distress.

Bombay benevolence, however, was not confined to succouring human beings; an endeavour was made to save the cattle also. A fund, called the Bombay Cattle-saving Fund was raised, and by means of it many cattle were saved. The fund amounted to 10,000 rs., and 2,000 beasts were gathered in the Sholapur Mills compound, having been purchased at from two annas (threepence) to six annas (ninepence) per head, whilst many were driven into the compound for nothing, the owners not being able to provide them with food. On October 31, 15,000 cattle were for sale in the Sholapur market, but there were no buyers and no fodder. As the cost of keep of each animal was eight annas (one shilling) per day, of course it was obvious that the Bombay Cattle-saving Committee could not last long or do much with the limited funds at its disposal. Indeed, it was only intended as a temporary measure, to continue at work until the permission of Government could be obtained to send the cattle to certain grazing-grounds on the hills which belonged to the State. Permission was given with the promptitude which marked the procedure of the Bombay authorities in regard to famine matters; and further, a large number of people on relief were set to cut fodder, large quantities of which were sold to those engaged in conveying grain into the interior.

At a meeting held later on, in November, at Sholapur, Mr. Morarjee Goculdass, an enthusiastic Parsee of a good English type, who seems to have been the spring of the philanthropic movement in Bombay,[1] made what the journals of the day called a 'slashing speech.' He attacked the greed of the Bunniahs in maintaining famine prices at a time when people were dying of want, and combining for inordinate profits when all others were freely opening their purses. 'If they do make large profits,' he said, 'the money will be cursed and never be of use to them, while they will incur the just displeasure of God.' He gave several instances of such wicked greed recoiling on the heads of the speculators, referring more especially to the profits in Bombay, at a time when cruel war was decimating America. But the most forcible argument he employed was, that his friends in Bombay were determined to battle with these combinations to the death, and were prepared, as a matter of business, not of charity, to bring up ten lakhs' worth of grain if it were needed. A contractor at Bombay, Mr. Nagoo Sayajee, lent the Sholapur Committee 10,000 rs. to be employed in

---

[1] In recognition of his public spirit, Mr. Morarjee Goculdass was made a 'Companion of the Order of the Indian Empire,' on January 1, 1878.

buying grain at Bombay, and selling it in the distressed districts plus carriage and expenses only. The cost of distribution and organisation he also bore. By these means the capital would remain in full for buying and selling throughout the whole period of the famine.

Sholapur, the scene and centre of much that was interesting and exciting during the famine crisis, has the honour of initiating a mode of relief which, when attempted in Madras eight months later, under the designation of ' Day Nursery,' attracted much attention in other parts of India and in England. Mrs. Grant, wife of the collector, busied herself on behalf of the suffering creatures around her, almost as much as did her husband. She urged the ladies of Bombay to raise a special fund to feed and tend the starving little children and to clothe the almost naked women. Many children were deserted, others had to be cared for, whilst their parents were on works ; others again needed the scanty food their parents could not afford whilst food prices were so high, supplemented by at least one meal a day. A dhood khana was, therefore, started for children under eight years of age ; funds were obtained to clothe the women. The admirable arrangements of General Kennedy, in providing for children on works as well as their parents, before long did away with the necessity for the dhood khana, so far as one class was concerned. It was greatly needed, however, for others. An officer employed on the works, writing to friends in England, describes the following scene :—

' The strangest sight in my famine work is to see the little children mustered. I am paying all children belonging to the labourers, who are too small to work, six pies a day ; so their names are all entered, and they have to answer them at muster. Some are so small they could hardly tell their names if asked, but they very soon learn to tell the sound of them when read out, and run up and sit down in line with much more apparent intelligence than their fathers. Each little beggar has to receive his or her own pay, too, at the weekly payment of wages, and they do it with no end of dignity and independence—up to the point of turning to walk away with it, when they usually end with a rush to hide in their mother's garments.' [1]

The native journals highly appreciating Mrs. Grant's efforts, and one of them (the *Rast Goftar*), after warmly eulogising the dhood khana, said Mrs. Grant's kindly intervention was a truly benevolent arrangement, which would bear favourable comparison with the schemes emanating from professedly religious men in Bombay and elsewhere.[2]

The special correspondent of the *Times of India*, writing on November 13, gives a most graphic and interesting description of the works of mercy carried on, which may be quoted in full as typical of much effort put forth during the whole period of the distress. He writes :—

' I spent Sunday most fitly in carefully examining the different works of mercy that, with one exception, have all been originated since I happened to come here. As in my last letter, I will give a meaning more or less clear to my rough notes. First we will go to the dhood khana, in the old military hospital, where Mrs. Grant looks after the infants. The notes I transcribe were in reality made on Saturday morning, but most fittingly come in here. The dhood khana was opened on Friday.

---

[1] The *Guardian*, London, January 26, 1877.

[2] The reference here, evidently, is to a proposal made by the Protestant Bishop of Bombay to take famine orphans and train them in the Christian faith, which the Native journals strongly condemned.

'On Saturday, at eight in the morning, then, I found Mrs. Grant and three other ladies at the door battling almost hopelessly against three hundred hungry mothers and hungry children. It was almost impossible to keep order, or to tell those who were fed until Mr. Grant, who had been showing Mr. Rogers other pitiful sights, came up, and reorganised matters by closing the door on the hungry, howling crowd, and after careful selection letting in some fifty at a time. These were made to seat themselves with their babies round the hospital walls. Then the ladies went round, like true sisters of mercy, feeding the little ones with milk, the older ones with rice, and with fresh jowaree cakes for some of the hungrier women. Even the newly-born babies, whose mothers were too starved to do a mother's duty, were not forgotten, and the feeding-bottle was in great request till some clumsy native broke it. Then it was pretty to see the English ladies kneeling and trying to feed the little swarthy dot with a spoon, and the mother's look of gratitude. Cups and small earthen pots were provided, and most of these, I am sorry to say, were stolen; and we saw one woman snatch the cup of milk from her baby's clutching fingers and drink it off herself. When the first batch had finished, they were kept apart at the end of the room, so as to prevent them, like Oliver Twist, from "asking for more," but one girl I saw climb out of a window, and she was not detected. The rest were admitted in similar lots, and at the third lot the Hon. Mr. Rogers took from me a girl of about five, who, as he tenderly led her up the room, looked the very impersonation of infantile "scarcity." There were not three pounds of flesh on that child's bones.

'Mr. Rogers—to prove his interest in Mrs. Grant's Children's Fund—subscribed liberally, and I learn that the indefatigable Mr. Morarjee Goculdass has succeeded in getting additional monthly subscriptions of 90 rs. at Poona, and a monthly subscription of 250 rs. at Bombay, this bringing the total up to about 500 rs. per mensem.

'Mr. Grant permits me to say that Lady Staveley, without knowing Mrs. Grant, has written to her, and most kindly offers to influence the Poona ladies in starting a kind of Dorcas Society to make rough garments for the poor women here. This Clothing Fund, it may be remembered, is allied to the Children's Fund. Much clothing has already been given away. The women are miserably clad, and girls of seven or eight go about without a rag upon them. Many must sleep out in the cold night air. Lady Staveley's example must surely find followers in Bombay. If we may judge by the ladies here, there is a common feeling of womanhood, and a sympathy with maternity, but then Bombay is so far off, and that miserable " scarcity " is so misleading. Still even a scarcity of garments ought to be remedied, when it is accompanied with a want of house-roof.

'From here we go to the school-house down in the town—remember that it is Sunday now. Older children, who have quitted milk as a vanity, and old people are fed here for the first time to-day, and in all 1,100 appeared. There is a good organisation here and a proper severity. All round the large compound they are made to sit in one continuous thin line. Then the committee go round. I may not call this a starvation hospital without provoking fresh letters from Poona, but I will call the sufferers patients. Each patient, then, is provided according to age, with a quarter of a seer of rice, or with half a cake of jowaree bread—thin like coarse oat-cake and slightly cooked like that on a griddle—there is a little boiled grain in the middle to make it palatable ; this is put on by a man who follows with a long ladle, in a Dotheboys Hall fashion. The quantity is carefully regulated so as to harm no patient after an unwholesomely long fast. Three times, where some slight delay occurred, the long rows of patients could stand it no longer and made a frantic but ineffectual rush at the stores in the centre. There was a good deal of snatching one from the other, and a strange look of satisfaction in the eyes when the hand has firm hold of the food. The difficulty in dividing the patients between Mrs. Grant's establishment and this is apparent enough, if we think that a mother's children vary in age. Here, for instance, I saw a baby, who ought to have the feeding bottle, crawling on all fours towards a little pile of rice which its sister held in her lap.

' From this we went to the store-house, where 2,000 recognised poor of the town present themselves every Sunday morning from six to eleven, and receive 7 lbs. of jowaree, which has to last them the week. New comers to the town are supplied daily here with bread; 500 of the lame, halt, blind, and maimed also received their weekly pittance to-day, and a dolorous lot they were, representing every disease under the sun, and making a trade of it. From this we cross over to the dispensary, where the representatives of the Bombay Fund are retailing various grains in the compound. The compound is piled high with sacks, and all day long the hungry crowd stare through the iron railings at the tempting heaps. Outside here this morning, as I drove past, a fearful scene occurred. A gentleman who was with me unluckily and unwisely gave a blind beggar a few coppers. In an instant we were mobbed by hundreds, in the terrible way they have here, some falling down with their faces in the dust (even isolated people do this if you relieve them), men showing how lean their stomachs were, and women uncovering their babies to attract attention. They clung round the tonga, and we had to drive our way out by force with a shrieking mob chasing us. Such scarecrows of figures, such pinched features and staring eyes, such shrivelled limbs and wasted breasts!

'I may as well go right on to the evening labours of the native committee for distributing bread. On this (Sunday) night, I was particularly requested to go round with them. I called for the secretary at half-past seven in a gharry. Another gentleman was with us. We started with a basket containing 75 cakes of bread, and no one is to receive more than half a cake, (I will again copy out my notes scribbled off under the sepoy's lamp); but I was told that four similar allowances of food had already been taken round.

'In the first "dharamsala" (rest-house) we find 10 people. One child is sick. An old woman gets up and tells us that the work we are doing is a good work. Rounding the corner we came upon 13 people, who confess to having been fed already. They have come from a village 36 miles off, and mean to stay here for work. Another lot of seven from the same place indignantly repudiate any previous food, and when cross-examined try to carry this abstinence back for five days. Sixteen more, who also give the distance of their village as 36 miles, have no food since the morning, "want work," but say they "don't know where to get it." The committee enlighten them, with a hint that if they do not know where to get work in the morning they will not know where to get food in the evening.

'We then go to the dispensary, travelling through the town with a couple of score of hungry wretches after us, probably professional beggars. Here eight of the patients had been fed in the afternoon. The man I mentioned previously was better, but his little girl died yesterday. If my telegram did the worthy doctor any discredit I am heartily sorry for it. He refused to admit this case simply on the plea that the disease— " want," or what you like—from which the man suffered was not recognised by the faculty. But eventually he did admit him, and though the man recovered, the child died, proving there was something wrong somewhere. The authorities have made it very clearly understood that they will stand no fine distinctions of this sort, and everyone tells me that the doctor is working night and day among the people in this district.

' We stop at a well of sweet water and lower the bucket ; people have been dipping all day long, and there are only about seven inches of muddy fluid left. But the water will come in the resting-time of night.

' Next we call on the subordinate judge, president of the grain committee, partly to see if he will join us, and partly, as he is an expert, to check your correspondent's prices from Poona. .As I anticipated, he said it was impossible that grain could be dearer at Poona than here. On the day your correspondent must have written, grain was half-a-seer more—all difference of measure fairly considered—than at Sholapur.

' We drove back by the dispensary ; there are 15 people outside to be fed. The armed sentinel stalks in to guard these precious grain-bags lying out in the open. Then outside the walls we pass a group of labourers camping under a tree : one child died to-day of cholera. Another man has been noticed here for two days with those old symptoms, is held up to the lamp's light, and is told he must go to the hospital ; says he would rather die. Then passing through a narrow wicket, we enter the court-yard of the big or dagum dharamsala. In the compound there are three brothers who have been to Narsala (towards the Nizam's dominions). They have four bullocks left ; they have sold eight and given four away ; heard there was no grass there, and so have returned. Would go to Poona when we told them of the Government offer, because their wives are starving at Saugola. Inside the dharamsala there are 103 people. We spoke to all of them.

'Here are a few cases :—One child, who has been vomiting and purging, arrived here yesterday with her mother after a journey of 40 miles ; the husband died on the road ; she cannot work until her child is well or dead. A man, woman, and five children, came from Avutee, 36 miles off ; the man, an invalid, had a quarter-seer of rice this morning ; the other nothing ; can't work ; his wife can. One woman and five children, from Izerwaddy—one child vomiting and purging. Still eats a bit of bread, and held it out afterwards to two little brothers. The woman can't work till her child is well. A little one wakes up out of the mass of children and cries out that it is hungry. All are miserably thin. Woman from Sattara, with a grown-up son and three children. Her husband has died, not recently : come for work ; have been fed an hour since ; all swear they have not. Man, woman, and six children ; man detected this morning offering his handful of rice for sale in the bazaar. Wife says he is mad ; he says he is a Brahmin—and he is—and refuses our food. Has also been detected buying a starved bullock with 8 annas, to carry his children on ; says they cannot walk. Give him money.—Another high-caste man who will not eat our bread.—Another.—One woman, one man, two children, came 20 miles for work, have spent their last two pies in grain ; have nothing but a little water in a pot ; the baby stops crying when bread is put into her mouth. One man, one woman, and child came 14 miles for work ; went begging this evening and got no bread.

As we came back they were munching at what we gave them.

'Then we drove for about a quarter-of-an-hour to another retreat. Party of 21 people and 11 cattle. Have had a little money to buy food for the last three days. Will go "wherever they can get food, and cattle may feed." Tell them of Poona; they are delighted ; give them food and one rupee for fodder ; and tell them to come to the mill compound and we will take care of their cattle till the trucks are ready.

' So ends our pilgrimage, and it is eleven o'clock. I can scarcely tell how much I admire the unassuming energy of the Secretary to the Relief Fund, Mr. Vishwanath Narayen. He was feeding the children this morning at seven ; he is leaving me now, and has worked all through the intervening time. The deputy collector seems almost omnipresent ; his name is Davathan, but after the way all the committees are working now, it seems as invidious, as it certainly is an idle compliment, to particularise any individual.

' There have been many cases of real Asiatic cholera. Four cases, and three fatal cases, at the mill. This morning, just before breakfast, I was called to look at two bodies—one that of a child, one of a woman—lying under two neighbouring trees close to the town gates. It was no good taking down the miserable story of the mother, who, as if I could help her, was brought up to me sobbing to tell her tale. I gave her something, and, like all the other poor wretches, she put her face on the ground.'

Similar scenes to these, and even more unpleasant, were to be witnessed occasionally throughout the period until famine declined.

Another form of relief, undertaken both by the

Deccan and Khandeish Committee, mainly through officials and the Sarvajanik Sabha, was helping the people to recover their former position. Seed-grain was supplied to those who could not obtain from Government, advances for sowing ; aid was rendered in purchasing bullocks and in repairing houses. The committee, through its agents, and by the aid of the Sabha, had distributing agencies in the following places :—

Sholapur	Yeola	Miraj
Pundarpoor	Sircophal Tank	Kaladji
Madapoor	Hubli	Akulkote
Mangalvadha	Saugli	Ahmednuggur
Mâhe	Madhivelal	Belgaum
Karsuala	Saugola	Kokisren
Dharwar	Malsiras	Poona
Bigapoor	Rutnagiri	Surat
Gudug	Dalrivadee	Broach
Barree	Tasgaum	Sattara

In Bombay city, also, assisted by an 'anna fund,' which was started in August 1877, much relief was afforded.

The agencies named, however, do not exhaust all the means of relief which were adopted. The Maharaja Scindia, of Indore, whose territories join the Bombay Presidency, spent much money in helping to feed those who were in want. The Sarvajanik Sabha, in one of their narratives, made this the subject of a comparison unfavourable to Government. The motives of the Government, it was admitted, were noble, and strenuous efforts had been made to provide for the people, but this had not been done in such a way as to 'rivet the claims of the Government to be regarded as their protector by many millions of its grateful subjects.' That is, the authorities had not adopted the Indian mode of indiscriminate feeding. It was complained :—
'The charity expenditure of Government has hardly yet exceeded 1,35,000 rs., while His Highness the Maharaja

Scindia's expenditure on account of the numerous poor-houses opened by him in Nassik, Trimbuk, Poona, Nuggur, and Pundherpore has overtopped this amount, while purely private expenditure through the relief committees and other independent channels has been four times as much.'

Some of the members of Government were not enamoured of Scindia's mode of action. The Hon. Mr. Gibbs strongly stigmatised the charity afforded by the Maharaja, which he says was expended on religious mendicants and lazy people who would not work. In fact, he remarked in his Minute, written when the famine was over, that he was so impressed with the waste and demoralisation caused by such uncontrolled relief that if the famine had continued for another year, as was at one time feared it would, he intended proposing that all charitable relief—unless strictly controlled by Government—be at once and peremptorily stopped. Sir Richard Temple did not share these views of his councillor, for, in his Minute, he expressed himself very warmly regarding the mode in which the people directly unaffected by famine had come forward to the aid of their suffering countrymen, and to the gift of charity had added sympathy and kindness. There may have been mistakes in affording relief ; idle and beggarly persons to some extent were supported, but, taken on the whole, the manifestation of charity in the Presidency of Bombay was of the order of highest mercy which blesses him that gives as well as him that takes.

II.—MADRAS.

The general public of Madras, as well as the Government, were taken aback by the rapid manifestation of distress in October–December 1876,[1] and no organised measures were taken of a nature adequate to meet the need. The Friend-in-Need Society, a charitable institution for the relief of poor Europeans and Eurasians, strengthened its organisation, but this was all. For the natives nothing was done on a scale commensurate with what was wanted. A suggestion was made that in Madras subscriptions should be raised and non-official aid secured in relief measures, but the idea was looked upon coldly, or actively opposed, as in one of the daily journals of the city, where it was pointed out that the disaster was so terrible that only a great organisation like that possessed by Government could hope to cope with the difficulty. Consequently, nothing was done in an organised manner. Nevertheless, much charity was being displayed, particularly amongst the natives. There was scarcely a family which had not some poor relatives from the country who looked to them for food, which was cheerfully given—not for a few weeks or months only, but in many cases for more than a year. Conversation with native gentlemen on this point has served to bring out many cases of heroic self-sacrifice ; half-rations were cheerfully sacrificed by respectable people, so that their relatives might share with them such food as they had. Even, however, when all the 'wanderers' who had kinsfolk in town were provided for, there were still many people who had no food, and in accordance with religious teaching and the promptings of their own hearts, several Hindu gentlemen in the Northern Division of Madras fed daily a large number of people. Two members of the Chetty caste fed 2,000 each ; one Mudaliyar 2,000 ; two Chetties 2,000 and 1,500 respectively, and others

---

[1] A description of the manner in which the villagers flocked into Madras will be found in chap. i. vol. i.

smaller numbers, making altogether 11,400. The food supplied has been described as of a very poor character, being thin gruel or conjee of rice or ragee poured into their hands and supped up more like cattle than human beings.[1] In addition to these, hundreds of poor people, congregated on the beach, were laying up for themselves a day of cruel reckoning by living on the grains of rice sifted from the sea-sand. Early in December the Government felt they were bound to grapple with the distress manifested in the chief city of the Presidency, and issued an order to the Commissioner of Police, directing him to open camps, and in various ways—e.g., giving cooked food at various depôts to respectable but indigent poor, to provide sustenance for the multitudes. In this Order of Government the following tribute was paid to the generosity which had been exhibited by certain Hindus :—'His Grace in Council has observed with much satisfaction the efforts made by all classes to relieve by private charity the existing distress among their fellow-townsmen. Conspicuous among these efforts are those of the Friend-in-Need Society and of the native gentlemen marginally noted,[2] and His Grace the Governor-in-Council resolves to grant to the Friend-in-Need Society a monthly donation equal to the special collections for relieving the poor, and to request the gentlemen above-mentioned to accept for distribution in food a monthly sum equal to the sum expended by them in feeding the poor, the only condition appended to these grants being that the money distributed for the Govern-

---

[1] Report by Col. W. S. Drever, Commissioner of Police, Madras. Col. Drever also says:—'This diet was, I am professionally informed, more calculated to induce disease than to sustain already exhausted nature.'

[2] Hugee Mahomed Padsha Saib, A. Armooga Moodeliar, N. Ramalinga Pillay, P. Moonesawmy Chetty, P. S. Ramasami Moodeliar, Venkatasawmy Nardi.

ment shall be applied to feeding those only who by age and infirmity are incapable of labouring for their livelihood, and that the establishments where the poor are fed shall be open to the inspection of an officer deputed by the Government.'

Madras town relief thus passed, in December 1876, into the hands of the police, who frequently had as many as 20,000 people daily to feed, and whose work was done with a thoroughness beyond all praise. Thenceforward, for nine months, only fugitive acts of charity—save through the Friend-in-Need Society—were exhibited ; the public, save as tax-payers, had no part or lot in the efforts which were being made to save the perishing multitudes.

What had happened in Madras was characteristic in a measure of all the large towns in the Presidency : all were crowded with infirm, sick, aged, and destitute poor. Attempts were made, unofficially, to relieve these. The collector of North Arcot reports that at Arconum the European railway officials and some of the native community 'subscribed handsomely' to provide a fund whereby the poor might be fed daily. In Gudiathum also the native community, of their own accord, and without solicitation or advice from European officials, established a relief committee. In these places, however, as in many others, the relief committees merely paved the way for the formation of relief camps entirely supported by Government and under official control.

On February 10, Mr. L. R. Burrows, president of the municipal commission, Madras, wrote a letter to Government in which he propounded a scheme of divisional inspection for relief of any distress which the present system failed to reach. The agency to be used was, mainly, that of ward representatives as they would be called in England, commissioners of divisions in

India. Government, however, was not prepared to accept the suggestion, and it was allowed to drop for a time.

Taking a glance over the whole area of distress—though noble efforts were made in places like Bellary, Trichinopoly, Salem—the non-official public generally do not seem, at this period, to have been sufficiently mindful of their duty toward the starving; a good deal of the apathy exhibited, however, was owing to the action of Government in not, at an early stage, taking the public into their confidence ; the evil wrought was increased by the visits and action of Sir Richard Temple, who rather pooh-poohed the idea of much and great distress. Of the feeling in his district the Collector of Salem wrote (January 16th) to Government: 'Private charity, never very prominent in Salem has, I regret to say, done little or nothing to alleviate suffering. A meeting was held in the town a short time ago, and some 2,000 rs. subscribed by those present, and probably another 2,000 rs. or 3,000 rs. may be collected.' In Trichinopoly, where several Europeans and Eurasians reside, and where a detachment of European troops is stationed, more exertion was shown. In January a meeting was held for raising funds, and a subscription list was put in circulation, both among the European and native gentry. Mr. Stokes, collector of Trichinopoly, writing on January 7, says :—' About 3,200 rs. have been subscribed by natives as donations. The European gentry came forward with a monthly subscription of about 150 rs., and 600 rs. in the shape of donation. I expect more subscriptions and donations. We started two relief houses in the town here on the 19th of December last with the aid of the 1,000 rs. out of the Prince of Wales's Entertainment Fund, which the native public has placed at the disposal of the Famine Relief Committee. Two more relief-houses have been started, one at Musiri and another at Kulittalai kusbah stations, in view to feed the distressed from Salem and other parts who pass through those taluks in great numbers.'

Among the difficulties encountered in affording relief was that of giving assistance to those whose caste rules prevent them leaving their homes or showing their faces to anyone. Prominent in this class were the Gosha females of Mohammedan families. Many were known to be in direst want, but death was preferred by some to exposure. Early in the famine, relief was given in Madras to Gosha females, but only to those above fifty years of age, and they received from one rupee to one and a half rupee per month. They were visited by paid Mussulmans (known as Hammamis) who made house-to-house visitation and reported to the Relief Agent employed by the Commissioner of Police, certain Mussulman gentlemen being security for the reality of the distress to be relieved. When the subject of the relief of this class came up in Arcot and Vellore, where the collector apprehended deaths from starvation, it was suggested by the Board of Revenue that the relief need not be entirely gratuitous. 'Many of the women are of good birth, and would prefer earning a pittance to being inscribed on a pauper roll. Some work, such as silk-reeling or the like, might be found for them.' This suggestion does not seem to have been generally adopted.

The natives of Cuddapah, at the beginning of the distress, held a meeting whereat it was decided that, in consequence of the increasing suffering, a subscription should be commenced for the purpose of opening a relief-house in the town. 1,410 rs. were contributed at once, and the merchants agreed that they would give, as their share towards the charity, three pies upon every bag of rice brought into the town. This voluntary taxation was continued for several months, and many people were relieved thereby. Among the more earnest workers in voluntary charity, from the first, were the Rev. W. P. Schaffter, of the Church Missionary Society, and his successor, when he was compelled to proceed to England, the Rev. J. Davies Thomas. They laboured in the Chingleput district, to the south-west of Madras city, and the last-named gentleman evidently obtained great influence over the people, one amusing instance of which was shown in March 1878. Among the petitions presented to the Chingleput Committee was one from a schoolmaster and his wife, in which they asked how they could ' commit suicide without offending the Deity or the Rev. J. Davies Thomas.' Their distress, they continued, was so great that death was to be preferred to life under the conditions described.

In all cases where subscriptions were raised—and to those mentioned must be added Coimbatore, Kistna, and Kurnool—Government gave an equal sum. The same policy was adopted in regard to the relief operations of zemindars, such as the jaghiredar of Arnee, who fed 700 people a day for several months. In Tinnevelly the propriety of private charity was pressed, by the collector, upon the people. Having established a relief camp for the thoroughly destitute, Mr. Pennyngton issued the following instructions to certain native officials in a non-distressed part of the districts :—' I think it would be as well if each tahsildar in the river valley were to raise subscriptions in the kusbah and surrounding villages for feeding the destitute poor who are wandering about in search of food. In the outlying villages a good deal must be left to private charity, but village munsifs should be relieved by them at the expense of Government, an immediate report of expenditure being sent in to the tahsildar, so that he ma make inquiries, and, if necessary, provide the applicant with a ticket for relief in the same village. It is time to make some attempt to put a stop to so much wandering about of half-starved paupers. It is probable that distress will gravitate towards the kusbahs chiefly, and there tahsildars must make quite sure that they are prepared to relieve everyone who comes. If any one of them appear to be fit for work, intimation should be sent to the nearest range officer, and he will no doubt make arrangements for giving them employment.

'In the river valley the famine has been quite a godsend to the ryots, and they have prospered amazingly, so that I think they may fairly be called upon to support their less fortunate brethren from other parts, though, of course, in the last resort all who require food and cannot get it otherwise will be fed as usual at Government expense, even in the river valley.

'I may mention, in conclusion, that the merchants in Tuticorin (who have also profited largely by the famine) have long since spontaneously opened a relief-house there and feed considerable numbers at their own expense.'

Thus, in a fitful fashion, throughout the earlier period of distress, scope for the exercise of private charity was recognised, and many generous deeds known only to giver and recipient were done. But when an estimate is taken of all the efforts made—and it is believed that reference is made in the foregoing pages to all organised attempts—they are miserably poor compared with the area affected. That more was not done is surprising. Sir John Strachey in making his Financial Statement in the Viceregal Council in March 1877, said: 'The task of giving relief to all those who suffer offers the noblest opportunities of doing good to well-applied private charity, and intelligence, and zeal: but it cannot be undertaken by the State.' Only in an incomplete manner was this truth apprehended by the people of Madras; when, however, later on, they awoke to their responsibilities, the splendid unselfish service given atoned for previous neglect.

III.—Mysore.

The famine policies adopted while the disaster of famine was simultaneously prevalent in the Madras and Bombay Presidencies, and in the Province of Mysore, were very dissimilar so far as private charity is concerned, until the visit of the Viceroy in August-September 1877 produced homogeneity. In Bombay private charity was altogether outside the plans and operations of the Government: it was recognised in a sense, but it was not aided nor controlled. In Madras the principle was played with for ten months. Fitful manifestations of private effort were made, when made they were encouraged in so far that grants from State funds from time to time helped to maintain a feeble circulation. But no attempt was made to develop and utilise the sympathy and zeal of a large non-official population. In Mysore, on the other hand, under the inspiration of the Government of India, from the first, private charity was a recognised detachment of the forces deployed to meet the famine. So great a part did private charity play in the campaign that it is not possible to tell in separate narrative the history of each. The one was inextricably woven in the other. For a description, therefore, of private charity in Mysore, the reader is referred to the narrative in Volume I. devoted to the distress in Mysore.

CHAPTER III.

THE APPEAL TO ENGLAND.

A GENERAL meeting of the Directors of the Monegar Choultry at Madras, sitting in a small dark room in which the meetings are generally held, had in the month of July, 1877, concluded its business and was about to break up when the Chairman, Deputy Surgeon-General Van Someren, was asked, 'Is there not a minute from one of the Directors to be read?'

'Oh! yes,' replied Dr. Van Someren, 'Mr. Krishnama Charriar has sent a minute about the high-caste poor, who, he says, are suffering greatly from high prices, and who will die rather than go into relief camps, or receive cooked food, and suggesting that the Choultry should undertake the support of such.'

'We can do nothing for them,' remarked a director. 'Our means are already straitened. We shall need helping ourselves.'

. 'Perhaps we had better forward the minute to Government, and leave the authorities to deal with it,' said the Chairman.

This was agreed to, and the subject disposed of, so far as the Choultry was concerned.

By the time that the minute reached the Governor in Council, distress had intensified, the south-west monsoon persistently holding off. His Grace and the members of Government had been brought face to face with much suffering consequent upon high prices ; the suggestion from the Choultry, therefore, received prompt attention. The authorities saw plainly that they could not deal with lower middle-class distress ; it was more than they could do to grapple with absolute destitution. It was, therefore, resolved to revive the plan proposed in the previous February by Mr. Burrows, President of the Municipal Commission, and relieve the distressed through committees formed of the commissioners. Also, as a part of this scheme, it was determined to change the policy hitherto adopted, and instead of deprecating public subscriptions, to ask for them, for every rupee contributed Government giving another. A grievous mistake was made at the outset in the mode adopted to appeal to the public for aid. Municipalities are new institutions in India, mainly noteworthy for harassing the people in the persons of the tax collector and the sanitary inspector. The yoke is borne uneasily, and a scheme floated by such an agency is doomed to grudging support. A meeting of the commissioners was held to determine upon the steps to be taken to meet the views of Government, which had been communicated. Conversation was somewhat desultory, but some definite arrangements were made: (1) a Central Committee was formed, which representative men were to be asked to join; (2) it was agreed that Divisional Committees should be appointed at a meeting to be held on the Saturday following, July 28; (3) subscriptions were to be invited.

Colonel Drever asked, in the course of the meeting, ' Where is the money to come from to meet the necessary outlay? It will take a great deal to keep up relief several months.'

' There are a good many wealthy people in Madras,' said Sir William Robinson; ' if they are applied to, they will be willing to assist. It is incumbent on us to do what we can ourselves and enlist sympathy.'

'Government has made it very hard to collect subscriptions in Madras,' remarked the Rev. J. M. Strachan, M.D. ' Some months ago the Government said subscriptions were not wanted and discountenanced private relief operations. Consequently the public have become demoralised. Further, everybody has suffered from the famine, and cannot afford to give. Why not ask that a relief fund be raised at the Mansion House in London, or in Calcutta ?'

The suggestion was received in silence, and discussion ' harked back ' to ' the Government,' the one fact in India. The native gentlemen present then expressed their views.

Somewhat periphrastically, Mr. Vanoogopaul Charriar said the relief was proposed to be distributed by the public and the commissioners ; their time was all they could be expected to give. ' It is, therefore, evident that the source from which the funds should be expected for the relief now under proposal should be the same as that now provided at the relief camps.'

' Eh !' interjected Sir William Robinson, ' is that what you call fulfilling your duty to the poor ?'

' It is the duty of every citizen to support his poor in one shape or another,' said the Hon. V. Ramiengar, C.S.I. ' The Government has spent all it can spend, and no land revenue is coming in ; new taxation must, therefore, now be faced. It is a sacred duty on the part of a man so to limit his expenses as to provide for his own poor.'

With talk of this kind, continuing till nearly eight o'clock in the evening, it was decided to do something, the meeting on the Saturday following to come to a definite understanding on this point.

On Saturday a meeting largely attended was held. It was then stated that it was intended to confine the proposed relief to the actual residents, and not to ' wanderers' daily arriving in the town; to those who were unable to avail themselves of the relief provided through the present system, and those who, from self-respect or other causes, were prevented from going to the camps ; as well as providing for other poor who, if not afforded immediate relief, would die of starvation. Certain rules had been framed, and related principally to matters of routine. One anna money-payment would be made to every adult, and six pies to every child, to be given daily by one of the members of the committee. This was subsequently altered to weekly payments—eight annas to an adult, four to a child.

After eight committees[1] had been appointed, for the several divisions of the town, aggregating nearly two hundred gentlemen, it was decided that an appeal for subscriptions should be made in the city.

' Why?' asked a gentleman present, when a resolution had been passed that the balance of the Madras contributions to the Bengal famine should be made available, ' Why should the Central Committee not put itself in communication with the Lord Mayor of London and seek English assistance to meet the terrible distress around us? There are many institutions in England which would help us—the Chambers of Commerce, for instance. They take a great interest in India, when the reduction of the cotton duties is on the *tapis*; it is not unreasonable to suppose they would be equally interested if an opportunity were given them in which they might confer benefit instead of receiving it. The English people have not the remotest conception of the horrors in our midst; if they were made acquainted with them, much help would be rendered.'

---

[1] For seven months these committees laboured most zealously in their various divisions, personally distributing week by week the dole provided. The work was arduous, but it was most cheerfully done.

' If we ask at all,' said Captain Heming, Deputy Commissioner of Police, ' we must ask for the whole Presidency and not for Madras only.'

' As a central committee in the chief town of the Presidency,' replied the first speaker, ' I conceive we can speak and act for the whole Presidency.'

' I quite agree,' remarked Sir William Robinson, ' with all that has been said about the necessity of making the English people acquainted with the fearful distress that exists. I am convinced the people at home do not know, or much help would have flowed to us. The proof of the want of knowledge in Great Britain is seen in the fact that only one donation has been received, viz., one hundred guineas from Lady Hobart. Still, I am not quite certain that the present is the right time to make a move, nor am I sure as to the way in which it should be made.'

' Let us do what we can ourselves before we appeal to England,' said Mr. Shaw, a merchant. ' I was in England when the Bengal famine occurred, and I have a lively recollection of the manner in which public sympathy was manipulated by sensational telegrams.'

' The two cases are not parallel,' was the retort; ' whatever there may have been of sham in the Bengal famine, there is none in Madras. Besides we can give what we have to give ourselves, and ask England to contribute at the same time. It is certain that we cannot contribute all that will be needed.'

There seemed general acquiescence in the spirit of these remarks, but as there was no definite motion before the meeting, nothing was then done.

Being satisfied that the course he had suggested was the right one, the gentleman who mooted the matter, through the daily journal of which he was editor, strongly urged the advisability of such a step being taken,

and remarked that if the aid of the public were wanted
it should be sought in a public meeting, and not through
an institution so little liked as a municipality.   He also
ascertained that, if solicited, his Grace the Governor
would not be averse to presiding over a public meeting
whence an appeal might be made to England.   The
following resolution was therefore prepared for submission to a meeting of the Central Committee, which
was called for Tuesday evening, July 30 :—'That the
Central Committee of town relief for Madras arrange
for a public meeting being held at an early date in the
Banqueting Hall, over which his Grace the Governor be
asked to preside.   That at this meeting resolutions be
submitted which shall show the extent of distress
throughout the Presidency, and that the aid of the
communities of Calcutta, and other Indian cities where
no abnormal distress is being experienced, be sought.
Also that the Lord Mayor of London and the English
Chambers of Commerce be communicated with, and
that the India Office be asked to place all available
communications regarding the famine at the service of
the English press.   As the local Government undertake
to keep the people alive, as far as possible, it be suggested
that the funds raised in England and elsewhere be employed in supplementing Government aid, and in providing implements for agriculture and seed-corn for
sowing, during the approaching north-east monsoon
season.'

A great many obstacles to the calling of the meeting
were raised, but after much difficulty they were overcome, and the resolution, with some slight amendment,
was passed.   The remarks made in support of the resolution by the gentleman who brought it forward were
as follows :—(1) Was the object contemplated in the
resolution needed?   On this point there could be no

question whatever ; the necessity was only too evident to everyone. Government had done its best to provide work and food for the people, but, at length, found the distress was assuming such magnitude, people of the higher castes were starving, and it had been determined to call upon the public for help. Distress so widespread as that in Madras could not be grappled with by themselves as they might wish to grapple with it, or as adequately as it ought to be. The scope was too wide for the people or the Government of Madras to deal with. Clearly, then, an appeal for outside help was needed. (2) Was it desirable that such an appeal should be made? The answer to this question was really involved in that which they had already considered and answered in the affirmative, viz., that it was needed. It was desirable that this should be done, as much in the interests of the English people as of the Indian. What would be said in England when the famine was over, and its terrible mortality known, if no appeal for aid were made? The questions would be asked, ' Why was not our aid sought? Why were we not given the opportunity of helping to alleviate distress?' This was the principle acted upon with regard to friends. If any of those present met an acquaintance or friend, who had passed through great distress, of which nothing was known till it was over, the reproachful remark would inevitably be, ' Why did you not tell me of your strait? I should have been glad to render you some assistance.' This was what the English people would say if the opportunity for them to give of their substance was not provided. · That same people gave towards the Bengal famine, in which only twenty-three people died of starvation, more than fourteen lakhs of rupees. There was not a relief camp in the Madras Presidency in which there were three thousand people, who, when they rose in the

morning, did not leave thirty corpses on the ground.
Granting, then, that an appeal was needful and desirable,
the speaker proceeded to ask, (3) Who should make it?
Clearly not the Government. It was no secret that there
had been injustice done to Madras with regard to this
famine, and a greater disposition evinced to believe what
Sir Richard Temple had said about the local Government's exaggeration of distress than to adopt the views of
the authorities themselves. For that reason Government
could not move in the matter. But there was another
and stronger reason. The famine had passed into a
stage when the assistance of the public was sought, and
if further help were wanted there must be an appeal
from people to people, from the people of Madras to the
people of England. Such communications were more
seemly if they proceeded from non-official sources than
from the Government. Of course, as members of society,
Government officers would help forward such a movement, but they could not so well undertake it as non-
officials could. (4) The need for early effort was very
great. A portion of the resolution alluded to affording
help to the people in planting during the north-east
monsoon season if the rains came. To ensure aid being
received in time, not a day was to be lost; time enough
would be consumed in communications, and if the aid
was to be really effectual it must come soon. Illustrations in support of this were cited. (5) There could
be no question that the appeal would be successful.
Some of those present were Englishmen, and knew the
thrill of sympathy which ran through the whole British
people when there was suffering among any race. And
the sympathy was not confined to a nervous thrill, but
it went farther and the pocket was dived into for practical support. This was so in regard to human beings
in want anywhere; but the benevolence would be in-

creased on behalf of fellow-subjects of the Queen-Empress.

Other resolutions were passed at this preliminary meeting, directing that his Grace the Governor should be asked to preside over the meeting, and a requisition to the Sheriff to convene an assemblage of citizens for August 4 was signed by six of the gentlemen present. The Governor having consented to preside, the requisition was sent to the Sheriff.

' The resolution is not very largely signed,' said the gentleman who forwarded it ; ' there are only ten names appended.'

' Quite sufficient,' replied Sheriff Munsie, ' I am satisfied that there is a general desire that the meeting should be held, and the names given will suffice.'

Three days later a meeting, which has now become a prominent feature in Southern Indian history, from the consequences which ensued from it, was held in the Banqueting Hall, under the presidency of his Grace the Governor, and an appeal was telegraphed to the Lord Mayor of London and the chief municipal functionaries through *The Times* newspaper.[1] Of the difficulties encountered in convening that meeting nothing need be said beyond that they were very great ; Anglo-Indian apathy seemed greater than it has been described to be,

---

[1] The message was as follows :—

To London *Times*.—From Madras Sheriff's Meeting.

Please publish information Lord Mayors London, York, Dublin, Mayors Birmingham, Bristol, Liverpool, Manchester, Provosts of Edinburgh, Glasgow, public meeting, Governor presided, resolved appeal British public for aid population Southern India. Severity famine increasing, distress great, rainfall continues insufficient, population affected 20,000,000, numbers absolutely dependent charity Madras Presidency 1,075,000, daily larger; increased mortality already reached nearly half million; distress now reaching better classes owing increased price grain double prevailing Bengal famine. Matters become worse rapidly. Under most favourable circumstances of weather, which is still unfavourable, pressure must continue till crops are gathered January. Necessity assistance most urgent pressing.

but a word or two descriptive of the assemblage may be not unfitting. The attendance of European gentlemen was large; native gentlemen were conspicuous by their absence. The seats in the body of the hall were filled, but the empty aisles and a great vacant space from where the seats ended to the door were calculated to exercise a depressing effect upon the promoters of the gathering. The Governor's speech was judiciously prepared and emphatically delivered; it cannot, however, be claimed that from an oratorical point of view the meeting was a success. This was of minor importance, as what was wanted was not so much to rouse those present to generosity as to provide a statement for presentation to the people of England. This was obtained in the speeches of his Grace the Governor, Dr. Cornish, and Colonel Drever, and the following resolutions, which were unanimously adopted:—

I. That the increasing severity of the distress arising from the famine necessitates an appeal to public charity.

II. That with the view of obtaining the aid referred to in the first resolution, the Lord Mayors of London, York, and Dublin, the Mayors of Bristol, Birmingham, Liverpool, and Manchester; the Lord Provosts of Edinburgh and Glasgow, and the communities of Calcutta and other cities and stations in India, and the editor of *The Times*, London, be at once informed by telegraph, and more fully by letter, of the urgent necessity which exists for assistance, and be solicited to adopt such measures as they may think most suitable for making the condition of the Presidency known to the public.

III. That the existing Town Relief Committee with its Divisional Committees be requested to continue in office, and that a Central Committee be formed to undertake the general management of the Famine Relief Fund.

A committee of about fifty gentlemen was appointed, and a meeting was held on August 6, in the Magistrate's Court at Egmore. Sir William Robinson was elected chairman, and Mr. Digby honorary secretary. Colonel Hearn, Inspector General of Police, demurred to the last appointment; the gentleman named had only been a few months in Madras; some one who knew the country well, and was acquainted with all the officials, was needed for such a post. Notwithstanding the objection, the nomination was agreed to without further remark. An executive committee, consisting of twelve European and native gentlemen, was appointed,[1] and the form of appeal, which should be addressed to England, was decided upon. Amongst other matters considered, was a brief draft appeal, drawn up by the Right Rev. F. Gell, D.D., Bishop of Madras, who, in his second paragraph, said : ' Pecuniary assistance on a very large scale is needed to meet the present and prospective wants of the very large population who, under the heavy judgment of Almighty God, have been reduced so low.' Simultaneously with the movement towards invoking private charity in Madras, his Lordship had communicated with his Grace the Governor as to the advisability of private relief being afforded. On July 28, the Governor wrote : ' I can see no possible reason why private charity should not be called in aid of the dire distress at the present time, in clothing the naked and housing the homeless. There is open, alas!

[1] This committee was afterwards increased to twenty-five. The names of its members were as follows :—

Sir W. Robinson, K.C.S.I. (*Chairman*).

G. Thornhill, C.S.I.	C. A. Ainslie.
G. A. Ballard.	W. W. Munsie.
R. K. Puckle, C.I.E.	Ven. Arch. C. R. Drury.
Col. F. Weldon.	Very Rev. J. Colgan, D.D.
Col. J. G. Touch.	Rev. J. M. Strachan, M.D.
Hon. A. Mackenzie.	R. G. Orr.
Hon. J. G. Coleman.	F. Rowlandson.
Hon. E. Ramiengar, C.S.I.	A. Cundasawmy Mudaliyar.
Hon. Mir Humayun.	F. Ramachendra Rao.
Jah Bahadur.	P. Srinwassa Rao.
J. Jones.	H. Cornish.

W. Digby, *Honorary Secretary.*

an ample field for the most liberal efforts of charity in England and here.'

Throughout the week the telegrams from England to the local newspapers were anxiously scanned for information as to whether the appeal had been effectual. Days passed without any sign being apparent of success. Six days after the meeting had been held, viz., on August 10, the Duke of Buckingham and Chandos received a telegram from a friend in London, which ran as follows : ' Suggest privately to President, famine meeting, to telegraph direct appeal to Lord Mayor. Success then certain ; meantime, movement hangs.' This message was communicated to the executive committee, and at its meeting on Monday, August 13, action upon it was taken. One gentleman (Mr. J. Jones) suggested the telegram to the Lord Mayor should be in these terms : ' Position extremely grave; monsoon failed ; crops withering, cattle dying. Famine must intensify during the next few months. Hundreds dying daily of hunger. Government and officials working manfully, but cannot prevent terrible mortality. Private assistance urgently needed.' Though it was conceded this was vigorous enough, it was not felt to be sufficiently explanatory, and, after some discussion, a draft was determined upon, which was as follows : ' Committee earnestly solicit your Lordship's powerful influence in support of an appeal for assistance for the afflicted population in Southern India. The position of affairs is extremely grave. Very great and increasing mortality from want. notwithstanding the utmost efforts of Government. The monsoon is again deficient; difficulty will certainly last till January. Cattle perished in large numbers. All labouring classes are in very great destitution. Property sold for food. Villages largely deserted, and the poor are wandering in search of sustenance. The resources of the lower middle classes are exhausted, owing to famine prices. Prompt liberal sympathy and assistance may mitigate suffering. Particulars forwarded to *The Times* a fortnight ago.'

This was sent to the Lord Mayors of London, Dublin, and York ; to the Lord Provost of Edinburgh, and the Provost of Glasgow; and to the Mayors of Birmingham, Blackburn, Bradford, Brighton, Cambridge, Manchester, Liverpool, and Sheffield.

Simultaneously with the receipt of this telegram in London, the Queen's Speech at the prorogation of Parliament was published ; in it appeared a paragraph relating to the sore and grievous distress in Southern India, which served to concentrate attention upon the disaster. In a manner worthy of its best traditions, *The Times* took up the cause of the famine-stricken, and, in a leading article on the subject, provided a passage with which Sir Thomas White, Lord Mayor of London, in initiating the Fund, gave point to his remarks. No sooner had the Lord Mayor received the message from the Madras Committee than he took action upon it. Contrary to the usual practice in England, where a public meeting seems indispensable to establish any enterprise whatever, no meeting was called, but quietly, unostentatiously, a Fund, destined to be one of the marvels of the year, was started at the dullest season of the year, when Parliament had risen, and all the wealthy and well-to-do folk had made preparations for touring and holiday-making. In the justice-room at the Mansion House, an Indian gentleman being seated by Sir Thomas White's side, and giving point by his presence to the cause to be advocated, the Lord Mayor, on August 12, with a few remarks, read the telegram he had received from Madras. ' This telegram,' said the Lord Mayor, ' speaks for itself, and I can only add to it the concluding words of a leading article in *The Times* of to-day : " Let not the appeal now at length made to us fall unheeded. Our countrymen at Madras call upon the municipalities at home, and their cry must be heard. We have hitherto been too little concerned with the awful trial that has befallen our fellow-subjects; let us redeem the past by keeping it before our eyes and in our minds and hearts until all that we can do is done, in order that it may be overcome." I shall be delighted to receive at the Mansion House, and to remit to the Duke of Buckingham and the other public authorities in India, any sums which the generous public may feel inclined to entrust to me ; and I sincerely hope that the urgent appeal which I now make for funds will be promptly and liberally responded to.' A day passed, and subscriptions began to flow in very rapidly, the first contribution being from a gentleman named Cash. Lord Northbrook, late Viceroy of India, sent a cheque for £500 ; the Earl of Beaconsfield sent the following autograph letter to the Lord Mayor :

2, Whitehall Gardens, August 5.

Lord Beaconsfield, with his compliments to the Lord Mayor, has the honour to enclose a cheque for £50 in aid of the Indian Famine Fund, over which the Lord Mayor has so kindly and wisely offered to preside.

The first list published showed two donations of 1,000*l.* each, two of 500*l.* each, one of 210*l.*, and several of 50*l.* each. Prominent among the names of subscribers were ' old Indians,' and the relatives of such. The Marquis of Salisbury, Secretary of State for India, and Lord Derby, the Foreign Minister, contributed, and, five days after the Fund was opened, it was put on a sure basis by a letter from the comptroller to his Royal Highness the Prince of Wales, in which a cheque for 500 guineas was enclosed. The Prince desired General Probyn, his comptroller, to add how sincerely his Royal Highness trusted that the Lord Mayor's appeal to the public 'for the relief of our starving fellow-creatures in Southern India may meet with the prompt and generous response it deserves.' The Princess of Wales sent 100*l.*, and Sir Thomas Biddulph, on behalf of Her Majesty, forwarded 500*l.* Prince Leopold, the Princess Imperial of Germany, Princess Alice of Hesse,[1] the Duke of Edinburgh, and other members of the Royal Family also contributed to the fund in its earlier stages. Within a week from the date of the appeal, 24,000*l.* had been received, and the sum was forwarded by telegraph to Madras, the Eastern Telegraph Company liberally offering to send messages free of charge. Associated with the Lord Mayor was a committee of gentlemen, chiefly merchants and bankers of the city, whose names will be found in Appendix D.

It is time to turn to India, where circumstances of a more or less interesting and exciting character were occurring. In India the response which was made to the appeal for subscriptions was very pleasing. The first notable sum received came with such promptitude that good heart was at once put in all interested in the movement. Acting on a telegraphic account of the meeting in Madras, which was published in the *Times of India*, the Government of Baroda telegraphed a

---

[1] The Grand Duchess of Hesse accompanied her subscription with a letter, of which the following is a copy:—

'Darmstadt, September 20.

'My Lord,—The Grand Duchess of Hesse, entertaining a lasting attachment towards her native country, was deeply moved by the sad reports which came from the Queen's Eastern Empire; and her Royal Highness's sympathies are fully shared by her husband, the Grand Duke, whose interest in everything that concerns the Queen and the people of Great Britain, is no less sincere. Their Royal Highnesses are anxious to send a small contribution towards the Indian Famine Relief Fund, which is being collected under your Lordship's auspices, and they have, therefore, directed me to forward the enclosed cheque of £50 for that purpose.

'I have the honour to be your Lordship's obedient servant,

'DR. E. BECKER.'

donation of 10,000 rs. The Prime Minister of Baroda, Sir Madava Row, K.C.S.I., was a native of Madras, and had not forgotten, in his elevation, the scene of his early struggles. It was hoped that the example of Baroda would be generally followed in India, and that in the great cities meetings would be held and subscription lists opened. But a difficulty soon occurred, the first sign of which was indicated by Mr. L. C. Probyn, Accountant-General of Madras. Writing to the Honorary Secretary of the Famine Fund Committee, on August 13, Mr. Probyn stated that he thought the objects for which contributions were asked should be more precisely defined. He said:—' It would, of course, be useless for private subscribers to compete with Government in this matter, or to attempt to set up an independent agency, and I gather it was not the wish of the meeting that this should be done. But people, perhaps less interested in the matter than I am, will, I think, very likely refuse their subscriptions on the grounds that they are asked to undertake the work which Government has already undertaken, and for which doubtless the Indian tax-payers will eventually have to pay.'

The subject had engaged the most anxious consideration of the committee, who were fully alive to the impolicy of clashing in any way with Government forms of relief. No definite rules of relief had, however, been formulated, at the immediate outset of operations, but it was clearly understood that the money subscribed would be expended in aiding those whom Government organisations could not reach. There was no wish or intention in any form to attempt to relieve those classes for whom the authorities had made themselves responsible. The committee looked upon themselves as occupying a position analogous to that of the

Red Cross Society in a warlike campaign. The organisation of armies of civilised states provided medical officers and ambulances, but when a battle occurred it was always found that there was more than enough work for both official and voluntary medical men and nurses. The famine had already shown that, beyond the limits which the most philanthropic Government must be careful not to overstep, there were multitudes who needed a helping hand extended to them to prevent them sinking into hopeless poverty ; there were hundreds of thousands of others who, when rains came, would need assistance in the provision of grain for sowing, in aid towards purchasing oxen and ploughs for preparing the land, and thatch for the roofs of their houses. These views were formulated in a series of resolutions passed at a meeting of the general committee held on August 24. They were as follows :—

(1.) Contribution in aid of local committees for relief of necessitous poor not reached by Government aid :

(2.) Contribution towards the care of destitute children in (a) orphanages ; and in (b) day nurseries ; and the like :

(3.) Providing clothes for destitute women and children :

(4.) And, to make allotments towards any other special objects which seem to come within the scope and ability of the fund.

It had also been determined that committees should be formed in all the districts affected by famine, in accordance with a resolution which set forth that 'collectors and European and native gentlemen in the distressed districts be requested to form themselves into local committees for the distribution of such aid as it may be in the power of the general relief committee to place at their disposal.' Circulars were addressed to all the affected places with most unsatisfactory results. The Government of India had adopted an attitude towards the fund which absolutely paralysed all the efforts which the committee were making. In India the Government is all in all. Any effort upon which the authorities look deprecatingly, or to which they give doubtful support, withers as though smitten with a plague. In the present instance, however, all effort was not checked, as the supreme and local Governments were at variance: the minor gods on the spot were propitious ; it was only the occupants of the far-off Olympus who were opposed (under a slight misapprehension of existing circumstances) to private charity being exercised. Some people there were who dared consequences, and five mofussil committees were formed during the month of August. But, generally speaking, the movement hung fire. The way in which the misunderstanding between Simla and Madras became public was this :

In common with other Indian cities, in regions where famine did not exist, the authorities in Calcutta had been asked to convene a meeting of the citizens, and ask for subscriptions. No response was made to this appeal for a while. Neither was any reply vouchsafed by the members of the Supreme Government at Simla, of whom subscriptions were asked. In a somewhat circuitous manner it soon oozed out that the Viceroy and his Council were not well pleased with the action which had been taken in Madras. The public meeting in the Banqueting Hall and the appeal to England were looked upon as the acts of the Government of Madras, who were represented by a journal which professed to speak the mind of the Government of India, as being in open revolt against their superiors. They were also charged with acting insubordinately in not asking permission of Lord Lytton to make the appeal; and further, in making it they had virtually confessed the inability of the authorities to cope with the disaster. It was a confession of defeat, a surrender by a general of division when the Commander-in-Chief had no thought of surrender, but believed his forces capable of overcoming all difficulties. This reasoning was fallacious, but for a time was very powerful. The action that had been taken was not the action of the Government of Madras, who it was felt by the chief movers in the matter could not as a Government appeal to the people of England or of any other country for assistance. But it was felt that the people of Southern India could open communications with the people of England, and that such a course would be right and proper. The movement, in its conception and carrying out, as has already been shown, was entirely non-official, and the Governor of Madras was asked to preside over the proposed meeting, not as Governor, but as the chief citizen of the Presidency, who, from his position, was peculiarly acquainted with the need that was alleged to exist, and who would be able to give such tidings as would carry weight. Yet further, not supposing for one moment that their desire to ally themselves with the Government could be misinterpreted into antagonism to the supreme authorities, it never entered the minds of the promoters of the movement to ask the Viceroy's countenance, which was assumed as certain to be rendered. It must, however, be conceded that there is something to be said from the point of view of the Government of India, the members of which were made by the appeal to appear wanting in a due appreciation of the facts. What reasons Lord Lytton and his Councillors had to urge for their action will appear in due course.

The vague and unauthenticated statements which

had been current for some time were confirmed towards the end of the month, and, just before the Viceroy left Simla, by circumstances which transpired in Calcutta. A meeting was held in the house of Sir Richard Garth, Chief Justice of Bengal, at Calcutta, to consider measures to be adopted towards raising public subscriptions in Southern India. The effort had a wet blanket thrown upon it at the beginning by Sir Richard Garth stating that since the invitations had been issued he had received a communication from the Lieutenant-Governor of Bengal to the effect that the Government of India was not desirous that any action should be taken in the matter by private agency at present, as the Government felt quite confident of being able to deal with the sufferers by the famine satisfactorily. It was also urged that as Her Majesty and the Secretary of State had sanctioned the desire of the Viceroy that the resources of the Empire should be placed unreservedly at the disposal of the Government of India for famine purposes, nothing need be done at present, and nothing was done.[1] It would be difficult to describe the indignation

[1] A 'communicated' paragraph to the Calcutta *Englishman* gave the following details of the meeting:—'At the private meeting held by special invitation at the house of Sir Richard Garth, on Saturday afternoon, to consider what measures should be adopted towards raising public subscriptions for the relief of the sufferers from the famine in Southern India, as suggested by the circular of the Committee appointed by the public meeting lately held at Madras, all classes of the community were represented. Sir Richard Garth opened the business of the meeting by explaining that since the invitation had been issued, he had received a communication from the Lieutenant-Governor to the effect that the Government of India was not desirous that any action should be taken in the matter by private agency at present, as the Government felt quite confident of being able to deal with the sufferers by the famine satisfactorily. Several gentlemen present expressed then their views on the subject. But, it appearing to be the general opinion that the position of Government had been improved by the sanction received from Her Majesty and the Secretary of State for India to place the resources of the Empire unreservedly at the disposal of the Government of India for famine purposes, it was decided to take no steps to appeal to the public at present. At the same time, it was decided to intimate to the supporters of the move-

and excitement which were aroused in Southern India when these facts were known. First and foremost, it was pointed out that H. M. the Queen-Empress, the Prince and Princess of Wales, the Secretary of State, the ex-Viceroy, were all put in the wrong as subscribers to the fund by this statement. It was deridingly asked whether the Government indeed could deal ' satisfactorily ' with the famine in its intensified aspect when, up to June 30, half a million of people had died from want, and want-induced disease. The Government of India were charged with teaching a new gospel, the gospel of inhumanity, while the people of Calcutta were called upon to revolt against such a doctrine. This, by the way, they were doing in the shape of contributions raised through the missionary conference and for the day nurseries, which had been established in Madras. In many ways the feeling of annoyance and vexation which had been engendered found expression, and amongst other instances may be quoted the following ' skit,' in which the practice of the Government of India of publishing draft bills in the *Government Gazette* was satirised: —

ACT XVI. OF 1877.

AN ACT AGAINST HUMANITARIAN PRACTICE.

The following Act and Statement of Objects and Reasons accompanying it are published for general information, under the 22nd of the Rules for the Conduct of Business at Meetings of the Council of the Governor-General of India for the purpose of making Laws and Regulations :—

---

ment for raising private subscriptions that at any future time, if it becomes necessary, the committee is willing to give its services to devise the best means of carrying out the proposals, and to devote all its energies to the cause of public charity.'

No. 16 of 1877.

THE ANTI-HUMANITARIAN ACT, 1877.

An Act to define and amend the Law relating to charitable contributions during Famine Periods.

Whereas it is expedient to define and amend the law relating to charitable contributions during Famine periods. It is hereby enacted as follows :—

Preamble.

CHAPTER I.

PRELIMINARY.

Short Title.

1. This Act may be called ' The Anti-Charitable Contributions Act, 1877 :'

Local extent.

It extends to the whole of the Madras Presidency :

Commencement.

And it has already been put into execution, viz., from August 6, 1877.

2. On and from that day the Laws specified in the schedule hereto annexed were repealed. But all powers conferred under either of such instructions be deemed to have been conferred under this Act.

Enactment repealed.

And all references to either of such Laws shall be deemed to be made to this Act.

These Laws are as follows :—

(*a*) The Bible, in use among Christians, particularly those portions relating to giving of alms.

(*b*) The Koran.

(*c*) The Hindoo Sastras and all traditions which counsel the support of life by charity.

(*d*) The Buddhist Banas.

CHAPTER II.

OF THE CONTRIBUTIONS WHICH ARE TO CEASE.

3. A contribution is a sum of money, or any quantity of food, or piece of clothing given to persons in deep and dire necessity.

CHAPTER III.

OF THE NON-NECESSITY WHICH EXISTS FOR CHARITY.

4. It has at length been recognised by the Supreme Government that distress exists in the Madras Presidency, and seeing that Famines occur with frequent regularity, and must be fought on system, the Government is prepared to deal with

Non-necessity for aid.

all distress that arises. It has been stated that half a million people have already died of Famine, but the Supreme Government has not seen each of these corpses. It is, therefore, enacted that it will henceforth be penal for any person to allude to this so-called 'fact,' the penalty in case of non-compliance with this order will be the same as in dacoity and other crimes of violence. (See Acts relating to Dacoities.)

CHAPTER IV.

OF WHAT CONSTITUTES AN OFFENCE UNDER THE ACT.

5. It will be considered an offence within the meaning of this Act and be punishable to the full extent of the penalties, if any person shall,— _{Definition of offence.}

(*a*) Give a contribution (1) to the General Relief Fund of the Madras Presidency, or (2) to the Town Relief Fund :

(*b*) Giving food or nutriment of any kind to people who are in search of sustenance, and are found anywhere outside their villages :

(*c*) Writing to friends in England from India, or other parts of Her Britannic Majesty's dominions, soliciting aid :

(*d*) Or any deed which can be construed by the servants of the Supreme Government into a charitable act. [All moneys subscribed will be impounded to pay the salaries of the large numbers of such who are already in the service of the State.]

Illustrations.

A, a resident in Madras, has given 500 rs. to one of the Funds named ; B, a Mofussilite, has done similarly, and, in addition, belongs to a Local Relief Committee ; C, a resident in London, has given 10,000 rs. ; A is to be heavily fined, B imprisoned for life, and C warned that, if he ever comes to British India, he will be arrested and tried on the charge.

A, a lady living in Namteypett, Madras, was discovered feeding a number of little children every morning with milk and brown bread. A is punishable with a fine of 500 rs. on the first occasion, and imprisonment, at the discretion of the magistrate, on all subsequent occasions, when the heinous charge is proved.

B, another lady living in Rayda, Madras, has established a number of Day Nurseries for babies and children who can scarcely run alone, whose mothers are engaged on relief works. This is considered a very bad case, and the magistrate has discretion to fine and imprison to the utmost possible limit. Half the fine recovered, or half the property of the prisoner (which will be confiscated) will be given to the informer.

A, third lady [it is anticipated that the ladies will be the grossest offenders], visits a Relief Camp, and gives 2-anna pieces to the poorest and most emaciated of the children. She also clothes some. On her first visit she finds she has not a sufficient number of 2-anna pieces, and sends several rupees worth by a friend D. This is a very gross transgression. A should be transported to the Andamans—not so much for the original offence, but for inducing D to break the law. D should be imprisoned for six months, and receive fifty lashes.

C (in the employment of Government) is reported to have given Liebig's Extract to a starving man, and recovered him. This, C did, knowing that there was a Relief Camp a mile and a half beyond his dwelling. C may plead that it was a wet night when he did this and the starving man was greatly exhausted, but this aggravates the offence, as, when camps are provided, nobody ought to be outside them. C will, of course, be imprisoned for twelve months, will be degraded, and his past service not be allowed to count for pension.

All cases that may be brought up are to be dealt with in the spirit of these illustrations.

THE FIRST SCHEDULE.

(*See Section* 2.)

This is unnecessary, as the laws, human and divine, which are to be abrogated have been already set forth in detail.

THE SECOND SCHEDULE.

A.—*Forms of Plaints, &c.*

There are to be no forms of plaints. The evidence of an informer that A or B, to the end of the alphabet, has been guilty of the crime of aiding or abetting in any way charitable relief, shall be sufficient to secure a conviction. No defence is to be allowed to prisoners, who are to be considered as *non compos mentis*, which they clearly are, if they give of their substance, and expend their sympathy upon the starving and the dying, when Government has taken the task in hand.

STATEMENT OF OBJECTS AND REASONS.

The object of this Act is to amend and codify the law governing the giving of charitable allowances on the part of the general public during a time of famine, and, indeed, at all other times. The want of a definite system of law upon this subject has long been felt. This want, it is hoped, will be supplied by the present Act. The Act is based mainly upon the Law of the Utilitarians, men who have no hearts and only diseased brains; no deviations from that law have been made, but some provisions have been adopted from the Pandemonium Codes, which were drawn up by that excellent gentleman, Mephistopheles, aided by Diabolus, the Advocate, whose art in making the worse appear the better part has been strained to the utmost in this case. The occasion for it was a dark and dreadful conspiracy among sundry and divers malicious persons residing in Southern India generally, but mainly in Madras. They seem to have conceived that it was their duty to supplement Government aid towards sufferers from famine during the trial of a great experiment, and based their action, among other things, on the weak plea that half a million of people had died through want, although Government was doing its best. But that best was only put forth by a Local Government too fond of having its own way : the supreme authorities have now girded their loins, and are entering into the conflict. The public will see what they will see. The mischief of such acts as those which this enactment will put a stop to is that the experiment which Sir Stra Johnchey has watched with such great interest is vitiated, and we shall have to fight another famine *de novo*. This is not to be tolerated : hence this enactment, which all are commanded to obey.

STOTLEY WHIKES,

Secretary to Government in the
Legislative Department.

INHUMANVILLE, August 8, 1877.

Whilst feeling was thus being aroused and expressed, the executive committee of the relief fund, satisfied as to the necessity for their action, had bated ' not a jot of heart or hope,' but had continued appealing for subscriptions, meeting claims for aid, and laying the foundations of a widespread scheme of relief to extend wherever distress existed in India.

As the time approached for His Excellency's arrival in Madras, there was much interest as to the course His Excellency would adopt towards a movement which had by this time given promise of attaining great pro‹ portions.

'Has the set of the current in His Excellency's mind become fully determined?' men asked each other. 'Is his famine policy absolutely decided upon?' 'Has it become as hard as the palæocrystic ice which barred the way of English seamen to the Pole?' If so, it was felt that His Excellency had better never have come to Madras. 'Instead of being the deliverer of Madras, he would become the destroyer of the people,' said one of the exponents of public opinion, which further continued, 'If Lord Lytton has imbibed the Temple notions about rations—and there is an ominous appearance of it— then we tell his lordship that he will have to stand at the bar of Indian and English opinion to answer for the guilt of a terrible mortality.' 'Adopt those reduced rations,' said the leading medical authority in this Presidency a few days ago, 'and your awful death-rate in the relief camps will be terribly increased.' In an issue of *The Times* recently to hand it was remarked, 'If there is such a mortality in Madras as there was in Orissa, there will be no mercy or forgiveness this time for those who are responsible. The policy of the Madras Government will prevent that terrible mortality. The policy Lord Lytton is credited with will bring it about. We beg his lordship to be warned in time, and not be seduced, by a hope of saving half a million sterling, into the adoption of such a policy, when every pound sterling of the amount that is saved will mean a human life untimely and unnecessarily squandered.' There are assumptions in the foregoing passages which were not borne out by subsequent facts, particularly with regard to the rival policies, but the remarks are quoted to show the direction and force of the currents of local opinion at the time. The new policy had not the effect which was feared.

The Governor of Madras proceeded to Raichore— the boundary-line station between Madras and Bombay

—to meet the Viceroy, and together the Governor-General and Governor travelled to Bellary, where a day was spent. The discourse between Lord Lytton and the Duke of Buckingham and Chandos was of relief works, relief camps, total expenditure, and kindred subjects, but not a word was spoken of the interrupted public meeting at Calcutta or of the alleged ability of the Government to deal satisfactorily with all affected by famine. The Governor of Madras left the Viceroy at Bellary and returned to Madras to receive the Viceroy at the chief city of the Presidency.

On the day preceding the Viceroy's arrival, a telegram was received from the Mansion House Committee stating that a report had appeared in *The Times* from Calcutta stating that in the opinion of the Government of India private subscriptions were not wanted. It was asked whether there was any truth in the statement, and it was added that unless speedily contradicted the success of the fund would be imperilled.

'The appeal to England has been very successful so far,' said his Grace the Governor, to a member of the executive committee on the morning of August 29, when on the platform of the Madras station the Viceroy's train was being awaited. 'I received a telegram last evening announcing the despatch of 25,000*l*. That makes 45,000*l*. altogether. The fund will probably be large. The "whip" will be successful.'

'That is very satisfactory, your Grace,' was the reply. 'But is not the charity of England likely to be checked by the telegram of *The Times* Calcutta correspondent, respecting which the Mansion House Committee has telegraphed?'

'It may have a temporary effect,' said his Grace, 'but I do not think it will do much harm.'

'Your Grace had an interview with the Viceroy

yesterday. May I ask whether his Excellency said anything about the fund ?'

' No. Not one word was said on the subject.'

' Seeing the prejudicial effect which certain statements purporting to have the authority of Government had in Bengal and now have in London, does your Grace not think the relief committee might seek an interview with the Viceroy, to come to a clear understanding about the matter ?'

' Yes ; I think the committee is bound to do this.'

The train came up at this moment and the conversation was interrupted.

Under eyes which scanned him closely, the Viceroy stepped from his carriage and proceeded with the Duke of Buckingham and Chandos to Government House amid the state and magnificence with which the present rule of Madras is marked.

On the following morning in a semi-official manner the honorary secretary of the committee had interviews with Colonel O. T. Burne, private secretary, and other members of the Viceroy's staff, and it was understood that Lord Lytton would be willing to meet the committee and discuss with them the question of private subscriptions and the scope for private charity. A statement of this fact was 'circulated'[1] during the day to members of the executive, who were to meet that evening in due course, that they might become acquainted with the business for consideration. With one exception, all the members who saw the notice were in favour of an interview which, it was hoped, would do away with the misunderstanding that existed. But when the committee met in the evening a different spirit was evinced. This will appear from the following passages

---

[1] 'Circulated,' in the fashion in which so much Indian committee work is done. Anglo-Indians will understand the allusion.

extracted from No. 1 of the 'weekly statements' of the Famine Committee :—
The following telegrams from London were read :—

From Lord Mayor, dated August 27.

Twenty thousand pounds further herewith. Telegram in to-day's *Times* from Calcutta deprecating private efforts as Government will do all necessary. Injurious. How does your Grace propose to distribute our fund? During last famine a Local Committee was appointed.

From Sir Nathaniel Rothschild, dated August 27.

By desire of Lord Mayor remit through Chartered Mercantile Bank further twenty thousand pounds. *Times* states this morning from Calcutta Government deprecates private charity. Unless officially contradicted will prevent further subscriptions.

It was resolved that the following telegram be at once sent to the Lord Mayor of London :—

Action Supreme Government unaccountable. Here notorious no Government efforts can reach certain distressed classes, private agency can. Central Committee Madras manages fund, controlling Local Committees interior. Operations quite distinct from Government, not conflicting but supplementary. Large funds urgently required, delay disastrous.

An entry in the minute-book of the committee shows that a telegram of the same purport as those from the Lord Mayor and Sir Nathaniel Rothschild had been received by a firm in Madras.[1]

The meeting was held late in the evening, and what followed was not a little dramatic in its incidents. The honorary secretary called at the telegraph office on his way from the meeting, forgetful of an arrangement which had been made, viz., that in consideration of the interest which the Governor had taken in the move-

---

[1] It is only fair to Sir William Robinson, chairman of the executive committee, to state that he was not present at the meeting whence it was decided to telegraph 'Action Supreme Government unaccountable.'

ment, his Grace should see all messages before they were despatched to the Mansion House, London. Later in the evening, letters were sent to the private secretaries of the Viceroy and the Governor respectively, containing copies of the telegram, and an account of the decision the meeting had come to, viz., not to interview Lord Lytton, but, instead, had determined to despatch a telegram to London, copy of which was enclosed. The letters were delivered just a sa party given in Lord Lytton's honour was breaking up. As at Bellary so in Madras, whilst all other conceivable topics in connection with the famine had been well threshed out in discussion, nothing had been said on the subject of private charity. It was not 'official' business, and, though doubtless uppermost in the minds of all, was not referred to. All parties were shy of bringing it forward, but with such a telegram as that which had gone to London, in which the conduct of the Supreme Government was described as 'unaccountable,' and their statement of being able to satisfactorily meet all distress distinctly denied, there was no possibility of further 'fencing.' The Duke started in search of the Viceroy, and the Viceroy proceeded to look for the Duke. They met, and, rumour has it, discussed the question in all its bearings till long after midnight, the outcome being a message to the Lord Mayor from the Duke of Buckingham and Chandos, couched in the following terms:—'Message from the committee this evening went without approval, before I had opportunity of conferring with the Viceroy on the subject of *The Times*' report respecting statement at Calcutta to which you refer. Viceroy entirely concurs that every facility be afforded to contributions of private charity towards relieving those cases of distress amongst famine-stricken people of South India which Government organisation does not propose to, and cannot undertake to meet, but was, and is, averse to Government calling meetings for levying subscriptions from Indian people who may have to bear heavy famine taxation. Hence probable origin of report. Funds will be managed by a central relief committee at Madras, and local committees, and not applied to relief of that distress which Government, by providing work and village relief, can meet.' A copy of this message was forwarded to the executive committee next morning. The Mansion House Committee managed their share in the unfortunate difference very skilfully, and served to allay the suspicion which was being aroused in England that disputation and wrangling were going on in India.

Three days later, in a *Gazette of India Extraordinary*, announcing the new arrangements made for the campaign, two letters appeared which—reluctant as the writer is to burden his pages with long documents—from their intrinsic importance must be quoted in full. They are as follows :—

THE COLLECTION OF PRIVATE SUBSCRIPTIONS AND THEIR DUE EXPENDITURE ON OBJECTS OUTSIDE THE SCOPE OF GOVERNMENT OPERATIONS.

No. 773, GOVERNOR-GENERAL'S CAMP, MADRAS, August 31, 1877.
From   S. C. BAYLEY, ESQ., C.S.I.,
        Additional Secretary to the Government of India.
    To
THE SECRETARY TO THE GOVERNMENT OF MADRAS.

Sir,—I am directed to forward, for the information of the Governor of Madras in Council, the accompanying copy of a letter which, under the direction of his Excellency the Viceroy, I have this day addressed to the Government of Bengal, in regard to the question of applying to the public for subscriptions in aid of famine relief.

2. The immediate object of this letter was to explain to his Honour the Lieutenant Governor of Bengal somewhat more fully than

had been in the telegram of August 12, the views and wishes of the Government of India in regard to appeals by Government for public subscriptions, and it is desirable that his Grace should also be informed of the considerations which led his Excellency to adopt these views.

3. With reference to paragraph 7 of the enclosed letter, I am directed to state that his Excellency finds on the proceedings of the committee[1] held on August 24, a resolution that the fund should be devoted (1) to contributions in aid of local committees for the relief of necessitous poor not reached by the Government; (2) To contributions towards the care of destitute children; (3) To making allotment towards any other special objects which seem to come within the scope and ability of the fund. The whole discussion tends to show that it was the desire of the committee to adapt its work to objects and measures of relief other than that already covered by the action of Government, but in considering the terms by which the committee define the objects to which their funds will be devoted, the Viceroy fails to gather such complete and specific information on the point as he could desire. He has no objection whatever to the benefits of private charity being directed towards those necessitous poor whom the action of Government cannot reach, and accepts it as quite probable that among women of the respectable classes, among persons on very small fixed incomes, and even among agriculturists who are struggling to remain at their homes, there may be cases, which ought not to come within the scope of Government action, but which may very properly be relieved by private charity wherever private charity has the necessary agency at its disposal. Similarly in regard to children, though Government is in one way or another endeavouring to keep alive all destitute or orphan children that may be thrown on its hands, there may well be room for private charity in regard to children not within this category, and moreover the work of providing for and supporting such children hereafter, either by grants to orphanages or to those who will receive such children, is obviously a fit subject for private charity. His Excellency understands it was not the object of the committee to express, in a general resolution, specific rules or detailed instructions, but doubtless these will be drawn out hereafter. In the meantime, as Lord Lytton learns that the subject has been under the consideration of his Grace the Governor, he will be glad to receive information as to the conclusions which the Madras Government have come to, and to learn not only what are the specific objects in detail to which funds are to be devoted, but also what agency the Committee propose to employ both in large towns and in the interior for the attainment of those objects. In large towns there will no doubt be plenty of volun-

[1] General Committee, Madras Famine Relief Fund.

teer agency available, but in the villages his Excellency apprehends that, outside the chain of relief organisation subordinate to the collector it will be difficult to find the requisite agency, and Lord Lytton deprecates the diversion of this organisation to purposes other than those of Government relief. This objection is not based on imaginary grounds. Experience has shown that, when the Government relief organisation has been placed under the orders of a central committee, it has led not only to the collectors being burthened with additional work, having to submit double sets of returns, and to correspond with an additional master, but also to a considerable amount of friction and some unseemly discussions between Government officials and their superiors. His Excellency hopes therefore that the Government of Madras will be able to direct the operations of the committee into some line where the agency to be employed will not be that of the overworked establishment already employed by Government.

No. 772, GOVERNOR-GENERAL'S CAMP, MADRAS, August 31, 1877.

From S. C. BAYLEY, ESQ., C.S.I.,
  Additional Secretary to the Government of India.

To

THE SECRETARY TO THE GOVERNMENT OF BENGAL.

Sir,—The attention of his Excellency the Viceroy has been drawn to certain correspondence which has passed between the Lord Mayor of London and the General Committee, Madras Famine Relief Fund, in regard to a private meeting held in Calcutta for forming a famine relief committee; and from this correspondence it appears that considerable misapprehension exists as to his Excellency's views on the subject of appeals to the public in aid of famine relief. I am, therefore, directed to communicate to you, in continuation of the Viceroy's telegram of August 12, the views of the Government of India on this important subject.

2. The Madras Government have undertaken to keep people alive by all available means within their power; they undertake to relieve the famine-stricken by giving work to those who can work; by giving food and attendance either in relief camps or kitchens to famine-stricken people who cannot work, and they distribute relief in the shape of a money-dole to nearly a million of people at their villages; but in order to do this the whole available organisation of the country

is strained to the very utmost, and it is impossible to place this organisation at the disposal of any irresponsible committee.

3. Before, therefore, the Government of India could properly ask for, or even accept, the charitable assistance of the public, it would be necessary to ascertain what measures of relief, other than those already adopted by Government, the central committee propose to adopt, and what organisation, other than the Government organisation, is at their disposal for carrying out those measures.

4. The Viceroy in his telegram of the 12th explained that he was unwilling 'to appeal for public subscriptions in aid of the efforts which Government was making to keep people alive,' that is to say, he was unwilling to ask for public subscriptions in order to supplement the Government expenditure on the same lines, for the same ends, and through the same channels of organisation as the Government had already occupied. To have done this would be merely asking for public subscriptions in aid of the Indian revenues, and it was unlikely on the one hand that the public would have cared to subscribe for this purpose, while on the other the assistance which such subscriptions could have given would have borne but an infinitesimal proportion to the expenditure of half a million sterling a month which the Government has already to defray on account of famine.

5. There was another consideration which, in his Excellency's opinion, rendered it specially inopportune to appeal to the Indian public for subscriptions in aid of Imperial expenditure on famine, so long especially as the objects and agency of such charity are not distinctly and definitely separated from the objects and agency of Government expenditure. It had become manifest that, in order to meet the heavy drain on the finances of India, which the Madras and Bombay famines were already causing, the Government would sooner or later be obliged to resort to increased taxation over the whole country, and it followed necessarily from the nature of the case that the very class from whom subscriptions might be expected would have to bear the burthen of taxation; the Viceroy was, therefore, unwilling to ask for public subscriptions from the same persons who would hereafter have to bear a heavy burthen of taxation for precisely the same objects as those to which their subscriptions were to be devoted.

6. This last consideration of course applies only to subscriptions raised in India, and in no way to appeals made in England; but its importance is increased by the fact that in addition to the destitution in Madras, the Government have to face anticipated scarcity also over a great portion of Northern India.

7. His Excellency in his telegram of the 12th instant added that, 'If any definite objects can be specified which are beyond the scope of

the operations of Government, and to which the subscriptions of the public can be usefully applied, there can be no objection.' At that time the Government of India had received no communication on the subject from the Government of Madras, and the newspaper reports of the public meetings left it quite uncertain whether the objects to which the committee destined their funds were those already provided by Government, or not : in fact, the telegram sent home by the committee to the Lord Mayor[1] leaves the question still open to the utmost doubt, and points rather to the assistance being devoted to relief works and relief camps, than to any fresh field of action. His Excellency has now, however, had an opportunity of conferring with the Government of Madras, and learns from his Grace the Duke of Buckingham that the committee propose to devote the funds received by them to special objects not coming within the scope of Government relief, two of which objects are understood to be the relief of those who are not yet so reduced as to leave their villages or to apply for Government assistance, and the support of orphans and destitute children not reached by Government agency. His Excellency is now in correspondence with the Government of Madras with a view to formulating somewhat more precisely the objects to which private charity will be devoted and the agency through which it will be applied.

8. While therefore it remains in the Viceroy's opinion undesirable for the Government itself to ask those who will hereafter have to bear the burthen of taxation on account of famine expenditure, to give their private subscriptions also towards the same object, his Excellency desires that every encouragement may be given to spontaneous efforts which may be made in this direction. Lord Lytton is very far from desiring to impede the flow of private charity, and is only anxious to secure that it should be devoted to useful purposes apart from those already taken up by the State, and that it should not be diverted into a simple contribution to the revenues of the State.

The reply of the Government of Madras to the letter sent to them was prompt and effective in showing that the relief movement was not an official one. It ran as follows (being signed by Mr. Garstin, Secretary to the Famine Department) : ' I am directed to acknowledge receipt of your letter of the 1st instant, No. 776,

---

[1] 'Committee earnestly solicit your Lordship's powerful influence, support, appeal, assistance, for afflicted population Southern India. . . . Property sold for food; villages largely deserted; poor wandering search sustenance; resources lower middle class exhausted owing famine prices; prompt liberal assistance sympathy may mitigate suffering.'

and to state that the Madras Government have taken no part in the matter of applying to the public for subscriptions in aid of famine relief, although, at the request of the citizens of Madras, the head of the Government consented to preside at a public meeting convened by the sheriff to consider the advisability of appealing to England for such aid.

' I am to add that your letter will be communicated at once to the general committee of the Madras Famine Relief Fund, with whom rests the duty of administering the funds raised, with an intimation that the officers of Government in their official capacity will nowhere be allowed to be disbursers of any funds which may be placed at the committee's disposal, although the Government have no reason to suppose that the committee are relying on the agency of State establishments for the administration of their private funds.'

When referred to the relief committee, the correspondence was simply acknowledged, with an observation that ' the committee note the remark of Government, that Government servants in their official capacity will not be permitted to dispense the funds of the committee, and that the wishes of the Government will be carefully observed.' This was clearly not the right answer to send. The Government of India asked for information, and they received a bald acknowledgment. Much inconvenience was subsequently caused by a want of frankness at this stage of affairs.

As soon as money had been received in large sums the claims of other parts of India outside the Madras Presidency were considered. Early in September a grant of one lakh of rupees was made to Mysore, and half a lakh to the Deccan and Khandeish Committee at Bombay. Willingness was also expressed to send aid to Hyderabad, but Sir Richard Meade, the Resident, after conferring with Sir Salar Jung, came to the conclusion that assistance was not needed. Grants were made on two occasions to Sir Henry Daly for distribution to famine-stricken people in Central India.

With the month of September a new departure was made by the committee in the direction of more efficiently and widely disbursing the funds which had been entrusted to them. Owing to various causes the process of forming committees in the mofussil was very slow, and it was determined to send two gentlemen — one north, the other south—into the districts for the purpose of reporting upon the state of affairs and forming committees. The delegates chosen were the Rev. J. M. Strachan, M.D., of the S.P.G. Mission, and F. Rowlandson, Esq., a solicitor of Madras. Their travelling expenses were provided for, and an honorarium of 1,000 rs. per month each was accorded. The instructions given to the delegates were that they were to organise as far as possible local committees in different parts of the various distressed districts, to be in direct communication with the general relief committee at Madras for distribution of famine funds. Also to organise special agencies where local committees could not be formed, or sub-agencies were likely to be more efficient.

They were reminded that 'the fund was designed to relieve the necessitous poor whom Government cannot or do not reach, and care is necessary to avoid even indirect interference with Government operations. Under the above designation may be included those who are not ordinarily reckoned poor, but who are rendered dependent by the present distress. While Government operations have for their object the salvation of life, the funds may be legitimately applied to the mitigation of intense suffering.' The general committee, they were informed, would be prepared to make pecuniary provision, if necessary (within reasonable limits), for preparing local accounts, and for all necessary expenses connected with the distribution of the funds.

These and other points were noticed to indicate generally the committee's wishes, but the deputation were left a wide discretion, and the committee relied on their making the best arrangements which the circumstances in each locality admitted of, within the scope of the funds and the general principles above enunciated. The committee looked to the deputation for practical suggestions for the more efficient and prompt distribution of the funds, and the objects to which they or the local committee desired to apply them. Copies of these instructions were sent to the chief places in each district in advance, to prepare the way of the delegates, and were of much service in this respect.

Even this measure did not serve to remove all the difficulties in the way of forming committees. The Government of India were believed to be still averse to private charity, and official and *quasi*-official assistance was therefore not given; indeed, more than negative harm was done—positive evil resulted. The executive committee, on September 19, therefore determined to take advantage of the Viceroy's continued presence in the Presidency, to procure permission for officials in their citizen capacity to render service. His Grace the Governor was with his Excellency the Governor General at Coimbatore when the following telegram was despatched from the executive committee in Madras : ' Famine relief committee respectfully suggest publication of an announcement by your Grace's Government that there is no objection to the cordial co-operation on the part of Government servants in the distribution of the almost national charity of the English people which is reaching this committee. In the absence of such announcement the committee anticipate great difficulty in meeting the expectations of subscribers. Mofussil committees can scarcely be formed without the aid of collectors, judges, and others. Our information shows that officers of all grades seem doubtful as to the propriety of co-operating under existing circumstances. It is very desirable that this doubt should be removed.' Letters were also sent officially to Government embodying the foregoing statements. The Governor conferred with the Viceroy, and at a meeting of the executive committee held in the following week, the Chief Secretary of Government, Mr. D. F. Carmichael, attended, and handed in a copy of a notification just issued from the press—damp to the touch, as all freshly printed matter is—which was as follows : ' It is the desire of Government that public servants of all grades should give all the assistance they can render, without detriment to their official duties, to the formation of local committees, and generally to promote the object which the famine relief committee and subscribers to the famine relief fund have in view.' This removed all doubt and difficulty, and with one or two exceptions Government servants most zealously assisted in the work of relief. Conspicuous among them were the sessions judges, whose labours in North Arcot (Mr. C. G. Plumer), South Arcot (Mr. O. B. Irvine), Tinnevelly (Mr. F. Culling-Carr), Trichinopoly (Mr. E. Forster Webster), Tanjore (A. C. Burnell, Ph.D.), Chingleput (Mr. J. Hope), Coimbatore (Mr. F. M. Kindersley), Salem (Mr. J. Gordon), Kurnool (Hon. J. C. St. Clair), were beyond all praise.

Early in October the executive committee determined (on the suggestion of the honorary secretary) to publish a weekly statement of their proceedings, for distribution in Great Britain and elsewhere, and generally in India. It was determined to publish reports from local committees and other information likely to be of interest to subscribers as well as calculated to help the various committees in carrying on their work. A 'statement committee' was appointed to arrange for the periodical publication of the statement. It consisted of two members and the honorary secretary, but one of these declined service, and only one gentleman (the Very Rev. J. Colgan) saw the proofs of the statement before publication. The 'Weekly Statement' was of foolscap size ; its average contents covered 60 pages— ranging from 40 as a minimum to 88 as a maximum. It was a source of great satisfaction to the committee to know that their efforts to make public all their proceedings proved very gratifying to subscribers. The full publication of facts was also likely to be of benefit should similar efforts be needed in the future. Materials now exist which can be used as a guide. Had such been available during the famine in Madras more good might have been done with the money subscribed, with less delay than occurred. The executive committee had to ' make ' its experience.

Early in October the committee, finding it had control of nearly fifty lakhs of rupees, and that its existing system of making grants in response to applications did not provide adequate means for disposal of the money, determined to make allotments proportionate to districts. Thirty-six lakhs were taken for this purpose, and the remainder reserved to meet claims outside the scope of the allotments, such as the proportion for Mysore, Bombay, and other places. It was also understood that as the amount subscribed increased the amounts could be proportionately added to. Mr. G. A. Ballard, member of the Board of Revenue, who was upon the committee, expressed his willingness to prepare a statement in accordance with these suggestions. This was done, the basis of allotment being the intensity of distress as revealed in Government reports. The method of calculation adopted was briefly this ; the number of persons in Government relief of all sorts was taken and compared with the total population as indicating the intensity of distress in the various districts. The proportion of agriculturists to the general population was taken fron the census returns. Onethird of the 36 lakhs was apportioned to non-agriculturists, whilst the remainder (24 lakhs) was apportioned to the agriculturists paying under 50 rs. Government assessment.

The results worked out a fair idea of distribution. They had been modified to some slight extent from general information available, and it was believed the statement given below might be accepted as being an equitable allotment. On further consideration it was found there were not data for properly distributing the sums to subdivisions or taluks, and it was thought that operation might safely be left to the local committees, assisted as they were by Revenue and other Government officers of experience. Particulars were as follows :—

DISTRIBUTION OF 36 LAKHS OF FAMINE RELIEF FUNDS.

District	Allotment to non-agriculturists	Allotment to agriculturists, generally pattadars under 50 rs.	Total
	Rs.	Rs.	Rs.
1. Bellary . .	2,25,000	6,75,000	9,00,000
2. Salem . . .	1,60,000	2,90,000	4,50,000
3. Kurnool . .	1,80,000	3,20,000	5,00,000
4. Cuddapah . .	1,60,000	3,40,000	5,00,000
5. Coimbatore .	1,19,000	1,81,000	3,00,000
6. North Arcot .	95,000	1,55,000	2,50,000
7. South Arcot .	18,000	82,000	1,00,000
8. Chingleput . .	75,000	1,25,000	2,00,000
9. Madura . .	53,000	97,000	1,50,000
10. Nellore . .	1,15,000	1,35,000	2,50,000
Total . .	12,00,000	24,00,000	36,00,000

This plan was adopted, and applications then before the committee were dealt with on the basis of this scheme. For the guidance of local committees it was decided that a letter should be prepared, of which the following is a copy of that sent to the honorary secretary of the local committee at Kurnool :—

The Madras general famine relief committee believe that their operations and those of the respective local committees will be facilitated and rendered more effective if a fairly definite idea is arrived at as to the amount of relief to be distributed in different localities.

2. The general committee find they are in a position efficiently to allot sums to collectorates, and perhaps to taluks. The arrangement of the farther more minute territorial and individual allotments will fall to the local committees and sub-committees under the general principles that have been, or may be from time to time, indicated.

3. Local and sub-committees had been pretty generally formed already, but the general committee is not satisfied that all parts of the distressed tracts come within their action. If there are any tracts that have been hitherto omitted it is very desirable they should now be arranged for either by bringing them under an existing local committee, or by a new committee or agency being forthwith started.

4. The general committee find that the sum for apportionment over the Kurnool collectorate will not fall short of five lakhs of rupees. The committee consider this sum may be best utilised by distributing approximately one-third to relief of the general distressed population, and two-thirds to assist agricultural operations by money grants for hire of bullocks, for seed grain, implements, &c. Generally the relief should be given to ryots whose puttas are under 50 rs.

5. In the Kurnool collectorate there is one local committee at Kurnool. Does this committee operate over all the taluks noted [1] directly or through local sub-committees or agencies? If not, I am to request your committee will be good enough to take the earliest possible opportunity of conferring with the collector, and with the collector's concurrence, if necessary with any of the division or taluk officers, and arrange either for bringing the taluks where relief has not hitherto been provided for within the scope of your own operations, or recommend to this committee how the said taluks may best be reached and receive their due share of relief.

6. The committee will be glad to have the local committee's

---

[1] 1. Pattikonda. 2. Ramulkota. 3. Nundikotkur. 4. Markapur. 5. Cumbum. 6. Nundial. 7. Sirwel. 8. Koilguntla.

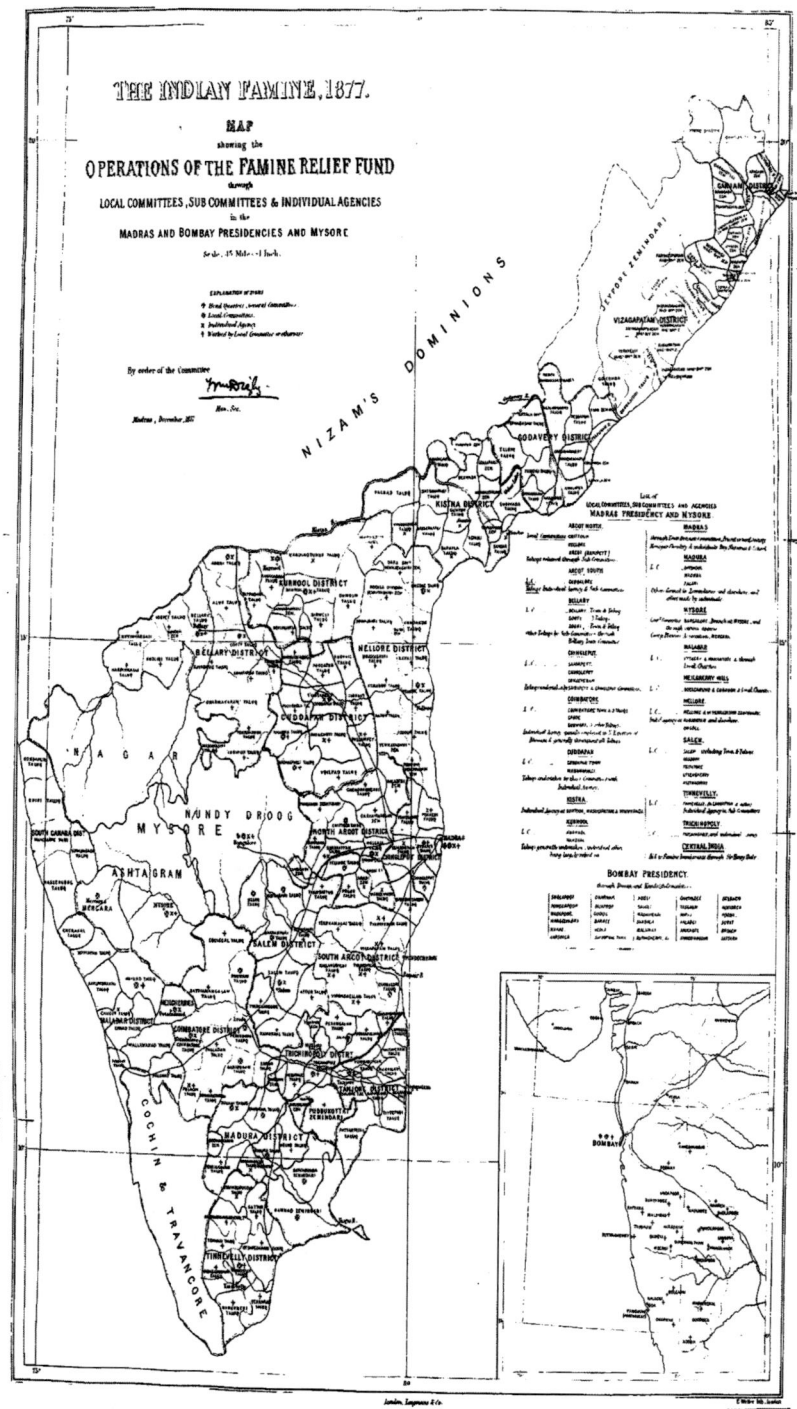

THE INDIAN FAMINE, 1877.

MAP
showing the
OPERATIONS OF THE FAMINE RELIEF FUND
through
LOCAL COMMITTEES, SUB COMMITTEES & INDIVIDUAL AGENCIES
in the
MADRAS AND BOMBAY PRESIDENCIES AND MYSORE

remarks as to proportionate allotments to different taluks. It will tend to avoid confusion if revenue territorial divisions are adhered to as far as possible in apportioning grants to committees and agencies.

By the first week in November the task of organising local committees, sub-committees, and agencies was complete, and the two gentlemen who went on deputation returned to Madras. Their labours had been very successful : where committees were already in existence the delegates were useful in stimulating and directing action, particularly with regard to the outlying taluks, whilst, where no committee formerly existed, good working bodies of members were formed. The consequence was that, speaking generally, there was not in November a taluk in the whole of the distressed districts which was not, more or less completely, feeling the benefit of the unexampled generosity of England, the Colonies, and some Continental countries, in the latter being included France—which subscribed through the Catholic missionaries,—and Germany and Switzerland— the two countries last named sending nearly 40,000 rs. to the Basel missionaries who labour in the western portion of the Madras Presidency and in the southern districts of Bombay. From the Kistna river to Cape Comorin most active relief operations were proceeded with, some of the distributors labouring in their self-imposed task with much energy and sacrifice. One gentleman spent over a week in a bullock cart visiting the distressed villages in a part of the region covered by the committee to which he belonged, giving aid to those whose cases had been previously investigated, and making further enquiries himself. This solitary instance would need to be multiplied vastly if justice were done to the zeal and discretion with which the funds were distributed. The various proceedings of committees published from time to time showed the wisdom of many of the arrangements made by sub-committees. The general committee felt that the discretion given to the sub-committees had been most wisely used, and the determination early arrived at, not to fetter their action with rules which local circumstances might render inoperative or *mal à propos*, was justified by events. By the first week in November over twenty-two lakhs of rupees had been placed at the command of local committees. The feeling, however, was general in the executive committee, that the money was not being distributed fast enough ; and at a meeting held on October 25 a minute by Mr. Ballard, indicating the necessity for a prompt and early distribution of the funds, was read. It was as follows : —

1. At page 5 of the 'Madras Famine Weekly Statement,' No. 5, will be seen a distribution of 36 lakhs of famine relief funds over ten distressed districts. The principles on which this distribution was arrived at are briefly indicated.

The arrangement as a whole was adopted by the executive committee, it being understood that in distributing the sums to districts, any considerable amount (say amounts aggregating over 1,000 rs.) should be deducted and the balance only allotted.

2. It was also, I think, pretty generally understood that approximately two-thirds of the above amount should be devoted to assist agricultural operations. There were various reasons for this resolution. I do not see them anywhere succinctly recorded, so it may not be out of place to indicate them here.

3. Non-interference with Government relief has all along been strongly insisted on by Government and desired by the committee. After the General Order of September 24 last, it was understood that Government particularly desired that famine relief funds should not be given (without the most careful discrimination) to persons who had previously been on Government relief, but who under the action or spirit of that order ceased to be relieved. Numbers who were struck off village dole, and discharged from open camps and small relief works, refused to go to close camps or large relief works at a distance from their villages. It was argued that to support or assist these people from famine relief funds to any great extent would tend to defeat the purposes of Government.

But if this large class, and the distressed still receiving Government relief, are eliminated, it seems clear that a comparatively small number of distressed will remain, save amongst the lower middle or poor agriculturists proper, *i.e.*, amongst the ryots.

It seemed that large numbers of these, if not actually starving (though instances of starvation were not wanting), were in very poor physical condition, whilst still larger numbers were bereft of all means of carrying on agricultural operations.

It was felt that if these could be reached *in time* many would be kept from the necessity of leaving their homes for Government works. Many would be enabled to cultivate their fields, sensibly helping towards increasing the food supplies of the country, and that thus by helping them liberally with money from famine relief funds an amount of direct and indirect benefit would be done not only individually but collectively which could hardly be achieved in any other way. The relief to the agriculturists must be given *now*. That to other classes can be extended over the time that pressure lasts. The communications the committee have received from Government officers, private individuals, missionaries, &c., show remarkable consensus of opinion that relief could be most efficiently given by distributing *largely* to the agricultural population.

But all agree that *the money should be put in the hands of the people with the least possible delay.*

4. The distribution of one-third and two-thirds of the allotments amongst agriculturists and non-agriculturists was accordingly proposed as, though an arbitrary, a fair, practical basis to work upon.

The essence of the success of the scheme, however, as far as the agriculturists are concerned, is to get the money forthwith into their hands, so as to keep them at home and help on with their cultivation during the present season.

5. I think the position indicated above has been theoretically taken up by the committee. Practically we seem to hesitate to act upon it. When any considerable grants are proposed there seem lingering doubts as to whether we are justified in making them now, whether we should not only make small disbursements at present, whether we should not husband the relief funds so that they may extend over four months or so, and that we may continue paying in driblets over that period.

6. It is open to us still to adopt this latter system if we please. Only, if we are to do so, let us adopt this and reject the other deliberately. At present there does seem some danger that whilst the former plan stands approved in principle, the time for carrying it out may be allowed to slip away by mere indecision in action.

7. I therefore intend proposing at next meeting as a formal resolution :—

   i. That the full allotments to agriculturists (generally puttadars under 50 rs.) entered at page 5 of the 'Weekly Report' No. 5 (deducting allotments aggregating 1,000 rs. or upwards in any case) be sent out to the respective local committees forthwith, with injunctions to arrange individual distribution in the taluks with the least possible delay.

   ii. That 25 per cent. of the allotments to non-agriculturists (with similar reservation as to sums already sent) be also sent out at once to the local committees, with intimation that balances are available to make them further similar remittances. That these further remittances will be made in communication with the local committees, but that this committee requests it may be borne in mind that casual assistance may be required to relieve distress till January or February.

8. I am only too well aware that the agricultural season may almost be considered as passed in some places, and is rapidly passing everywhere. Still, in my humble opinion a more efficient use of our funds cannot be made.

As the question is one of the gravest importance, I have put it in this form. If the resolutions are seconded and carried, they can be acted on at once. If they are not approved, I trust that amended resolutions or other resolutions may be put forth and adopted for action to be taken on them.

9. Even with the immediate distribution proposed, 15,00,000 rs. will remain for distribution in Madras districts not included in the above, in Mysore and elsewhere—and to supplement, if necessary, the sums now recommended to be distributed.

I do not think I can be wrong in appending to these remarks a General Order just received. It seems to me that by putting money at once into the hands of the ryots we can most efficiently aid what Government here desire.

GOVERNMENT OF MADRAS :—REVENUE DEPARTMENT.

Famine Relief.

No. 489. Proceedings of Government, dated October 15, 1877, Famine Relief, No. 2,331.

The Governor in Council has, by a telegraphic order of the 13th instant, called the attention of collectors to the importance of utilising to the utmost the present favourable change in the season. The recent rainfall has materially restored the condition of growing crops; many crops are being now harvested; land is nearly everywhere in a fit state for cultivation; and the rains of the north-east monsoon may be shortly expected. Prices have been gradually declining. In this state of the country it is of the utmost importance to its future prosperity that every exertion should be at once made to induce, encourage, and facilitate the return of people to their own homes and ordinary occupations. There may not unnaturally exist some feeling of hesitation amongst many, especially amongst those who have wandered from their own districts, to leave their present shelter, but the interests of the country demand that every available hand shall be turned to agriculture, and every exertion used to increase and expedite the growth of the newly-sown crops, on which the people must rely to restore the prices of food-grains to a normal state.

2. That this necessity is appreciated by the people is evinced by the fact that large numbers have already of their own accord left works and camps for agricultural employ, and that in many districts the area cultivated is larger than usual at this period. Yet in these districts more, and in others much, can be done, and no divisional officer should feel satisfied while any available land in his division remains uncultivated.

3. The Governor in Council desires also to impress on collectors the urgent necessity for reducing, as rapidly as may be, the numbers who are receiving State charity on relief works, in relief camps, &c., and consequently of diminishing the heavy drain on current expenditure.

4. The general principles on which relief is to be administered are already laid down in General Order of September 24, No. 2,847. The Government have spared no pains to relieve and sustain, and also to provide employment for, the people; now, however, agricultural or other usual employment is obtainable, and district officers must take care that the measures which were necessary for relief of the famine-stricken are not converted into a prolonged demoralising and pauperising charity.

5. A judicious but firm application of the tests and limitations laid down in the Government Order referred to will prevent the danger while meeting any necessity; but laxity or indecision in any district may not improbably result in the continued dependence of a large pauperised population on State aid through another year.

6. Where the numbers on relief works are materially diminished,

proportionate diminution should be made in the establishments, and labour should be consolidated so as to economise supervision. When the numbers in camps are materially diminished, subordinate establishments should be also diminished or otherwise utilised, permanent officers of the districts being allowed to resume their ordinary work. The general relief organisation of a district, however, is not to be reduced or broken up until further instructions from the Government, the nature of which will be regulated by the advent and extent of the monsoon rains.

7. The Governor in Council has had before him applications for sanction for many new works of a petty and local character, the possible benefit to arise from which can only be of a purely temporary character. He considers such works undesirable, but does not, however, desire to fetter the discretion of collectors, and therefore will not generally refuse to sanction works recommended by them ; but the sanction will only be accorded upon the distinct understanding that collectors, before recommending any works for sanction, satisfy themselves that such works are essential to the proper extent of relief, and are not urged from motives of purely local interest, or instigated by subordinates who hope for an opportunity to make an illicit gain from the relief expenditure.

(True Extract.)

(Signed) J. H. GARSTIN,

Additional Secretary to Government.

To the Collectors of Kistna, Nellore, Cuddapah, Bellary, Kurnool, North Arcot, Chingleput, South Arcot, Tanjore, Trichinopoly, Madura, Tinnevelly, Coimbatore, Salem, Commissioner of the Nilgiris, Board of Revenue, with a copy of telegram, dated October 13, 1877, No. 28 ; Financial Department, with a copy of telegram, dated October 13, 1877, No. 28 ; Public Works Department, with copy of telegram, dated October 13, 1877, No. 28.

After some discussion the resolutions were agreed to, and a third added in the following terms :—' The general committee, whilst indicating the above proportion of distribution, do not wish to bind the local committees by any hard and fast line. The general committee leave to the local committees, and look to them to exercise, a judicious discretion in making actual distribution both in regard to classes of the population and in regard to individuals.' These resolutions were printed as a memorandum and forwarded to all committees and agencies next day. Thenceforward the work of distribution proceeded with little delay or interruption.

A most pleasing feature of the period under notice was the *entente cordiale* which was renewed between his Excellency the Viceroy and the disbursers of the relief fund. This was made manifest in the following letter to the honorary secretary :—

Government House, Simla, Sept. 30, 1877.

My dear Sir,—The Viceroy desires me to write to you in regard to the intimation, which he conveyed to you when at Madras, of his desire to subscribe to the general relief fund as soon as the objects to which the fund is to be devoted should be specially defined.

His Excellency has now ascertained from the Madras Government, and from your instructions to the delegates of the committee, the general purposes on which the fund will be expended; and although he hopes to learn hereafter that these purposes have been somewhat more minutely defined in communication with the Madras Government, he is satisfied that they have been planned with a careful desire to avoid clashing with those of Government organisation, and that they are such as the Government of India can fully approve. His Excellency regrets that there has been some delay in obtaining this information, but he is anxious to lose no further time in adding his name to the subscription list of the relief fund, and I am accordingly directed to enclose, with the expression of his Excellency's best wishes for the continued success of your efforts, a draft for ten thousand rupees.

I remain, my dear Sir,
Yours faithfully,
O. T. BURNE,
*Lt.-Col. and Private Secretary
to the Viceroy.*

Wm. Digby, Esq.,
Hon. Secretary, Famine Relief Fund.

G 2

CHAPTER IV.

THE COLLECTING COMMITTEES.—THE MANSION HOUSE.

NOTHING could have been simpler than the procedure adopted by the Mansion House Committee in its direction of the vast national fund which was speedily raised. This was in keeping with the manner in which the movement was started—quietly, unostentatiously. The promoters, however, were pleaders in behalf of real distress and much suffering, such distress and suffering as served to touch the British heart very closely. For once the remark, 'A trifling casualty nigh at hand absorbs more attention and occupies more interest than the welfare of hundreds of thousands at a distance ' was proved untrue. Space was annihilated, and with the absence of all sensationalism, or anything that could be called such, a real and lively interest was established between the British and the Indian people which continued at the flood for many months. According to the testimony of the Mansion House Committee, much of this interest was created by the means used by the Madras executive committee to keep all interested *au courant* with the condition of the people and the efforts made to alleviate distress. Among other means adopted were weekly telegrams which, upon receipt, were posted outside the Mansion House, and sent to all the newspapers. The following are messages sent out at the dates named; they will serve to show the impressions formed by the disbursing committees of their work:—

To the Lord Mayor, London.

This week has been the busiest in the committee's experience. All through the distressed districts the utmost activity is being displayed by the relief committees, who are disbursing the funds most carefully. An enquiry from house to house in the villages has been made, and the lists have been scrutinised with the greatest care. The reports from the local committees and agencies give most interesting descriptions of the gratitude shown by the recipients, and particulars of the benefits derived from the fund. These reports appear in the 'Weekly Statement' posted to England to-day. The recipients are made clearly to understand that the relief comes from English friends. One distributor writes :—'I should like you and your friends in England to see the expression of thankfulness upon their dark, careworn, haggard faces. A chord has been struck which probably never was touched before.' Some cases of agriculturists, especially in the Nellore district, are most disheartening. In the first sowing the seed rotted ; in the second the young plants were eaten by grasshoppers. In these cases advances had been made by Government, and now a grant from the relief committee has put new life in the people, and courage to try again. The mortality returns of August are still coming in. They all tell the same story of a greater number of deaths that month than in any other period of famine. In South Arcot, for instance, the increase over the average of that month of the last five years is 10,033 ; Chingleput, 7,613 ; Cuddapah, 9,340 ; Kurnool, 6,769 ; Madura, 7,198. Next week we hope to have the complete returns for August. In Mysore the destitution and death-rate have been very bad ; but though the actual statistics are not yet to hand, an improvement is reported. Weather fine, with passing clouds ; wind north-east, but rain holding off. Reports from the Ganjam and Kistna districts show that the rain is greatly needed there, the Godavery river, fed by the southwest monsoon, having been lower than in any previous September in many years. Irrigation in the Godavery system much affected in consequence.

Madras, October 23.

To London, to Lord Mayor.

Operations being continued. New tracts, Trichinopoly and Tinnevelly, been brought within scope action. One president of committee writes :—'The closer you look into matters, and the better you know the people, the more you see how fearfully widely spread is the present, distress, borne by the poor creatures in dumb resignation to fate, and with scarcely a murmur.' The general committee's delegates have visited all districts. Now there is not a taluk or zemindary not included in range operations. Arrangements made by taluk committees many cases admirable, the most deserving of the people being reached and assisted. Utmost advantage is being taken of favourable rains interior, and the aid from England enabling cultivators very small holdings commence sowing, &c., is simply incalculable. Every exertion is being made by central, local, and sub-committees and agencies to make most present opportunity. Ascertained death-rate, August, largest on record. Letters from England received mail, especially Mansion House and Manchester, much appreciated. Wind, weather Madras variable. Partial showers general and frequent throughout Presidency, except Madras. Rainfall above Ghats more steady and general ; prospects improved, save parts coast in Godavery, Delta, Kistna, and Ganjam. Further aid been allotted famine immigrants Central India through Sir Henry Daly. Small allotment unofficial efforts in Nizam's dominions.

October 27, 1877.

To London, Lord Mayor.

All possible exertions are being made to turn the favourable weather to good account. The organisation is now complete. Over 100 committees are actively at work, with excellent results. In the interior, where the greatest difficulty as to the disbursement was anticipated, generally satisfactory arrangements have been made. The members of the committees are making the most self-denying and earnest efforts to bring the maximum number of people within the scope of the fund. One European gentleman lived for a week in a bullock 'bandy' among villagers, disbursing aid to people whose cases had been previously enquired into. This is but a sample of earnest and energetic efforts of the committees. At Trichinopoly, when the committee was formed, the late Prime Minister of Travancore, Sheshai Sastri, proposed that the Madras Committee should convey to the English public the high sense of thankfulness and gratitude of the people of Trichinopoly for their noble liberality in having come forward to aid the inhabitants of India in this distress. Weather 'monsoonish' and favourable in most districts. Latest Government reports, dated October 31, say of Ganjam—' Here, rain urgently wanted. Crops withering.' Of Godavery there is a similar report. The favourable season leads to a rapid reduction of people on Government relief, yet this month (November) began with

1,362,329 people on works and gratuitous relief. Our committees forecast that relief will be required to support life till February, when crops are expected. Already eight lakhs of rupees have been allotted to Mysore, of which five have been actually remitted. Australia is rendering appreciable assistance.

Madras, November 3, 1877.

To London, Lord Mayor.

Reports from all districts of committee's operations continue satisfactory. Excluding Bombay, thirty relief centres, but including Mysore with Madras Presidency nearly 150 committees; probably three or four thousand English, Eurasian, Indian gentlemen engaged in work of relief. Amount expended and in course of expenditure to date over 300,000l. sterling. During next few months till crops reaped operations will continue, and munificent generosity Great Britain, Australia, New Zealand, Mauritius, non-distressed portions India—eighty-two lakhs in all—will enable general committee, Madras, meet all demands. Impression produced by marvellous generosity, especially England, most profound. Perfect and entire unanimity between officials and our committees exists; the maximum of good attainable is being secured. Weather continuing favourable ; many people leaving Government relief, returning to agriculture and trades. Majority these need help to begin life again, being absolutely homeless, without clothes, without money. In some parts too much rain falling. Seed sown late rotting in ground; dry crops part of Bellary district quite spoiled, necessitating help to those who month ago seemed beyond assistance. Committees will continue weekly telegrams of progress if wished, and reports published each mail-day will be forwarded till distress over. Please wire this Lancashire and elsewhere.

Madras, November 10, 1877.

The Mansion House Committee met weekly, but arrangements were made for the receipt of money continuously, and the officials of the fund were kept very busy day by day, as contributions flowed in fast. Many letters breathing the deepest sympathy with the sufferers were received by the Lord Mayor, from amongst which that from Miss Florence Nightingale may be selected. She wrote:—

London, August 17, 1877.

My Lord,—If English people know what an Indian Famine is— worse than a battlefield, worse even than a retreat; and this famine, too, is in its second year—there is not an English man, woman, or child, who would not give out of their abundance, or out of their economy.

If we do not, we are the Turks who put an end to the wounded, and worse than they, for they put an end to the enemy's wounded; but we, by neglect to our own starving fellow-subjects; and there is not a more industrious being on the face of the earth than the ryot. He deserves all we can do. Having seen your advertisement this morning only, and thanking God that you have initiated this relief, I hasten to enclose what I can—25*l.*; hoping that I may be able to repeat the mite again; for all will be wanted. Between this and January our fellow-creatures in India will need everybody's mite—given now at once—then repeated again and again. And may God bless the fund.

Pray believe me, my Lord, ever your faithful servant,

FLORENCE NIGHTINGALE.

The Right Honourable the Lord Mayor.

By way of extending operations, communications were opened with all the provincial mayors and provosts throughout the United Kingdom, and there were few who did not respond, some in a very generous manner. A similar appeal—a circular setting forth in brief terms the distress being experienced— was sent to the ministers and clergy of all denominations, asking them, if practicable, to have collections in their respective places of worship. By these means, in small sums, millions of people became partakers in the act of charity, making it truly national. Communications were also sent to the chief municipal functionaries of Australasia, with great results of good. Most of the British Colonies, however, contributed without being solicited to do so. The work of the Mansion House Committee was kept very practical in its aims and efforts through the presence upon it of Indian administrators like Sir Henry Norman and the Earl of Northbrook, and of a number of Indian merchants.

By way of experiment, a money-box was, early in September, attached to the railings of the Mansion House during the business hours of the day, and the result was the collection on that day of 10*l*. 12*s*. 10*d*. in coin of all kinds. A noticeable subscription paid in on one occasion was that of 2*l*. from the children of the Board Schools in Sun Lane, Norwich, and with it was sent the suggestion that if a similar collection was made in the 14,000 schools of the kingdom a sum might be obtained that would equal, if not exceed, the church offertories. Another contributor urged that a public appeal should be made for 'a million sixpences.' 'Connaught Street, W.' wrote that a house-to-house subscription in that street of fifty-nine houses resulted in one day in 20*l*. 5*s*. being added to the Lord Mayor's fund. Seven householders had already subscribed through other channels, and fourteen were away from London. He suggested that if responsible persons in other parts of the metropolis would likewise visit all the dwellers in their streets and explain the nature and urgency of the crisis, the result could not fail to be a very handsome addition to the fund. A Wesleyan minister at Birkenhead, who sent 24*l*. from his Sunday scholars, suggested that an appeal should be made to the Sunday schools. He said : 'I cannot but think there would be a handsome response. Have we not 20,000 schools that could send 1*l*. each?'

At a meeting of the Common Council of the City of London it was unanimously resolved to contribute the sum of 1,000*l*. towards the fund. Mr. Hodsoll

Heath, speaking upon the question, expressed his opinion that private charity, munificently as it was being bestowed, would go but a small way to meet the vast requirements of the famine-stricken population, and that it was the province of the Government, primarily, to undertake effectually the work of relief. It was impossible to relieve sixteen millions of people by private subscriptions. The Lord Mayor's conduct in opening the fund was warmly approved, and his Lordship took occasion to thank the generous subscribers to it, and especially the local mayors who were working hard in the matter. The Government, he added, were doing what they could.

Several influential weekly newspapers opened lists among their subscribers and materially added to the fund. On one day, early in the history of the fund, two Grecians called at the Mansion House and paid in 28l. which had been subscribed by the scholars of Christ's Hospital. There were very few public schools —or private ones either, for that matter—which did not make contributions to the fund. An interesting fact in the history of the fund raised in India was that the students of Bengal, through the Rev. K. S. Macdonald, contributed largely. The children of Anglo-Indian parents at school in the United Kingdom were very active in contributing to a fund which was to relieve the race to which their ayahs and bearers belonged. Everybody who had little ones at home had some story to tell of the kindly feeling evinced by their children : from among the multitude of stories told one may be selected. Three children were at school in England and heard of the distress in India; the two elder ones (girls) at once agreed to give up a trip to the sea-side that the money might be sent to the Mansion House. They also asked to be allowed to do without butter on their bread and sugar in their tea, that the money might be sent to the fund. This was permitted. 'I don't want butter or sugar,' said their little brother. So he was allowed to take the self-denying ordinance, and continued bravely for a week, when he went to the relative in whose charge he and his sisters were, and said:—'Auntie: isn't the famine over yet? I think it is.' Of course it came to an end at once for that warm-hearted little fellow.

The Chief Rabbi of London called upon his co-religionists to subscribe ; in the course of his appeal he said:—' It is but a few days ago that our congregations were asked to alleviate the misery of the unhappy victims of the war ; and I am glad to learn that the appeals on behalf of the Turkish Sufferers' Relief Fund are being satisfactorily responded to. But the calamity which has befallen our fellow-subjects in Southern India is of such magnitude, and the need for immediate help is so pressing, that I dare not delay making this request to you. During the sacred festivals which are approaching you will on several occasions address your congregation. I ask that on the day you deem most fitting you would plead to your congregants on behalf of the millions who are suffering by the dire and dreadful famine that is raging in India. You will, then, I am sure, point out to your hearers how necessary it is that the efforts of the Indian Government in coping with this terrible calamity should be supplemented by private bounty. You will impress the sacred truth upon your worshippers that with our sincere penitence and devout prayer must be combined practical benevolence, and you will remind them of the inspired bidding of the prophet which he proclaims in discoursing of the fast acceptable to the Lord : " Is it not to deal thy bread to the starving ? " I leave it to your judgment and the discretion of your wardens whether it be advisable to make a special collection among the members of your synagogue, or whether you will call upon them to forward their generous contributions direct to the Mansion House fund, or, in the case of provincial congregations, to the local fund. May the Lord speedily remove the scourge of famine from the Indian Empire, and grant us all a year of happiness, a year of peace, prosperity, and salvation.'

By the first week in September money was received at the Mansion House at the rate of 7,000*l.* per diem, but the tide was only rising, and shortly after 10,000*l.* per day were received for several days. The amount was received in sums varying from the copper coin dropped into the box outside the Mansion House to a cheque for 1,000*l.* from a London banker or merchant; 164,000*l.* was raised in three weeks. The maximum sum received on any one day was 12,000*l.*, on September 21. In barely six weeks the sum of a quarter of a million sterling was received. This amount was the spontaneous and voluntary offering, not only of the merchants and bankers of the City of London, but of all classes throughout the country, from Her Majesty downwards; and was a remarkable proof—if any such were needed—of the heartfelt sympathy with which their fellow-subjects in India were regarded at that most critical period. The collection of so vast a sum naturally cast a good deal of anxious work upon the chief magistrate, his secretary, and the small staff at the Mansion House, but, with the aid of the energetic committee, everything proceeded successfully. A telegram announcing that a quarter of a million had been exceeded, and that the fund was still likely to increase, was despatched to Her Majesty the Queen by the Lord Mayor, and a formal communication of the fact was made to the

Prime Minister.[1] The Empress of India acknowledged the intimation of Sir Thomas White by a telegram through the Home Secretary, which stated that Her Majesty felt deeply the readiness with which the sufferings of the people in India had touched the hearts of the people at home. Lord Beaconsfield thought the result 'a splendid instance of national sympathy,' and added, 'I will express my hope that this generous aid may still be extended, because although the action of the Indian Government at present is not hampered by want of funds, without doubt the assistance administered by private hands reaches localities and classes which the necessarily more formal help accorded by public authority does not and cannot touch.'

The sympathetic feeling of the English people did not need much stimulus, but a great deal of help was undoubtedly afforded to the fund by the letters which his Grace the Governor of Madras wrote to the Lord Mayor from time to time. One of them was as follows :—

Government House, Madras, September 10, 1877.

My dear Lord Mayor,—I venture to express to your Lordship the heartfelt gratitude which already begins to pervade the minds of natives of this Presidency for the exertions your Lordship has made and the response which has rewarded your kind interest.

The emergency is indeed great. Realise the position of the English people with the quartern loaf ranging from 2s. 6d. upwards, and at the same time an utter scarcity of every green thing—of everything with which food can ordinarily be supplemented—and you may form some idea of the scarcity and the terrible position of the classes even above the poor labourers and cultivators. To see those classes aided and, if possible, saved from falling into the abyss of pauperism from which in all countries it is so hard to emerge, is one of the principal objects I hope to see attained by the aid of English charity. Government may do much, but, working necessarily under rule and regulation, cannot do much that should be done. Working side by

[1] *The Times*, September 27.

side with a powerful organisation of private charity, it can do much, very much more than will be due to the mere amount of money expended. I have directed returns of the increasing distress and pressure in the various districts to be sent to your Lordship; the mortuary returns sent home officially disclose too plainly the sufferings of Southern India.

Believe me, your Lordship's faithful
BUCKINGHAM and CHANDOS.

The Right Honourable the Lord Mayor.

At a meeting held on October 22 the Lord Mayor referred in terms of high appreciation to the efforts made on behalf of the fund by the mayors and local authorities throughout the kingdom, and said that from the Lord Mayor of Dublin he had received no less than 22 remittances of 500*l*. each. He also stated that about 800*l*. had been collected in the Roman Catholic churches of the metropolis, and would be paid in within the next few days.

An extract from the minutes of the Mansion House Committee of November 5 will show how the fund was stopped :—

'A meeting of the executive committee of the fund now being raised at the Mansion House for the relief of the sufferers by the famine in India was held in the Venetian Parlour for the despatch of business.

'The fund was reported to amount to 446,100*l*., of which 405,000*l*. had been remitted to India.

'While the committee was sitting a telegram from the Duke of Buckingham, the Governor of Madras, dated that afternoon, was received by the Lord Mayor. It was in these terms :—

'Your Lordship's exertions have brought such liberal aid from all quarters that, under the present favourable prospects, we gratefully say the collection may cease. In this the executive relief committee concur.

'Another telegram, addressed to Mr. Soulsby, the secretary, was simultaneously received from Mr. Digby, the secretary of the relief committee, stating :—

'" With reference to the Governor's telegram, please remember that

we shall continue active operations with the munificent funds supplied
to us till January or February."

'On the motion of Mr. S. P. Low, seconded by Sir Nathaniel de
Rothschild, M.P., it was unanimously resolved to send the following
telegram in reply to the authorities at Madras :—

'The Mansion House Committee will make no further appeal.
They will collect all subscriptions from local committees and other
sources with the least possible delay. The accounts will be audited
and the balance remitted. Twenty thousand pounds, making 425,000*l.*,
is to-day forwarded.'

It was not easy, however, to stay the flow, and for
nearly six months after this date the Mansion House
Committee continued to receive subscriptions and to
remit them to Madras.

A strong feeling of cordiality existed between the
chief collecting and the chief disbursing committees,
and when the time came for Sir Thomas White, as Lord
Mayor, to give place to another, the Madras executive
committee telegraphed to his Lordship in these terms :—
' On the approaching termination of your tenure of high
office, we desire to express on behalf of the people of
Southern India the deep and warm gratitude which is
felt among all races and creeds for your Lordship's
active benevolence, and for your great and successful
exertions in promoting the munificent sympathy of the
people of Great Britain with the sufferings of the famine-
stricken populations of India.' The Lord Mayor thus
replied by telegram :—'I return you my warmest thanks
for your telegram just received. It will ever form a
most pleasing recollection to me that, in my official
position as Lord Mayor, I was made the medium of
forwarding to Southern India the generous alms contributed by all classes of my fellow-countrymen for the
relief of the famine-stricken people. I take no credit to
myself for the splendid response made to my appeal, but
I rejoice that my office here enabled me to originate

the fund and to take some part in its collection and distribution.'[1]

LANCASHIRE.

No part of England responded more eagerly to the appeal for contributions than did the county of Lancashire. This was the more pleasing from the fact that through its trade there is no portion of the United Kingdom brought so much into contact with India as the great cotton-manufacturing county. Public meetings were held in Manchester, Liverpool, and other places, and subscription lists opened. A letter from the Rev. S. Alfred Steinthal, honorary secretary of the Manchester and Salford committee, epitomises the action taken in Lancashire. Writing on October 4, he said :—

'I have had the honour, in behalf of our committee, of sending you various sums: on September 5, 10,000*l.*, on September 19, 5,000*l.*, on the 26th, 3,000*l.*, and to-day I am happy to remit another 3,000*l.*, making in all 21,000*l.* I trust before this reaches you to have sent still more to relieve the sad suffering of our fellow-subjects in India. My chief object in writing to you to-day, in addition to confirming my previous telegrams, is to inform you that our chief Lancashire towns have agreed that their subscriptions are to be all placed under one heading as "Lancashire Indian Famine Relief Fund." We are all mindful of the generous help given to our factory workers during the cotton famine by friends in India, and are very desirous that it should not be thought that we were ungrateful for

---

[1] One further instance of good feeling may be mentioned :—Prior to leaving the Mansion House, the late Lord Mayor (Sir Thomas White) entertained there at dinner the members of the committee by whom he had been assisted in the collection and distribution of the Indian famine fund. The banquet was served in the Long Parlour. After dinner 'the health of the Madras Committee' was proposed by Sir Thomas White, and a telegram, wishing them success in their arduous labours, was despatched to his Grace the Governor. Mr. S. P. Low replied for the Mansion House Committee, and Mr. J. Fleming, C.S.I., proposed, in flattering terms, 'the health of Lord Mayor White,' under whose auspices the fund had been raised, with a result so successful.

that generous assistance. We bear it constantly in mind, and one of the few gleams of comfort that we can derive in the midst of this sad visitation arises from the fact that it enables us, in some small degree, to give expression to the sense of obligation we shall always feel under to those generous friends who helped us in our need.

'Some of our Lancashire subscriptions have already been paid into the Mansion House fund, but we shall try and make a complete list of Lancashire contributions, and shall feel much pleased if you can by some means let our county work be known; as we feel a special tie to India, above what can be felt by other parts of England, with the exception of the cotton manufacturing part of Cheshire lying near us.

' While I am writing, might I be bold enough to ask you to be kind enough to send me all possible information as to means which men of experience in your Presidency believe may be adopted to avert such calamities in the future ? Our committee have resolved as soon as the pressure of work arising from the appeal for money is over to try and arouse such public feeling as shall help the Government in carrying preventive measures, even at the cost of public money, and all advice which comes to us from men residing in India must be of great service to us.'

The money contributed—nearly £100,000—was only a small part of the sympathy shown by Lancashire. Through public meetings and in other ways pressure was brought to bear upon the English Government to devise remedial means to prevent future famines.

Two Lancashire towns—Bolton and Blackburn—preferred to keep their contributions distinct, and did so. The sums sent by them respectively were £5,150, and £3,500.

At one of the weekly meetings of the Manchester Committee of the Indian Famine Relief Fund the Bishop of Manchester laid before the committee the following letter, which is worthy of permanent record, as showing the spirit in which the fund was contributed :—

Manchester, September 11.

My Lord,—I have been requested by a deputation from the work-people employed by Messrs. S. Schwabe and Co. at Rhodes, near Middleton, to bring the following under your Lordship's notice :—A desire having been expressed by many of the hands employed at the above works to contribute to the above fund, some of their fellow-workmen convened a meeting of the whole body. At this meeting, of which Mr. C. B. West was chairman, it was resolved unanimously that every man, woman, and child employed at the Rhodes Printing Works should contribute one-fifth at least of a week's wages. In order that the payment of the contribution should not press too heavily on any contributor, it was arranged that the collection should be made fortnightly during a period of eight weeks, or, say 5 per cent. at a time. Mr. West and the cashier at the works having entered in a book the names of the whole of the people employed at the above works, with the amounts due weekly to each placed opposite, the workpeople were invited to sign the book as proof of their willingness to contribute the percentage of their wages agreed upon. This was done in nearly all cases with the greatest alacrity and cheerfulness, some giving more, and few less fortunately situated a little less than the stipulated 20 per cent. The first collection, which will be the largest, as it includes extra amounts, summed up to 44*l.*, and a cheque for that amount has been placed in my hands. The total of the subscriptions will, it is expected, reach 110*l.* or 120*l.* Now, were similar steps to be taken at all our mills and manufactories with like results, what a noble contribution Lancashire would make to the fund for the relief of the famishing Indians. The gentlemen who have waited upon me believe that it is in your Lordship's power to bring about such a striking proof of the sympathy felt by the workpeople of Lancashire for their suffering fellow-subjects in India. Were you to use your influence with the workpeople at even only a few of the many mills, railway depôts, &c., these gentlemen believe that the movement would spread rapidly and a grand result would accrue.

Yours, &c.,
J. G. MANDLEY.

In closing accounts and forwarding the balance, Mr. Watson, secretary to the Blackburn committee, wrote :—

At the last meeting of our committee it was decided that the Madras committee should be asked to express their opinion in an elaborate minute as to the best means of preventing the recurrence of famine in the districts over which they have so laboriously distributed the relief funds.

It is the opinion of this committee that the experience acquired in the various districts over which your committee have distributed relief; the knowledge they have gained of the cause of famine, and their opinion as to the best means of preventing the recurrence of a similar calamity, will be of the highest importance to us.

Any assistance that we can render by the diffusion of sound opinion and information on the subject will be most willingly and zealously given.

This is the duty of the Famine Commission appointed by the Government of India, rather than of the Madras committee, whose task was one of relief and not of remedy.

Bradford also had communications direct with the Madras committee, and contributed £8,500.

SCOTLAND.

Scotland, proportionately to her population, has, perhaps, sent more sons to India than any other part of the United Kingdom, and her interest in all that concerns the Empire is proportionately great. Edinburgh worthily took the lead in Scotland in raising contributions, and the famine relief fund there was appropriately inaugurated at a meeting over which the Lord Provost presided, and at which such representative 'Indians' as Lord Napier and Ettrick, once Governor of Madras, and George Smith, Esq., C.I.E., LL.D., late editor of the *Friend of India*, took part. Dr. Smith was made co-secretary with two other gentlemen, and for a time the attention of the dwellers in the Modern Athens was concentrated upon India and her woes, Lord Napier and Ettrick serving to maintain the interest by giving a lecture on Indian Famines to the working men of Edinburgh. A *précis* of the report issued by the Edinburgh committee, at the close of their operations, will serve to show the scope of their operations :—

This fund was opened, on a telegram from his Excellency the Governor of Madras to the Lord Provost of Edinburgh, received on August 15, 1877, appealing for public sympathy and help.

The action of the Lord Provost and Town Council of Edinburgh, in response to the appeal, was approved of by a most influential meeting of the citizens and representatives of the adjoining counties, held on September 3, 1877. In a letter from the late Viceroy and Governor General of India, the Earl of Northbrook, who was passing through the city, the nature of the distress was urged as especially suitable for private benevolence, and the opinion was expressed that ' Edinburgh would not be behindhand in the good work, while it would be warmly supported by the whole of Scotland, where there are so many and so honourable associations with the Indian Empire.' A large committee under the presidency of the Lord Provost was then nominated to raise subscriptions on a general scale. This acting committee was formed with the distinguished ex-Governor of Madras, the Right Honourable Lord Napier and Ettrick, K.T., as vice-chairman. This committee met five days a week all through September and October, and thereafter weekly, till the close of the year. The City Chamberlain from the first freely and zealously gave the movement the benefit of his experience and energy as honorary treasurer.

' Spontaneous subscriptions of comparatively large sums began to flow in as the result of the publicity given to the Madras appeal all throughout the country. The honorary treasurer, however, lost no time in addressing (1) special circulars to some 3,000 citizens and residents in the country, which in most instances met with a prompt and liberal response. This was followed (2) by a somewhat similar representation sent to no fewer than 24,000 addresses in the local Directory; (3) the banks and insurance offices, other public offices, and some shops, received subscriptions. The acting committee desire to express their gratitude to these agencies for their hearty co-operation, and especially to the Banks, both in the city and country, for the arrangement made for cashing drafts free of cost, and to the Bank of Scotland for their remittance of sums to Madras also free of all the usual charges. (4) Considerable sums were paid into the office of the honorary treasurer, at the City chambers (5) A special movement was organised among the working and trading classes, chiefly through the Edinburgh United Trades Council, with whom Mr. Harrison and other members of the committee held conferences; and also directly in several large establishments. In order to promote this most desirable end Lord Napier and Ettrick delivered a lecture on India, which attracted a crowded audience to the Free Assembly Hall towards the close of September, and was warmly appreciated. The report of the lecture had a powerful influence in promoting the general subscriptions. His Lordship more recently delivered a second lecture in the Literary Institute, on the prevention of famine. Though living at a considerable distance from town, Lord Napier and Ettrick continued to preside at the principal meetings every week. Mr. Duncan M'Laren, M.P., attended nearly all the meetings and guided the movement throughout by his great experience and zeal. (6) Individual members of the committee promoted the subscription in the neighbouring towns. On October 22 a circular was addressed to all the boroughs and municipal bodies in Scotland who had not up to that time taken part in the national subscription, communicating to them the proceedings of the Madras central committee, and offering to remit any amounts raised free of expense. (7) Finally, on the return to town of many families at the close of the autumn holidays, collections were made by church congregations and in schools. These formed most important, and, at that stage, most valuable feeders to the general stream of benevolence.

'The result of these and other agencies, such as lectures, has been the subscription of 23,216l., chiefly in the two and a half months ending November 18, when the assured fall of the north-east monsoon in all districts save Ganjam and Vizagapatam largely removed the fear of the continuance of famine beyond the next harvest of February 1878. This sum is, with one exception, the largest raised by Edinburgh for any public purpose. To the Patriotic fund after the Crimean war this city was the means of adding 16,000l. For the relief of distress in Lancashire, to which, it should not be forgotten, the people of India liberally subscribed, Edinburgh raised 35,000l. The Edinburgh Famine fund of 1877 is also proportionately larger than that contributed by any other city of the Empire, so far as present statistics show. The Mansion House fund has exceeded the unparalleled amount of half-a-million sterling, a fact which has called forth the congratulations of the Queen on the " magnificent result." This sum has been drawn from all the provinces of the Empire, including the Colonies and some parts of Scotland. Dublin contributed 13,000l., which it sent to London. Glasgow raised 22,390l., of which it forwarded 4,310*l.* to Bombay and 17,632*l.* to Madras. Manchester and Salford, Liverpool, Blackburn, Bradford, Bolton, Oldham, and Greenock, also remitted to India direct. But no one can assert that either Edinburgh or the whole Empire—which, including India itself, may be said to have given 650,000*l.*, or, what is equivalent in Indian currency and in purchasing power to above three-quarters of a million sterling—has done more than its duty. The whole sum acknowledged in Madras up to December 15 last from India itself as well as the rest of the British Empire, is 7,908,714 rs., or nearly 800,000*l.* at the par of two shillings the rupee.

'The valuable analysis of the Edinburgh fund by the honorary treasurer reveals some interesting details. The number of separate donations to the Mansion House fund is stated at over 16,000; from the comparatively small area of Edinburgh, and those parts of Scotland which remitted through it, there have been 3,608 personal subscriptions, yielding 12,057*l.*, or rather more than half the whole. Church collections came next; 428 congregations gave 7,400*l.*, or a third of the whole, if the allied sums from 89 schools and 9 lectures be added. These two classes make 19,823*l.* of the total 23,215*l.* The balance is made up by 250*l.* from the working classes in 86 establishments, 293*l.* from 14 corporations and societies, and 2,848*l.* from 14 county or town districts.

' Of the total number of 4,265 subscriptions, there were 2,984 from the city of Edinburgh, yielding 11,337*l.* This is at the rate of 3*l.* 15*s.* each. Almost the same rate prevailed in Leith, where 283 subscribed 1,035*l.* The landward subscriptions of the county of Mid-Lothian numbered 167, and amounted to 1,200*l.* Towns beyond Mid-Lothian sent 5,368*l.* in 342 contributions, and counties other than Mid-Lothian 3,377*l.* in 330 contributions. From counties beyond there were 21 subscriptions amounting to 100*l.* The highest subscription was anonymous, 500*l.* from " M. S. S. D." Perhaps the most significant is that of 5*l.*, the spontaneous offering of the boys of the Wellington Reformatory. A few givers sent monthly subscriptions to the fund as long as the pressure lasted, an example followed in India in times of famine, and worthy of general adoption. In addition to the church collections above stated, the United Presbyterian Church raised 2,630*l.* as a special fund for sufferers in Rajpootana, and the Free Church 802*l.* for orphans in Bombay and Hyderabad.

' After careful consideration of the claims of Bombay, of Rajpootana, and of a mission in Hyderabad, the acting committee resolved to send all remittances in the first instance to the central committee in Madras. That body is in the heart of the greatest suffering; it represents all classes and creeds; it established a careful system of distribution and control, and it has done its work well. At the same time, seeing so many of the subscribers to the Edinburgh fund were interested in other places than South India, the acting committee recommended the Madras Agency to give careful and generous consideration to applications from the places named. The committee do not know if an appeal was made to Madras from Rajpootana, but the Madras grants to Bombay, Mysore, and elsewhere, seem to have been satisfactory. In this as in all previous famines it has been proved that the best, and in many cases the only agents of the bounty of this country, and of Government itself, are the missionaries, both Protestant and Roman Catholic, next to the overburdened district officers. The calamity in South India has told heavily on the millions of Christians there, as shown by the official proceedings sent to the Edinburgh committee every week. The sum of 20,000*l.* was sent to his Excellency the Governor of Madras in six remittances, of which the last reached on December 3. This yielded no less than 225,412 rs., owing to the gain by exchange at from 1*s.* 9½*d.* to 1*s.* 8⅞*d.* per rupee. When the net amount of 22,300*l.* or thereby has reached India, it will be found that this is really equal to about 25,000*l.* or more, according to the purchasing power of the rupee on the spot.

'The total cost of collecting this amount has been 925*l.* The bulk of this, 855*l.*, is due to advertising (630*l.*) and circulars and postage (225*l.*), without which the money could not have been raised. The money allowed by the committee for the services of clerks is 60*l.* The amount of the City Chamberlain's intromissions as honorary treasurer of the fund is herewith submitted as brought down to the 12th instant, and docqueted by Mr. Thomas Dall, C.A., as honorary auditor. The City Chamberlain has considered it a privilege to organise and direct the movement under the acting committee, a privilege which the three honorary secretaries—Messrs. Skinner and G. Harrison, and Dr. George Smith, C.I.E.—have been delighted to share.

'So far as the official reports of the Government of India show, the following sums have been raised for the relief of the people in recent famines :—

Year	Place	From British Empire	Famine Deaths	Cost to	
				State	People
1861	Upper India . .	£ 165,000	500,000	£ 650,000	4,000,000
1866	Orissa, Behar, and North Madras	121,000	1,500,000	1,500,000	Enormous but not reported
1869	Rajpootana and Central India	U. P. Ch. sent 23,000	400,000	very little	1,000,000
1874	Behar	230,000	a few	7,500,000	Unknown, but little
1877	S. India and Bombay . . .	650,000[1]	697,804 For nine months in Madras only, will be double this at least.	9,250,000	Not yet estimated, but three times that in 1861 at least.

'In the twelve months ending November 1877, 900,000 tons of grain were imported into the ports of the province of Madras, to feed the people, or 5,600,000 lbs. a day. This seems to be over and above the large import inland by railways from the north. With this an average number of three millions of peasantry, labourers, small artisans, and the respectable and high-caste poor were fed daily by Government, while food was supplied, in addition to the stocks of the country, to all who could pay for it. In the interior there were villages where food was not available at any price, while it was brought up as fast as the railway could carry it to the dying, at rates which seem to have risen above four hundred per cent. In Mysore and Bellary the horrors of famine seem to have reached their height. The records of the police tell of cannibalism and mortality over which humanity draws a veil. But it is pleasing now to read this extract from a letter received by Dr. Smith, from the centre of Bellary, where the suffering was most terrible. The date is December 22 last:—"After this wonderfully favourable weather, we have heard the district is looking perfectly beautiful. Agriculture and crops are most favourable, grass for cattle is abundant, and there is any quantity of water in the tanks—10 or 12 months' supply without requiring almost another shower."

'In resigning their trust the committee do not feel that it is their province to urge the adoption of any one panacea, such as irrigation, or railway. They are satisfied that, in the last ten years at least,

---

[1] Over 820,000l. were received before the fund was finally closed.

since Lord Lawrence's great scheme came into force, as large a sum
has been devoted to such public works as the revenues of India can
bear, but they are not prepared to say that the money has always been
spent in the wisest way. They believe that much more could be done
for the mitigation of famine than at present, by such an administration
of the land tax as would leave the peasant less in the hands of the
money-lender, and might develop habits of thrift and comfort. It is
in the people themselves as much as in the Government, that in India,
as in other lands, power to withstand famine must be sought. The
committee observe with satisfaction that the present Government of
India has departed from its early policy so far as to resolve that not
less than one million-and-a-half sterling shall be provided by every
Budget as a reserve for famine relief. But whether India, as it is, can
bear the strain of this as well as of adequate public works; whether
canals cannot yet be made to pay as well as railways, and if so, how
far they will protect vast populations who have no permanent source
of water supply; and whether the land tax and land tenures cannot
be dealt with in the spirit of Colonel Baird Smith's report and Lord
Canning's orders after the famine of 1861—these and other such
questions are for the solution of a Parliamentary or Royal Commission.
In conclusion, the committee rejoice in the abundant evidence supplied by official assurances of the Viceroy and the Madras and Bombay
authorities, by the detailed reports of the Madras relief committees,
and by the vernacular and English press, that the aid sent from this
country has not only largely saved human life, mitigated human
suffering, and enabled the surviving peasantry to stock and sow now
their little holdings, but has bound more closely the political ties
between the people of Great Britain and their fellow-subjects in the
East. There still remains the great question of the support and train-
ing of thousands of orphans to be dealt with. But, believing that the
Christian benevolence of this country will more effectually act on the
movement through other channels, the committee do not recommend
the prolonged continuance of the Edinburgh fund for relief of the
famine of 1877.'

. Glasgow and Greenock both opened separate funds;
from the former city £17,622 were received, and from
the latter £1,840.

THE COLONIES.

In Australasia the movement for relief was taken up
with great heartiness, and as soon as efforts were com-

menced a telegram was sent to the Madras committee, asking whether aid would be preferred in grain or money. The latter was considered the more preferable mode, and the Australasian committees were so advised. Public meetings were held in the chief cities and country towns ; most sympathetic and eloquent speeches were made. Particularly was this the case in Sydney, where the Roman Catholic Archbishop caused a great sensation by his generous oratory. The amounts raised in the various colonies were as follows :—

Victoria	£28,600
New South Wales	18,000
New Zealand	13,000
South Australia	11,450
Tasmania	3,900
Queensland	3,000
Making a grand total contributed by Australia and New Zealand of	£77,950

The population and contribution per head of the people in each province are given in the annexed table :—

	Estimated population Jan. 1, 1878.	Contribution per head.
South Australia	237,536	11½d.
Tasmania	106,000	8¾d.
Victoria	861,500	7⅞d.
New Zealand . . .	417,532	7½d.
New South Wales . . .	665,000	6½d.
Queensland	203,095	3½d.
Total .	2,479,880 making 7½d.	

the average contribution per head in all the colonies.

At the antipodes of Great Britain, as in Great Britain, most earnest and self-denying efforts were made to render assistance. A description of what was done in South Australia will serve as an indication of the activity and zeal displayed. On Wednesday, September 19, 1878, a meeting convened by the mayor of Adelaide (Mr. Caleb Peacock) was held in the city, and a committee formed to organise a scheme for sending speedy relief to the famine-stricken districts in India. This committee, together with a few other gentlemen whose names were added subsequently, had the general oversight of the movement, but the practical organisation and working out of the scheme was entrusted to an executive sub-committee. The final report issued says :—' After careful deliberation the sub-committee considered it undesirable and unnecessary to make— as they were strongly urged to do—a house-to-house canvass in Adelaide and the suburbs for subscriptions. Active measures, however, were taken to disseminate information respecting the famine and its sad results, and to distribute subscription-lists and books for the collection of contributions. The sub-committee received great assistance in their labours from the proprietors of the *Register* newspaper, who printed free of cost 50,000 copies of an article on the famine compiled from authentic sources ; also from Messrs. Scrymgour and Sons, who gratuitously printed a large number of lithographed letters, with which they communicated with persons in the city, suburbs, and country districts. Aid was also afforded by Mr. Dobson (of the Temple of Light), who presented to the committee a number of copies of photographs received from the mayor of Melbourne, portraying the sad effects of the famine. To all these gentlemen, and to many others whose zealous co-operation involved the expenditure of much time and attention, the committee on behalf of the public generally desire to record their most sincere thanks.

' Lists were distributed to all parts of the country as follows :—To local committees, 103 ; corporations, 67 ; district councils, 380 ; post offices, 69 ; public-houses, 570 ; sheep-stations, 222 ; police-stations, 85 ; public institutions, 56; private institutions, 173; banks, 81 ; local courts, 6 ; churches and chapels, 76 ; societies,

20—1,908.   A total number of 1,908 lists and 58 books
were issued in this way.

'The interest which was taken in the movement by
the public generally in South Australia was manifested
by the ready response which was made to the appeal—
a response which enabled the committee to remit within
a fortnight a first instalment of 3,000*l.* This credit
was sent by telegram, so that it was immediately available in India.   Within six weeks a further remittance
of 5,000*l.* was in like manner sent to Madras, and
on December 4 an additional 3,000*l.* was forwarded.
The total amount raised has been 11,450*l.*: deduct
amount already remitted, 10,000*l.*; expenses incurred,
260*l.*—10,260*l.*; leaving amount in hand to be remitted
about 1,190*l.* Reckoning bank interest on the current
account and the exchange on drafts, the sum of 11,450*l.*
subscribed here will be equivalent in India to an amount
exceeding 12,000*l.*'

To Victoria belongs the honour of having contributed the largest donation to the fund of any individual
contributing.   Mr. W. J. Clarke, a wealthy squatter,
gave 2,000*l.*

From Canada, Jamaica, and other West India Islands,
Natal, British Guiana, Mauritius, Hong Kong, the Straits
Settlements, Gibraltar—in fact, without exception from
every part of the British dominions, contributions were
sent.   The solidarity of the British Empire was exemplified in a most pleasing manner by the sympathy and
aid which the relief fund called forth.   India was the
centre of attraction in every part of the world, and a
stronger bond than administrative acts could weave
cemented all parts of the Queen's dominions as they had
never been cemented before.[1]

---

[1] The Norfolk Islanders, descended from the mutineers of the 'Bounty,'
who settled first at Pitcairn, and were then moved to Norfolk Island,
contributed 51*l.* to the Madras famine relief fund.   Dr. Selwyn, the

In India the sum raised was, comparatively, not large, but the explanation is to be found in the fact that distress was general everywhere save in Bengal, and that the high prices of food and other articles made large donations impracticable. The following details should be of interest :—

Contributions from Indian Princes.

	Rs.	a.	p.
H.H. the Maharaja of Baroda	10,000	0	0
H.H. the Maharaja of Travancore	8,000	0	0
H.H. the Maharaja of Cochin	5,000	0	0
H.H. the Raja of Venkatagiri	2,000	0	0
H.H. the Maharaja Holkar	10,000	0	0
H.H. the Maharaja of Mourbhurj	5,000	0	0
H.H. the Maharanee of Shorna Moye of Cossimbazar	2,000	0	0
H.H. the Begum of Bhopal	1,000	0	0
H.H. the Maharaja of Vizianagram . . .	1,000	0	0
H.H. the Maharaja of Purnea	1,000	0	0
H.H. the Maharanee of Rarjat Koer Ticari . .	1,000	0	0
H.H. the Raja of Poodoocottah	500	0	0

Regimental Contributions.

	Rs.	a.	p.		Rs.	a.	p.
2nd Regt. M.S. Cav. officers and men .	132	11	0	8th Regt. N.I. . .	127	2	0
2nd Regt. M.N.I. .	115	0	0	9th Regt. N.I. . .	142	9	0
2nd Regt. Ghoorkas	93	8	0	10th Regt. M.N.I. .	95	0	0
3rd Regt. Sikh . .	153	11	6	16th Regt. M.N.I. .	142	14	0
4th Regt. B.I. . .	257	5	0	20th Regt. N.I. . .	149	0	0
4th Regt. M.I. . .	282	13	0	25th Regt. N.I. . .	256	11	0
4th Regt. P.C.H.C. .	90	0	0	26th Regt. N.I. . .	136	2	0
4th Cav. H.C. . .	236	4	0	28th Regt. N.I. . .	196	8	0
5th Regt. Ghoorkas .	350	0	0	40th Regt. . . .	110	0	0
				89th Regt. H.M. .	375	0	0

Bishop of Melanesia, states in a letter to the Bishop of Madras, that the whole community does not number 400 souls. 'They are by no means well off, and derive their money chiefly from whaling, which is carried on for about six months of the year, and from the sale of their produce to chance whalers, and also by the sale of cattle to New Caledonia. But the story of the famine has touched their hearts deeply ; and as they took advantage of the day of intercession to use it also as a day of thanksgiving for their safety during the whaling season, their offertory may be considered as in part a thank-offering.'

MANSION HOUSE INDIAN FAMINE RELIEF FUND.

Committee.

The Right Honourable Sir Thomas White, Lord Mayor (chairman).
The Right Honourable the Earl of Northbrook, 4, Hamilton Place, Piccadilly, W.

Sir N. M. de Rothschild, M.P., New Court, St. Swithin's Lane, E.C.

Lieut.-General Sir Henry Norman, 16, Westbourne Sq., W.

K. D. Hodgson, Esq. M.P., 8, Bishopsgate St. Within, E.C.

E. C. Baring, Esq., 8, Bishopsgate St. Within, E.C.

Sir C. H. Mills, M.P., Lombard St., E.C.

H. M. Matheson, Esq., 3, Lombard St., E.C.

Baron de Stern, 6, Angel Court, E.C.

L. Huth, Esq., 12, Tokenhouse Yard, E.C.

C. Arbuthnot, Esq., 33, Great St. Helen's, E.C.

J. S. Morgan, Esq., 22, Old Broad St., E.C.

J. Fleming, Esq., C.S.I., 18, Leadenhall St., E.C.

S. Morley, Esq., M.P., Tonbridge

Alderman Sir W. A. Rose, 66, Upper Thames St., E.C.

Alderman Sir Robert Carden, 2, Royal Exchange Buildings, E.C.

W. R. Arbuthnot, Esq., Great St. Helen's, E.C.

Mr. Alderman Hadley, City Flour Mills, E.C.

Mr. Alderman Sidney, Bowes Manor, Southgate, N.

F. W. Buxton, Esq., 62, Threadneedle St., E.C.

Hon. H. L. Bourke, 18, Finch Lane

Henry Bayley, Esq., P. and O. Company, Leadenhall St., E.C.

S. P. Low, Esq., Parliament St., S.W.

W. Scott, Esq., 6, East India Avenue

M. Girod, 144, Leadenhall St., E.C.

E. H. Hardcastle, Esq., 144 Leadenhall St., E.C.

J. Sands, Esq., 50, Old Broad St., E.C.

J. Pender, Esq., M.P., Eastern Telegraph Company, Old Broad St., E.C.

Charles Teede, Esq., College Hill, E.C.

P. Macfadyen, Esq., Great St. Helen's, E.C.

G. Parbury, Esq., 87, Newgate St., E.C.

Thomas Gray, Esq., 34, Fenchurch St., E.C.

J. H. Crossman, Esq., Rolls Park, Chigwell

T. J. Reeves, Esq., 11, King's Arms Yard, E.C.

C. B. Dowden, Esq., 19, Cullum St., E.C.

A. T. Hewitt, Esq., 32, Nicholas Lane, E.C.

G. Arbuthnot, Esq., 40, Threadneedle St., E.C.

G. Smith, Esq., 14, Bride Lane, E.C.

J. N. Bullen, Esq., 65, Old Broad St., E.C.

F. W. Heilgers, Esq., Chartered Bank of India, Australia, and China, Hatton Chambers, E.C.

W. Mackinnon, Esq., British Steam Navigation Co., E.C.

H. S. King, Esq., 65, Cornhill, E.C.

Principal Subscriptions received in London.[1]

	£	s.	d.
Her Most Gracious Majesty the Queen-Empress . .	500	0	0
His Royal Highness the Prince of Wales . . .	525	0	0
Her Royal Highness the Princess of Wales . . .	105	0	0
His Royal Highness the Duke of Edinburgh . .	100	0	0
Her Royal and Imperial Highness Duchess of Edinburgh	50	0	0
His Royal Highness Prince Leopold	50	0	0
His Royal Highness the Duke of Cambridge . .	50	0	0
Her Royal Highness the Duchess of Cambridge . .	100	0	0
The Crown Prince and Princess of Germany . .	100	0	0
The Grand Duke and Duchess of Hesse . . .	50	0	0
The Grand Duke and Duchess of Mecklenburg Strelitz .	30	0	0
His Grace the Duke of Bedford	500	0	0
„ „ „ „ „ Northumberland . . .	500	0	0
„ „ „ „ „ Devonshire	500	0	0
The Duchess Dowager of Cleveland	500	0	0
The Most Noble the Marquis of Salisbury . . .	500	0	0
The Earl of Northbrook	500	0	0
Lord Leconfield	500	0	0
The Earl of Pembroke and Montgomery . . .	500	0	0
The United Grand Lodge of Masons	1,050	0	0
The Governor and Company of the Bank of England .	1,000	0	0
Messrs. N. M. de Rothschild and Sons . . .	1,000	0	0
Messrs. Baring Bros. and Company	1,000	0	0
Messrs. Coutts and Company	1,000	0	0
The Corporation of London	1,000	0	0
The Grocers' Company	1,000	0	0
The Mercers' Company	1,000	0	0
The Clothworkers' Company	525	0	0
The Merchant Taylors' Company	525	0	0
The Fishmongers' Company	525	0	0
The Goldsmiths' Company	500	0	0
The Oriental Bank Corporation	500	0	0
The Widow of the late George Ashbourne, of Calcutta .	500	0	0
Messrs. J. S. Morgan & Co.	500	0	0
Messrs. Arbuthnot, Latham, & Co.	500	0	0
Messrs. Stern Brothers	500	0	0
Messrs. Glyn, Mills, Currie, & Co.	500	0	0
The Commercial Sale Rooms	1,698	16	0
The Baltic	1,899	0	0
Members of the Stock Exchange	1,525	10	0
Lloyds	2,300	2	6

[1] This list is prepared chiefly to show the large sums given by individuals,

Towns, &c.

	£	s.	d.		£	s.	d.
Aberdeen . .	3,702	10	6	Butterworth .	177	15	4
Aldershot . .	131	18	6	Bridgenorth .	535	6	5
Ashford . .	160	1	2	Beverley . .	153	3	0
Aston upon Mersey	60	19	1	Bromsgrove .	93	12	11
Atherstone . .	105	0	0	Buckingham .	150	0	0
Aberystwith .	162	18	2	Barnsley . .	897	0	11
Alford . .	118	6	10	Bridgwater .	150	0	0
Alyth . .	109	16	0				
Alsager . .	81	3	1	Cheltenham .	1,561	16	1
Arbroath . .	460	12	10	Colchester . .	806	14	0
Aberdare . .	64	13	3	Carlisle . .	949	14	2
				Canterbury. .	962	7	11
				Cambridge (Town)	969	1	6
Burslem . .	400	0	0	Cambridge, (Uni-			
Bridport . .	302	7	1	versity) . .	765	3	4
Bristol . .	5,430	7	2	Coventry . .	763	2	6
Bury St.Edmunds	488	1	4	Cork . . .	1,143	19	9
Bath . . .	1,783	13	6	Chester . .	1,500	0	0
Boston . .	400	0	0	Cardiff . .	1,021	0	0
Brighton . .	2,985	0	0	Cleckheaton .	600	0	0
Belfast . .	3,050	2	1	Chesterfield .	314	4	9
Basingstoke .	275	6	0	Carnarvon . .	280	0	0
Banbury . .	261	7	10	Congleton . .	300	0	0
Batley . .	350	0	0	Couper Angus .	250	11	3
Birmingham .	7,922	13	2	Chichester . .	300	5	1
Bodmin . .	121	15	0	Cirencester . .	331	5	9
Bromley . .	60	1	7	Chard . .	137	3	6
Burnley . .	1,803	3	7	Cowes . .	75	2	0
Beaumaris . .	61	4	7	Croydon . .	213	19	10
Bedford . .	859	0	0	Chatham . .	328	6	2
Banff . . .	1,208	5	3	Crewe . .	395	11	0
Barton on Humber	259	17	2	Chipping Norton	50	0	0
Blairgowrie .	286	5	7	Chippenham .	124	0	2
Brockley Road .	56	3	1				
Beverley Minster	55	5	4	Dublin . .	13,000	0	0
Brighouse . .	175	15	3	Dundee . .	4,148	14	4
Barrow in Furness	776	4	3	Doncaster . .	962	1	9
Burton on Trent .	214	11	0	Derby . .	1,912	15	7
Battle . .	178	6	6	Devonport . .	815	15	5
Belford . .	82	4	0	Dewsbury . .	700	0	0

and the amounts contributed through the Mansion House by towns in Great Britain, by collections in places of worship, and from the Colonies. The broad base of the magnificent contribution of £820,000 may be estimated from the particulars here recorded.

Towns, &c.—continued.

	£	s.	d.		£	s.	d.
Dorchester . .	420	7	7	Glossop . .	203	14	6
Dudley . .	724	2	1	Guisborough .	100	0	0
Dover . .	637	19	7	Goole . .	113	5	1
Durham . .	340	7	2	Giggleswick .	140	6	8
Devizes . .	269	5	9	Glastonbury .	75	0	0
Denbigh . .	148	0	0	Gillingham . .	50	0	0
Deal . . .	109	13	6	Guernsey . .	387	3	6
Dawlish . .	125	0	0				
Daventry . .	100	0	0	Hull . .	4,746	0	5
Darlaston . .	67	0	0	Halifax . .	3,225	11	9
Dunstable . .	75	19	8	Huddersfield .	3,750	0	0
Dalton-in-Furness	52	0	0	Heywood . .	1,144	1	6
Dumfries . .	61	11	6	Hanley . .	1,000	0	0
Dartmouth . .	50	0	0	Harrogate . .	845	0	0
				Hereford . .	468	14	10
Exeter . .	2,560	0	0	Huntingdon .	460	3	4
Elgin . .	483	10	9	Holmfirth . .	401	4	7
Exmouth . .	321	5	0	Hertford . .	254	4	2
East Retford .	169	14	7	Horncastle . .	244	5	5
Eye . . .	87	1	8	Hawick . .	490	0	0
East Looe . .	83	13	10	Hallaton . .	76	3	6
				Hove . . .	67	5	1
Faversham . .	135	4	5	Hendford . .	86	8	4
Falmouth . .	198	4	3	Harwich . .	218	14	1
Forfar . .	173	18	4	Horbury . .	100	0	0
Fenton Urban Sa-				Hungerford .	90	13	1
nitary District	280	0	0	Haverfordwest .	250	14	3
Faringdon . .	111	12	9	Hitchin . .	176	0	1
Folkestone . .	265	5	6	Hythe . .	70	3	0
Fazeley . .	61	14	2	Hayling . .	50	0	0
Farnham . .	103	6	6				
				Ipswich . .	724	1	3
Grimsby . .	730	0	0	Isle of Man .	492	10	0
Grantham . .	682	10	0	Ivy Bridge . .	52	0	0
Gloucester . .	594	10	0	Inverness . .	548	9	3
Great Yarmouth .	509	13	8				
Guildford . .	363	1	10	Jersey . .	256	4	5
Great Driffield .	397	6	0				
Gravesend . .	416	4	8	Keighley . .	1,645	0	0
Gainsborough .	264	14	6	Kendal . .	1,689	12	10

*Towns, &c.—*continued.

	£	s.	d.		£	s.	d.
Kilkenny . .	414	10	5	Middlesborough .	200	0	0
Kircaldy . .	330	1	2	Monmouth . .	73	6	6
Kidderminster .	351	12	9	Market Drayton .	50	0	0
King's Lynn .	290	13	4	Market Weighton	50	0	0
Kirkenbright .	187	0	8	Maidenhead .	58	0	0
Kingston-upon-				Mafferton - with -			
Thames . .	242	8	5	Wansford .	100	0	0
Knottingsley .	133	4	5				
Knaresborough .	127	8	4	Norwich . .	2,192	12	3
Kingsbridge .	150	6	10	Nottingham .	2,408	5	0
Kington, Hereford	63	15	5	Northampton .	1,555	5	11
				Newcastle - upon -			
Leeds . . .	7,243	13	0	Tyne . .	5,446	7	4
Leicester . .	3,427	9	3	Newport, Isle of			
Longton . .	621	14	2	Wight . .	233	18	4
Luton . ·	239	8	3	Newcastle- under-			
Lewes . .	703	0	0	Lyme . .	372	1	4
Lincoln . .	600	0	0	Newport, Mon. .	803	16	4
Lichfield . .	422	6	2	Newcastle, Staf-			
Lymington . .	238	2	3	fordshire . .	100	0	0
Ludlow . .	151	2	9	New Malton,			
Louth . .	478	17	9	Yorkshire .	361	13	9
Launceston . .	203	4	11	Neath . .	383	9	8
Leek . . .	253	16	6	Northallerton .	190	7	10
Loughborough .	130	0	0	Newark . .	231	5	4
Lyme Regis .	85	0	0	Newton Abbot .	470	0	0
Littlehampton .	55	0	0	Newbury . .	261	0	1
Luton Hoo . .	68	12	4				
Lynn . . .	88	11	2	Oswestry . .	380	3	0
Lostwithiel . .	70	0	0	Ossett . . .	200	0	0
Littleport . .	50	3	0	Ottery St. Mary .	105	7	9
Maidstone . .	1,071	16	0	Perth . . .	3,175	0	0
Macclesfield .	350	0	0	Portland . .	120	0	0
Matlock . .	331	6	7	Plymouth . .	2,216	11	10
Margate . .	289	7	6	Portsmouth .	732	1	11
Mansfield, Notts .	290	14	0	Pontefract . .	405	5	6
Morpeth . .	155	7	6	Penzance . .	390	0	0
Montrose . .	140	0	0	Penrith . .	550	0	0
Motherwell .	73	7	3	Peterborough .	499	11	5

Towns, &c.—continued.

	£	s.	d.		£	s.	d.
Preston . .	4,655	15	0	Sutton Coldfield .	267	10	0
Petersfield . .	89	16	0	Southampton .	1,382	6	2
Paisley . .	1,000	0	0	Shrewsbury .	1,668	9	7
				Stafford . .	578	2	7
Runcorn . .	584	5	6	Sittingbourne .	100	0	0
Rochdale . .	2,000	0	0	Salisbury . .	1,040	5	3
Rothesay and				St. Austell . .	211	2	4
Bute . .	475	10	0	South Shields .	124	15	0
Rochester . .	319	18	5	Sudbury . .	150	9	1
Romford . .	356	11	11	Seaham Harbour	135	0	0
Reigate . .	550	7	10	St. Helens . .	738	8	6
Reading . .	737	14	7	Shipton-on-			
Romsey . .	159	15	7	Craven . .	449	3	11
Redditch . .	50	0	0	Swansea . .	358	15	5
Ripon . .	406	0	0	Staines . .	165	18	7
Royston . .	252	15	10				
Ramsbottom .	300	0	0	Torquay . .	950	0	0
Richmond (York.)	318	4	5	Taunton . .	667	10	0
Rotherham . .	1,039	8	1	Tynemouth. .	877	19	11
Rhyl . . .	164	10	2	Tiverton . .	194	0	0
Ross . . .	82	2	6	Torrington . .	59	14	7
				Tamworth . .	341	11	10
Sheffield . .	6,700	0	5	Teignmouth .	414	7	4
Stockport . .	1,847	4	0	Tipton . .	200	0	0
Stamford . .	313	0	0	Tavistock . .	252	7	4
Sidmouth . .	245	19	1	Tewkesbury .	112	9	0
Southport . .	1,532	6	7	Tenby . . .	305	5	6
Scarborough .	818	12	0	Turnham Green .	120	15	2
Sandwich . .	128	15	7	Totnes . .	56	11	8
Stoke-on-Trent .	610	19	7	Truro . .	300	4	2
Stourbridge. .	541	14	3	Tenterden . .	57	8	6
Stourport . .	106	14	11	Towcester . .	70	18	3
Sunderland. .	1,791	5	5				
Stonehouse (De-				Ventnor . .	51	15	6
von) . .	180	0	0				
Saffron Walden .	404	10	7	Winchester . .	782	1	0
St. Stephen's .	228	10	0	Wigan . .	1,575	0	0
St. Margaret's .	68	10	0	West Bromwich .	703	7	3
Saltash . .	67	12	5	Warwick . .	4,553	15	11
South Molton .	120	15	5	Windsor . .	172	1	0

Towns, &c.—continued.

	£	s.	d.			£	s.	d.
Wolverhampton .	1,034	4	1	Wycombe . .	78	18	3
Wakefield . .	1,500	0	0	Wisbech . .	164	4	6
Whitby . .	748	14	5	Wraxall . .	132	17	6
Walsall . .	467	2	7	Whitehaven .	799	10	4
Wells . . .	183	18	8	Wednesbury .	394	9	11
West Hartlepool	603	9	8	Weymouth . .	273	5	5
Wuerdle and Wardle,				Wrexham . .	286	4	11
Rochdale .	180	0	0				
Wilton . .	196	2	0	York . . .	2,506	10	6
West Abbey .	140	0	7	Yeovil . .	100	0	0

Colonies.

	£	s.	d.
Auckland, New Zealand	500	0	0
British Guiana	2,000	0	0
Coquimboo	38	9	6
Freemantle (Western Australia) . . .	43	11	8
Hong Kong	140	16	2
Hobart Town	1,553	8	4
Invercargill	500	0	0
Jamaica	1,024	10	0
New Plymouth, New Zealand . . .	540	10	4
New South Wales	17,740	0	0
Otago, New Zealand	4,010	0	0
Pietermaritzburgh	860	0	0
Wanganui, New Zealand	517	3	7
Wellington, New Zealand	1,994	5	1
Per Sir J. Vogel, Agent-General for New Zealand -	2,094	2	6
Collected at the British Vice-Consulate at Fiumé	21	3	4

Churches, &c.

	£	s.	d.
Westminster Abbey	140	0	7
St. Paul's Cathedral	147	9	3
Holy Trinity, Paddington	461	2	8
St. Paul's, Paddington	424	15	2
St. John's, Paddington	402	10	4
St. Mary Abbotts, Kensington . . .	333	5	8
St. Mary Magdalene, St. Leonards . .	246	2	2
Holy Trinity, Tunbridge Wells . . .	239	18	3

Churches, &c.—continued.

	£	s.	d.
St. Jude's, South Kensington	231	15	6
St. Stephen's, Westbourne Park	228	10	0
Christ Church, Highbury	224	4	3
St. Paul's, Onslow Square	223	8	5
Camden Church, Camberwell	214	13	7
Matson Church, Gloucester	213	9	2
St. Mark and St. Andrew's, Surbiton	202	18	10
St. Augustine, Highbury New Park	142	10	6
St. James', Kidbrook	110	14	1
St. Paul's, Beckenham	134	16	6
Quebec Chapel	116	0	4
St. Stephen's, Canonbury	100	0	0
Christ Church, Streatham	146	14	2
Beddington Church	112	2	6
St. Bartholomew, Sydenham	181	6	0
St. Michael's, Blackheath Park	128	7	2
St. Mary's, Balham	100	5	0
St. Luke's, West Holloway	100	0	0
St. James' Parish Church, Dover	102	0	0
St. Jude's, Mildmay Park	103	9	7
Otley Parish Church	126	0	0
Monken Hadley Church	100	10	0
Parish Church, Holy Trinity, with St. Saviour's Chapel of Ease	123	0	0
St. John the Evangelist, Penge	155	10	0
St. John's, Blackheath	113	10	4
Christ Church, Lee	139	1	5
Mortlake Church, with Christ Church, East Sheen	117	8	9
Christ Church, Tunbridge Wells	120	16	8
Christ Church, Folkestone	170	9	0
St. Stephen's, South Dulwich	130	6	9
Ackworth Church	176	8	2
Bath Abbey	134	12	0
St. Peter's, Bayswater	183	0	5
St. John the Baptist Church, Hove	100	1	2
St. Mark's, Lewisham	100	3	4
St. Mark's, Hamilton Terrace, N.W.	136	6	5
St. Michael's, Highgate	108	2	4
Christ Church, North Brixton	149	2	9
St. George's, Bloomsbury	125	14	6

Churches, &c.—continued.

	£	s.	d.
Temporary and Parish Church, Cheltenham	182	19	6
Trinity Church, Weston-super-Mare . .	159	13	9
Parish Church, Weston-super-Mare . .	108	11	1
Christ Church, Crouch End, Hornsey . .	105	17	8
St. George's, Bickley	101	19	1
Foundling Hospital Chapel . . .	105	9	9
St. Margaret's, Lee	133	6	7
Church Eaton Church	126	3	0
St. Mark's, Tunbridge Wells . . .	105	1	6
St. Matthew, Croydon	123	15	10
Beverley Church	114	12	0
Earley Church, Reading	142	3	10
Holy Trinity, Kilburn	102	3	8
Christ Church, Surbiton	132	9	10
Trinity Church, Eastbourne . . .	175	15	0
Parish Church of Holy Trinity, Sydenham	180	0	0
Christ Church, Worthing	116	17	0
St. James', Holloway	165	1	10
Eton College Chapel	146	0	0
Satterthwaite Church	122	12	0
St. Mary's, Chelmsford	124	2	10
Christ Church, Malvern	105	16	2
St. George's Chapel, Kemp Town . .	147	8	2
St. James', Westmoreland Street, Marylebone	111	17	0
St. Peter's, Belsize Park	166	12	8
Rugby School Chapel	101	0	0
Christ Church, Gipsy Hill	143	12	2
Christ Church, Chislehurst . . .	122	12	2
St. Michael's, Paddington	158	9	6
Weybridge Parish Church	116	3	10
St. Mary's, Christchurch, and St. John the Baptist, Wimbledon	176	12	8
Holy Trinity, Swane	136	8	4
St. Paul's, Hamlet Road, Upper Norwood .	110	5	0
Ford Church, Northumberland . . .	143	0	0
St. Michael's, Highgate	111	19	8
Richmond Church	105	16	2
Oswestry Parish Church	135	10	0
St. Leonard's Parish Church . . .	113	16	8
Immanuel Church, Streatham . . .	190	5	2

Churches, &c.—continued.

	£	s.	d.
Trinity Church, Cheltenham . . .	115	2	9
St. Mark's, Reigate	100	0	0
Christ Church, Brighton	189	10	0
St. John the Divine, Kennington . .	106	8	10
Holy Trinity, Bournemouth . . .	162	0	11
Downs Baptist Chapel, Clapton . . .	113	14	7
Camden Road Baptist Chapel . . .	118	9	0
Metropolitan Tabernacle	270	18	0
Regent's Park Baptist Chapel . . .	129	7	2
Chelmsford Congregational Chapel, London Road	102	0	6
Blackheath Congregational Church . .	163	14	6
New Court Congregational Church, Tollington Park	103	1	6
Craven Hill Congregational Chapel, Tollington Park	100	0	0
Lewisham Congregational Church, Tollington Park	130	13	5
Brixton Independent Church . . .	103	11	10
St. John's Wood Presbyterian Church . .	117	7	2
St. Paul's Presbyterian Church, Westbourne Grove	141	10	0
Marylebone Presbyterian Church . .	133	9	1
Central Synagogue	183	11	0
Roman Catholic Churches and Chapels .	832	10	0
Primitive Methodist Connexion . . .	554	19	5
Welsh Calvinistic Methodists . . .	1,060	18	4

CHAPTER V.

THE DISTRIBUTING COMMITTEES: INCIDENTS IN THE WORK OF RELIEF.

THE record of the labours of the various local committees and sub-committees of the Madras Presidency covers nearly fifteen hundred pages of foolscap, in most cases printed in small type. It is obviously impossible to do more than give a general idea of the manner in which the money contributed was spent, and this could not, perhaps, be better done than in the words of the reports submitted from time to time. To these reports of committees may usefully be added incidents of interest gleaned from the pages of the ' Weekly Statements of the Executive Relief Committee.' At the outset the general committee in Madras determined, whilst laying down broad lines of relief arrangements, to leave details to local committees. These committees proved themselves worthy of the trust reposed in them. This will appear from a few illustrative particulars:—

MODE OF RELIEF IN THE MOFUSSIL.

The taluks of Tripatore and Uttengerry, which are in charge of the head assistant collector, Mr. LeFanu, contain a population of about 350,000 in 740 villages. The Uttengerry taluk is as large again as the Tripatore taluk, and is suffering from famine as severely as any taluk in the district except Darmapoory.

The mode in which the committee proposes to work these taluks for relief purposes is the following :—The taluk of Tripatore is divided into eight and that of Uttengerry into sixteen divisions, each division containing about thirty-four villages on an average. The members of committee have each undertaken to visit all the villages in one or more divisions, to go from house to house and to inquire into the circumstances of every householder, and to enter on the spot in a book made for the purpose the name of the person entitled to relief, the amount of kist paid on his land, and the amount within 20 rs. to be given him. If his case be such as to require more help than 20 rs. a note is to be made of it for the favourable consideration of the committee. Then a ' ticket' is given to the individual with a number on it corresponding to the number opposite his name in the book, and he is told to come to the taluk town any day after the 20th instant to get the sum allotted to him. The object of fixing this date is twofold— 1, that sufficient time be given to the delegates to prepare their lists and get them passed by the committee ; and, 2, that sufficient time be given to the Madras committee to arrange for remitting the sum asked for. The method entails much labour, but we are convinced that it is the *only efficient plan* of carrying out the intention of the relief committee. The list of gentlemen who have volunteered to carry out this plan in these taluks, which I append, will show you that money placed at the disposal of this committee will be utilised in the best possible manner to meet the necessities of the distressed.

The urgent necessity of having the money placed *at once* at the disposal of the committee arises from the fact that unless cultivators are assisted within fifteen days to sow their fields, the season for sowing will have passed away and the opportunity of helping them lost for the present. I trust, therefore, that the sum asked for will be sanctioned without delay.

Our calculation of the probable sum required is made as follows :— From inquiries made by me in some villages I conclude that an average of ten cultivators in each village will require help on an average of 15 rs. each. In 740 villages this will amount to 111,000 rs., which is a little more than the sum asked.

This committee agree with the Madras committee that it is very desirable to have some general standard by which grants to ryots in a collectorate should be regulated. But this is very difficult, and indeed impossible under the circumstances, if our aid to ryots is to be of real value. The time required for conference and discussion by committees before such a standard could be arrived at is the very time in which the ryots should sow their fields, and hence in which the aid of the committee would be of any permanent value to them. Besides, the necessities of ryots in different parts of the same districts vary, and hence the average amount to be given must also vary. When I wrote my letter of the 13th my calculation of the probable sum required for these two taluks was based on my experience in some villages in the southern part of the district. In those villages I found that small cultivators had either died, left their villages, or had lapsed to the class of coolies ; and that only the more respectable had remained at home, greatly reduced in circumstances; in fact, in a state of great destitution. Hence I calculated that there would be an average of ten persons in every village who would require help averaging 15 rs. each. I have been this week visiting villages in this taluk every day, in order to prepare a list of such as are entitled to relief from the committee, and I find that the average number in each village is as much again, but that the average sum required by each person is less by one-half. That these villages are not a fair sample of all villages in the taluk I feel certain, for they are those which have suffered least from famine.

The general principles on which this committee give help to cultivators are these :—

1. Not to help such puttadars as can obtain a loan from Government.
2. Not to give anything towards buying bullocks.
3. Not to give money to any man unless the village munsif and others testify that what he says about his circumstances is true and that he will use the money given him for cultivation.
4. To help cultivators who have cattle to procure seed grain.
5. To help such as have neither bullocks nor seed grain to buy the latter and hire the former.
6. To help those whose houses are either wholly or partially destroyed.

Our plan of operation, which I sketched in my letter of the 13th instant, is such as to secure full and correct information of every cultivator, and so of enabling us to give according to the relative wants of each individual, from 1 r. to 20 rs.—*Tripatore Committee.*

I enclose an English copy of 'Instructions' which we issue in Tamil to the agents of the local committee. After defining the classes Government provide for, these instructions sanction the five following kinds of relief :—

1. Persons in great distress who are not entitled to Government help.
2. Friendless children and orphans not reached by Government.
3. Hire of two ploughs for a day, or one plough for two days, in cases of great poverty—equivalent to a grant of 12 annas.
4. Where the roofs of houses have been sold for fodder, or have been sold for the sustenance of the owner, or have been

burnt, three days' cooly for a man and a woman may be given when the need is great—the object being to give support while the work is being done.

5. In extreme cases clothing may be given during the cold season—three yards of rough cloth to an adult, and one and a half for a child.

The maximum aid per diem to be given to an adult is the value of 1 lb. of rice (equal to 1 anna 3 pies at present) and 3 pies in money, and for a child half that amount.

No aid in excess of 5-8-0 rs. per mensem is to be given to one family without the express sanction of the Committee.—*Dindigul Committee.*

At no better place than this perhaps could the testimony of the Government of India to the good work done by the local committees be stated. Writing to the Secretary of State, the Viceroy in Council said: ' In their " Weekly Statement " of October 20 the committee laid down the general principles which have since guided their expenditure. With the assistance of the Government officials in the districts, and by the agency of two of their own delegates, they established sub-committees and agencies all over the country, numbering by last reports no less than 110; and to these sub-committees they entrusted the expenditure of their funds, with the general instructions that two-thirds of the sums supplied were to be expended in giving to agriculturists the means of starting afresh in their calling, by assisting them to rebuild their houses, and to re-purchase bullocks and implements of agriculture, &c.; and one-third was to go towards relieving the destitute classes not reached by Government agency. How this latter part of the scheme has worked, and whether it has clashed in any way with the relief given out of Government funds, we have no information; but as the district officers must of necessity be the backbone of the sub-committees, and as the instructions of the committee have been precise and explicit, to avoid all appearance of interference with the action of Government, we presume that, although the operations of the committee must at some points have overlapped those of Government, yet, on the whole, the money has been usefully expended, and that no friction has taken place. In regard to the main scheme, however, of setting up agriculturists, we have explicit testimony, borne by several officers, to the excellent effect it has had in preserving the self-respect and position of the ryot, saving him from sinking to the position of a day labourer, and enabling him to turn to the best advantage the favour-able prospects of the season. We do not think a more judicious method of expending the bulk of the vast sums placed at the disposal of the committee could have been devised, and it has doubtless done incalculable good. Our heartiest acknowledgments are due to the committee for this result, and for the care they have taken to avoid friction or interference with the measures of Government.'[1]

The nature of the relief actually afforded may be gathered from the following extracts:—

Dindigul, November 17, 1877.

We are now progressing well with the work of distributing the funds placed at our disposal. We have already sent out into the villages 18,000 rs., most of which has been distributed, leaving us at this present with a balance of 7,000 rs. in hand. It has already been necessary to modify our original plan of distribution. In that we depended principally upon the services of the village officials for the distribution of relief, their work being controlled and attested by honorary members of the committee, consisting chiefly of the principal ryots residing in the villages. We soon found these officials were not trustworthy. In most cases there was delay in bestowing relief, and greater delay in submitting reports and returns. During the famine these men have had much extra work thrown on their hands; for

[1] The despatch from which the above is taken was written in reply to one from the Secretary of State, dated November 8.

example, the distribution of money doles in their villages, while their only pay was a piece of *manippa* land, which in the famine brings them in nothing, and is a loss to them by the amount they have expended upon it. Is it surprising that with daily facilities for misappropriating money, and with the pressure of the famine upon them, they recouped themselves for their work and time by retaining money which should have relieved needy villagers? I have no hesitation in saying that the village officials have been demoralised during the famine. It would have been money well spent if funds which have gone to import men and horses from other parts of India had been employed in rewarding these wretchedly remunerated village officials for the substantial and responsible work they were called upon to perform. As it was, a short experience proved that it was inexpedient to employ them; and the honorary members, who were appointed without a reference being first made to them, proved in the majority of cases either unwilling or incompetent to do our work.

In this state of things we had to look around for other agencies which were fortunately at hand. The Rev. J. S. Chandler, of Battalagundu, undertook the distribution of funds, directly, or by the aid of his catechists and teachers, in sixty villages. The Rev. E. Chester allowed his subordinates to take charge of forty-one villages. The Rev. L. St. Cyr and the Rev. A. J. Larmey, Roman Catholic priests, had the distribution in thirty-one villages allotted to them; and the special deputy collector, Subba Iyer, undertook relief operations in forty-three villages; while I employed agents in seventeen villages. This makes a total of 197 villages thus provided for out of 204 in the taluk. The distributors are all strongly urged to avail themselves of the local knowledge of the village officials and principal ryots while bestowing relief.

We find this plan works very well. The committee appoints the proportion of relief to be given in each village. Special cases needing extra assistance must be referred to the committee. Occasionally a village headman refuses to attest the registers and tickets because he is not paid for it and it is not Government work; but a substantial ryot can always do this duty. At times the distributor has been urged to divide a certain proportion of the funds with the village officials, and in one case the goomastah of a village munsif kept back a portion of the money dole, on the pretext that the persons owed money to him. We have not yet met with any case where the distributors have taken a part in, or connived at, wrong-doing of this sort. This committee acknowledge with pleasure the earnestness and promptitude with which the various distributors have entered upon this charitable duty.

The suffering in the district is still great, and must needs be till after the harvest is gathered in. At Rettiappetty, during the short time the agent of this committee was there bestowing relief, three persons died of starvation. Out of thirteen children sent to me a fortnight ago, five have already succumbed, and others remain in a very precarious condition. I have started an orphanage, in which there are at present 124 children. Within the next week the number will reach 150. Some of the children sent from the outlying districts are in a most deplorable condition, and the utmost care and attention fails in many cases to save them.

There are villages where special help is needed. In some places almost the entire village has been burned down by thieves who hoped to profit by the confusion. For example, the village of Malliappanpatti consisted of two or three streets of Roman Catholic and one row of pariah houses. The houses were fired and all destroyed, with the exception of the pariah houses. This happened some months since, yet many of the villagers have been unable to rebuild their houses, and seek aid from us.

We are thankful for the means placed at our disposal for relieving the general distress, and trust that, as the sum already allotted to us will soon be expended, the general committee will give us a further grant of 10,000 rs. for the month of December.

P.S.—I had scarcely completed this letter, when a communication from a member of the committee came to hand, from which I extract the following paragraph :—

'A young man died at our church-door last night. A Chakklia boy died, and the body was left unburied for five days in Pangalapatti. In Athoor, when they were distributing relief, a man who stepped forward to receive his dole at the call of his name died from the effort before receiving the dole.'—W. YORKE.

Coimbatore, November 25, 1877.

I have the honour to submit another report on the working of the local committee at Coimbatore; and I trust that the general committee will be satisfied that the funds are being distributed and aid afforded to those requiring it with as much rapidity as is possible. My former report shows the modes of relief to which we are giving our particular attention, and it is unnecessary to recapitulate them.

2. In the town of Coimbatore the expenditure during the past fortnight has been 3,632 rs. 12 annas, as shown in the following table :—

Form of Relief	No. of persons	Amount
		Rs. A.
Support of life, money dole, &c. . .	5,279	2,468 8
Day nurseries	4,718	515 12
Clothing	295	217 15
Repairing houses	72	272 4
To cultivators for seed, &c. . . .	3	28 0
Miscellaneous charity.	243	77 3
Office expenses	—	3
		3,632 12

The averages will be found to be as satisfactory as in my former report. A sum of 283 rs. 9 annas has to be deducted from the cost proper of feeding the children in the day nursery, for that sum was expended in building the three sheds required and in fencing the same; a lump sum of 28 rs. 10 annas was also paid for some Swiss milk, of which very little, however, has yet been used. Making allowance for these sums, the averages are approximately $7\frac{1}{2}$ annas per head for money doles; $8\frac{1}{2}$ pies for the day nursery; 15 annas for clothing; 3-12 rs. for repairing houses; 9-5-4 rs. to cultivators; 5-1 annas for miscellaneous charity.

3. I mentioned in my last that we contemplated starting a large day nursery, or, more properly speaking, a feeding-kitchen for poor children: and we find it working admirably. The number of children has increased, and, as will be seen, the daily average of children fed numbers 337. Two of the ladies of the station have most kindly undertaken the superintendence of the kitchen, and are indefatigable in their attendance and care for the children who flock to the place. There are still many cases of most fearfully emaciated children, some still coming, whose chances of life seem quite gone; and since October 12, when the kitchen was first commenced, thirteen children, who were too far gone when brought to the kitchen, have died. But numbers of children have benefited, and been saved by this timely aid; some have so improved that they have been removed from the list, and others are rapidly improving; and it is a pleasure to contrast their appearance now, bad as in many cases it still is, with their general appearance some few weeks back.

4. The reports from the various sub-committees among whom the town was divided are all most cheering, showing that, though distress still prevails in parts, and will continue until the harvest is got in and prices fall, the general condition of the people is much improved, and the numbers receiving weekly doles will probably be soon reduced;

though the expenditure for clothing and repair of houses may increase.

5. The item of miscellaneous charity is given to help strangers back to their villages, and also to those who have no fixed residence in town and yet require immediate relief.

6. In the Coimbatore taluk the returns show an expenditure of 8,147-8 rs. ; the averages being nearly 1 r. per head for money doles ; 4¼ annas for clothing ; 7-3-3 rs. for repairing houses ; 6-2-10½ rs. to cultivators ; and 8–10⅔ annas for miscellaneous charity. The average for money doles is higher than in the town, but that is owing to the fact that in many cases money doles have to be given for two or three weeks at a time, as the villages cannot be constantly visited, while in the town the doles are given weekly.

Form of Relief	No. of persons	Amount
		Rs. A.
Support of life, money doles, &c. . .	5,289	5,342 10
Clothing	133	76 10
Repairing houses	215	1,548 8
To cultivators for seed, &c. . . .	199	1,229 12
Miscellaneous charity	90	50 0
		8,147 8

7. The reports from the sub-committees of this taluk show that almost all lands are now under cultivation save those purposely reserved for pasturage ; that the growing crops are very fine, and that prospects are most cheering : at the same time, in some outlying villages where Government aid had clearly never penetrated, there is still much distress and much emaciation, especially among the children, and help will be needed till January. Besides the money doles the chief aid now to be given is for repairing and rebuilding houses, many having been totally destroyed.

8. In Pulladum taluk the expenditure has been 13,949-4 rs.; and the averages, as far as can be estimated, for the number of persons relieved has not always been given, is 11-10 annas for money doles ; 1-8 rs. for repairing houses ; 6-1-6 rs. to cultivators ; 5-8 annas for miscellaneous charity. The sum shown for clothing is the amount expended in the purchase of cloths, which are being gradually distributed ; and the returns do not show the number distributed up to the 15th instant.

Form of Relief	No. of persons	Amount
		Rs. A.
Support of life, money doles, &c. . .	3,046	2,254 5
Clothing	—	524 14
Repairing houses	118	177 0
To cultivators for seed, &c. . . .	1,793	10,922 11
Miscellaneous charity.	—	60 12
Office expenses	—	9 10
		13,949 4

9. From this taluk the report shows the prospects to be good; cultivation progressing steadily, the cholum and cumboo crops promising to be very fine. But in many cases ryots still want help, having spent their all in bringing their lands under cultivation, and not being, of course, able to go to the Government Relief Works, since they must continue to watch and tend their growing crops.

10. In this taluk I regret to say that there have been very serious complaints of the extortions practised on the poor ryots by the officials, the monegars and curnums. It has been reported that in many cases the monegars and curnums have extorted one-half of the relief given to the ryots; and in one case where 6 rs. were given to a lad for his support and to enable him to repair his house, no less than 5 rs. were said to have been taken by the village officials, the reason for such an exaction being that the lad had at first refused to give anything. This last case was, I am glad to say, at once brought to the notice of Mr. Gnanabaranom Pillay, one of our committee members, who was visiting the taluk, and he at once brought it to the notice of the magistrate, who has taken up the case. The magistrate has written to me that on his taking up the inquiry a large number of similar complaints were made to him; and our committee member, Mr. Gnanabaranom Pillay, is going out to the taluk to prosecute such cases as may be brought to light. I hear that the prompt action of the magistrate has had an immediate good effect, causing the restoration of a great part of what had been extorted, and I trust that any true cases may be successfully prosecuted, and this wholesale plunder by village officials be put a stop to.

11. In the taluk of Oodoomalapettah the expenditure has been 11,297-1-6 rs., the averages being 2-5-7 rs. for money doles; 1½ rs. for clothing; 3-12 rs. for repairing houses; 4-0-3 rs. to cultivators; 1-11-1 rs. for miscellaneous charity. The average for money doles may seem high compared with other taluks, but it is to be explained by the doles being given to last over some weeks, as the villages cannot be constantly visited.

Form of Relief	No. of persons	Amount
		Rs. a.
Support of life, money doles, &c. . . .	746	1,753 8
Clothing	75	84 4
Repairing houses	797	738 0
To cultivators for seed	2,158	8,667 4
Miscellaneous charity.	30	50 12
Office expenses	—	3 5
		11,297 1

12. The sub-committee hope that by the end of the month they will have disbursed all the money received. They report that, as in other taluks, cultivation is general and prospects excellent, the fear now seeming to be that there may be too much rain.

13. The return from Pollachy taluk has not been received by me, it having been returned to that sub-committee for amendment; but the distress there is very little and the amount expended is consequently small, while Mr. Moonesawmy, the assistant surgeon there, who has joined our committee, reports that he still has sufficient funds in his hands.

14. I think the general committee may rest assured that the funds are being distributed wisely and expeditiously. What has occurred in Pulladum taluk shows the difficulties that stand in the way of distribution, even where the committee members are on the spot and pay the money personally into the hands of the recipients of relief; and shows how impossible it is to delegate the distribution to others than the committee members. It is also reported that in many cases the village officers report lands as uncultivated which on inspection are found to have growing crops; so that it is impossible to rely on reports without personal inspection to test their truth. Committee members being, then, the only reliable agents for the actual distribution of the money, the distribution must necessarily occupy some little time. But in spite of all these difficulties I think the funds are being well distributed. The only complaints we have had have been from the Pulladum taluk; and I do not think the general committee need fear that there has been any delay such as to affect the cultivation, seeing that from every taluk we receive reports that all lands are under cultivation.

15. The ryots have certainly shown well in these trying times. In many cases they have literally sold everything in order to be able to sow their lands; and though the lands are sown the ryots must be supported until the harvest is got in. They well deserve it, and such,

as I gather from one sub-committee's reports, will be one principal form of relief for the next month or two.

P.S.—Our fortnightly return will be sent as soon as the amended return is received from Pollachy.

Trichinopoly, December 11, 1877.

I have the honour to forward my report on the operations of the Trichinopoly Local Committee to November 30, to go by to-morrow's post together with the prescribed returns and a printed copy of our Proceedings, dated November 29, 1877.

There was a short delay in our getting to work in the outlying portions of the district in consequence of the exceedingly heavy rain which fell last month and made travelling a matter of difficulty everywhere, and in some places impossible, but the task of distributing funds has been pushed on with vigour and we have already brought relief to the doors of a vast number of indigent persons.

We commenced work by dividing the whole district into circles, and to each circle one member of our committee was appointed to go from village to village and from house to house, administering relief to those persons who were in want of food, making advances to ryots for the purchase of seed and for the hire of ploughing cattle and giving clothes to the naked.

The general condition of the district was even worse than we anticipated, and from nearly every side we have received reports showing how severe and widespread was the distress. Mr. Pattabiram Pillai, the collector's sheristadar, and a member of our committee, writes of the Manapparai circle as follows : ' The people are in as wretched a state as could be imagined.' ' Three-fourths of the houses in Poyampatti are roofless.' In another village ' 35 houses have been deserted.'

In Melayadupatti and its suburbs ' I saw the same thing over again—ruined houses, emaciated men and women, and skeleton children, a sad spectacle.' ' The state of these people and of those whom I had the good fortune to relieve in the Manapparai circle cannot be realised by any who have not seen them. . . . I was surrounded by hundreds of females and children with scarcely a cloth to cover them.' Speaking generally of the condition of a group of 15 villages in his circle he says, ' The people were eating wild-grown greens which the late rains have produced—their huts were in ruins and afforded them no shelter, their clothes were all rags, and most of them were almost naked.'

Your committee will see from these brief extracts how terrible was the distress in his circle, and what energy it required to bring relief surely and swiftly to every man's house. Mr. Pattabiram has devoted the whole of his time to this work with the most gratifying results.

K 2

In his last reports he writes, 'Crowds of ryots went in for the purchase of paddy, grain, and cumboo seeds in the fairs which are held in their vicinity. . . . They have set about repairing their houses, ploughing their waste fields, sowing seeds and preparing seed beds.' The clothes sent by the Trichinopoly Committee (200 pieces, each 40 yards long and 1⅜ yards wide) were of the greatest use. The people prized them highly.

The commissioner for the Kuttalai circle, a pensioned tahsildar, writes that many of the ryots are in a very reduced condition without seed or money to pay labourers or to maintain themselves.

From the Musiri circle accounts are rather more cheering. Mr. Salisbury writes that there is a fair average of land under cultivation in the 68 villages visited by him.

From Arealur, Mr. J. Arivanandam Pillai writes that the standing crops in some 50 villages have been utterly destroyed by locusts. He describes the state of one village, Thiranypoliem, as follows : 'The whole of the ryots, including the village munsif, presented such a ghastly appearance that I never saw anything like it during the whole of the famine. I was somewhat thrown back in my ardour by the remarks of the tahsildar and the deputy collector, who were of opinion that there was no great famine in their taluks ; but when I actually went to the villages the ravages of the locusts, the emaciated bodies of the ryots, the tottering condition of their huts, the torn rags which covered their nether limbs, all these told me a different tale. The distress is beyond description.'

Our operations in Udayarpollium taluk were checked by a letter dated November 7, addressed to our Vice-President, Mr. Seshiah Sastri, C.S.I., by the tahsildar, who writes as follows : 'On a careful enquiry into the condition of this taluk I find that there is very little necessity at present for affording any relief whatever to any class of poor people here.'

Further enquiry, however, into the actual state of the taluk placed under his charge led the tahsildar to alter his opinion, and on December 4 he writes again to ask for money for ryots who have no food and no means to buy food.

The general result of our work in the taluks for the period ending November 30 is as follows :—

In Manapparai 10,829 persons have received 5,339 rs. for support of life ; 1,779-15 rs. have been spent in providing clothing, 1,525 rs. for repairing houses, and 2,928 rs. for purchase of seed, &c.

In the same circle Tahsildar Sambamuti Ayar distributed 2,221 rs. for support of life ; for clothing, 1,196 rs.; for repairing houses, 897 rs. ; for purchase of seed and bullock hire, 1,310 rs

In the Musiri taluk 824 persons received 1,992 rs. for the support of life; 342 were clothed (411 rs.); 176 rs. were given for the repair of 51 huts, and 11 cultivators received 102 rs. among them for the purchase of seed grain.

In Arealur 636 persons received support, and 48 persons were clothed. These numbers, however, represent but a very small portion of the whole work that has to be accomplished in this circle, and which is being proceeded with as fast as circumstances will allow.

In the Kuttalai circle 49 persons received 233 rs. for support of life; 97 were clothed; 40 houses were repaired; 377 persons received 1,791 rs. for purchase of seed, &c.

In Thatchenkurchi circle (Trichinopoly taluk) 1,439 persons received varying sums of money for support of life; 1,214 were clothed; 208 received sums of money for repairs of houses; 444 received advances for the purchase of seed.

The Rev. Mr. Joyce, Roman Catholic chaplain; Mr. Seshiah Sastri, C.S.I.; Mr. Adolphus; M.R.Ry. Perriasamy Mudaliyar, and the Rev. Mr. Guest undertook the duty of looking after the poor of the town of Trichinopoly.

Mr. Seshiah Sastri and Perriasamy Mudaliyar have disbursed 5,457 rs. for the support of life for about 700 families of Gosha women containing 2,107 souls. Some of the money was intended for repairing houses destroyed by the rains, and some 200 rs. were distributed to the poorest boys in the Government Normal School.

The Rev. Mr. Guest has distributed money to 2,033 persons for support of life; 72 persons were clothed; 30 rs. were advanced to 3 cultivators.

The Rev. Mr. Joyce has relieved 1,682 persons, and 200 were clothed; 33 rs. were given for repairing houses.

From the Rev. Mr. Adolphus 280 persons have received advances for support of life; clothes were issued costing 25 rs.; 17 rs. were given for repairing houses.

Mr. Webster has spent 597 rs. for subsistence of 121 ryots, purchase of seed, hire of bullocks, &c.

Mr. Parsick, C.E., has distributed among 1,440 persons, chiefly the children and women of coolies attending the relief works, clothes valued at 1,000 rs.

By the Rev. Mr. Nicholas 162 rs. were distributed for support of life, and 10 rs. were spent on clothing in the Udaiyarpolliem taluk.

The reports received from these gentlemen tell the same tale of great distress and suffering and of gratitude for timely relief afforded. The narratives of distress in the town are all touching and painfully interesting. Of one section of people, the Gosha women, Mr. Seshiah

Sastri writes as follows : 'Some of the dwellings are respectable, but the generality are wretched hovels, which, with the household utensils, are not worth more than a few rupees. In them dwell Gosha ladies with their numerous families, eking out a miserable subsistence out of their own earnings from lace-work, and making gold thread, making up flower garlands and green bangles and out of any earnings of their husbands, descended of once well-to-do families, but now sunk to the position of jutka drivers, menial servants, punkah pullers, or in receipt of a scanty and uncertain income from nominal religious service at mouldering tombs and half-ruined dargahs. The tale of famine as we read it in the condition of these Gosha women and of their wretched huts was in many cases most heartrending. Some families represented the nobility of the days of Chunda Sahib : Dewans, commandants, killedars, royal physicians, and palace high priests.' The condition of other classes of people in other quarters of the town is vividly painted by the Rev. Messrs. Adolphus, Joyce, and Guest.

Extracts from these reports and from those received from the taluks are forwarded with this letter, and will, I believe, be perused with great interest by your committee.

We are still in full swing and have plenty to do before our work comes to a close. It is not yet too late to make advances for the purchase of seed grain, and we have many poor persons who are still in need of clothing. Mr. Seshiah Sastri having telegraphed to Bombay, Madras, and Negapatam, found that the latter place afforded the cheapest market, and we have already obtained 500 pieces of cloth from that town.

Kalastri, February 1878.

To check the application of relief the committee have appointed four supervisors who receive weekly a list of grants made, with their objects, and who, after inquiry, report as to the use which the recipients have made of the money received.. The grants for seed grain and bullocks are the most important, and the report on these, though weekly continued, cannot be completed until next month, i.e., until after sowing time is over.

The reports received to-day may perhaps be taken as typical. They show that out of 14 villages for which reports are received to-day, the whole amount of land for which advances have been made has been cultivated in eleven cases : in the remaining three cases advances have been given for sowing 44 kawnies, of which 23¾ kawnies are already sown, and the rest of the land is ploughed ready for sowing. The total expenditure thus far is, then, grants for seed grain and bullocks. Ryots understand thoroughly the gratuitous nature of the grant. Fully one-half of the cultivation now on the ground is from seed grain bought with Mansion House money.

The expenditure thus far is as follows :

		Rs.	a.	p.
(1) For seed grain and bullocks	. . .	30,995	14	0
(2) „ Money doles and cloths	. . .	1,284	4	5
(3) „ Office charges .	. . . .	206	1	5
(4) „ Contingencies .	. . . .	24	15	4

This leaves a balance of 2,487-12 rs. in the hands of the Kalastri Committee.

This balance, together with the 5,000 rs. now asked for, the Committee propose to expend thus :

	Rs.	a.	p.
(1) Seed grain and bullocks	4,500	0	0
(2) Money doles, houses, weavers' cloths .	2,380	0	0
(3) Office charges	580	0	0
(4) Contingencies	27	12	0
	7,487	12	0

As giving an indication of the suffering caused by high prices, the following letter, written by the Honourable A. Seshiah Sastri, C.S.I., once prime minister of Travancore, is instructive:—

Trichinopoly, December 5, 1877.

I take the liberty of writing a few lines, touching the condition of the poor people residing in the Fort and suburbs of Tanjore, to which place I paid a visit the other day, and request the favour of your laying the same before the President and members of the committee at your earliest convenience for their consideration.

2. I am a native of the Tanjore district—served there upwards of three years, now ten years ago, residing in the town of Tanjore, and, during the greater portion of that time, held the honorary office of Vice-President of the Municipality, the duties of which brought me face to face with every class of the residents and took me to every nook and corner of the town. I have thus had ample opportunities of observing and knowing the condition of the people dwelling therein, and may therefore be trusted in the statements which I am about to make.

3. Moreover, during my recent brief visit, I met many of my old friends, both in and out of the service, and derived much information from them as to the present distress among the poor of the town.

4. The Mahrattas of Tanjore, both Sundras and Brahmins, form a

singularly isolated community, whom the adventures of war, two centuries back, threw suddenly into the possession of one of the richest and finest kingdoms in the Carnatic, and time and distance have almost completely cut off their connections with their mother-country —Maharashtra.

5. Once in possession of the principality which fell to them for the asking almost, they seldom had further occasion for the exercise of military virtues, and, as a people, they soon relapsed into an easy and luxurious life, and everything which could contribute to finery and luxury was cultivated to a perfection which to this day has not been attained in the court of any other native prince in India.

6. Leaving out the members of the Royal Family, the families more distantly related to it, the dignitaries of the palace, all of whom contented themselves with basking in the sunshine of royal favour and grace, and deriving the means of living in splendour direct from the Sovereign's bounty—leaving out the numerous class of officials, high and low, who, in the plenitude of unbridled power, derived a boundless income, the mass of the Mahrattas derived an easy, comfortable subsistence, some by betaking to service, almost nominal in many cases, on the numerous establishments of the superior class above alluded to, as bearers of swords, maces, lances, flags, and various other emblems of power—as sepoys, as peons, as mahouts, as drivers, as household stewards, &c. Others by betaking to professions not requiring severe manual labour, such as making flower garlands, lace-work, embroidery, and tapestry; and similar refined occupations too numerous to mention.

7. On the cession of the principality to the British about 80 years ago, the wealth and affluence of many, chiefly of the official class, disappeared. But as most of the members and dependents of the Royal Family and the grandees and dignitaries of State always lived within the town, their condition was not very seriously affected, so long as the Raj was maintained and supported by the Punjum Hassa allowance.

8. When the Raj, however, became extinct, scarcely a quarter of a century ago, the fall became to them a reality, and in spite of arrangements considerately made by the British with a view to break the fall, ruin and wretchedness have been overtaking them year after year; for the impoverishment of each nobleman's family involved in the ruin perhaps a dozen poor families, their servants and dependents. The pensioned class have been, for years, bearing up against the severe pressure of high prices. Those engaged in occupations I have already described have been sinking deeper and deeper in poverty, both by the falling off of their trades and by the high price of food grains.

Though a few families have emigrated, still the mass cling to their homes, trying to make a subsistence out of almost nothing.

9. Simple, artless, ignorant, and credulous in the extreme, knowing and caring to know nothing of the world outside, unaccustomed to severe work, and addicted to an idle and luxurious life, and proud of historical associations yet too fresh to be forgotten, they have been, with very few exceptions, in a very wretched condition of late years. As one of them very pithily said to me, 'We cannot work—we will not steal—we must not beg—we are left to starve.'

10. In several families, of even the poorest, the females are quasi-Gosha, and are utterly unproductive members. I mean unproductive in an *economic* sense—for otherwise, poverty and progeny seem to go only too much hand in hand !

11. Now, I think, it will be easy to conceive the effects of a terrible famine on a population so situated—a famine which has taken away all the surplus produce of the district, and sent up the cost of the food grains to at least three times the normal prices. I have been informed that the present condition (as indeed their past ever since the famine began) of at least a thousand families is deplorable in the extreme, and I, who know the people so well, can well realise it.

12. It is nothing against the argument of my cause, if the district of Tanjore yielded a fair crop last year, or if a bumper crop is maturing on the ground in the present. Naboth's vineyard is indeed laden with fruit—but what of it to the poor neighbours, who cannot get or buy a share of it. This is exactly the position of the bulk of the poor of Tanjore Fort and suburbs, and it is on their behalf I venture to appeal to the general relief committee at Madras, who are so nobly administering the charity of the English nation. I feel confident that no portion of the Mansion House fund could be better spent than on the mansions of fallen greatness in Tanjore or in the tottering hovels where poverty reigns supreme. I feel sure that a grant of 75,000 rs. will go a great way to bring relief home to them and send into many a poor man's hut a ray of cheerfulness in a night of darkness. I also think I could organise a thoroughly respectable and trustworthy agency to carry out the distribution of relief, should my proposal meet with sanction.

The system adopted in Mysore, where district officers were more freely employed than in Madras, will be seen from the two tables appended:—

Extract from diary of Mr. VENKET Row, Special Relief Officer,
Kolur District.

Monday, January 7.—Visited (3 miles) Ellavoopally P. Census work occupied me from 7 A.M., to 3 P.M. During which relief was given to 4 families. 90 rs. were distributed among them as follows:—

House No.	Rs.	Name	Purpose
2	25	Akki, with a brother and two daughters. Her condition was enough to touch even the hardest heart. Pays 12 rs. Kandayam, had 2 bullocks and 2 cows last year	For a pair of bullocks
3	15	Mooneaka, with two grown-up sons and 2 pairs of bullocks and 30 sheep last year, has one bullock. No house	For one bullock and to build a hut
6	30	Baswa, with two brothers, a sister and mother, all were in the Sriniwaspoor Relief Camp. Had a pair of good bullocks, 4 she-buffaloes, 15 sheep. Pays 7 rs. Kandayam. His land is not cultivated; has no house	5 rs. for hut 5 rs. for food 20 rs. for a pair of bullocks
8	20	Hanama, by caste Vaddar, a son and two miserable daughters lately returned from relief camps, now lives by begging. Has no house	5 rs. for a hut 5 rs. for food 10 rs. for a pair of buffaloes

The relief afforded to the two last cases was an incalculable blessing to them, for they never even dreamt that, in their present desperate condition, to which they had been inured for 18 months past, a relief of this kind, enabling them to settle once more in life with their relations, would come to them so unexpectedly.

Returned home at 4 P.M.

Wednesday, January 9.—Visited two villages, Sataandhalli and Gunganahalli. 205 rs. were distributed among 17 families in both the villages, as follows:—

House No.	Rs.	Name	Purpose
4	25	Vengti, with a grown-up son and two children, her husband died of starvation. Pays 8 rs. Kandayam	25 rs. for a pair of bullocks
6	10	Vengatrama, has one bullock. Pays 8 rs. Kandayam	10 rs. for a bullock
10	5	Timmi and her daughter . . .	2 rs. to patch up hut, 3 rs. for food
12	20	Mooniga, his mother and wife. Pays 7 rs. Kandayam, has become a day labourer, his land is waste	20 rs. for a pair of bullocks
13	13	Venketrama, has one bullock, pays 7 rs. Kandayam	10 rs. for a bullock, 3 rs. to patch up hut
15	10	Mooniga, has one bullock . . .	10 rs. for a bullock
20	5	Naga, weaver, and three dependents, has a loom	5 rs. for materials
20	35	Venketramu, and nine members, all in miserable condition, has 20 acres of dry land and no bullocks, had a pair of bullocks and 3 cows last year	25 rs. for bullocks, 10 rs. for food
22	10	Lutchmi and three others . . .	10 rs. for a bullock or a cow
29	10	Dassa and four others, pays 5 rs. Kandayam, has one bullock	10 rs. for a bullock
33	5	Moonehanooma, and three others . .	5 rs. for clothing
33	10	Lonna, weaver low caste, has no loom .	5 rs. for loom, 5 rs. for materials
11	7	Byah, has no house	5 rs. for house, 2 rs. for clothing
30	4	Moonigah, weaver, has a loom . .	4 rs. for materials

INCIDENTS IN RELIEF.

(A PAGE FROM A DELEGATE'S NOTE-BOOK.)

THE ryots are a very simple race, with child-like habits of dependence on whomsoever finds them the pittance they require to borrow now and then to form the trifling capital requisite for their rude operations in husbandry.

At one place the notices convening a famine meeting had been issued sufficiently early to allow some idea of the purposes of the Madras Committee to get abroad in the bazaars and through the villages. The meeting was held, and it was decided to apply for funds for distribution. In the afternoon a band of some 250 ryots appeared in the compound of the house, and sent in word that they had come for their money. A message was sent back to them that no money was as yet available for distribution ; when they sat down in ranks, apparently with the intention of being on the spot to secure the promised aid the moment it should arrive. As time passed on, and night fell, there was no clamour, but the poor fellows slipped away by twos and threes till the place was empty. Probably each of them has ere this been gladdened by the receipt of a dole sufficient to give them a start, and has had his faith in the committee fully restored.

I wish I could paint a picture which would show the English subscribers the following scene:

A window in an old public building opening into a

courtyard—time 6.30 p.m., so that the Indian apology for twilight is almost over. On the window-seat is a flickering candle by which sits a pale Englishman, one of the best known of our civilian judges. Standing by him another judge—perhaps the best native lawyer in the Empire ; behind them, looming in the shadowy background, several members of committee, native and European, and your "delegate." Just below the candle on a ledge along the wall is an energetic East Indian gentleman, who takes now and again a ticket from the holder below. In the courtyard is a motley crew of all sorts. Gap-toothed crones and younger women deformed or sickly ; old men tottering with age and young men with palsy; children of both sexes homeless, friendless, and foodless. Then a sprinkling of *mauvais sujets*, professional beggars, and here and there a sturdy old mendicant of the Ochiltree type, who considers himself prescriptively entitled to a share of any 'awms' which may be going anywhere in his beat.

This is the Local Committee inspecting, as a body, the applicants for relief to whom individual members of their body have given tickets.

The children are the class *par excellence* which the grisly old giant Famine delights to run 'amok' amongst. You can tell at a glance the poor wee bairns that have been in his cruel grip. The head looking unnaturally large by contrast with the emaciated trunk, the shoulder blades projecting as if they had been inserted by mistake in too small a carcase, the arms and legs shrivelled to the size of their bones, except at the knees which are swollen. Then the expression of the bleared little faces. The vacant fixed look in the eyes, the drawn cheeks and lips, and the premature air of resignation, which one sees sometimes in a monkey when it looks up at you with the mournful face of an old man whose troubles had told on him.

At one place the faces of some of the children haunted us so much that orders were given for 200 of the worst cases to be collected. You should have seen them, for I could not hope to give you an adequate idea of their misery. In some the last forces of their system seemed to have been expended in growing, and I never saw folk out of Doré's drawings whose length was so hideously disproportionate to their breadth.

Others were tiny and wizened every way, as if an attempt had been made to see into how small a compass a suffering body and soul could be compressed.

The whole party, after we had inspected them, were marched off to a camp, but as it was impossible of course to coerce them, over 100 slipped away, and only 96 reached the new home. The poor wee runaways preferred, I suppose, the evils they knew of, bad as they were, to the horrid vague. unknown. Those that allowed themselves to be taken care of, were fed *ad lib.*, and in one part at least of each little body that line of beauty, the curve, was substituted for the hideous famine angles.

But the hunger had got too strong a hold on them to be dislodged by one meal, however good and large. So during the night the small sinners crept under the tatties into the hospital for adults, and stole the rations supplied to the patients.

And yet when morning came each little maw was as ready as ever for food—maybe the more ready for the stolen sweets of the midnight meal, for in convalescence most surely ' *l'appétit vient par le mangeant.*' —F. ROWLANDSON.

Scenes by the Wayside.

On a recent tour, I heard directly of not less than 30 deaths from starvation, in five or six villages. I also saw several in a starving condition, some of whom have since died. In one enclosure I saw a man, willing and strong to work, but, from hunger, lying upon his back, with arms and legs extended, apparently insensible. The emptiness of the abdomen showed the cause of his trouble. A little distance from him lay his wife, in a half-conscious state, with an infant trying to extract nourishment from its mother's breast, and an older child lying a little way off, in the same condition as the mother. I have heard that the man died soon after. In the same village, the day before I was there, a young man climbed a tree in search of half grown fruit, became dizzy from weakness, fell, and was killed.

I was told by three men, each of different caste, in another small village, who mentioned the names of deceased persons as they counted them over, that in four families of potters in that village, containing 20 individuals, there had been nine deaths from starvation. And that of 16 houses belonging to people of another caste, only six are now occupied, and that in these 7 persons had died from hunger.

I was also told by the same men and another belonging to a little village near, that 11 of the 18 houses in this latter village are now empty, and that in the remaining 7, six have died from want of food.

It is for the relief of persons thus situated that assistance is requested.

My duties as a missionary call me to go much among the people, bring their wants to my notice, and give me opportunities to help them had I the ability.

The rains that have fallen have afforded relief to some, in some respects, already. They also give promise of future harvests. These however, from the lateness of the rain and other reasons, will be less abundant than in ordinary seasons. Till the time of harvest the price of grain must continue to be very high.—Rev. J. HERRICK, *Madura*.

Extreme Wretchedness.

Mr. Dawes, the deputy collector in charge of the Ootenghiri taluk, was one of the passengers, and I had much useful conversation with him. He took me to see a 'kitchen' near the Morapoor station, but a stream running across the road was so swollen by the heavy rains that we could not reach it. A number of the people, however, gathered about us, and I have seen nothing in the camps near Madras to compare with their wretchedness. Small-pox has been very rife. and one poor woman by the wet road-side appeared to be dying of it. The emaciation of the sufferers was the more striking from their nakedness, which, in many cases, was almost wholly uncovered. Mr. Dawes asked for clothes, seed grain, and bullocks.—F. ROWLANDSON, *Sept.* 25.

A Day's Work by an Honorary Secretary.

The work of dispensing aid as per your rules, enclosed in your letter of the 18th instant, has gone on well. The plan we here adopted is briefly as follows :—

(1.) I *personally* pay out all funds and as far as possible to the individuals receiving the aid. Gosha women and sick persons of course have the aid sent to them by trustworthy friends.

(2.) The other members of the committee examine and inquire into the needs of all applicants for relief except Christians, and those accepted are sent to me with a note giving some particulars, &c.

(3.) From 7 A.M. to 10 A.M. I receive all who have the notes of my colleagues, and take the liberty to inquire into any applications which may be made after those having the 'chits' are cared for.

(4.) All members of the committee are bound by promise to exercise every precaution to keep out the unworthy, and each is personally responsible for all whom he may send.

(5.) The amount which each applicant may receive is left entirely to me.

Of course these brief rules are subject to alteration if found to be contrary to your wishes or undesirable.

(6.) My accounts are subject to inspection by any member of the committee. I have up to this evening distributed 1,384 rs. to 352 families. Consequently I have only 616 rs. now in my hands, and this will go off at the rate of 200 rs. or more per day.

Poor ryots by scores, and others of every caste, creed, and profession armed with 'chits,' stating the urgency of their case, from the village munsif and kurnam where they reside, from near and afar come here daily for aid. Each 'chit' generally tells a sad tale of bullocks dead, house tumbled down or burnt up, seed grain required, or a widow and destitute children, or orphans, or of sickness and distress in the family of the bearer, whose whole demeanour shows that the letter is only too true. Thus come the wails from the villages day by day. Each member of the local committee has assured me that the importunities of the crowds about his house or office daily, for an order that they may get money to relieve their need or distress, is *perfectly excruciating*. Personally, it is not too much when I say that frequently 1,000 persons are in or about my compound, each trying to get an opportunity to press his claim for aid. The rush is so great that I have to have a police constable and two or three trusty men constantly on duty to keep order. But I think I succeed pretty well in giving to the deserving and in getting rid of the drift. I first receive all applicants for aid sent by my colleagues on the committee ; (2) those sent by village munsifs and kurnams; (3) those known to me personally or to some one of my trustworthy native assistants ; (4) all those sent by any responsible person, known to be such by any one of us; (5) I then look over the company of other applicants and listen to what each has to say for himself ; of course in the case of many a look is enough. I have no idea that our plan is the best possible, but it is the best I can think of, and it seems to work well. While we do not do all we should like to do, and while, no doubt, we are sometimes deceived, thousands are aided who otherwise would either soon be in sad distress or dead.—Rev. J. E. CLOUGH, *Ongole.*

Difficulties in Distribution.

A few of the incidents that one meets with may be interesting as showing the condition and disposition of the people. In Rammeracherd we met a small farmer who had been very well off; he had spent a great deal of money in buying fodder for his cattle; but prolonged drought baffled his efforts to keep them alive ; he had lost every one, had no means to cultivate his land, he was badly off for clothing, his house had become quite desolate, his wife had died some days previous to my visit ; and the poor man was thoroughly dispirited. I gave him a blanket and a little money for the purchase of seed grain. In other instances I have found that there was great need of careful enquiry in giving help. In one village I found two families, cultivators, extremely poor, receiving the Government money dole. I asked if they had not sown their lands. The reply was that all their cattle were dead and they had no means whatever to sow their fields. I visited their houses and saw the empty stalls, and ploughs lying idle. It seemed a worthy case for help ; but on further enquiry where the fields were, the kind of soil, what seed they proposed to sow, &c., I discovered that the nature of the soil was such that it was useless to sow it this season, as the cold weather crop would not grow in it ; and that it would be therefore quite useless at present to give any help for ploughing the land.

In a neighbouring village to which this news had spread, I was met the same day by a number of farmers who pleaded for help, as they had no means to cultivate their land. One man in particular said he had 60 acres, and had not been able to cultivate a foot, he was so poor. I said I would go and see his land, and was then told by an on-looker that the man had let it, that it had been cultivated and the crops on it doing well.—Rev. E. LEWIS, *Bellary.*

Taluk Triumvirates.

Gooty, October 2, 1877.

I believe the following is an outline of the scheme we agreed on this morning.

Operations to be entrusted to the 'taluk triumvirates' (as I may call them) composed in each case of (1) the taluk relief officer, (2) a selected native gentleman, and (3) myself.

The names of the taluk officers and native members you are aware of. The forms of relief to be two, viz.:—

1. The feeding of children in day nurseries.
2. The relief by money pittances of persons who by reason of social position are deterred from accepting Government relief on works or in close camps, and yet are legitimate objects of charity.

There will be no difficulty in deciding upon the claims of children, inasmuch as the mere fact of obvious need will be a sufficient qualification.

The task of selecting proper objects for the second kind of relief will be much more delicate and difficult. Our object will be to relieve the sufferings of persons who may reasonably be excused for persistence in shrinking from the tests of need which Government have imposed.—W. H. GLENNY.

An Audacious Suggestion.

At the Erode meeting it was proposed by some of the native gentlemen present that one of the committee's operations should be the lending of money at a low rate of interest to the more wealthy ryots, *i.e.*, their own class, as they complain that they have to pay high rates now. I did not understand that the loans were asked for with any idea of indirectly benefiting the population generally, but gathered that these gentlemen were seeking simply to enrich themselves from your funds. This incident throws some little light on the difficulties which attend the distribution of our funds in outlying places.— F. ROWLANDSON.

Suffering among Classes beyond Scope of Government Operations.

For some months past the evidence of suffering in regard to the families of certain classes has been quite clear, and the scheme of Government out-door relief in cooked food, though meeting the necessities of the old and feeble, has not been brought home to the great bulk of the poor requiring food. It is well known that food is distributed daily at the Government feeding house and camps, one meal a day to from 12,000 to 16,000 persons ; but although these feeding depôts have been increased since February, so scattered is the area of the town that it is quite impossible for parents who may be in service and earning small wages to absent themselves and accompany their children to the feeding depôts. The consequence is these children, in very large numbers, have suffered and are suffering from the usual consequences of chronic starvation, and unless means can be devised to supply the children of the industrious poor with food in excess of the means of the parents, many must die before food supplies return to their normal value.

Some weeks ago, one of the very worst cases of starvation I have ever seen came under my notice, and on enquiry it turned out that the poor little victim was not a waif and stray from a famine village, but simply the child of the widow of a domestic servant, out of employ, who had been fighting the battle of life for years, almost within a stone's throw of my own residence. This child was simply a living skeleton, with every bone and ' anatomical process ' distinctly marked, and so weak that she could not stand alone. In this instance the effects of starvation were too far advanced to admit of remedy, but investigation showed that there were many others travelling along the same road to premature death, and who were not, and who could not be, reached by the Government scheme of relief. Recent inspection of the recipients of money dole from the town relief committee in Madras (the classes who are ordinarily in no way depending on charity) convinces me that the food deficiency is affecting very seriously their condition, and that the young children of these classes must be helped with a liberal hand if we would preserve their lives for the benefit of the commonwealth.—DR. CORNISH.

Horrors of the Famine.

Allow me to add some incidents supplied by one member of the committee, the Rev. J. S. Chandler, of Battalagundu, who writes :— ' On Friday, the 19th instant, a child died in my compound that had been picked up in the streets, after having been deserted by its mother for three days. On Saturday, the 27th instant, another child died from the same cause. On the morning of that day my school-boys found the body of a famine-stricken woman in the Battalagundu river. On the day previous, Catechist Anthony found a body in the Venkadasthri Kottai river, and had it buried. He reports having seen twenty-five or thirty bodies that had been brought down the river.

On the 29th instant I overtook a starved weaver tottering along the road two miles from his home. He had a fresh wound on the top of his head produced by a recent fall. I placed him in my bandy and conveyed him home.

' On the 21st instant, on visiting a hamlet, I was pained to see that all the children there were in a starving condition, yet none of them were beggars.

' A few days later, the catechist above mentioned was sitting in a public place in a neighbouring hamlet, when a boy came along with a bunch of greens to be cooked for the family. As he was slowly passing by, he exclaimed, " My eyes are dim," and falling to the ground, died in a short time.

' Recently the corpse of a woman was carried along the road slung to a pole like an animal, with the face partly devoured by dogs. The other day, a famished crazy woman took a dead dog and ate it, near our bungalow.'

This is not sensational writing. The half of the horrors of this famine have not, cannot, be told. Men do not care to reproduce in writing scenes which have made their blood run cold. Yet it is necessary, time and again, to allude to these sufferings, that people beyond our borders may know that the famine is still a dreadful reality.— W. YORKE, *Dindigul.*

Female Nakedness.

I have been much struck by the absence amongst the famine subjects of that modesty which so generally prompts the native women to cover their breasts, and have been assured by more than one officer that it is the result of their intense misery. It is true one native gentleman on the Salem committee (himself I believe a Madrasee) told me that this modesty was not as habitual in the Salem district as in the neighbourhood of Madras; but a district officer told me that in normal times the women always keep themselves covered unless when about the doors of their houses or at work in their own fields. Another consideration is that in Salem the Government have been giving employment to the large weaver community, and have now in stock so enormous a quantity of cloths that it will be difficult to avoid the sale of them becoming, for a time at least, a Government monopoly when trade in the commodity recovers its normal activity. Possibly some arrangement could be made by which the naked can be clothed and the danger threatening the weavers' trade be averted.—F. ROW-LANDSON.

Insect Pests in the Fields..

A great calamity has befallen a large tract of some 50 villages in the Perambalore taluk—a calamity greater than the famine. The ravages of locusts was something fearful—there was not a grain of cholum, cumboo, or varagu left on the stalk. My road was crossed by swarms of these, and the road was actually covered by them 100 yards before me. The young ones hop their march while the winged ones lead the army. When they alight on fields, the young ones stick to the root and cut the stalk down, while the bigger ones take their position on the ears and eat away the grain. You see a field after their devastation—the sight is most melancholy—as if a row of sticks were stuck in the ground; no blade, no ears, and no freshness in the plant, as if their vitality had departed from them. One ryot determining to cut his crop, green as it was, to save at least some of it, had collected labourers to do so the next morning; but to his amazement, the whole had been eaten up during the night; and the locusts stuck to him in such numbers as threatened to eat him up alive.—*Member of Trichinopoly Committee.*

The Patience of the People.

My immediate object in writing to you is to warn you that applications hitherto made for relieving distress in this district do not represent anything like even a tenth part of what we want. I believe the acting collector's committee applied to Madras for 1,000 rs., and perhaps you have sent one or two more thousands to the district. Now, in one taluk alone there are upwards of 5,000 ryots, holding puttahs of 10 rs. and under, whose crops have failed. Supposing, then, we give these men 10 rs. a head, that will represent 50,000 rs. I know this district well, and, as you know, I can converse with the people in Tamil, and I tell you that everywhere in the uplands of this district there is a very great mortality among their cattle used for ploughing, and a very general inability among the people to provide themselves with new bullocks or to buy seed. There are also many cultivators who have never been and who never will go to a relief house, and who would rather die at home than leave their villages and seek Government gratuitous relief. These men are simply pining away slowly, and to make proper use of the funds at our disposal it is necessary that those persons should be sought out in their own homes and relief given them then and there in the shape of a small money donation. In truth, the closer you look into matters, and the better you know the people, the more you see how fearfully widely spread is the present distress, borne by the poor creatures in dumb resignation to fate, and with scarcely a murmur. I dare say you have received reports of the cultivation prospects of the coming year, in their general tenor very favourable. I advise you to distrust them. It is quite true that at the commencement of the cultivation season a very great deal of land was ploughed and sown, and it was then, as of course you know, that the kurnum's accounts were drawn up and sent on through the taluk to the collector's office; but as far as I can ascertain, no account has been taken of the subsequent loss by drought, and in my wanderings about the villages I should say in this neighbourhood half the dry land is still lying waste, as the crop planted in July failed for want of rain later on, and then mortality among the cattle and poverty among the people prevented a second sowing of crops.—E. FORSTER WEBSTER, *Trichinopoly.*

Disappointments; Gratitude.

The first sowing, after the rains came in September, very generally rotted; the second sowing, as soon as the young plants were above ground, has generally been devoured by the grasshoppers. Ryots during the past few days and now are trying to sow again, but the poorer ones are sorely pressed for seed, I assure you. Every hour of the day, yes, every half-hour, and frequently much oftener, I receive 'chits' from some one of my colleagues travelling in the district, or from Government munsifs, which read like this—'The bearer of this chit is a ryot living in the village of ——. Before the famine he was well-to-do, but three of his four bullocks are dead. He cultivates —— acres of ground. He sowed one half of jowalee and the seed rotted. He sowed it again, and the grasshoppers ate up the plants as soon as out of the ground. He has *no* means to purchase seed grain, and no one will sell to him on credit. His family is also suffering for want of proper food. Please help him all you can,' &c. Or another chit reads thus—'The bearer of this note is a widow who resides at ——. Her husband died of cholera some months ago. She has a little land and two buffaloes are yet alive. If she can get a little seed grain she hopes to get some of her neighbours to sow a small piece of her ground at least. She is very poor; has four children, and two of them are sick. They all need cloths badly. Please do for this poor woman all you can,' &c.

These are not fancy sketches, but like applications, either by letter or in person, are dozens every day. As I give 3 rs. or 5 rs. or so to such as described above and tell them, '*This is charity given by kind-hearted generous Englishmen to you who are suffering and starving. Take it and try for another crop with all your might, that you and your little ones may live and not die,'* I should like you and your friends in England to see the expression of thankfulness and gratitude upon their dark, careworn, haggard faces. A chord had been struck probably never touched before.

I hope you will send me a large donation this time. I now frequently sit to receive applicants from 7 a.m. until 4 p.m., with a recess of twenty minutes for breakfast only. 10,000 rs. put out here just now would (D.V.) do a grand work for this section, the beneficial effects of which would last through a generation. My colleagues are helping with a will that does them all great credit. Government munsifs from near and afar are begging for the privilege of sending in people for aid. As funds at my disposal heretofore were limited, of course I have had to go slowly. I can now distribute, if health continues, and *put it just where it ought to go* (a few exceptions no doubt) 1,000 rs. per day, five days per week. Please ask the committee to give us here this time 5,000 rs. *at least if possible.* We should like 10,000 rs. to meet the emergencies described above, but don't want to appear selfish. I am keeping the *name* of each individual, *caste, age, village, taluk, district, amount given and why.*—J. E. CLOUGH, *Ongole.*

Gratitude.

Children and even infants in arms have had relief put into their little hands by me, one rupee, half a rupee, or a quarter of a rupee, all in silver, as each case needed—the parents in the same family being separately provided for with larger sums. In making this distribution I told the parents they would see from this that their emaciated little children too were cared for by the ladies and gentlemen and even the children of England; school children, too, of England having contributed to the bounty. In every case the money has been paid by me direct to every individual, old as well as young.

On the part of the recipients of the bounty, the most heartfelt expressions of gratitude have been addressed to me, and every possible outward token, indicative of the inward feeling, exhibited, both by Hindu and by Mussulman, by male as well as by female. I give here some of these grateful tokens exhibited *after* receiving the relief, because these are genuine expressions, deliberate dictates of the heart; expressions of respect, &c., *before* receiving relief, I consider mostly perfunctory and commonplace; these I do not mention. Complete prostration of the person; bowing the head almost to the ground; kneeling down, clasping both hands before the chest and throwing them over the head, and salaming from the foot to the head over and over again ; throwing themselves at my feet unexpectedly— this I always restrain when •I see it coming, but it has been difficult to do so. There have been more touching tokens also in the grateful tears of Hindu and Mussulman widows who may have handled rupees when their departed husbands received pay, but who have not had that gratification I know not for how many years—ten, fifteen, twenty, thirty—and in all probability never expected that gratification again in this world. When such as these actually held in their hands hard, shining, full rupees (the Treasury had fortunately supplied me with many new ' Empress' rupees) two, three, four, or more which they could call their own, for themselves and starving children, it was but natural that they should ever and anon open the palm, take a glance of the money, then close the palm as if sure of the money, and after a while repeat the process of taking another glance, all the while their and their children's names, &c., were being entered in the register. These in particular retired with fervent protestations about lighting especial lamps in their homes in honour of the kind donors, and praying the Almighty to bless the donors and their offspring.

Some poor creatures declared they had been living on greens, and they quite looked it, and now, they said, they would get a little meat or fish. Some old women between sixty and seventy had longed for a little mittoy, a luxury they enjoyed in better days, which days had now so long passed away, and now, for once—they would treat themselves to some and gratify their longings. (This reminded me of the patriarch Isaac.) Such and similar were the outpourings of heart on the part of these poor creatures in the comparative seclusion of my verandah where they received the money. It so happens that I can speak Hindustani as well as Tamil.

When thanks, loud and repeated, were expressed to me with professions of my being their visible Sami—a notion which of course I instantly checked—I have told them, using an Oriental illustration which would be well understood by them, that they (the famine-stricken people) were the dry fields and dry garden-beds perishing for want of irrigation ; that the ladies and gentlemen of England were the grand lake or large tank which contained the water supply. It was to them that, under God, the thanks were due, and not to me who was a mere channel, and nothing more, through which the precious liquid flowed.

This always led to a fresh outburst of hearty good wishes; that the British nation might flourish for generations to come, and the British flag wave over the land for hundreds and hundreds of years. —*The Rev.* T. P. ADOLPHUS, *Trichinopoly.*

Extortion by Village Officials.

Extortion by village officers of portions of doles given to the poor has been very general [in this sub-division]. In only one case did there seem sufficient evidence to make prosecution advisable. In that case the defendant (a village headman) was sentenced to six months' rigorous imprisonment, and a fine of 50 rs. or four months more. The difficulties of getting convictions in such cases were strikingly illustrated in this one. In the first place the detection was quite accidentally made by the European officer himself. And the conviction took place in the face of the refusal by the principal witness to give evidence. Fortunately the officer had on the spot caused this witness's complaint to be recorded. The defendant's father actually, by bribing a Government peon, detained the witness on the way to court and delayed the trial for a week, and but for very energetic personal exertions by the famine officer would doubtless have spirited the witness away altogether.—W. H. GLENNY, *Gooty.*

Dislike to Relief Camps.

I heard of men and women being harnessed to their ploughs in place of their lost bullocks, and of other poor agriculturists, who not having even ploughs, were seen dragging large branches of trees over their little plots of land. The recent excellent fall of rain has brought up all over the country a weed with a bulbous root, which although in ordinary years it is only used in small quantities, owing to its unwholesomeness, is now being eaten largely by the poor, forming the staple of the only diet they can procure outside of the Government closed camps, which appear to be as much disliked as is the 'workhouse' by the respectable poor at home.—F. ROWLANDSON.

The Goodness of the Poor towards each other.

A great deal too much is said about the readiness of the poor to sponge on the bounty of Government, or of private charity. Half of the tales on this subject are untrue and the other half garbled or exaggerated. Exceptional cases have been known, but the general experience of the Teynampett nursery, and I imagine of others, is, that mothers, aunts, grandmothers, or neighbours will bring children up to be fed, and, though in want themselves, never express by word or sign a desire to share in the help they know is meant only for young children. Big boys will bring little boys, and, though lank and hungry, and casting longing eyes on the food, are only intent on seeing their charges get their allotted ration. For six weeks past a little girl of ten or eleven has been bringing up two sickly children twice a day, nursing them with the tenderest care and never asking for bite or sip on her own account. She showed no signs of starvation until the last few days, when I noticed that she was beginning to go down, and I have asked the lady in charge of the nursery to bring her on the list of those to whom one good meal a day may mean the salvation of life.—DR. CORNISH.

Practical Help.

I would venture to make a suggestion on one point in which private charity could in the interior of the district be employed with the utmost advantage, and afford relief which (though urgently required) cannot be given by Government. Many hundreds of cases of poor ryots have come to my notice whom this famine has reduced to absolute destitution. They have lost their cattle, sold or mortgaged their lands and their little personal property. Hitherto they have managed to live by working on roads, but when ordinary times return and works are closed, they will have simply nothing to face the world with, and their condition in fact will be worse when the famine is over. For such as these (and they are painfully numerous) Government can do nothing beyond having kept them alive hitherto by providing work and by keeping them alive till the end of the famine. But private charity could do a great deal of real good by making small grants to such persons, and by enabling them again to start in life when the present hard times are over.

I can imagine no better object for private charity than this, and I would earnestly bring it to the notice of the committee. There are, of course, many other excellent and legitimate objects to which private charity can be devoted. But if the committee's funds are limited, far more good will be done in the interior of the district by devoting as much money as possible to one comprehensive and useful measure, than by dividing it among many schemes however beneficial in themselves.—W. A. HOWE, *Divisional Officer.*

Personal Investigation of Relief Lists.

On the whole I am of opinion from what I have seen that the best way of doing the most good with this money in this estate, where there is such a dead level of poverty in all the villages, with all castes and classes, is not so much by giving large sums to a few persons, as small amounts to a great many, to enable them to get their lands already sown weeded, or to re-thatch their houses, which are roofless, or to have a small sum in hand to maintain themselves till January. My procedure is very simple. I know the general state of each village as well as anybody else. I select as many of the worst as possible with reference to the amount allotted, making no distinction whether they are owned by the zemindar or by private persons. The headmen are directed to prepare a list of persons deserving and wishing to receive a small assistance, and not holding more land than five kalems of seed land and ten gurukoms of dry land, or possessing more than one bullock. This list is submitted to the tahsildar, and when the day is fixed, the ryots come up for distribution. A few questions are asked on each case, and sometimes it happens that a kurnam has included all his own friends and servants and excluded the others. When the list is gone through, I ask to see the remainder of the villagers, who have come up to watch proceedings; and some of these I select on personal enquiry. In fact I believe that I have got some of the most deserving cases in this way. As the ryots must often come with some of their family, each ryot is asked to bring up his own people with him; and in this way I have seen a vast number of families in a more thorough manner than I could have done at any other period of the last eight months. The majority of the women and girls of the lower castes, and indeed some of the Sudras as well, seem to be barely covered with decency; and I should be glad to have more to give away in cloths; but I quite see that there is great danger in this of the same women following from camp to camp ; and getting a double or treble share.—J. LEE WARNER, *Ramnad.*

The Inadequacy of Funds.

The population of the taluk is 320,723, of which 12,818, or close upon four per cent., are in the town of Dindigul, and 3,753 are in the hill villages where no relief is required. The remaining 304,152 are distributed in 204 villages in the taluk. Now, reserving 1,000 rs. to be spent in the town of Dindigul, we have 7,000 rs. for each of the months of November and December to be spent in the taluk, being 23 rs. per 1,000 inhabitants, and for October and January, only half that amount. We are already learning how difficult a thing it is to take 23 rs. into a village containing 1,000 inhabitants and render efficient aid to the distressed there. It is only sufficient to aid about five cultivators out of the 1,000 inhabitants. What are these rupees among the many people who have been plunged in poverty by the severity of the famine ? The same sum will re-roof four or five houses only in a village of about 330 houses, leaving nothing for other cases of distress. The donations appear generous when we speak of the

lump sums, but when we examine the distribution in detail, we then
realise how very little it will do to mitigate the general distress.
From one village of 1,000 inhabitants, well-authenticated petitions
for 105 rs. were presented in one day. We were able to send them
23 rs. as their proportion for the month of November. Such illustrations might be multiplied to any extent. From all sides the representation of the distributor is that the grants we allow are nothing
like adequate to meet the distress. I write thus, not with a desire on
the part of this committee, or of myself, to complain of the allotment
made by the general committee to us, but to represent the actual
facts, and to express the hope that the general committee will be in
a position to give us additional aid for January and February.—W.
YORKE, *Dindigul.*

My grants to individuals have been almost ridiculously small; but
the general poverty of all classes on this large estate is so great that
there is no other course open. I will give an instance. At a place
called Karencottai I held a distribution taking in 20 odd villages
which have been much afflicted by the famine. When the money
was nearly all exhausted, there remained a great number of applicants
whose names had not been included in the prepared lists. All these
persons held out their puttahs, pleading most lustily for help. Their
appearance gave unmistakable signs of long privation. When I explained to them that the money is a free gift and that it cannot be
made to go farther than it does, the whole chorus shouted that they
might at least have a rupee apiece, and return to their villages. Even
this I was unable to do for them. Numbers are beginning to return
to their homes from Ceylon, many of them dreadfully emaciated.
Their story is always the same. They went over in the summer
months to escape starvation. The planters took advantage of the
numbers to lower their rates for labour; and hundreds only obtained
one meal a day, and are now returning with nothing saved and a
blank future before them, unless they can get assistance.—J. LEE
WARNER.

A Lively Sense of Gratitude.

Both in Coimbatore and Salem fine rain has fallen, and much land
has been already brought under cultivation, but I am sorry to say
that a large number of puttadars (ryots) are still present in relief
camps, having lost their bullocks, their implements, and everything
they possessed (including their health and ability to work).

The present season, so far, is the most favourable that has been
known for years past, and with small advances to the poorer ryots to
buy seed grain, or a pair of bullocks and a plough, an immense

amount of good might be done. Whatever the committee may see fit to allot to district committees with the object of helping the poor but respectable ryots should be given without delay, for it is essential in these dry districts that the ploughing and sowing should be done before the setting in of the north-east monsoon.

I was present yesterday at Sunkerrydroog when Mr. Longley, the collector of the district, enquired into the circumstances of a ryot.

The man attracted my attention, amongst thousands of starving creatures, by his extreme emaciation. He holds a puttah of land, for which he pays ten rupees a year. A portion of this land he managed to plough and sow with the help of his friends. His own bullocks died in the hot weather. He has had no food or means of support for months past, and applied at the camp for relief, simply to keep life in his body. This poor fellow was so attenuated that the circumference of his arm in the thickest portion measured only four and a half inches, and his thigh in the middle nine inches, and, although a well-built and tall man, measured only 25 inches round the chest. His present condition is such as to render him physically unfit for any exertion. Mr. Longley told him he should have an advance of 15 rs. to buy seed and bullocks, and the man was quite happy and ready to go back to his own village, though literally at death's door from long starvation. I saw another case this morning of a man who pays 30 rs. a year to Government—who has lost wife, children, bullocks, and everything that constitutes a native's enjoyment of life, but who is in better health and strength for work, and who will be helped by an advance.

There are thousands of cases of this description in Coimbatore and Salem. The Government officials have been already overwhelmed with applications for advances from respectable landholders, and after discussing the matter carefully with the officials in Coimbatore and Salem, I can only come to the conclusion that the bountiful private charity of our fellow-countrymen cannot be better bestowed than in helping the class of small landholders to set themselves up again in the implements and accessories of a husbandman's career. No time should be lost in the allotment of grants for this purpose if the committee are satisfied that the object is one coming within the sphere of relief contemplated by them.

The class of persons to whom this relief is applicable are well known to native and European officials. They are the tillers of the soil, and non-migratory in their habits. Relief can be apportioned without the slightest difficulty to the necessities of each case.—DR. CORNISH.

Absurd 'Scares.'

In anticipation of the approval of the committee, I am authorising my colleagues to grant estimated cost of cultivation to ryots paying less than 20 rs. of annual land assessment whose kharif crops have been entirely destroyed by the recent excess of moisture. The marked fall in temperature indicates that the rain has at last ceased. We can now see what amount of irreparable damage has been done. Whole fields of kharif crops—cholum and cumboo—have been utterly destroyed : some half harvested, some untouched by the sickle, but which were almost ripe for it ten days or a fortnight ago.

I submit that no class are more legitimate objects of assistance than these poor people who, after seeing their crops safely through the perilous days of July and August, and giving promise of a bounteous harvest, have at the last moment been disappointed of the fruit of their enterprise and industry.

There can be no doubt or deception in these cases. Nor can there be any suspicion or fear on the part of the recipients. I should think that gifts of this kind may perhaps at least force upon the ryots the conception that these grants of money do not come from Government, but from the English people. Hitherto, in the majority of cases the donees have received with manifest incredulity our assurance that ' the Sircar' has nothing to do with the matter. In one instance a number of people who had actually ploughed their lands declined at the last moment to receive the money from Captain Hopkins. They admitted that they suspected some new device to screw revenue out of them. Another scare remains at this moment : doubtless it will shortly be overcome by a little management. The Goondacul nursery is empty, owing to an idea that the nurseries are intended as traps in which to catch children to be carried away to Madras or across the sea to be christianised. On October 1 ten thousand people on our works deserted to a man simply because of a rumour originating in the idle chatter of a subordinate, that all the coolies were to be carried off to forced labour in the Nilgiris. I mention these occurrences to illustrate the necessity of cautious dealings with this population in the present matter.—W. H. GLENNY.

Unselfish Children.

There were 943 children, some of whom were quite, and many nearly, naked.

Probably they would be equally so in normal times at their own homes, but then in the wet and cold they can get warm shelter, and need not leave it for their food. But in the camp it is necessary to collect all the inmates in pens for feeding, and there is no shelter from the wind and rain, either as they make their way across the wide spaces between the sheds, or as they sit on the wet ground. I went down the rows and selected 187 children to whom the sub-committee will give cloths.

I was struck by the goodness of the elder children to their orphaned little brothers and sisters. I noticed, as they flocked in, two or three lads staggering along under the weight of a chubby little one, reminding one of 'Sloppy' and 'The Minders.' As I went down the row I found a small damsel with her portion untasted before her. On questioning her I found she was a caste girl, and could not eat until she had first performed her ablutions. She could not have been more than seven years old, and looked a healthy child and likely to have a good appetite.—F. ROWLANDSON.

A Selfish Reason.

As we were leaving the village they brought forward a boy of about 14, and told me he had wet land but no means of cultivating it, as his elder brother had sold off everything and gone away. I asked how many bullocks they had in the village, and was told 22 pairs! I then asked the richest man in the village if he would help the boy with the loan of some bullocks, but he entirely refused. I learnt subsequently at the committee meeting that owners of cattle here will neither lend nor hire them to landowners who have none. 'Of course not,' was the remark; 'if they can prevent the others from cultivating they will ge t so much the better price for their grains.'—F. ROWLANDSON.

Typical Cases of Distress.

Case I.—Narasami, widow of Raghavachari, aged 38, Vishnava Brahmin, has dependent on her (1) son Kistnadu, aged 12 years, (2) son Copaludu, aged 10, (3) son Samadi, aged 8, (4) daughter Seetamma, aged 5, (5) daughter Alamelu, aged 12 months, and (6) Seshamma, her sister, aged 40. Her husband died two months ago. He was up to his death pusari (priest) of the Vishnu temple, for which he got 5 rs. per mensem. The widow has a dilapidated house, and half a cawnie of land, which cannot be cultivated, as she has no male relation or cattle. She cannot, according to her caste rules, leave her house for twelve months after the death of her husband.

Case II.—Nagamma, widow of Subba Row, aged 36, Brahmin. She has a father-in-law, Chedambari Row, aged 75, and blind. Six months ago he went to Tripatti to borrow money on land already mortgaged, but she has not heard of him since. She herself has no land. She lives in her own house, which is mortgaged. Her husband's grandfather was tahsildar of Chittoor. She has one brother, who gets his living by begging, and who occasionally helps her.

Case III.—Chengamma, widow of Siddappa, aged 42, Karamala caste; has one son Annasami, aged 6. Has no property or house to live in; lives in a chuttrum; is reduced to weakness by the famine. She had village relief dole, but this had been discontinued by Government; she will not go to the relief camp on account of caste prejudices.

Case IV.—Lutchami, widow of Rama Reddi, aged 28, Reddi caste. Her husband died five days ago; has a son Thalwa, aged 6. Has now neither land nor house; all were sold owing to the famine.

Case V.—Sayamma, widow of Chunga Reddi, aged 52, Reddi caste. Lives in the house of another, having no property of any kind. She looks weak, did work on the roads, but is now unable; her feet are swelling.

Case VI.—Chengamma, widow of Subbamma, aged 80, Pariah. Has no one to support her, has no property, will not go to the relief camp, as she thinks 'there is no one to feel for her.'—*Rev.* J. M. Strachan, M.D.

'Real' Charity by the Taluk Triumvirate.

We are much in want of more hands, but perforce have to do without them. There are no non-official Europeans in the division. Among the mercantile community there may be fit persons, but we do not know of any. The agriculturists, with whom we have constant intercourse, have many excellent qualities, and are, under normal circumstances, honest enough. But recently we have had, in the way of our public business, conclusive proof that it is unwise to subject their temptation-resisting power to too severe a strain. Be it understood that our native colleagues are altogether exceptional men. Any one of them is a richer man than any of his European colleagues ever will be. This, however, is a minor matter. All three are men of unblemished character and eminently charitable dispositions. Jutur Subba Reddy's reputation is local, but the fame of the good works of Sanjiva Reddy of Joharapuram and Nigi Reddy of Goondacul has, I believe, reached England. The munificence of these gentlemen, be it observed, has manifested itself in deeds quite different from the extremely 'other-worldly' performances which form the staple Indian variety of 'charity.' These gentlemen have actually spent their

money in feeding the hungry—the clean and the unclean : a thing
that no Hindu ever did *pour faire son salut.*—W. H. GLENNY.

Evil of Indiscriminate Charity.

Spending money is a simple matter. For instance—let it be
known in a village that a charitable gentleman will present a cloth to
every old woman who approaches the presence with a plentiful lack
of raiment. The rustic murmur will spontaneously spread abroad ;
and everywhere he halts the charitable gentleman will not only have
opportunity of attiring files upon files of ancient dames, but his expenditure will be assisted by a rise in the local cloth-market of anything from five-and-twenty per cent. upwards. If the evil effects of
unthinking and short-sighted benevolence were confined to the con-
genial sphere of the elderly female portion of the community, one
would let it pass without serious criticism. But the affair assumes a
darker complexion when it is a question of sapping the self-reliant
and industrious character of a valuable population, and holding out
rewards for success in deception.

We wish that our leisure had been greater, so that we might
have done more. But we humbly claim for our work the modest
merit of careful execution. No doubt, with all our care, we have
occasionally been egregiously imposed upon. With less care there
would have been more imposture.

Every case was separately enquired into, by the light of the best
information available, and every rupee delivered, with all circumstances of publicity, into the hands of the grantee, by or in presence
of a European officer, and each case is recorded in detail. I speak
chiefly of 'agricultural cases ;' there was no analogous need for details
in giving people cloths, for instance. Doles and donations 'in support of life' were not granted without very thorough investigation.
Grants of money for cost of cultivation were, as far as time allowed,
followed as well as preceded by enquiry ; with the result that in some
cases it was discovered that the money had been obtained by false
pretences. The mendacious recipients were in such event called upon
to disgorge : which they invariably did, through fear of unknown
consequences. One poor fellow of his own motion came from some
distance and delivered up his grant, saying that he had changed his
mind about cultivating. He was probably afterwards ascertained to
be a fit subject for a donation ' in support of life.'—W. H. GLENNY.

Scene in a Relief Camp.

This morning I visited the relief camp of Chittoor. Formerly there were in it over 3,000, now about 1,000. The situation of the camp is most picturesque; not far from a beautiful tank, which reminds one of a miniature Scotch loch, it is surrounded by hills, whose crags and grassy crevices looked beautiful in the light of the early sun. Not far from the entrance is a graveyard full of nameless graves; and on enquiry I found it was the convicts' graveyard; this time last year there were not many graves in it, but about last Christmas cholera came and the yard was filled. I went carefully through each line of the inmates of the relief camp, and I can bear witness to the fact that the able-bodied have been weeded out. I saw very few indeed that did not bear the unmistakable stamp of starvation. A group might easily have been formed as ghastly as any that have been photographed. Their ' bones speak ' as the natives expressively say. About 50 cloths were given away, and many of the recipients fell down on their faces and touched our shoes in token of their gratitude. I visited the hospital and found it clean, but very damp owing to the heavy rains. There were the usual cases of starvation-diarrhœa. In the women's ward we came to a fair young girl, covered nicely in her cumbly, her hand under her head, apparently sleeping comfortably, but on trying to feel her pulse, I found her dead. In the men's ward, a well-built young man was found *in extremis*, his eyes sunk, his cheeks drawn, the slow, laboured heaving of his chest, all showing that the end was not far off. A stimulant was administered, but he was beyond the reach of remedy, beyond hope. In passing through the lines of the women, I saw one with a baby, and asked to see it; its skinny form was nestled to its mother's breast; I told her it was dead; and then she gave a look of suffering that went through one's heart, and burst out into a wail that told a mother's suffering at the loss of her last, her only, child. I saw also three other bodies—that of a young man, a young woman, a young girl, who had died during the night. The young woman's mouth was wide open and her eyes were dreadfully staring, as if craving in death for food. After visiting the camp, I went and saw about 500 ryots who had come in from the villages for seed grain, all of them willing to cultivate and yet obliged to stand idle.—Rev. J. M. Strachan.

From Drought to Deluge.

Camp Kamuthi, December 15, 1877.
I am more cheerful to-day, and therefore think it the best opportunity to write to you again what has happened in this part of the estate. There was an unusual fall of rain all the night of the 6th, and in consequence all the rivers were in high flood. Suddenly and simultaneously almost, a great many tank bunds in this and the neighbouring estate of Sivagunga gave way : and all these waters, taking the direction of the sea-level, were poured upon the Kamuthi taluk, and the Vizgai, which takes its course through the Ramnad taluk. All the tanks of these two taluks had already received an abundant supply, and the ragi harvest was almost ripe, and the ryots were cheerfully looking forward to the termination of last year's sufferings in the cutting of the crop, some of which would support them, while the sale of the remainder would enable them to buy fresh paddy seed for the second crop, or bullocks if they had already got seed, or to clear their debts. In one day all the standing water, and the works which held it in, were swept away, and in some places the crops lost or materially damaged. This is not all, unfortunately. At Tornchali and Kamuthi, two large villages, and one of them almost a town, the floods passed over the towns, and in many cases, besides throwing the houses down, swept everything out of them. The people were already in a miserable condition enough ; and now many of them are turned out into the open. In Kamuthi, where I am now writing, having got here after the greatest difficulties, 379 houses, including 65 terraced and well-built houses, have been knocked to pieces. In the hamlets round it 200 more houses have been swept away, and from this place down to the sea every village has its tale of distress. The loss of human lives is not very great so far as I can ascertain, but all the cattle which were grazing on the open fields (the whole country is a plain down to the sea for 25 miles) seem to have been swept before the flood. The shepherds of one village, besides their houses, lost their whole stock, 1,500 sheep, 37 oxen : therefore, I think that if you have a large surplus at your disposal, you will cheerfully give me an additional grant. I think what you have already given me would have been enough for all my wants, without this additional disaster, but now I cannot fix the exact amount which I really may want, as till the water subsides it is so difficult to follow the track of the flood ; I should say that another 10,000 rs. would be enough. My horse has been nearly drowned twice in this tour in mud and quicksand, and I have repeatedly had to do a march on foot, wading in mire, and to get to Kamuthi at all I had to take my clothes

м 2

off. Really I am not exaggerating the misery of this small town when I say that it is sickening to see it, and not have the funds to alleviate it all. If you send me another small grant, I can alleviate some of it, though, of course, I am writing to the collector of the district, and I do not know what help the Government is inclined to give.—J. LEE WARNER.

THE 1-LB RATION

CHAPTERS I.—IV.

THE 1-lb. RATION.

CHAPTER I.

THE QUANTITY OF FOOD NECESSARY TO SUPPORT LIFE.

Long familiarity with the dismal duty of fighting famine in India has not yet led to certitude in modes of conflict. The experience of former disasters has not yet been formulated and made easy of access. Consequently each new catastrophe presents the spectacle of schemes attempted which afterwards have to be amended; indeed experience has to be 'made' instead of a few broad lines of policy being followed, adapted to meet particular circumstances, which, in time of scarcity, are pretty much the same in all parts of India. In 1873-74, when the scarcity in Behar was occupying much time and attention, one of the chief subjects of consideration was the amount of food required daily by the people who were to be fed at the State's expense. Lord Northbrook, the Viceroy, on the data that if 1½ lb. is enough for an adult, 1 lb. per head will feed a population including children of all ages, put the quantity at half a seer, or one pound of grain for each man, woman, and child. Sir Richard Temple, who took over charge of the famine portfolio when he succeeded Sir George Campbell as Lieutenant Governor of Bengal, put the quantity at three-quarters of a seer, or 1½ lbs. In urging the adoption of this standard, Sir Richard said :—

This rate ($\frac{3}{4}$ of a seer, or about $1\frac{1}{2}$ lbs. per head, for men, women, and children), at which grain should be provided, was assumed after due consideration and discussion. The lowest diet provided in Bengal gaols for non-labouring prisoners is equal to about 1 seer, or 2 lbs. The ordinary diet of a labouring adult in Bengal is taken, after statistical enquiry, to be 1 seer of rice, besides $\frac{1}{4}$ seer (about $\frac{1}{2}$ lb.) of fish, pulse, pepper, or other condiments. The diet prescribed for adult Bengalee emigrants on shipboard and for Bengalee sailors, always exceeds one seer a day in total weight, and in some cases it reaches 2 seers a day. Many of the poor people for whom grain was to be provided would be labouring hard on relief works during inclement and exhausting weather. Nearly the whole of the Government provision of grain consisted of rice, which contains less strength-giving qualities than wheat and some other grains. It was known that each bag of the expected consignments of Burmah rice would contain from 8 to 20 per cent. of innutritious husk. In view of all these considerations I framed my estimates of total requirements on the basis that each person to be relieved would on the average require $\frac{3}{4}$ of a seer ($1\frac{1}{2}$ lbs. of grain) a day. In practice it is found that even to ordinary paupers, who did not do any work, local committees had to give $\frac{2}{3}$ of a seer of rice daily besides one pie ($\frac{3}{8}$ of a penny) for the purchase of salt and condiments; to women in delicate health and to persons reduced by previous hunger, a still larger daily dole had to be allowed.

The Duke of Argyll was at that time Secretary of State for India, and when the question came before him, he supported the larger estimate and ordered its adoption. His Grace argued that it was better to err on the safe side, and give the people a fraction more than was absolutely essential rather than a fraction less.

When distress, in 1876, occurred in Bombay, as is stated in the Bombay narrative, in vol. i. of this book, a system of works of two kinds, viz., professional agency, in which 75 per cent. of an ordinary day's toil should be done, and Civil agency, in which 50 per cent was required, was adopted; those who worked hardest were best paid. The rates which were decided upon have been already given, but they may be repeated here. They are:—

Public Works Department Scale.

MAN.	WOMAN.	CHILD OVER 7 YEARS OF AGE
1 anna, plus the value of 1 lb. of grain.	½ anna plus the value of 1 lb. of grain.	½ anna, plus the value of ½ lb. of grain.

Civil Agency Scale.[1]

½ anna, plus the value of 1 lb. of grain.	¼ anna, plus the value of 1 lb. of grain.	¼ anna, plus the value of ½ lb. of grain.

In Madras the Board of Revenue, dealing with certain proposals then before it, prescribed the following, with reference to the existing orders of Government as to addition of condiments or equivalent in money, to grain wages.

	Maximum in money.	In grain and money.
	RS. A. P.	
Men	0 2 0	1⅓ lbs. and 3 pies.
Women and grown boys	0 1 4	1 lb. and 2 pies.
Children	0 0 10	0¾ lb. and 1 pie.

The quantity of rice which the maximum rate, 2 annas, would purchase in most districts at that time was from 1·7 to 2 lbs., and 3 pies would purchase about ¼ lb. Hence the 2-anna rate, which was very generally in force, left about 1½ lbs. over and above what had to be bartered for condiments. This the Board considered excessive.

The orders from which the above rates are quoted go on to say:—

The Board will therefore prescribe 1⅓ lbs. and 3 pies as the grain and money wage of a man cooly, and rule that when prices rise so that anna 1-9 will not buy 1⅓ lbs. of second sort rice, the grain and money scale is to be introduced. The following will be substituted for the draft rule 10 in certain instructions submitted for sanction:—

Wages paid in money are not to exceed 2 annas for a man, anna 1-4 for a woman or boy between twelve and fifteen years, and 10 pies for a boy or girl between seven and twelve years old. Boys over fifteen are paid as men, and girls over twelve as women. Children under seven are not to be employed on relief works. When local

[1] It should be borne in mind that there were never more than 10 per cent. of the people on Civil Agency works: nine-tenths were on the Public Works scale.

prices rise so high that anna 1-9 will not purchase $1\frac{1}{3}$ lbs. of second sort rice (38·98 tolahs=1 lb.), arrangements are to be made to pay in grain and money on the following scale :—

Men	$1\frac{1}{2}$ lbs. + 3 pies.
Women and grown boys	1 „ + 2 „
Children	$0\frac{3}{4}$ „ + 1 pie.

It will be noted that the Board have throughout taken rice as the grain with reference to the price of which wages are to be adjusted. This is favourable to the cooly, as the other grains which are the ordinary food of the bulk of the labouring classes are still cheaper than rice. Government had not then specified what grain should be taken.

When the correspondence came before the Madras Government on January 12 (his Grace the Governor had not returned from Delhi), the Government approved the Board's proceedings, with the exception of the rule regulating the rate of grain wages, in which they considered $1\frac{1}{2}$ lbs. should be substituted for $1\frac{1}{3}$ lbs., and they directed that when 2 annas would not buy $1\frac{1}{2}$ lbs. of second sort rice, or other grain in general local use, wages were to be paid in grain, together with a small money payment for condiments, thus:—

	lbs.	pies.
Men	$1\frac{1}{2}$	+ 3
Women and grown boys	1	+ 2
Children	$0\frac{3}{4}$	+ 1

It was added : 'The adoption of rice as the grain with reference to the price at which wages are to be adjusted is approved. Collectors will, of course, understand that so long as the local market rates for other staple grains will provide the prescribed ration for the money wage, the change to grain wage need not be made.'[1]

[1] The officer (Mr. J. F. Price, assistant to the collector of Bellary, soon after made acting collector of Cuddapah, where, during the distress he did most excellent service) upon whose comments this order was passed,

This was practically the ration which was being granted in the Madras Presidency when Sir Richard Temple hurriedly arrived in the Presidency—'like

gave the following reasons why at least two pounds of grain per day, and condiments, should be given:—

First.—The coolies are not in good condition. One cannot positively call them emaciated, but they are below the mark, and getting any decent amount of work out of them will, unless they are fairly fed, end in the appearance of sickness; certainly cholera, and probably fever and dysentery, which will soon cut them off by hundreds. The recent outbreak of cholera, which made its appearance after a slight shower of rain, showed how prone the coolies were to take disease.

Secondly.—There are no relief houses on the works, and all that is given in the way of relief is to persons who are too much emaciated to work, or who (according to your verbal instructions to me) are blind or maimed. We employ only those able to work, and the coolies have from their earnings to support a brood of children, and perhaps an aged relative or two. If the allowance is cut down, the working members of the family, as they have either to do their tasks or to receive reduced wages, must eat what they get, and the family must go hungry. As the State will not allow them to starve, it must maintain them by that pernicious institution (relief houses) which I look upon as an incentive to pauperism and rascality of all kinds. To say nothing of their evil effects, the cost of relief houses would be a far heavier charge upon the public purse than that of the small extra allowance of rice given to the actual working coolies.

Thirdly.—Not giving an amount of food which will allow of the working members of a family keeping those who are too young or too old to labour produces want, and its sequence crime, and the latter, as far as the district is concerned, not of the ordinary petty class, but of a serious type. The interior arrangements of gaols are nowadays so comfortable that people in these famine times often prefer the regular, plentiful, and varied diet, the easy work, and comfortable quarters which accompany a sentence of imprisonment, to the hard life of the free man. Persons with these views are not, as the present state of the district gaol shows, very few, and they will cost the State many hundreds of pounds long after the famine has become a thing of the past. The Bellary taluk, I may in support of my view mention, is free from anything but petty crime.

Fourthly.—The price of everything here is so high, that by the time that a coolie has bartered a portion of his day's wage of grain for salt and condiments, which he must have, or eventually die from the simple fact of his eating rice; he has less than half of what is considered amongst natives to be the ordinary amount of food which a labourer in hard work, such as digging gravel or breaking stones for eight hours a day, can consume.

Having been for two months brought in constant contact with a very large body of famine coolies whom I have carefully observed, I consider it my duty to state why I think that the present scale of payment should be adhered to. If another is ordered, I will at once introduce it, but I feel bound to express my conviction that it will lead to much misery and want, an arrow released from the bow,' as one collector described his advent and progress—about the middle of January.

Sir Richard Temple left the presence of Sir John Strachey on January 9, strongly impressed with these ideas above all others, viz. (*a*) that no waste was to be permitted ; (*b*) that extravagance was to be sternly checked ; (*c*) that lavish expenditure was not to be sanctioned for a moment; (*d*) that, in a word, the State's resources were to be carefully husbanded. The Delegate pondered this counsel, and, ten days after, when in Bellary, saw means by which he thought he could reduce probable expenditure by 25 per cent. The people were receiving more food than they needed; it might be cut down by at least one-fourth. So on January 19 he wrote, with a confusion of expression[1] not creditable to an ' experiment' of such vast importance, as follows:—

The present rate of wages is fixed at 2 annas per diem for an adult, and proportionately lower for women and children. This rate is fixed upon the supposition that it will purchase 1½ lbs. of grain per diem—a quantity which is deemed essential for *a man while at work.* There might indeed be a question whether *life cannot be sustained* with 1 pound of grain per diem, and whether Government is bound to do more than sustain life. This is a matter of opinion ; and I myself think that 1 lb. per diem might be sufficient *to sustain life,* and that the experiment ought to be tried. Possibly the gangs might not perceptibly fall off in condition. After a week or fortnight of experience it would be seen whether they so fall off or not; if they were to seriously fall off, then the point could be considered. . . . . . The people are in very good case. A reduction might now be demanded in the interests of financial economy, and might be attempted for a

to the necessity for opening relief-houses, and to increased crime and disease, and that it will eventually add to the burden which the State has taken upon itself.

[1] See passages italicised in the succeeding extracts.

time at least without danger ; at all events the trial might be made
for people at taskwork, and especially with those who are not really
at taskwork and who, though nominally at some sort of taskwork,
are doing very light or nominal work. One pound of grain ought to
be made to suffice. At the present prices, a rate of one anna and a
half would purchase a pound of grain, and would leave a small margin
for condiments, vegetables and the like. It may be that Government
would be willing to allow more than a pound a day of grain if its
financial means permitted ; but the demands of economy seem to require that at all events a trial should be made as to whether a pound
a day might not be made to suffice for the one purpose which is admitted, namely, the staving off of danger by starvation.

A copy of this minute was sent to the Madras
Government at the same time that the original was
forwarded to the Government of India. The suggestion was received in divers ways by the different
authorities. By the Supreme Government, solicitous
for the financial aspect of the question, it was cordially
welcomed ; by the Madras authorities, anxious to save
the people alive and in good heart, it was looked
upon with hostility, and, for a time, resisted. In his
journeyings through the Presidency, the Delegate
arrived at Madras at the end of January, and had
repeated conferences with the Governor and his Council,
in which he urged, with much force and persistency,
the desirability of adopting his suggestion, which was
that one pound of grain plus half an anna (three
farthings) be the daily ration. The Madras Government were prepared to give all due consideration to
the arguments for economy, and the problem they
found difficult of solution was whether the quantity of
food proposed would suffice to keep the multitudes in
fair health. Their medical officers, when consulted,
gave a most emphatically adverse opinion ; other
officers—those in charge of camps—were equally emphatic in condemnation of the proposal. Such statements as the following from Major A. G. Murray,

special relief officer, were before the Government, and
naturally caused hesitation on the part of the Council.
Major Murray, writing to the collector, Mr. Barlow,
said:—

> The hospital assistant in medical charge of the camp at the Red
> Hills assures me that 1¼ lbs. of raw rice per diem is no more than is
> absolutely sufficient for an adult person, whether he be old and infirm
> or no, and I quite hold the same opinion.
>
> A less amount of food might sustain life, but would not be sufficient
> to save the recipient from hunger, which in feeding these persons is, I
> suppose, the intention of the Government.
>
> The complaint of the able-bodied adult doing a day's work is that
> he receives no more for his day's work than this bare allowance of
> food.

At length, with a desire to be loyal to the Supreme
Government and in sympathy with the wish for
economy, the Madras authorities yielded, and on
January 31 an order of the Governor in Council
was issued, in which Sir Richard Temple's proposal
was adopted, and the amount to be given to labourers
on relief works fixed at the value of one pound of grain
plus half an anna.

CHAPTER II.

THE CONFLICT BETWEEN THE DELEGATE AND
DR. CORNISH.

No sooner were orders issued for the 'experiment' of keeping the people on one pound of food per day than a great outcry was raised. In vol. i., chap. iii., of this book, reference is made to the feeling evoked in India generally, but particularly in Madras. Further instances need not be given here, but attention may at once be directed to the controversy, in which the Sanitary Commissioner of Madras, Dr. Cornish,[1] was pitted against Sir Richard Temple. Of the argument between these two functionaries as complete a digest as possible will be given.

Sir Richard Temple's minute was gazetted on February 3 ; on the 15th of the same month Dr. Cornish had prepared a protest which he submitted to the Madras Government. He began with citing the passage in Sir Richard Temple's minute wherein he expressed the 'opinion' that the ration might be reduced. 'As the adviser of Government on public health questions in this part of India,' Dr. Cornish recorded his 'respectful protest' against 'opinions' which were in direct contradiction to the accumulated testimony of scientific observers in every country in which the question of the quantity and variety of food essential to keep a labouring man in

---

[1] 'A famine authority of whom all India will one day be proud,' was the expression used of Dr. Cornish by Sir W. Robinson, K.C.S.I., speaking in the Madras Legislative Council, in March 1878.

health and strength had been the subject of investigation. ' Sir Richard Temple's opinion was an individual one only, unsupported by evidence, scientific or otherwise, as to the sufficiency of 16 oz. of cereal grain to maintain a labouring adult in health,' whilst there was a large accumulation of facts which did not afford any support to such a theory.   Sir R. Christison, of Edinburgh, was of opinion that ' the adult human body requires 35 oz. of dry food per diem, arranged so that the carboniferous and nitrogenous principles may be in the proportion of three of the former to one part of the latter.'   This is seldom obtained in India, the nitrogenous principle in foods being defective.

In 1863 the question of the quantity and quality of food necessary in India was made the occasion for close and searching enquiry.   This enquiry was instituted at the instigation of the British Association for the Advancement of Science, and the reports of district medical officers and others on this point were submitted by Dr. Cornish to the Madras Government in the year 1864.   'It is a curious fact,' Dr. Cornish says, ' that amongst all the reporters there was this combined testimony, that the minimum grain allowance of a man in health and in work was *not less than* 24 oz., while the amount which a native of good appetite was capable of disposing of, estimated by natives themselves, was from 24 to 48 oz. per diem.   For Bellary and Cuddapah the average daily allowance of dry cereal for a labourer was reported to be 33 and 48 oz., respectively.'

The physiological needs of the adult human body, according to all scientific investigators, necessitate the expenditure of from 140 to 180 grains of nitrogen in twenty-four hours, *while the body is in a state of rest.*   In ordinary labour about 300 grains of nitrogen will be excreted, and under great physical exertion, such as that of walking for many hours consecutively, from 500 to 600 grains. Now, if this amount of nitrogen is not provided in food, it is obvious that the body must prey on its own tissues so long as any remain to be preyed upon, and this is, in fact, what happens when the food taken into the body is insufficient in quantity or quality to compensate for the constant waste that is going on in every organ and tissue.

The quantity of nitrogen in 16 oz. of rice may be from 68 to 80 grains. Dr. Cornish proceeded to remark that the quantity of food essential to maintain life is a question very much of the work expected to be got out of the eater. 'If we want to get a maximum of steam-power out of an engine we must feed the furnace liberally with coals, and in like manner a man would soon cease to have any power in his muscles if the food supplies were inadequate.' A feeble vitality might be maintained for a certain length of time on a diet the staple of which is a pound of rice per diem, but *labour* on public works on such a dietary is quite out of the question. As soon as the nitrogenous matters of the food cease to supply the normal waste of the muscular and other tissues, the body itself begins to die. If this slow death of the body goes on for too long a time, the Indian labourer finds himself precisely in the condition of the Edinburgh physiologist (Dr. Stark, who tested in his own person the effects of a reduced dietary); he is the victim of a form of starvation from which no amount of subsequent liberality in feeding can save life. Dr. Cornish urged that practically the important point was this ; any dietary which contains less than 200 grains of nitrogen for natives of India will not permit of severe labour or task work. 'The gaol diets in this Presidency are calculated to provide from 200 to 300 grains of nitrogen, and in certain instances these diets have had to be supplemented by extra meat and vegetables to prevent the

men from falling into a low condition unfitting them
for their daily task. It comes therefore to this ;
whether in the present dearth of supplies a man engaged
on task labour and paid at the rate of one pound of grain
per diem, and half an anna in cash, can with the latter
coin purchase a sufficient amount of nitrogenous nutriment (to say nothing of salt, oil, condiments, vegetables
and firewood) to make his daily ration equivalent to 200
grains and upwards of nitrogen.   The reply is, simply,
that neither in the shape of meat, fish, dholl, milk, or
buttermilk, can he procure a sufficiency to eke out the
defects of his grain ration.'

    In a previous letter (No. 105, dated February 7),
Dr. Cornish had pointed out that the effects of insufficient nutriment might not be immediately apparent, and
in regard to this question of a pound of grain being
enough, or not enough, they would never know the
results until the mischief resulting from a deficient
supply of nitrogenous food had gone so far that a
retracing of their steps would be powerless to save life.
'I cannot too often repeat,' he said, ' that it is the slow
and gradual form of starvation by defective nutrition in
the daily food that is the most difficult to deal with by
after-remedies.   It is easier in these cases to break down
the vital powers than to build up or restore.'   The
Sanitary Commissioner's final remark, in his letter,
indicated a blot in Sir Richard Temple's proposals. Dr.
Cornish said :—' If the 1 lb. of rice be inadequate for
the daily ration of a labouring man, it is sufficiently
obvious that if he attempt to divide this amount of food
with young children, or do without food for one day in
the week (on Sundays), the breakdown in strength will
come only the faster.'

    The Madras Government were much impressed
with the tone and spirit of this letter—strong on its
scientific side, powerful in its appeal to humane and

utilitarian considerations. The Governor in Council resolved to forward a copy of Dr. Cornish's letter to the Government of India and to the Secretary of State, with an intimation that the Madras Government were anxiously watching the effect of the scale of wages in force, and had directed that weekly, or, if necessary, more frequent reports of the results be submitted to Government. They also arranged that Dr. Cornish should personally inspect some of the working gangs in the North Arcot and Ceded districts, and report the results of his observations. The Governor in Council further resolved that a copy of Dr. Cornish's letter should be forwarded to the Board of Revenue and every collector and district officer in charge of relief operations, in order to warn them of the importance of the anxious duty confided to them of watching the effect of the tentative reduction of subsistence allowance, and directed that all Zillah surgeons at stations in the vicinity of which relief works were in progress, should, as soon as the new scale of wages had been in force for one week, report to Government, after careful inspection of the labourers, whether they could, or could not, detect any indication of loss of power or flesh in the coolies; they were also to maintain constant supervision, and forward periodical reports on the subject.

Sir Richard Temple was not slow to take up the gage thrown down. He wrote another minute, reviewing the objections of the Sanitary Commissioner, Madras, to the reduced scale of wages, dated Coimbatore, March 7, in which he remarks :—' Inasmuch as his (Dr. Cornish's) views, if these were to be adopted without adequate deliberation, might involve a large and unnecessary expenditure of public money, I would submit for the consideration of the Governments of India and Madras, a few remarks on these objections.' Into the purely professional part of his opponent's arguments Sir Richard would not enter further than to note that while no doubt abstract scientific theories of great value on the subject of public health are of modern growth, the Indian population with which they were then dealing had lived for centuries in disregard of them, and practically at the present date the poorer classes, even in countries much more civilised than India, did not actually obtain, either in food, lodging, or ventilation, the amount declared by scientific men to be necessary. Sir Richard further noted particularly that 'most of Dr. Cornish's observations refer to Europeans living in a cold climate, where waste is greater, and largely exceeding the natives of India in average weight, requiring therefore more food. The Edinburgh enquiries, which he cites, however applicable to European cases, and however valuable in the abstract, are not strictly and exactly applicable to the poorer classes of the Madras Presidency.' The practical question, however, was this : 'Can and does the new scale of wages suffice to keep the people with whom we are now dealing in fair health under present conditions and circumstances. More than this Government has declared itself unable to undertake.' The evidence of relief camps in the Madras Presidency showed that a native at rest can gain flesh on a pound a day.[1] Dr. Cornish apparently assumed that by the new scale a man could not obtain $1\frac{1}{2}$ lbs. To this Sir Richard replied:—'But in the first place it is to be observed, that at present prices throughout the greater part of the distressed district a man can, with the half anna which he receives in cash, buy an extra half-pound of grain a day, and still have a small margin over

---

[1] I was informed at Vellore that indigent adults admitted to the relief camp in consequence of their inability to work have improved considerably on a ration of a pound a day. Dr. Fox, the civil surgeon, and Captain Harris, the relief officer, were agreed on this point.—*Sir R. Temple.*

for condiments ; that is, he earns sufficient to allow him
the minimum quantity requisite to keep him in health
while at work. More than this, I submit, it is not in
the power of Government to do.'

It must be remembered (Sir Richard continued)
that in the Madras Government Orders of January 31
two rates of working pay are laid down, and that all
persons who do work amounting to 75 per cent. of
the Public Works rate, receive one pound of grain and
one anna in cash, while those who receive a pound of
grain plus half an anna (who alone are referred to by
Dr. Cornish) are only required to render task-work at
half the Public Works rate. Now the Public Works
labourers are paid by piece-work, and no definite task
is asked for ; they do as much or as little as they like,
and are paid accordingly. The minute proceeded :—

The result is that those who really undergo the severe physical
exertion described by Dr. Cornish do actually receive wages equal to
$1\frac{1}{2}$, perhaps even 2 lbs. a day, which is tantamount to what he recommends. It is only for those who do not undergo such exertion that
the lower scale, recommended by me, and ordered by the Government
of Madras, is intended. Practically, at this time, by Public Works
rate is meant the amount of work done per rupee, and relief labourers
on the first standard are expected to do three-quarters as much for a
rupee as common labourers, that is, supposing the Public Works
Department rates for earth-work to be 8 cubic yards per rupee, then
relief labourers of the 1st class have to do 6 cubic yards for the same
money ; and two annas being taken as the minimum wages on which
they can be maintained in health, $\frac{3}{4}$ of a cubic yard is the task assigned
to enable men in this class to earn their two annas. It is considered
(and this is in accordance with Dr. Cornish's views) that persons doing
less work than this can live on less, so while the 2nd class labourer
does only $\frac{1}{2}$ a cubic yard of earth-work daily, he receives in return $1\frac{1}{2}$
annas. But as observed, the Public Works rate is not a task but a
scale, and ordinary labourers are not content to earn 2 annas daily by
excavating one cubic yard, but as a matter of fact earn much more
than this. I was informed by Mr. O'Shaughnessy, the district
engineer of Nellore, that some of the gangs at work on the East
Coast Canal were earning 5 and even 6 annas a head daily, that is

were doing five or six times as much work as is demanded from the
relief labourers on the lower scale.

The objection to the new scale, which Dr. Cornish states in detail,
is properly formulated by the phrase a full day's wage (that is, something more than the 1 lb. and the ½ anna) for a fair day's work. But
the phrase postulates that there is a fair day's work, which is just
what the vast majority of the relief labourers do *not* render. Therefore they are not entitled to, and do not physically need, the full day's
wage. Where they render a really fair day's work, there they do
receive, under the new rules, more than the reduced scale. The rates
were avowedly recommended by me as experimental, and if they shall
be found insufficient they may be increased; but it appears to me that
they have not yet been found so, and that Dr. Cornish argues from
a mistaken premise which undermines his conclusions. If the poor
people were found to be falling off in condition, then I would at once
recommend an alteration in the rate; but at present we have no such
experience.

There was one point which Sir Richard felt he must
concede to Dr. Cornish's arguments. In laying down
the minimum scale, it was of 'course intended[1] that
each labourer should be able to consume his own wages,
and not have to share them with other persons of his
family. These members of the family should either
work for themselves, or if unable to do so should be
admitted to gratuitous relief. The case of young children who accompanied their parents to the works, but
were too young to work, that is children from one year
to seven years of age. had already attracted his attention, and he had recommended in a separate minute

---

[1] With respect to the remark 'it was of course intended,' &c., one of the
Madras papers at the time remarked, 'In his first order about reducing the
wages Sir Richard forgot the children. It is all very well to say that he
had always intended that they should be separately provided for, but if an
officer comes in with full powers to make a change, reduces wages, and does
not give the compensatory provision for the children (which would have left
matters very much as they were before) it is not surprising that the relief
was restricted to the actual worker, and not extended to their families. Mr.
Ross, of Bellary, expressly put the question as to whether he was to relieve
the children of workers, and was told that he was not to do so. How, then,
about the "intention" which was said to be cherished?'

that a subsistence allowance be granted to them. Sir Richard continued:—

Further I would urge, as the one motive common to the Governments of India and Madras and to all connected with the famine relief works, the preservation of life and the mitigation of extreme suffering at the smallest cost to the State consistent with the attainment of the object in view, that the enquiry as to whether the reduced scale of wages is sufficient to enable the people to tide over the next few months without serious danger to themselves should be decided not by preconceived physiological theories, but by patient practical examination of the people themselves, with a view to ascertain whether there is in fact any, or any serious, change in their physical condition under the new scale as compared with their average condition in ordinary times. Having carefully inspected during my tour in this Presidency thousands of relief labourers, I give it as my opinion that with very few exceptions, which are not as a rule traceable to insufficient relief wages, the general physical condition of the labourers is as good now as in ordinary years.[1] If, as already stated, I find after a little more experience, that the new scale of wages does seem insufficient to maintain the people in health, I will be the first to say so ; but so far, this has not seemed to be the case.

. In conclusion, it is not possible, I submit, to determine à priori on scientific data what amount of food is necessary to sustain the particular classes who come to our relief. The real point to be considered is whether in ordinary times they get more than one pound a day for a male adult. This is an economic question which can be determined by calculating the rates of wages in the rural districts—not the wages of trained professional labourers employed by public bodies, not the wages of stalwart men of the professional class of workmen, but men of lesser physique and lighter frame, such as that of the village poor —the wages received by the labouring poor in the villages of the interior; and then by taking the prices of common grains in ordinary years. Now from enquiries made in various districts of the Madras Presidency, I apprehend that the labouring poor in rural localities can hardly get more than one pound a day for a male adult in ordinary times. If this be so, then the reduced scale must be sufficient for these same people on the Government relief works, and need not be increased.

Another minute followed quickly from the same pen

[1] This assertion is shown to be baseless from the fact that during the month when this was written.the death registers showed 50,000 additional deaths, and, further, there were many deaths which were never registered.

in which Dr. Cornish's scientific argument was traversed.   After quoting certain passages from his
antagonist's letter, Sir Richard says :—'In the "Madras
Manual of Hygiene," compiled under the orders of
Government, and published in 1875, the main parts of
Dr. Cornish's theories are adopted.   It is stated, page
96 :—" The unavoidable internal work of the adult
human being, that is, the movements necessary for
respiration, circulation, and digestion require a minimum of 138 grains of nitrogen in 24 hours for their
maintenance.   In a state of idleness of mind and body,
the least amount compatible with health may be stated as
200 grains for a man and 180 for a woman.   In the
ordinary circumstances of the soldier, the artisan, the
field labourer, and the prisoner in most of our gaols, 300
grains will be a fair minimum.   Very great physical
exertion will demand 500 grains or even more." '

Sir Richard admitted that the opinion that 1 lb.
a day of grain might suffice for a relief labourer, together with some allowance for condiments and the like,
or some nutritious substance, was not indeed based on
scientific theory   It was founded rather on probabilities practically deduced from the condition of the poorer
classes in ordinary times, and on the results of general
experience.   It was not put forth with absolute confidence.   It was to be subjected to trial, not by theoretical data, but by the observation of its actual results.
He added : ' Certainly this opinion was not based on so-
called scientific evidence, apparently taken as proved on
the strength of experiments made on men of different
races and habits, living under different circumstances,
in an altogether different climate, and, probably, exceeding by a third in average weight the people to
whom the results of the experiments are with such
confidence applied.   For administrative and financial

purposes, I should not base my recommendations on such data, inasmuch as the question must be one extremely difficult of scientific ascertainment, and in respect to which even the best-conducted experiments, if made in different parts of the world, might lead to varying results. And in order to show how little these data can be accepted for these purposes, it is sufficient for me to refer to the " Madras Manual of Hygiene " itself.' Sir Richard proceeded :—

In an appendix, from page 361 to 380, are given the whole range of Madras dietaries for soldiers, sepoys, and prisoners—military and civil—under various circumstances of sickness and in health. They prove, first, that as regards natives of the country the carboniferous bear to the nitrogenous elements of food, the ratio of about 7 to 1, instead of 3 to 1 as in English dietaries (in the ration of the sepoy on foreign service the proportion is 10 to 1-26·70 oz. to 2·68, page 379), and as the absolute weight of food taken daily by natives and Europeans is probably about the same, it follows that the amount of nitrogen required by natives must be much less than that required by Europeans. And when the diets are examined this is found to be the case. The Madras sepoy, when ordered on foreign service, during which he may be, and often is, called upon to undergo severe physical exertion, receives a full ration from Government. According to the theory, he requires a minimum of 300 grains of nitrogen when performing ordinary duties, but when marching or undergoing severe labour he needs 500 or 600 grains. As a matter of fact, he gets (page 379) only 178 grains, little more than half the minimum required, and only about a third of what is declared necessary to him when called upon to do strenuous work. According to this theory, then, the Madras sepoy would be undergoing starvation at the hands of Government. But, in fact, he is not so reduced physically, nor does he fail that Government when it calls upon him for exertions compared to which the labour demanded from most of our relief labourers is as nothing. This case, I submit, makes very strongly against Dr. Cornish's theory, but a still stronger one yet remains behind.

The British soldier, to whom, if to any one, the theory should apply, requiring like the sepoy 300 to 600 grains under like circumstances, receives 242 grains of nitrogen in his full ration, that is, 25 per cent. less than the minimum required to keep him in health when in garrison, and less than half what he ought to have when marching or on service. But this is not all, for when his ordinary work is not demanded of him, as when he is in garrison or at sea, he receives only a reduced ration and, singularly enough, though the details of the two rations are altogether different (" Madras Manual," pages 364 and 369), the amount of nitrogen contained in each is identical, namely, 155 grains, about half of the amount declared to be the minimum necessary to maintain him in health, a quarter of what he should have when on service, and considerably less than the *least amount compatible with health* in a state of rest of body and mind, as laid down in the quotation from the " Madras Manual" already cited. According to this theory we should have to imagine that the British soldier is half starved on board ship, or that he is landed in India in a reduced condition physically, or in a state of health which could hardly be restored by subsequent nutrition. The actual fact is, of course, the reverse.

'These statements and estimates of the chemical constituents of the military rations, both for European and native troops, are not (be it remembered) made by me,' continued the Delegate, 'but they have been furnished by the "Madras Manual of Hygiene;" they are put in the simplest form possible, and can be verified by any one, though he may not be versed in the chemistry of food or the data on which the calculations are made. And I submit that they prove conclusively that the theories enunciated by English authorities, however eminent, and apparently adopted without additional experiment by the "Manual," do not in fact apply except in the most general way to Englishmen themselves, and cannot be at all accepted as valid reasons why Government should desist from a trial suggested by experience, which, if successful, will conduce to saving the people on the one hand, and to preventing unnecessary expenditure on the other. I should not have discussed this matter at all had not the scientific theory been propounded with so much decision and with such strongly-worded remonstrance against the disregard of it. But we see that the theory is not applicable, and cannot be implicitly accepted. If, as stated in my minute of 7th current, it is found on a deliberate and dispassionate trial that the new scale is insufficient, and that the labourers do not maintain their health, it can, of course, be revised. But I have sufficiently shown that this is a matter which may be left to careful observation of the condition of the people, and not deduced à *priori* from theoretical considerations which break down when subjected to plain criticism and are shown to be inapplicable to the case in hand. Though constrained to demur to the manner in which the Sanitary Commissioner applies certain theories to the proposed practice in our relief operations, I am fully conscious of the benevolent and charitable motives by which Dr. Cornish is actuated, and of his meritorious labours for the welfare of the people in this Presidency.'

The rumour was current in Madras that when Dr. Cornish received the two minutes of Sir Richard Temple, which were forwarded to him by the Madras Government, he exclaimed, with Cromwell just before the battle of Dunbar, 'The Lord has delivered him into my hands.' Certainly the Sanitary Commissioner girded his loins, and penned a reply which the medical profession generally considered smote the adversary hip and thigh. This rejoinder was written in a white heat of feeling, but, competent authorities assert, without being in any sense unfair to the antagonist's argument. A summary of the minute would not do justice to it, and, in spite of its length, a full abstract must be given.

In his covering letter, forwarding the reply, Dr. Cornish said :—

The Government of India, while giving every publicity to the minutes above referred to in the official *Gazette of India*, has not thought proper to give a like publicity to my letter No. 115 of February 13, to overthrow the arguments of which these minutes were especially designed. The subject involved is the sufficiency or otherwise of an arbitrary allowance of food to maintain the health and strength of the labouring poor. It is a practical question of the highest interest to men of science, political economists, and social reformers in every part of the world, and in the interests of humanity generally I venture to express a hope that the fullest publicity be given to my own part in the discussion as well as to Sir Richard Temple's, so that the public, and scientific men in particular, may have the subject of discussion before them.

This remonstrance produced effect, for Dr. Cornish's letters appear in the Blue Book on the Indian Famine, having been previously published in the *Gazette of India.*

Dr. Cornish, in the earlier paragraphs of his 'Reply to Sir Richard Temple's Minutes of March 7 and 14, as to the sufficiency of a pound of grain as the basis of famine wages,' is somewhat apologetic as regards his own action in bearding an official of the eminence of Sir Richard Temple. 'Sir Richard Temple thought,' he says, ' that the sufficiency or insufficiency of this grant of food was a matter of "opinion," and recommended that a scale of payment based on the price of a pound of grain should be tried " as an experiment" in the various relief operations throughout this Presidency, and the Madras Government had already acceded to the proposition, and issued orders for the enforcement of a reduced scale of wages, before I was aware that the subject had been before the Government. Under these circumstances there was a choice of courses before me : I might have held my peace, and in the event of subsequent calamity have sheltered myself under the plea that the Madras Government had not done me the honour of seeking my advice before sanctioning the reduced scale of wages ; or, knowing from long and painful experience the risks to the population resulting from inadequate food and nourishment, and the general want of accurate knowledge of subjects by most people, I might have ventured, unsolicited, to sound a note of warning to the Government, and to state my opinion in terms admitting of no misunderstanding. I chose the latter course, and I am very glad that I did so, as my letter has drawn forth two elaborate minutes from Sir Richard Temple regarding the basis on which he calculated that a pound of grain a day would suffice for a labouring man, and the subject can now be discussed purely on its merits by scientific men and the public at large, quite irrespective of the official positions of the parties contributing to the solution of the problem of feeding a people with the least expenditure of life and money.'

Then followed a thrust: 'I have, of course, been an attentive reader of famine literature, to which Sir Richard Temple has been so large and valuable a contributor. His most masterly " Narrative on the famine in Bengal and Behar in 1874 " lays down with clearness and precision the data on which the importation of grain was then determined, and I need not say that I agree almost entirely with every word Sir Richard Temple then wrote in regard to the quantity and quality of the food required for the maintenance and health of the people.' The passage which is quoted in chapter i. of this section is given in parallel columns, with extracts from the minutes of 1877, and Sir Richard Temple is convicted of inconsistency.

In his minute of March 7, 1877, Sir Richard Temple declines to enter into the ' purely professional arguments' advanced in Dr. Cornish's letter further than to note that, 'while, no doubt, abstract scientific theories of great value on the subject of public health are of modern growth, the Indian population, with which we are now dealing, have lived for centuries in disregard of them.' To this Dr. Cornish replies :—

I must confess that I am not quite clear as to the meaning of the above extract. I did not put forward any 'abstract scientific theory,' but merely stated a *fact*, that as the human frame, in every race and climate, disposes of a certain amount of nitrogenous matter every twenty-four hours, a like amount must be taken into the body in food to restore that waste, otherwise the tissues of the body will gradually disappear; and that in my opinion one pound of rice, containing from sixty to eighty grains of nitrogen, and a small money payment of six pice, or three farthings, would not suffice to enable a labourer to provide a sufficiency of nitrogenous food to restore his daily waste of tissue. In reply, I am told, in effect, that abstract scientific theories are very pretty in their way, but that the Indian people, who disregard them, manage to get on very well without them. But this manner of disposing of the subject does not seem to have satisfied Sir Richard Temple, for in a subsequent minute, dated March 14, he endeavours to grapple with the scientific objections to his proposals.

It was, however, with the practical objections of the first minute that Dr. Cornish preferred to deal at the outset. He did this by showing that the enquiries of 1863 proved that Sir Richard was in error in supposing that his (Dr. Cornish's) remarks had reference to the dietaries of Europeans, when he was at special pains to point out that an independent investigation, conducted by 20 or 30 medical officers in the mofussil civil stations, and checked by his (Dr. Cornish's) own independent enquiries and observations, showed that the minimum grain allowance of a man in health and in work was not less than 24 ounces, and that it was frequently double that quantity in favourable seasons. Moreover, in regard to the proportion of nitrogenous to non-nitrogenous food, the reference made to Sir Robert Christison's labours was simply to show the standard to which all successful dietaries should approach, and Dr. Cornish expressly admitted that in the food of an Indian people the 'proportions of 1 to 3 are but barely attained, and the tendency is always to a smaller pro-.

portion of nitrogenous food.' The whole experience he wished to bring forward on this question of food and health was Indian experience, and he expressed himself surprised that Sir Richard Temple, who knew so well in 1874 what the ordinary food of the people was, should write as if there had never existed any periodical medical literature in India, or that he should ignore the fact that every Indian medical authority who had written on the subject of food for prisoners was opposed to his recent opinions. ' One might think,' indignantly writes the Sanitary Commissioner, ' from Sir Richard Temple's minute, that men like Leith, Chevers, Ewart, Bedford, Strong, Mouat, Fawcus, Irving, Forbes, Watson, Mayer, Lyon, myself, and many others, whose papers I have not immediately at hand to refer to, had never thought out the subject of feeding in its practical and scientific aspects, and that gaol and other diets in India had been constructed without reference to the nutritious quality of the food grains, or to the proportions of the various kinds of food. It must be abundantly clear to Government that if this new theory of Sir Richard Temple's is correct, viz., that 1 lb. of grain and a small money payment equivalent to three farthings, is enough to keep a labouring man in health and strength while undergoing a fair daily task, then every administration in India has been for years past inciting people to break the law by providing criminals with a dietary beyond their actual necessities, and all the carefully recorded experience of the last 30 years, as to the effects of food on health in Indian gaols, must be discarded as worthless.'

Dr. Cornish would, he said, have occasion to show, however, that the carefully built up experience of the past must be the guide in this matter, in preference to the mere ' opinions' of a gentleman who, apparently unconscious of the cruelty involved in his proposals, would desire to begin a huge 'experiment' on the starving poor of this country, at a time and under conditions which would prevent the results of that 'experiment' ever being tested and recorded. Dr. Cornish continued (and in these passages he touched some of the vital points of the controversy, particularly in reference to the examinations of relief gangs periodically):—

What in fact was the proposition of Sir Richard Temple's to which I took exception? It was this. 'There might indeed be a question whether life cannot be sustained with one pound of grain per diem, and whether Government is bound to do more than sustain life. This is a matter of opinion, and I think that one pound per diem might be sufficient to sustain life, and that the experiment ought to be tried. Perhaps the gangs might not perceptibly fall off in condition. After a week or fortnight of experience, it would be seen whether they so fall off or not.'

If it were not so serious a matter as a blind experimentation on the limits of human endurance, it would be amusing to note the method by which Sir Richard Temple here proposes to test the results. 'After a week or fortnight of experience,' he says, 'it would be seen whether the gangs fall off perceptibly in condition.' Now what are the conditions abroad in the country by which such an experiment could be subjected to those rigorous tests which would satisfy practical men as well as scientific men? Our relief works are scattered over many thousands of square miles of country, they are but indifferently supervised, and in no instances are the native supervisors qualified to test the results of any special system of feeding or payment as regards the health of the people. To record the results of such an experiment with the accuracy required it would be essential to weigh every individual of a gang, to enter their names and weights in columns, and to repeat the weighing week by week for a period of several months,—to note also the condition of each individual, week by week, as to anæmia, pulse, tongue, heart's action, muscular power, &c. An 'experiment' of this nature might be carried out as regards a few persons under the constant observation of a medical man, aided by careful assistants, but it is obvious that the results on a large scale, according to the tests proposed by Sir Richard Temple, could never be ascertained. Sir Richard Temple does not seem to be aware of the fact that 'a week or two' of low living, while doing much mischief, might still give no results measurable by the eye or by weighing.

There is nothing more remarkable in connection with these famine relief works than the sudden changes and fluctuations in the *personnel* of the gangs. The people inspected one day may be away the next. The people falling ill and unable to work are replaced by others, and there is never any certainty that two inspecting officers going over the same ground within a short interval of time are seeing the same people. Any comparison of their observations or reports, therefore, can scarcely be gone into profitably while this uncertainty exists in regard to the identity of the individuals composing the gangs.

There is, however, a rough and coarse test of the results of the reduction of wages which may commend itself to the notice of Government. It is that while the numbers paid for and supposed to be employed on relief works in the first week in February were 907,316, they fell in the last week of March to 662,195, and that the numbers 'too weak for work, requiring cooked food in relief houses,' had increased from 38,163 in the first week of March, to 99,113 in the last week of the same month. From my recent inspection in Madanapalli and Royachoti I found these helpless and infirm people were increasing at the rate of more than 100 a day at each relief house, and if they continue so to increase, as I think is but too probable, the numbers to be fed in the Cuddapah district will probably reach 20,000 within the next two months, instead of 3,294, as in the last week of March. I leave it for others to determine whether the policy of instituting a bare subsistence wage on relief works has, or has not, contributed to the enormous increase of the sick and feeble, and of the gratuitous feeding throughout the distressed districts.

The condition of the labouring gangs varied very much in the several localities. Some had very little distance to go to their labour, and in such cases the collection of half a cubic yard of road material Dr. Cornish thought might not involve any unusual exertion. But even in these cases he had seen work attempted when the ground was as hard as iron, and with tools much too heavy for the strength of those who had to wield them, and officials of the Public Works Department had told him that in their contract rates no coolies would ever think of attempting work of this kind except when the ground had been softened by rain. In such cases the bodily wear and tear of moving half a cubic yard of material, or executing 50 per cent. of a Public Works Department task, was considerable, and especially in the case of weakly gangs. He had seen moreover very wretched and enfeebled creatures in the gangs who had come, some distances of four, six, and even eight miles to their work, some of them dragging their children to and fro with them, and he had no hesitation in stating that when these walking distances and carrying weights were taken into account with the day's work, the expenditure of force was far ahead of its replenishment in the shape of food wages.

With regard to the statement that the lowest scale of wages would permit in most instances of men buying 1½ lbs. of grain in addition to condiments and some other nourishment, however that might be the case in the Bellary district or in certain stations on the line of railway which Dr. Cornish had not then inspected, it was not so in the upland taluks of North Arcot and Cuddapah. At Goorumkonda the bazaar price of rice was only 13 lbs. the rupee, and at Royachoti about 14 lbs., so that one anna would not purchase even 1 lb. of grain. The mode of calculating the wages, too, in some districts had practically the effect of reducing the earnings of men from 1a. 6p. to 1a. 5p. or 1a. 4p., and what with deductions for short work, and the 'customary tribute' to the gangsmen, there was reason to fear that in a very large proportion of cases the labourers did not get anything like the whole of the reduced wage.

Dr. Cornish noted that Sir Richard Temple had made a most important concession to the famine labourers in consequence of his protest, and if no other good

had resulted, he felt bound to thank the Delegate for the
consideration given to the last paragraph of his letter,
in which he pointed out that a man must *eat*, even if he
had no *work*, on Sundays, and that a subsistence wage
ought not to be shared with young children.

Practically (Dr. Cornish continues), there is now very little
difference between Sir Richard Temple's wage-rate and my own recommendations. I have contended, and have given reasons for considering, that the basis of a pound of grain for a labouring man was unsafe,
especially when that wage was paid only for six days in the week,
and when helpless children had to share in the food. Sir Richard
Temple admits the weakness of this portion of his scheme, and by con-
ceding additional help to feed the young, has in point of fact yielded
all that I felt justified in urging.

According to my observation, though the ordinary wage rate
of 2 annas, 1–6, and 1 anna for men, women, and children respectively, may in some districts be too little to procure a sufficiency
of nourishing food to keep up health, yet in times like these the people
are ready enough to work for such wages cheerfully, and with a good
heart, getting payment for and doing work only on six days in the
week. Whatever deficiencies in their food there may be they supplement in their own fashion by using articles that, though not in general
use, may help at a pinch to sustain life, such as the seeds of the
bamboo, tamarind, &c., the pith of the aloe plant, and certain jungle
leaves like the Sethia Indica.

The actual wage receipts of a man, wife, and four children, on the
old and amended new scale of wages are given below

Ordinary Scale.

			R.	A.	P.
Man . .	6 days at 2 annas . .		0	12	0
Woman . .	„ 1½ „ . .		0	9	0
2 Children .	„ 1 „ . .		0	12	0
2 Children under 7 years of age . .		—			
	Total per week .		2	1	0

Sir Richard Temple's Amended Scale.

			R.	A.	P.
Man . .	7 days at 1½ annas . .		0	10	6
Woman . .	„ 1¼ „ . .		0	8	9
2 Children .	„ 1 „ . .		0	10	0
2 Children under 7 years ¼ „ . .		0	3	6	
	Total per week .		2	1	3

o 2

From this comparison it will be seen that in the case of a man with a family of four children, two of whom are workers and two non-workers, he is actually better off by three pies per week under Sir Richard Temple's modified reduced wage than he was when working six days in the week for ordinary wages. Mr. West, C.E., in charge of the Cheyar embankment works, informs me that to meet the views of the district authorities, and to avoid the appearance of competition in the labour market, he has reduced his rates from the ordinary two annas to the modified scale of Sir Richard Temple's, and paid for the Sundays, and that, practically, his disbursements per head average just the same as before.

The great financial saving, therefore, of ever so many lakhs of rupees is not likely to accrue from the introduction of the new scale of wage. It has given intense dissatisfaction to the labouring people, who could not or would not comprehend its terms; it has opened the door for abuses of various kinds, and it has not tended to economy in disbursements.

Sir Richard Temple asks if I will admit that a pound of grain a day is sufficient to maintain an adult native of India in a 'state of rest.' In reply, I have to state that I do not know of any cereal grain which would give a sufficiency of albuminous matter in a lb. weight to replace the daily waste of nitrogen from the adult native body, and consequently I am unable to admit any such proposition. The 'evidence' adduced by Sir Richard Temple in regard to this matter is in reality no evidence at all. Sir Richard says that in the Vellore relief camp Dr. Fox and Captain Harris were agreed that men had so improved on 1 lb. of grain; but when I came to enquire into this matter I found that the 'evidence' rested on general impressions, and not on periodical weighing and individual record of weight from time to time.

Even in the 'weight test' some caution is necessary, for many of the people who come into camps appear to be filling out and fattening, when in reality they are getting dropsical and in a fair way to die. I can easily understand that the people in the Vellore camp did better on 1 lb. of grain per diem than they did on 12 ounces, which was the scale in use a few weeks ago when Dr. Fox urged an increase.

I have thought it safer and more prudent in this matter to fall back on our experience in dieting non-labouring prisoners, and to recommend 20 ounces, or 1¼ lb. of cereal grain besides dholl, vegetables, condiments, &c., for adults fed in relief camps, and this allowance is now sanctioned by Government, and should be, I think, a minimum allowance, considering how much tissue these poor creatures have to repair before they can be brought into a state to do a day's work.

In a paper recently brought to my notice by Surgeon-General G. Smith, I find that at Nellore Surgeon-Major A. M. Ross has been weighing coolies on relief works, and their average weight is below that of average 'under trial' prisoners in gaol. Thus :—

In Gaol.

Men.		Women.		Children.
109·1 lbs.	.	92·3 lbs.	.	70·0 lbs.

Relief Works.

94·3 lbs.	.	77·6 lbs.	.	46·0 lbs.

These weights appear to indicate much wasting, but the weighings will be continued and reported on from week to week.

In the last paragraph of his minute of March 7, Sir Richard Temple states his belief that the labouring poor in Madras in rural localities can hardly get more than one pound of grain a day for a male adult in ordinary times. The enquiries on which this belief is founded were made, I apprehend, by Sir Richard Temple himself, in his rapid journey through the country.

But I should submit to any impartial person whether enquiries made in this way, to satisfy a foregone conclusion, can be compared in value with the careful statistical enquiry undertaken calmly and deliberately in the years 1862 and 1863, and which enquiry furnished the basis for all our subsequent arrangements in the dieting of the people under circumstances where they cannot have any voice in the choice of their own food. Most people in India are acquainted with the sort of answer a high official personage will get in reply to leading questions, and if Sir Richard Temple thinks he has got at the truth in this matter, I can assure him, after a close practical study of the food of the people of Southern India for the last fifteen years, that he is utterly and entirely mistaken, and that so far from the labouring adults living upon a pound a day, they eat on the average nearly double.

Dr. Cornish then proceeded to the consideration of Sir Richard Temple's second minute, of March 14, in which he entered upon the scientific questions involved in the objections to his diet scale. Here again justice will not be done to the argument save by copious quotations. Dr. Cornish says :—

In this minute Sir Richard Temple observes, paragraph 6 :—

' The opinion that 1 lb. a day of grain might suffice for a relief labourer, together with some allowance for condiments and the like, or some nutritious substance, was not indeed based on scientific theory. It was founded rather on probabilities practically deduced from the condition of the poorer classes in ordinary times, and on the results of general experience.'

I think it would have been more to the point if Sir Richard Temple had given something a little more precise than the vague term ' general experience.' I may ask, in return, whose experience? Not Sir Richard Temple's, surely; for in 1874 he assures us that the people in Bengal habitually use from one to two seers of grain (2 to 4 lbs.) per adult, and that even the people in relief houses, doing no work, got two-thirds of a seer (1½ lbs.) Sir Richard Temple records nothing of his travels in Bombay, showing that the people on relief works there lived on 1 lb. of grain a day. It was only on his arrival in the Bellary district that he evolved this strange doctrine, that a Madrassee could do, what the people in no other part of India can, thrive on 16 oz. of cereal grain a day.

A quotation was made from a letter by Sir R. Christison on the rations of soldiers ; the passage urged that ' unskilled constructors of dietaries in famine times' should be ' somewhat modest' in respect to their knowledge. It should make them especially cautious in the enunciation of new and strange doctrines such as ' that the amount of nitrogen required by natives must be much less than that required by Europeans.' Dr. Cornish proceeded :—

This is really the crucial test of the whole question, and I am afraid it cannot be definitely settled on the *ipse dixit* of Sir Richard Temple. In the scientific world we are accustomed to ask that any one bringing forward a new theory shall state the facts on which his theory is based; and in this case it would be quite fair to ask Sir Richard Temple whether by himself, or with professional aid, he has endeavoured to test his theory by estimating and measuring the amount of nitrogen which natives of ordinary size and weight eliminate from their bodies. The investigation is one of by no means a difficult character, and no one has any right to bring forward such a theory in proof of the sufficiency of a scale of food without first ascertaining, by repeated investigation and experiment, that the nitrogen excreted by natives is proportionately less than in Europeans. The consequences of our accepting such a theory without the clearest and plainest proof might be most disastrous, and the *onus probandi* remains with the originator of the theory.

I almost wish, in regard to Sir Richard Temple's reputation as a gentleman of many and varied accomplishments, that he had spared me the difficulty of dealing with his 'crucial tests' in paragraphs 11 and 12 as regards the alleged discrepancies in theory and practice as to the amount of nitrogen necessary to a successful dietary. It is not a pleasant thing for one in my position to point out errors of comprehension on Sir Richard Temple's part; but, however painful the operation, it must be done. Sir Richard Temple quotes from the 'Madras Manual of Hygiene,' a work of admitted excellence, by Surgeon-Major H. King, M.B., the composition of a scale of rations allowed to native soldiers on foreign service. He points out very truly that these rations, while yielding an abundance of carboniferous food (32 oz. of rice), are very defective in nitrogenous principles, the whole weight of food in fact yielding only 178 grains of nitrogen per diem. 'According to this theory,' observes Sir Richard Temple, 'the Madras sepoy would be undergoing starvation at the hands of Government. But, in fact, he is not reduced physically, nor does he fail the Government when it calls upon him for exertion. This case, I submit, makes very strongly against Dr. Cornish's theory.'

I have no excuse to make for this dietary of our native soldiers on foreign service. I gave it up fifteen years ago, and recorded my opinion of it in the following terms :—' The deficiency of animal food in the diet, and the excess of carboniferous material, is undoubtedly a fertile source of the prevalence of sickness in native troops on foreign service. The mortality of Madras troops on this diet in Burmah is more than double what occurs in Indian stations, where they find their own food.'[1]

The foreign service 'ration' in fact is a 'survival' from the time of the first Burmese War. It was formed in times long before sanitary commissioners or chemists learned in food-composition existed; and at the present time it is no more to be regarded as a typical 'diet' than are the buttons on the backs of our dress-coats to be regarded as a device for supporting a sword-belt. The ration is simply an 'aid' to the soldiers employed in a foreign country, and the men are put under no stoppages whatever on account of it, but draw the full pay of their rank, just as if they had to find every particle of food out of their pay. If the relief coolies in whose behalf I have protested had seven or nine rupees a month in addition to the pound

[1] *Madras Medical Journal*, vol. viii. p. 30.

of grain, I should have made no objections to the insufficiency of their rations.

The Government expect, in these settled times, with the Burmese markets well supplied with poultry, eggs, fish, and flesh, that the Sepoy can buy his nitrogenous food for himself, and practically he does so to such an extent that of late years the troops stationed in Burmah have been almost as healthy as when in Southern India.

But there are and have been exceptions. I need not go back to the very terrible mortality of native troops from bowel complaints in the first and second Burmese Wars. These things are matters of history, but no later than the year 1872 a detachment of native troops was sent from Burmah to occupy posts on the Arracan river in co-operation with the Lushai expedition.

In this locality the men had no market at hand in which to buy animal food, and in attempting to live on their 'rations' they sickened and died in large numbers. The proportions are given in the following table :—

Strength 184	Ratios of sick to strength	
Hospital admissions . . 901	per mille . . . 4,896·7
Deaths (12 from 'dropsy,' 5	Deaths . . . . 146·7
from 'debility') . . 17	

In this case and in all others demanding active service away from markets of supply, the native soldier on foreign service *does*, in fact, 'fail to do what the Government expects of him,' and simply because his 'rations' are unfitted of themselves to support his health and strength. The fact is acknowledged and admitted by every officer who has commanded in Burmah.

Then, again, the 'rations' of the European soldier do not, as Sir Richard Temple supposes, constitute his whole food. Every commanding officer knows that the British soldier habitually buys extra meat from the bazaar out of his ample pay, and there is no regiment in the country which has not a provision shop of its own in which anything, from a Yarmouth bloater to a truffled sausage, may be bought. The rations on the whole are fairly adapted for the British soldier, although there is no doubt that he eats more meat than the quantity contained in the ration.

I must confess that I was a little staggered by Sir Richard Temple's quotation of the scale of food allowed to 'European soldiers on board ship.' I was travelling at the time of receiving the minute, and away from all books of reference, so that I could not verify the composition of the diet as given in the 'Madras Manual of Hygiene'; but I knew that this diet had been framed under the advice of scientific men, and that it was not likely to err in the direction of giving too little nitro-genous food, and I was quite satisfied that some error had crept into the calculations, and that Sir Richard Temple had pitched upon this 'crucial instance' without thought of the possible inaccuracy of the figures. The explanation of the calculated quantity of nitrogen in this diet being only 155 grains per day is very simple. The diets which are valued in the appendix to the 'Madras Manual of Hygiene' are all taken from the 'Madras Medical Code.' The quantities of this particular diet will be found in the code, page 133, vol. ii. The transcriber instead of entering 4 lbs., or 64 oz. of 'fresh bread' for a week's ration, has made the mistake of entering 4 oz., and, as a conse-quence, all the calculations of albuminous and carboniferous food are below the actual truth.

There is also another error. The calculator of the nutritive values has assumed that 'salt-meat' contains less albumen than fresh, and has put down a less proportion of nitrogen for the salt-meat ; but this is not really the case, though in salt meat the albuminous matter may be less easily digested. The effect of salting meat is to harden the albuminous tissues, and to cause the watery juices of the meat to enter the brine ; consequently salt meat has more albumen in a given weight than fresh or preserved meat. On the whole I consider the ship-board dietary of the European soldier, containing as it does, according to my calculation, from 200 to 240 grains of nitrogen per diem, very well suited for a class of people who have nothing whatever to do. . . . . .

I feel bound, however, to protest against the line of argument advanced by Sir Richard Temple, that, as the British soldier only needs so much nitrogenous food, the native of India can do with two-thirds of that amount, or less. We have no grounds whatever for admitting so dangerous a theory, and all our practical experience tells just the other way. . . . .

The effects of improving the standard of diets in the Madras gaols in 1867, so as to raise the amount of albuminous food equal to from 200 to 240 grains of nitrogen per diem, has been to diminish the mean annual death-rate from 107 to about 22 per thousand for the eight years in which the new dietaries have been in force. This ought to be fairly convincing testimony, but there is more behind. A few years ago a gaol superintendent, who had been admonished by Govern-ment for over much flogging, was requested to adopt some other mode of punishment, and the punishment-book showed, in the course of a few months, some hundreds of entries to this effect : 'Half rations until he completes his task.' The result was great increase of sickness and mortality from the diseases such as now fill our famine camps, viz., sloughing ulcers, bowel complaints, dropsy, and impoverished blood. On discontinuing the food punishment, the mortality began slowly to subside to its normal proportions. So close is the connection in fact between a sufficiency of nitrogenous food and the health of the prisoners, that I never now hear of an increase of bowel disorders and dropsies in a gaol without at once suspecting tampering with the food or provisions in the district prisons. In talking the matter over with the Inspector-General of Prisons, I find that he has arrived at precisely the same conclusion. After the Bengal famine, I see it noted that the rate of mortality in the Julpigoree gaol was 27 per cent., chiefly from 'bowel complaints.' In Rungpore 17·6 per cent. In Gya, Tirhoot, and Chumparun the mortality was 17, 10, and 15 per cent. respectively. ' Dysentery was the most fatal disease.' The *précis* writer who compiles the sanitary statistics of the India Office does not appear to have had a notion of the connection of the undue gaol mortality with the famine, but notes that a ' special report has been called for' to explain it. Reading between the lines I can at once tell him that it was a mortality from starvation diseases.

With all these facts before me, I think myself quite justified in having given early warning of the danger of reducing wages to the basis of one pound of cereal grain a day, even admitting that my remonstrance was, as Sir Richard Temple states, ' strongly worded.' It saves time to state in plain terms one's actual meaning, and my meaning was quite evident when I showed that Sir Richard Temple's proposals were out of harmony with the experience of the Bengal famine, and with our actual knowledge of the effects of insufficient food.

Up to this point, however, Dr. Cornish had been discussing the question apart from actual facts furnished by the famine. In the remaining portion of his letter, which is quoted in its entirety, he deals with observed facts. He says :—

There remains yet one more point to be noticed with reference to differences of opinion in regard to the present condition of the labouring poor. On this point Sir Richard Temple states : ' Having carefully inspected during my tour in this Presidency thousands of relief labourers, I give it as my opinion, that with very few exceptions, which are not as a rule traceable to insufficient wages, the general physical condition of the labourers is as good now as in ordinary years.'

This is Sir Richard Temple's opinion, but not mine. I too have seen a considerable number of relief labourers, and have taken some pains to find out where the distress really is, and my experience is this, that if I want to see the darkest side of the famine picture, I must look for it elsewhere than amongst the ranks of those who have still strength enough left them to work. Consequently I make it a point of examining, wherever I can, the condition of the people fed in relief houses, lungerkhanas, and by private charity. I try to ascertain the condition of the poor who frequent the public bazaars and markets; and I pay special attention to the condition of the old and the young, whom I find almost invariably to be the earliest victims of distress. It is in this respect probably that my estimate of the effects of the famine on the health of the lower classes differs so widely from Sir Richard Temple's. My own view is briefly this, that the famine is pressing with peculiar severity upon certain sections of the labouring classes, who average from twenty to thirty per cent. of the population of the several districts; that amongst these classes there has been already a very large mortality, primarily due to bad and insufficient feeding; and that the condition of the survivors is in many cases critical in the extreme, as shown by the rapidly increasing proportion of persons who are unfit to work, and who have to be fed entirely at Government expense to keep the feeble vitality they have from being altogether extinguished.

Immediately the condition of a people becomes so low that they cannot work, the question of saving life becomes enormously complicated, and in plain language the time has then passed by when Government relief can do more than attempt to rescue a few possessed of the strongest constitutions. What has been our experience in this respect in the Madras relief camps now being established throughout the country? Sir Richard Temple, I observe, in his numerous minutes, has passed by this subject of the actual mortality of the famine-stricken, but as a public health official, I am bound to take notice of it.

The following figures show the mortality amongst this class of the population in the Madras camps for ten weeks ending March 31 :—

Mean strength	Total deaths	Annual rates per mille
11,005 . .	1,971 . .	. 930·8

This enormous mortality simply means an annual death-rate equivalent to 930·8 per mille of the population constantly under observation, and, in fact, is a death-rate which wipes out nearly the whole of the living within a year. The excessive death-rate going on in Madras is going on in every relief camp in the country. I find but little difference in the proportion of deaths, whether in North Arcot, Cuddapah, or Madras. And it must not be supposed that this excessive death-rate is due to cholera or small-pox, for the Madras camps have been singularly free of the former, and by means of vaccination the small-pox epidemic has been controlled. The deaths are almost entirely due to diseases which invariably, in India, attack under-fed and starved people, viz., extreme wasting of tissue, and destruction of the lining membrane of the lower bowel. This is a simple statement of fact. Thanks to the assistance of Surgeon-General G. Smith and his able medical staff in Madras, this question of the nature of the famine disease has been abundantly verified by post-mortem examinations. Surgeon-Major Porter informs me that the average weight of bodies of full-grown men he has examined has varied from fifty-seven to eighty-five pounds, and it is enough to record this fact to show the extreme wasting going on during life.

But if the condition of the labouring classes is so generally satisfactory to Sir Richard Temple, how is it, I may ask, that the death-returns of the famine districts are so much above what is usual? I have not as yet received the returns for February, but those for December and January are available for comparison with the average results of the previous five years. I must, however, note with respect to these district death-returns, that from personal investigation in the districts, I know they very much understate the real mortality of the last few months. The truth is, the famine has disorganised our village establishments to such an extent that the actual numbers who have already perished will never be known. Hundreds and thousands of people have died away from their homes, have fallen down by the roadsides, and their bodies have been left to be eaten by dogs and jackals. Mr. Gribble, the sub-collector of Cuddapah, in the course of a morning's ride of fourteen miles, came upon eight unburied bodies, and at Royachoti in January last Mr. Supervisor Matthews informed me that after an outbreak of cholera fifty-three dead bodies lay for days exposed in the dry bed of a river, near the works the relief coolies were engaged on. Walking over this ground two months after the event, the numerous skulls and human bones scattered on the surface convinced me that the statement was founded on fact.

With our village establishments panic-stricken, and the village messengers away at relief works, it is quite certain that the death registration has been most incomplete. At Madanapalli I found that the deaths in the civil hospital had exceeded those borne on the village register for certain months, and at Royachoti the deaths amongst the starving people sent into the relief shed in March had exceeded the registered mortality for the whole town. It is obvious therefore that the figures I now give do not represent the real truth of our losses; they are at the best approximate only.

Mortality in Famine Districts.

Districts.	Chingle-put.	Nellore	North Arcot	Kurnool	Cudda-pah	Bellary
Population	938,184	1,376,811	2,015,278	914,432	1,351,194	1,668,006
			Registered Deaths.			
Average of 5 years { December ending 1875 { January	1,892 1,404	2,007 1,794	3,445 3,943	1,420 1,371	2.336 1,933	2,585 2,253
Present season {1876, Dec. {1877, Jan.	2,865 6,094	5.644 11,142	6,046 13,686	11,862 6,253	6,612 13,861	7,440 6,361
Ratio per 1,000 of population per annum Average of 5 years (two months) Present season (two months)	21·08 57·2	16·6 73·7	21·9 58·7	18·3 118·8	18·9 88·7	17·4 60·4

Even these figures, which we know to be under the truth, show an appalling mortality in the famine districts during December and January. I have no reason to suppose that the state of things here indicated has much improved in February and March. But in our municipal towns, or in some of them at least, within the famine area, death registration is more efficiently managed, and the following figures will tend to show the gravity of the famine as exemplified in an abnormal death-rate. In Bellary I have long had reason to suppose that the registration was not properly done, and the returns of some of the Bellary municipalities are obviously imperfect. The first thing that attracted my attention in connection with the famine, on returning to duty in the end of January, was the abnormal death-rate amongst certain classes and certain localities of the Presidency town, and I lost no time in drawing the attention of Government to the condition of the people, and suggesting measures for combating the great destruction of life then going on. While the mortality of the Presidency town was exaggerated by the influx of starving immigrants, the experience of other municipalities shows that throughout the famine tract the death-rate has risen out of all proportion to its normal condition.

Mortality in the Municipalities of the Famine Districts.

Municipal towns	Madras	Conjeveram	Nellore	Vellore	Wallajahpett	Kurnool	Cuddapah	Bellary	Adoni	Gooty	Anantapur
Population	397,552	37,327	29,929	38,022	12,103	25,579	16,275	51,766	22,723	6,730	4,918

Registered Deaths.

		Madras	Conjeveram	Nellore	Vellore	Wallajahpett	Kurnool	Cuddapah	Bellary	Adoni	Gooty	Anantapur
Average of 5 years ending 1875.	Dec.	1,211	65	53	84	41	71	50	77	69	9	7
	Jan.	1,260	65	37	81	30	73	55	57	47	10	8
	Feb.	1,100	65	38	80	26	60	40	53	51	9	4
Present season	1876 Dec.	2,034	96	127	89	48	376	83	192	448	127	11
	1877 Jan.	4,059	367	169	146	66	147	82	114	180	24	9
	1877 Feb.	4,401	87	288	215	41	171	92	127	278	6	27
Ratio per 1,000 of population per annum Average of 5 years (3 months)		35·9	20·8	17·1	28·4	32·0	31·9	35·6	14·4	29·3	16·6	15·4
Present season (3 months)		105·5	58·9	78·06	47·3	51·2	108·5	63·1	33·4	159·1	93·3	38·2

The famine so far has already fallen very heavily on the old, the weakly constitutioned, and young children. It is still 'weeding out' from our labouring classes a large number of victims, and in consideration of the fact that diseased conditions dependent on insufficient food *follow many months after the cause has passed away*, I apprehend that a heavy and unusual mortality will continue, even after the period of drought and dearth of food has ended.

The survivors of the famine will be the strongest and best fitted of their race to continue the species, and when plenty again blesses the land, they will produce a vigorous race of descendants; but I think there can be no reasonable doubt that this food deficiency has fallen very heavily upon the ordinary agricultural labouring poor, and that many years must elapse before they will have made up the numbers who have fallen, and are still falling, victims to the combined famine and pestilence now in our midst. I have in former reports called attention to the fact, that the children born of famine-stricken mothers are nothing but skin and bone. My recent experience goes to show that the birth-rate is seriously diminishing, and that pregnancy amongst the distressed women is becoming a rare condition.

It is on these grounds that I cannot subscribe to the pleasing and hopeful telegrams in which Sir Richard Temple summarises the weekly progress of events for the benefit of the Home Government and the

English people. There are two sides to every picture. Sir Richard Temple, like a skilful general commanding in battle, naturally fixes his attention on the main points of attack and defence, and so long as these are safe, his main work is accomplished.

I, on the other hand, as a public health official whose special duty is to preserve life, am bound to listen to the cries of the wounded, and to note in what way the combatants suffer, and I should be wanting in my duty to myself and to the Government I serve, if I failed to state the facts coming to my knowledge, and the deduction drawn from those facts.

A few days before leaving the Presidency of Madras to assume the governorship of Bombay, Sir Richard Temple replied to Dr. Cornish's letter in a minute dated Cuddalore, April 18. It was comparatively brief, and was confined to a few points upon which he held exactly opposite opinions to Dr. Cornish. Having regard to the importance of the subject, Sir Richard refrained from 'making the objections which might ordinarily be made to the tone of some parts of the Sanitary Commissioner's minute as an official paper.'

Sir Richard accepted the Sanitary Commissioner's assurances that the 'Madras Manual of Hygiene' was wrong on the point upon which the Delegate had rested. He proceeded to indicate a weakness in the argument of Dr. Cornish. Sir Richard says :—' It is not necessary, however, to pursue this point, or any such like points, because I understand that the medico-chemical theories upon which the Sanitary Commissioner of Madras seems still to rely are not implicitly accepted by the highest sanitary authorities in India, and do not entirely coincide with the newest development of scientific thought regarding the carbonaceous and nitrogenous elements necessary for the nutrition of the human frame. Nor is it practically necessary to discuss further the Sanitary Commissioner's opinion regarding the sufficiency or otherwise of the reduced wage, because in his present minute he admits that, as now applied, it is sufficient. His previous objections appear to have been diminished by the granting of the wage on Sundays as well as week days, and by the granting of a small allowance for the support of the young children of persons employed on the works. I had myself always contemplated that the reduced wage should be allowed on Sundays. As regards the very young children, their case did not at first suggest itself for consideration, as all young children from seven years and upwards were admitted to relief. But as soon as the case of the children under seven years of age was brought to my notice, I recommended that they also should receive a small allowance. I found, however, that this had been already ordered by the Madras Government.'

On the main point of the sufficiency of the rate to support labourers on works, Sir Richard Temple would not give way. He had his own observation to go by. Seeing is believing. Consequently, he remarks: ' Though I do not undertake to pronounce any opinion upon a medico-chemical point, yet I do undertake to say whether thousands of relief labourers inspected by me are physically in fair working condition or not. And I adhere to the opinion previously expressed, that the many gangs which I inspected working on the reduced wage were in such condition, regard being had to the condition of such persons in ordinary times. In this opinion I was confirmed by the experienced medical officer on my staff who had seen the realities of famine in other parts of India. But in order that no doubt might remain upon the point, I asked for and obtained the opinion of the Sanitary Commissioner with the Government of India. And after inspecting in different parts of the country some 35,000 relief labourers, he pronounced them to be, with some individual exceptions, in fair condition. This, then, is the true test of the insufficiency or otherwise of the reduced wage, to which I have always appealed, and still appeal. According to this test the wage appears to be sufficient at present. If at any time any marked deterioration of the physical condition were to indicate that the reduced wage is insufficient, then I shall be the first to make a revised recommendation.'

Sir Richard drew a distinction between those employed on works and those in relief camps. He said: 'Inferences deduced from the condition of the recipients of gratuitous relief are wholly irrelevant if attempted to be applied to the conditions of relief labourers. If, unhappily, there be mortality among the inmates of relief camps, it by no means follows that there is any mortality among relief labourers. In point of fact there is no mortality among relief labourers except from cholera, small-pox, or other diseases, and when sometimes cholera has stricken and dispersed large gangs of relief labourers, there has never been any reason to suppose that the scourge arose from want of food. Again, if notwithstanding scientifically arranged diets the condition of the inmates of relief camps continues bad, no amelioration whatever could be afforded by raising the wages of relief labourers, who are a totally different class. These poor inmates have never gone to relief works at all.[1] Indeed the very reason of their admission to the relief camps is this, that they are incapable of going to relief works. They are diseased or infirm, or being indisposed to work have wandered about, or, passing by means of relief close at home, have wandered to a distance. Being thus helpless for one reason or another, they are picked up and

[1] This was shown to be entirely incorrect. Thousands went from works to camps, either immediately, or after an interval of starving at home.

taken care of; but when picked up they are often beyond the reach of human aid. No analogy, therefore, drawn from these persons can possibly be applicable to relief labourers, and to mention the two cases with any sort of parallelism and in any kind of connection, would be to produce confusion of ideas and other misapprehension. If indeed persons who were pale on being admitted to relief works were to become thinner and thinner and weaker and weaker, till at last they had to be drafted off to gratuitous relief camps as unfit to work, then that would be a reason for considering the wages, but this is just what has not occurred, and is not occurring. If I saw or knew of any signs of it occurring, then I should be the first to move. Many relief labourers indeed have left the works of their own accord, not so much, however, because the wage was reduced, but rather because task-work was enforced, or because the scene of labour was removed to a distance from their homes.'

With this the wordy warfare between the Delegate of the Government of India and the Sanitary Commissioner of Madras came to an end.[1]

---

[1] On more careful examination of the papers I find that the Government of Madras asked Dr. Cornish to reply to one of the paragraphs of Sir Richard Temple's minute (the last passage quoted above). The Sanitary Commissioner did so, and quoted the Delegate's own words and instanced his own acts in sending people from works to relief camps as the last thing Sir Richard Temple did in the Madras Presidency.

CHAPTER III.

EVIDENCE *PRO ET CON* AS TO THE SUFFICIENCY
OF THE RATION.

AFTER the scale of wages prescribed in the Government order of January 31 had been in operation six weeks, the Madras authorities had before them a mass of papers from district officers, which, in their opinion, proved that the wage was insufficient to maintain, in all cases, the condition of people working on relief works, while their Sanitary Commissioner considered the sustenance afforded thereby generally insufficient. Further, from a letter written by the secretary (Mr. C. E. Bernard, C.S.I.), to Sir Richard Temple regarding the Delegate's classification of gangs, it appeared that out of 94,250 persons inspected in the Madras Presidency, 28,850 were reported as middling, and 15,800 as indifferent, while of the gangs inspected in other provinces, numbering 3,100, 1,000 were reported as indifferent. It further appeared that in Mysore a larger food allowance per head than was permitted for Madras had been authorised. His Grace the Governor in Council carefully considered the papers proving the above statements, and also had the advantage of conferring with Sir Richard Temple thereon; he resolved to wait reports from other districts as well as further reports from the Coimbatore and Cuddapah districts, before finally deciding on the question of the adequacy or otherwise of the scale of allowances laid down in the Government order already quoted.

There was, however, no doubt, in the opinion of his
Grace in Council, from a perusal of the reports already
received, as well as from the personal observations of
members of the Government, that many persons were
to be found in gangs who were failing in strength
from insufficient nourishment or from other causes.
This might arise from their having been previously
weakened by insufficient or bad food before coming to
the works, or from their having been in bad health; or,
again, from the task of work exacted from them being
too heavy, having regard to the sustenance given. His
Grace in Council therefore directed the special attention
of all collectors and divisional officers to those predispos-
ing causes. Any persons found in working gangs whose
appearance indicated failing condition were to be at once
withdrawn from such gangs and given some lighter
work, or if, on any large work, such persons were found to
be numerous and no relief camp was sufficiently near, they
were to be placed together in a special gang and given
such additional allowance as might be found necessary to
maintain their health and strength. Where the members
of a gang generally showed signs of physical deterioration, it might indicate that the work had been too great,
the allowance of food too small, or possibly that they
had not received the full benefit of the allowance granted,
either in consequence of malpractices on the part of
maistries and overseers, or because they had dependents
living upon them, and sharing their bare subsistence
allowance, whose wants should have been discovered
and relieved, if necessary, by the village officers. The
order continued :—' In case of children on works, who
are found to be habitually weak or exhausted at the
end of the day, it may be necessary either to give them
increased nourishment. to reduce their work, or to relieve them altogether, if under ten years of age, of work

as a test. His Grace the Governor in Council cannot too strongly impress upon all divisional and relief officers the importance of the most vigilant attention to the circumstances of the people on relief works and in the villages under their charge. The success of any measures devised for the relief of present distress will mainly depend upon the personal exertions and vigilance of local officers, and the completeness of their detailed arrangements. One point especially must never be overlooked, but which has, it is feared, not received sufficient attention in some places, namely, the regularity and frequency of payments of wages.'

This order was communicated to all collectors and relief officers, and proved but the presage of another order issued six weeks later, doing away with the 1-lb ration altogether.

The reports from some of the officers were most adverse to the scale recommended by Sir Richard Temple. A selection from them may be made as follows :—

With reference to G. O. No. 329, of January 31, 1877, Mr. W. H. Glenny has the honour to say that, according to his own observations, and that of the officers assisting him, he does not think the physical condition of the people on relief has deteriorated in consequence of the reduction of wages. The gangs now, it is true, present a far poorer appearance than they did a month ago. But he conceives that this is owing to the elimination of persons of conspicuously well-nourished physique.

On March 21 I inspected about 1,500 coolies employed in making a road towards the Mysore frontier to meet a road in course of construction there leading from Colar to Muddanapully and Punganur. There were several gangs of Brinjaries and many Mussulmans employed. Of the 1,500 coolies, Mr. Clerk and myself picked out 250, or 16 per cent., who, in our judgment, were in very bad condition, and many of them more fitted for a relief camp than for labour on relief wages. There were about 50 men and perhaps 30 women out of the whole number in good muscular condition. The children were nearly all feeble, emaciated, and anæmic. The young girls who, from their ages, should have been women, were arrested in their development.

and showing no signs of puberty. A few women brought their infants with them to the works, and these youngsters were literally starving for want of nourishing breast-milk.—Dr. Cornish.

If, as the famine officers believe here (Bellary district), the able-bodied people have mostly other means of support than the subsistence wage, it is clear that their present physical condition is no guide to us in determining the point of the sufficiency of the wage. I am, however, inclined to the view that there has been a gradual deterioration in the physical condition of the people, and that the proportion of those who are weakly and emaciated must be fast increasing. I judge so from the condition of the labouring gangs which are considered 'able-bodied,' and note the almost complete absence of redundant flesh among them, and from the admitted fact, that, as the able-bodied are discharged from the road gangs, their places are taken by people who are physically reduced. I note, too, with some apprehension, the fact that, in the town of Bellary itself more than 10 per cent. of its population is receiving some sort of relief in the shape of partial meals of cooked food. It may be that this relief is abused to some extent, but on this point the local committees will hereafter report. Meanwhile, the applicants for relief amongst the town poor are increasing every day. But, besides the town poor, I saw yesterday at the feeding house in Bruce Pettah, more than 800 men, women, and children of the immigrant population who came and waited patiently for hours in expectation of getting a meal of cooked food. Amongst these were some terrible pictures of emaciation and misery, and at the least there were more than 50 children amongst them, who, if not taken into some home, and fed and nursed, will assuredly die within a short time.—Dr. Cornish.

There is no doubt that the labouring classes, as a rule, have fallen off greatly in condition within the last few months, and it must be remembered that we see none of the worst cases of destitution in the streets. All such cases are at once sent either to hospital or to the relief camps by inspectors who patrol the town for the purpose; but after all this weeding out, I can say most decidedly that the people I meet now in the streets are much thinner and poorer-looking in every way than those I saw six months ago, when even the poorest mingled in the streets.—*Surgeon-Major A. E. M. Ross, Nellore.*

I have the honour to report that I have ordered the following rates to be paid to relief labourers from Monday, April 23, except in the town of Adoni, where the existing scale will be adhered to :—

Men	.	.	annas 2	} To inefficient gangs for seven days.
Women	.	.	„ 1½	
Children	.	.	„ 1	} To ordinary gangs for six days.
Infants	.	.	„ ¼	

The reasons are, to meet increased pressure now visible in the condition of the labourers themselves. I have inspected carefully 24,000 of them within the week. Captain Hamilton has seen all the remainder, and agrees with me that the time for some relaxation has come.

This pressure is chiefly due to the advancing season and the time the people have been on the works. But there are other causes. The price of grain has risen and is rising, and sometimes it is not easy to get on the remoter works, while at places distant from Adoni the price fluctuates greatly. The evening storms which now frequently occur interrupt payments and cause much inconvenience to the labourers camped on the roads. Their clothes are getting very ragged. The great heat, at a time when generally they are not compelled to work, is trying; and the recruiting for Nellore has undoubtedly pressed very severely on the adult male labourers.

In fact, it is among the latter that the change is visible, and this accounts for the apparent disproportion in the new rates. The women still look much as before, as no direct pressure has been put on them to go to Nellore. Many of them are in excellent condition, sleek and fat. This cannot be said of any of the men.

I maintain the old scale at Adoni, as it is properly only a depôt to catch up persons who want work. There is a great tendency amongst the labourers to gravitate thither, and this can be best met by making outside works more attractive. Moreover, at Adoni grain is cheapest, and there is always shelter.—W. B. OLDHAM, B.C.S.

Here in Alur, however, I agree with Mr. Maltby in thinking that the people are decidedly thinner than they were.

I have thought it necessary, in anticipation of your sanction, to raise the rates in Alur taluk from 23rd instant by 3 pies all round.— W. H. GLENNY.

With reference to G. O. No. 1,088, dated the 15th ultimo, I have the honour to forward a copy of a letter No. 48, dated the 21st instant, from Mr. Oldham, in charge of the Adoni taluk, reporting that he has raised the wages of men, women, and children to 2 annas, $1\frac{1}{2}$ annas, and 1 anna respectively.

I also inclose copy of paragraphs 2 and 4 of letter No. 138, dated 20th instant, from the sub-collector, that he has raised the wages in the Alur taluk 3 pies all round.

2. I quite agree with them as to the necessity for this; a time of great pressure has arrived. The heat of the weather is very severe and the strength of the labourers is decreasing in consequence (with the bare subsistence given them).

3. But what I would most earnestly request is this: that Govern-

ment should be moved to allow this higher scale of wages everywhere in the district, at least during the ensuing month. Uniformity is most desirable, and the necessity is the same everywhere, for prices are rising.—J. H. MASTER, *Collector of Bellary.*

Judging from the present physical condition of the labourers generally, I think that they are failing in health and falling off in strength. Many who were working with pick axes a few weeks ago are now unable to use them, and they complain of debility, which their reduced and decaying forms and hungry appearance clearly indicate. I have seen some, between thirty and thirty-five, so feeble as to require a support to walk, and I learnt that they were a few days back in good health and were working on relief works for wages, but are now succumbing to inadequate food and defective nourishment.

Every labourer honestly complains of low wages and earnestly solicits an increase; and their cry that they are ill-fed and are starving and becoming feeble day by day is loud and general in every gang that I have seen. From careful observation and frequent and varied tests I am convinced that the mere individual subsistence allowance that we now give them as wages is barely sufficient for a single meal in these hard, hot days when they have to work under the burning sun.—C. RAGHAVA ROW, *Deputy Collector.*

In continuation of my letter No. 218, of April 8, and with reference to your foot-note to G. O. No. 757, of March 1, I have the honour to report, for your information, that since my arrival at Kottoor, Kudligi taluk, I have almost every day watched the manner in which the large crowds of the relief labourers on the several works about this place are working. No less than 2,080 coolies have come under my observation, not mere inspection, and I must say that the result has not been encouraging.

The female coolies outnumber the male beyond all proportion, and the bulk of them are of low physique, many adults and broods of young children looking pale and lank. The grown-up women, though of middle age, and some of their infants strolling about the place, pass for miserable moving skeletons. The mothers complain that the ¼ anna allowed to each of the children is not enough to buy sufficient nourishment for it, the pittance paid to themselves scarcely sufficing to buy them a good day's meal. Considering therefore the amount of exhaustion resulting from exposure to the burning sun of April and May, and the discouraging indications of the process of wastage among the relief labourers, I would respectfully suggest a gradual increase in the present rate of wages, until such a time as we could detect a change for the better in their physique. In making this suggestion for your consideration I have not lost sight of the importance of the difference to the treasury that would result from having to 'make the increase in the rates to over a lakh and a quarter of the labourers in my division,' but I feel bound to do so at any risk in furtherance of the liberal policy of Government declared in the Government order under reference.—MURUGESEM MUDALIYAR, *Deputy Collector.*

The weavers, on the whole, of whom there were many on this road, appeared to be the feeblest people amongst the gangs. Guinea-worm was very prevalent, and all classes of these gangs showed the tendency to scurvy indicated by swollen, spongy, and bleeding gums.

I learnt from Mr. Oldham that it has not been the practice hitherto in this taluk to pay the coolies for Sundays. In the opinion of this gentleman and Capt. Hamilton, there has been a perceptible change for the worse in the condition of the gangs of late, so much so that Mr. Oldham had determined on raising the rates from the beginning of the week on his own responsibility. Mr. Oldham had come to this decision without any communication with me on the subject, and stated that considering the prices of food and the condition of the people, he deemed an increase of wage to be necessary. I left Adoui on Monday afternoon for Goondacul.

At Goondacul I met Mr. Glenny, the sub-collector of the district, and Lieutenant Wilson, on famine works, and as the Honourable Sir Richard Temple was expected to arrive during the night, the inspection of gangs at Goondacul was deferred until next morning.

Goondacul.—On the morning of the 24th instant I accompanied Sir Richard Temple in the inspection of a gang of about 1,000 coolies at Goondacul; of these people 180 were men, and the rest women and children.

Of the 180 men present, Sir Richard Temple selected 41 (or more than 22 per cent.) as unfit for work, and directed that they should be fed at the neighbouring relief house. In looking over the remainder, I noticed eighteen others, who, in my judgment, were out of condition and unfit for hard work, though equal perhaps to a slight exertion.

It is not a little remarkable that Dr. Harvey, the private surgeon to Sir Richard Temple, in his memorandum published in the *Gazette of India* of April 14, page 993, should have noticed, on February 22, that the Goondacul gangs were the best he had seen. The majority of the Goondacul people, he observes, 'belonged to a class above the lowest, and were almost without exception in very fine condition, looking as though they had undergone no suffering, nor ever missed a meal.'

With regard to the forty-one men selected by Sir Richard Temple as too weak for work, it was ascertained that twelve of them had recently come upon the works, and the remainder had been from two to five months employed in the gangs. It was certain, therefore, that twenty-nine of the number had been living for some time on the reduced wages, and as Dr. Harvey specially comments on the fine physique of the Goondacul gangs on February 22, it would seem to follow that two months of reduced wages had produced the deterioration observed and commented on by Sir Richard Temple on April 24.

The women and children in these gangs far outnumbered the men. A few women were selected by Sir Richard Temple as unfit for work, and sent to a relief house. I noticed that many of the women were thin and worn, and others anæmic, and I should have selected from fifteen to twenty per cent. of them as below their normal condition. The tendency to a cachetic condition of the gums was noticed in these gangs also.—DR. CORNISH.

In Government Order May 5, 1877, No. 1,648, it is laid down that care is to be taken that no able-bodied coolies are to be retained in the camp. In this district, where relief works are available for the demand of labour, a famine camp thus becomes a large hospital where men reduced by starvation are fed and brought to a proper condition to enable them to work, which accomplished, they are discharged.

The diet laid down in the Government Order referred to is literally a subsistence diet, one upon which existence might be held for a prolonged period, but certainly not one upon which persons reduced by starvation could be expected to improve. Indeed, the diet conveys a sufficient amount of carbonaceous and nitrogenous material, but it has no provision for the conveyance of many salts which are equally essential for the due maintenance of health, the chief of which may be noted as the common adjunct of sodic chloride. Fresh vegetables and fatty matters are also absent. Without the former amongst people already reduced below the standard of health, infallibly scorbutic symptoms will rapidly become added to those of starvation, and the camp will become decimated by the most intractable forms of dysentery and diarrhœa.

Doubtless in camps in the open district vegetable matters would be supplied by the natives themselves by finding edible roots, &c., but here, in the midst of a large city, the camp inhabitants naturally diffuse themselves around the bazaars imploring the additional necessaries to this diet.—*Surgeon* W. G. KING, *M.B.*

I made enquiries and questioned many of the people, but I saw and heard of no case of their eating leaves, and everyone said that he or she had been properly paid. I do not think that famine coolies in these parts, though they may give the head cooly or maistry the customary 'dustoori' in order to have their names entered upon the rolls, allow themselves to be defrauded of their wages. They are open-mouthed enough in their complaints, but I have found that when anything was said against the head coolies or maistries, it was generally either that they worked the people up to their allotted tasks, struck individuals off the roll for being constantly absent, or else refused to enter children in a class higher than they should be. Mr. Cox, who understands and speaks Telugu remarkably well, and who is very ready to hear and patient in investigating every complaint, no matter how petty, has not been able to find any cases of the coolies having been paid less than was due to them. I have not the slightest moral doubt, nor has he, that Government has been considerably defrauded as regards the number of children receiving 3 pies per diem. Some cases of this brought forward by the assistant famine officer, Mr. Horden, are now under investigation, but I fear, from what I saw, that nothing can be made of them from a magisterial point of view.

Having read with much interest the remarks made by Dr. Cornish in the various reports submitted by him to Government, I have been much struck with their correctness. The famine is evidently telling, and telling heavily, upon the old and very young. The former are, with very rare exceptions, becoming shrivelled, flabby, and haggard in appearance, and the girls and boys who have arrived at the point of puberty show, in their faces and limbs, all the signs of insufficient feeding. They are 'spindly,' their arms are thin and flabby, their legs are wanting in flesh, the knee-joints, in the case of the boys, and of such girls who, having tucked their clothes up to work, allowed of my seeing their knees, stand out like knobs, and the insides of the thighs are flattened and loose. The busts of the girls have not filled out, and the chests of the boys show the bones, and they mostly tie themselves tightly round the waist, producing an unnatural and puffy appearance of the abdomen. Their skins, instead of being of a healthy smooth brown, have a nasty yellowish cast, and are frequently dull in colour. The infant population, i.e., the sucking children, are very much reduced, in some cases almost skeletons; their arms are like sticks, their ribs show distinctly, and their buttocks are perfectly flat; their legs are like their arms. At Porumamilla, the larger part of the children in arms were in this state or verging upon it. The payment of three pies for these can do no good. This sum will not provide the mother with a sufficiently increased supply of food to find milk for her little one. The nursing women must either have a special and considerably increased allowance, or the infants must die. This is a point upon which I have not the slightest doubt. I have questioned several women as to the reason of their children being in the state that I have described, and the answer has invariably been 'I have little or nothing for it.' The truth of this was apparent enough.

The Board know that I am not a sensational writer. I am simply stating facts, and the correctness of these can be proved if Government will send the inspecting medical officer just appointed to this district to visit the northern portion of the Budwail taluk.—F. J. PRICE, *Acting Collector of Cuddapah.*

The falling off among these coolies and among those at Kodoor was plainly the result of continued payment at the lower rate (Scale 2), and the falling off has been rendered more rapid of late by the exhaustion of dry grains in the local markets. Nothing but rice is now obtainable, and much of this is very indifferent in quality. A strict watch is, however, now kept by the police to prevent the sale of any which appears to be absolutely unfit for food. Still, I believe some such is secretly sold. A few days ago the tahsildar seized five bags at Rajampet (my present camp) which were utterly unfit for food and almost rotten from exposure to wet.—R. S. BENSON.

Having on May 8, while inspecting the road from Sundupalli to Rayaveram, mustered and examined the coolies on it, I beg to report as follows on the condition of the people there. I counted 752 coolies altogether in 16 gangs; of these 58 were old and 168 weak; of the weak ones, several old.

I also observed about 70 young children. A few looked plump, but these were rare objects, most of the little ones being ill-fed; some of them looked pale and had that peevish look resulting from privation. One case in particular I made a note of:—A woman had three children, none of them being fit to work; she herself got 1 anna 4 pies a day, the children together 9 pies, making a total of 2 annas 1 pie a day. Rice was sold at Sundupalli shandy on the 7th at 4 seers per rupee; it was slightly cheaper the week before. With her daily income the woman could not have got quite half a seer, or a very small fraction over 20 ounces (3½ ollocks) given to an adult pauper in the relief camp, who gets extras besides; the woman and children, I need hardly remark, were half-starved. Even if the woman had got the higher rate of 1 anna 5 pies, her condition would hardly be better. This may be taken as an individual case, but I am certain there must be many families in the same condition. The wonder is that the relief camp has not a larger number in it than it has.

That these low rates are telling much upon the condition of the p ople is clear ; how much longer the coolies can hold out on them is a matter depending entirely on each individual's personal strength.— E. V. BEEBY.

Mr. Money tells me that some of his superintendents are measuring the same gangs at stated intervals, and that all agree that the coolies are falling off.—J. D. GRIBBLE.

Adverting to paragraph 6 of G. O. dated January 31 last, No. 329, Financial Department, I have the honour to report on the physical condition of the coolies employed on relief-works in this district during the week ending Saturday, May 5.

The special relief officer says : ' The people who came under my notice as labourers in this district on the reduced scale of wage are still falling off; and it will be unnecessary that I should furnish any further weekly report on this subject, as I am fully convinced, and no further experience can alter this conviction, that the reduced scale of wage is insufficient to provide the labourer with the necessary food to keep up his physical condition and at the same time do any work.'

The deputy collector in charge of the Saidapet taluk has observed no changes, but the officers in charge of relief works in the Trivellore taluk state that there has been a slight deterioration in the physical condition of the coolies owing to the insufficiency of the scale of wages, but partly to the excessive heat of the weather.—R. W. BARLOW, *Collector of Chingleput.*

On the morning of April 13 I visited some gangs of labourers employed in collecting material for the repair of the Gooty road, about six or seven miles out from Bellary. There have been, until recently, some 6,000 or 7,000 persons employed on this road. On the morning of my inspection I examined nearly 3,000 labourers and children.

Many changes have been going on in these gangs, and only the day before my visit about 500 were selected as able-bodied and requested to go to Nellore. Some of these, however, had not left the works, and have since been given the option of transferring their services to the new railway works in progress within the district.

From my note-book I see that we examined 964 men, 1,189 women, and 244 working boys and girls. From 300 to 400 nonworking children were also inspected.

Condition of the Men.—The men are generally spare of flesh, though naturally broad-chested, well-built, and muscular. Guineaworm was prevalent amongst them ; many were anæmic and out of condition, and had spongy gums, and pale creamy tongues were more frequently present than absent in all the men of the gangs. Out of the 964 men, 169 were noted as being feeble, emaciated, and out of condition, or about 17 per cent. of the whole. Some of these were old, as well as enfeebled by privation.

Women.—Of 1,189 women examined, 245, or 20 per cent. of the whole, were noted as in weak health and emaciated more than usual. The women of this part of the country are mostly tall and spare of flesh, and I hardly saw one really stout woman amongst them. Many of them, besides the 20 per cent. above noted as in a reduced condition, were pale, anæmic, and evidently unhealthy, as shown by the condition of their tongues and spongy unhealthy gums.

Children.—The working children, to the number of 244, were fairly well nourished, and I did not see many that were emaciated, but, looking at their gums and tongues, it was clear that their health was generally low; more than half of the children had spongy and discoloured gums.

The non-working children, as regards the elder ones, were pretty well taken care of, but the babies in arms, in considerable proportion, showed that they were slowly starving from defective breast-milk of the mothers.

The labourers on this road, Mr. Howe informed me, were fairly representative of the able-bodied gangs in the district.

I have already alluded to the prevalence amongst these gangs of some of the earliest symptoms of scurvy. 'Land scurvy' has been known to prevail in India over extensive tracts of country during seasons of scarcity and famine. The opportunities, however, for studying the symptoms and nature of the disease of late years have not been taken advantage of, and very little is known about it. It would seem to be due, as in the case of sea scurvy, to some extent to the absence of fresh vegetables and acid vegetable juices and fruits in the diet of the people. The seasons that are noted for scanty production of grain and cereals are remarkable also for the dearth of fruits and green vegetables, which in ordinary seasons enter so largely into the dietary of the people. To what extent the population have undergone privation in this particular we shall never know, but a significant fact within my own experience may not be out of place in illustration. In travelling from Vellore to Cuddapah across country I was unable to buy a lime in any village or town bazaar that I passed through. Now as in ordinary times lime juice is used by every native in the preparation of his curry, it must be evident that the condition of the people in regard to anti-scorbutic fruits and vegetables must have changed very much for the worse.—DR. CORNISH.

Times of India, March 12, 1877.

. . . . What has been done in the Bombay Presidency in this way, where also this reduction, which is likely to prove so costly, was introduced as an experiment? Literally nothing. A few days after the introduction of the new scale we had just that kind of cheerful assertion from Dr. Hewlett about the ' remarkably good health ' of the labourer which the compassionate physician gives on leaving the room of a dying patient. As the people in the works sleep on the roadside or in pits, have no shelter by day or night, are clothed in rags, and live, but only the strongest of them, on 16 oz. of grain per diem, it was so difficult to see why they should be remarkably healthy, that Dr. Hewlett's assertions did as little harm as good. But for six weeks he has been strangely silent, and we have been afforded no mortuary returns save those for cholera.

We have now shown what Dr. Cornish, the adviser of the Madras Government on public health questions, thinks of the new scale of famine relief. Dr. Hewlett, the adviser of the Bombay Government, is on a journey we know; peradventure he sleepeth, with easy and approving dreams of the new policy, and for anything like a professional opinion we have no one else to look to but Dr. Weir, health officer of the city, not the Presidency. According to the communication from Dr. Weir, read at the town council meeting, the condition of the city promises to be bad enough, simply on account of the exodus from the famine-stricken districts which it were folly not to attribute to the reduction of wages. So long as the old daily wage of two annas was maintained in the districts, there was no influx into Bombay, which is too far away from the famine to be a goal for any but men seeking for food in real earnest. Now, Dr. Weir says, there are 10,000 of those unfortunate people who have arrived from Poona and Sholapur, ' and an increasing number are coming in every day.' Sir Frank Souter, the man of all others in a position to speak, said he ' was certain that people were flocking in from all parts, and considered their condition should be promptly looked to.' Dr. Blaney, whose long experience has given him a wide knowledge of the Bombay poor, declared the evil to be quite as serious as Dr. Weir reported. ' The increase of mortality was not ten or twelve per cent., but already fifty, sixty, or seventy per cent. among the Bombay poor.' Colonel Hancock also bore testimony that ' the numbers were increasing every day.' Dr. Weir's account of the condition of the famine-stricken people is most pitiable, and is singularly in accord with that of Dr. Cornish in Madras :—' Exhausted by travel, and without hope, they are smitten by every breath of disease, and even now the mortality from fever amongst them has advanced the usual death-rate of this city to an apparently alarming height. . . . Fever is the disease most fatal, and the unusual atmospheric conditions have been strangely favourable to its development. Famine-stricken people, overwhelmed by despair, are little capable of resisting the chills of this season; and I cannot conceal from myself that the damp of the monsoon will prove terribly fatal and destructive to those now seeking refuge in this city.'

The only witnesses to be cited on the other side, so far as the Presidency of Madras is concerned, are Surgeon-Major S. C. Townsend, officiating sanitary commissioner with the Government of India, and Mr. Lyon, of Bombay. The former visited the people on relief works near railway stations and inspected them; the latter dealt with the question mainly from a theoretical point of view.[1] Sir Richard Temple wrote a covering minute to be published with Dr. Townsend's report. In that minute he pointed out that the views of the Sanitary Commissioner of the Government of India on this important matter coincided with his own, which had been formed after inspecting nearly 200,000 people under relief in Southern India. Sir Richard, therefore, recommended the adoption of the opinion of Dr. Townsend, to the effect that there were not as yet any sufficient grounds whatever for any general raising of the relief wage rates in the Madras Presidency.

Dr. Townsend, in his report, recapitulates at length the history of the various rations tried in the Madras Presidency, and proceeds:—

The point in question cannot, in my opinion, be decided on physiological grounds. It is true that some years ago the doctrine on the subject was, that muscular exertion entailed waste of muscular tissue, and that in order to compensate this waste, food containing nitrogenous principles must be supplied in proportion to the labour undergone; but later investigations have, I believe, tended greatly to modify

[1] I am informed that Mr. Lyon never saw a famine cooly in his life.

this teaching, and certainly at the present time there is no theory on the subject so generally accepted or founded on data so incontrovertible that an economic question involving the expenditure of large sums of public money can be decided by it.

The question of the sufficiency or otherwise of any scale of diet can only be decided by observation of its effect on individuals and on masses of people, and observations of this kind in a time of scarcity like the present, if conducted impartially and without bias towards theories, cannot fail to contribute facts bearing on the question of the quantity of food of different kinds that is necessary to support the human system under certain conditions, which would be of great value, from a scientific point of view, as well as for guidance in the conduct of measures of relief in future times. I have no knowledge of the population of this Presidency, but considerable experience in other provinces leads me to believe that at all times signs of mal-nutrition are more or less visible among the power classes of the populations of India.[1] A loose and shrivelled skin, a pale and anæmic aspect, and emaciation will certainly follow privation and insufficient food ; but the same appearances may arise from defective nutrition resulting from constitutional debility or disease. Again, when famine presses hard on the population, diminutive and emaciated infants become numerous, and form one of the most painful evidences of the prevailing distress ; but in the best of times, if any large portion of the poorer classes were subjected to inspection, the number of these distressing objects would be considerable. Our statistics show that the rate of mortality of infants among the population of this country is as high or even higher than in the manufacturing districts of England, and it is more than probable that the number of women who are unable to nourish their infants is as numerous here as in other countries, while it is not the habit of the mothers to supplement their own defective supply by other food. In short, the scale of living among the population of this country is at all times low. Diseases resulting from mal-nutrition are common, and the rate of mortality compared with that of other countries is very high ; therefore when inspecting masses of people collected from the poorer classes with the view of estimating the effects of abnormal scarcity among them, a very large allowance must be made for what may be called permanent poverty, and which it is beyond the power of Government to remove.

The want of accurate information as to the extent to which the people on the relief works possess sources of support other than the

---

[1] To this the pertinent remark was made, ' But the " poorer classes of the populations of India " don't die at the rate of 25 per cent. every year.'

daily wage given them, is another obstacle in the way of forming a correct estimate of the sufficiency or otherwise of that wage to maintain them in fair condition. Where the gangs are encamped on works away from their homes, and where the men are equal to or outnumber the women, it is probable that the majority are dependent solely on the wages they earn; but when the works are near the larger towns and the gangs are composed to a very large extent of women and children, it may be assumed that the men are earning wages in some form elsewhere, and that the earnings of the women and children are simply accessory to the ordinary means of support. On the other hand, enquiry will often elicit the fact that individuals on the works are supporting with their earnings a child or relation at home besides themselves.

But notwithstanding these difficulties, it is possible by a careful scrutiny of large gangs of people in different localities, combined with information derived on the spot from the officers who have superintended the relief measures from the commencement, and have watched the condition of the people, to arrive at a fair estimate of the extent to which the people have suffered and are suffering from the prevailing scarcity of labour and dearness of food, and how far the measures adopted for their relief have proved successful.

The appended notes give the details concerning the several gangs that I have inspected in the course of my tour. I will here only direct attention to the points more particularly bearing on the question of the sufficiency of the reduced rate of wage. The first bodies of relief labourers that I inspected were at Sholapur in the Bombay Presidency. Here there were two bodies of labourers. A large body of upwards of 3,000 employed under the Public Works Department, and performing about half the task ordinarily exacted from able-bodied labourers. The men were receiving 1¾ annas, the women 1¼, and the children ¾ of an anna. Here there was no question as to the sufficiency of the food. Men, women, and children appeared in good condition, and there was no doubt on the part of the officers superintending the works that the wage was quite sufficient for the support of the labourers in health.

The other body of labourers was employed under the Civil authorities, and numbered about 300. A large proportion of them were above middle age, and they had come on the works in January in an enfeebled state. Some of these people had improved since they came on the works, but as a body they were much lower in condition than the gangs under the Public Works Department. The wage given was in both instances the same, with the exception that the men employed on the Civil works received only 1½ annas instead of 1¾;

in neither case was payment given for Sundays when no work was done. The lower condition of the Civil gangs was no doubt due chiefly to the circumstance that they had become more reduced before coming on the works. The average age of the adults was greater, and it is probable that at the best of times they were below the average in physique.

At Adoni I inspected nearly 13,000 relief labourers, the greater majority of whom had been on the reduced rate of wage for above a month. The task-work performed was very light, not more than $\frac{1}{10}$ of the task exacted from a coolie in ordinary times. The largest gangs employed on the Yemmogamir road were composed chiefly of inhabitants of the town of Adoni; the other gang contained chiefly people belonging to the agricultural population. As a rule, all these people were in fair condition, and in the opinion of the relief officer they had not deteriorated since the reduced rate of wage had been in force. There were of course exceptions, and weakly and feeble people were here and there picked out; but these exceptions consisted of persons who had never been in good health and condition, or it was found on enquiry that the individuals shared their wages with a child or other relative.

At Bellary I inspected upwards of 10,000 relief labourers. At the Hiriyal road, where a large body of 7,500 was employed, the men considerably outnumbered the women. Task-work was exacted, and if the task was not complete, less wage was given, and the great majority were receiving less than the reduced rate. There was, however, no sickness among them. The number whose appearance called for enquiry was very small, and the impoverished appearance of the individuals lighted on was usually accounted for in much the same way as at Adoni. The relief officer stated that these gangs had improved greatly in appearance since the works were established, and they had certainly not fallen off since the reduced rate of wage had come into force.

In Cuddapah I inspected two bodies of labourers : one numbering 590, employed close to the town and station, consisted chiefly of the inhabitants of the town, and the women greatly outnumbered the men ; and several of these women were the wives of syces and other servants of Europeans. The daily task exacted was light, and was commonly completed. In my opinion these people were in appearance little, if at all, below the standard of health common in the town populations of this country. Some were, no doubt, thin and anæmic, but the number was small, and in the majority of these cases the individuals had only lately come on the works or had been suffering from fever. The other gang, 800 strong, that I inspected in Cuddapah,

Q 2

was composed chiefly of the agricultural population belonging to the surrounding villages. Here also the women generally outnumbered the men, who were said to find work elsewhere. The general appearance of these people was very good. A very large number of the men and women were as stout and healthy-looking as they could be in the best of times; here and there thin and weakly persons were observed, but on enquiry it did not appear that their weak condition was attributable to want of food. The relief officer stated that when the people received the higher rate of wages they did not spend more in food than they do now, but saved the difference, and they have not deteriorated in condition since the wage was reduced.

At Vellore, North Arcot district, I inspected altogether about 3,000 people : 1,120 employed and 400 applicants for employment in the construction of an embankment on the Palaar river may be considered as samples of the population who have not hitherto been on relief, for those employed had been collected, some for about a fortnight, others for not more than a few days. The proportion of men employed here was small, being only 7 men to 28 women and children, and a very large proportion of the men were old or elderly. The task exacted here is 75 per cent. of the ordinary Public Works Department rates, and the people are paid at the following rates :—

Men   .   .   .   . 1 anna 11 pie.
Women .   .   .   . 1 anna 5 pie.
Children .   .   .   . 1 anna.

This is higher than the reduced rate given in other districts, and seven days' payment is given for six days' work. The elderly men were most of them of spare habit, but they were fairly muscular and their appearance healthy. The younger men were for the most part robust and in good condition. At the Sooriaghunta tank 1,600 people are employed, and here the proportion of men is very small, being only 3 to 35 women and children. This small proportion of men on the works is attributable to the circumstance that in this part of the country agricultural operations and other means of employment are not suspended to the same extent as in the Ceded districts, and that the able-bodied men are for the most part employed in the occupations that engage them in ordinary seasons ; but at the present prices of food their earnings do not suffice to maintain their families, and women who in ordinary times would not undertake coolie labour are on this account induced to come and earn additional means of subsistence on works which are conveniently near their homes. The gangs at the Sooria tank were first formed on November 24. From February 19 to March 25 they were on the reduced rate, but it has now been again raised to the same rate as on the Palaar embankment because the people did heavier tasks. As a body, these people were in fair condition, and, so far as I was able to ascertain, did not deteriorate or show signs of weakness during the five or six weeks that they were on the reduced rate of wages.

At the Vellore Relief-house 700 people who are incapable of work are fed. The proportion of men and women is about equal. Each adult male receives daily 1 lb. of dry rice cooked; 10 oz. of this is given at 10 o'clock and the remainder in the evening. To the evening meal is added half an ounce of dâl mixed with vegetable and condiments in the form of curry. In many of these people the effects of famine are very evident, particularly among a number of people who have come in from the Kalastri zemindari, but they are improving on the food now given them.

Taking the evidence that has come before me in the course of my tour, I can arrive at no other conclusion than that the rate to which the wage of the relief-labourers was reduced on the recommendation of Sir Richard Temple is sufficient to support them in fair condition, provided that care is taken that the individual recipient is the only person who is supported on it. And I see no reason why the wage should be raised unless an equivalent amount of work is performed.

Competent authorities in Madras did not scruple to express their dissatisfaction with Dr. Townsend's report, which was declared to be untrustworthy. He was urged not to leave the Madras Presidency without seeing something of the misery of the people in the camps and relief-houses, but he returned to Simla without seeing anything but gangs of coolies on works in various districts near the railway, and on this hurried inspection made his report.

Surgeon-Major Lyon, F.C.S., chemical analyser to the Bombay Government, prepared a memorandum founded on observations of prisoners in the Bombay House of Correction. To it were appended a large number of tables dealing with analyses of foods and kindred subjects. Two of these tables were as follows:—

TABLE IV.—DAILY NITROGEN AND CARBON OF EUROPEAN DIETARIES.

	Nitrogen Grains Daily	Carbon Grains Daily
1. Standard diet (Moleschott)	316·5	4,862
2. ,, (Parkes, Pavy, Church) .	300	4,850
3. Mean for ordinary labour (Letheby) . .	307	5,688
4. Hard-working labourers (Playfair) . .	389	6,086
5. Active labourers ,, . .	373	4,473
6. Active labourers, Royal Engineers (Playfair)	350	6,504
7. Moderate exercise (Playfair) . . .	291	5,094
8. English soldier, Home service (Playfair) .	293	5,164
9. ,, ,, (Parkes) .	266	4,718
English Government Convict Establishments.		
10. (*a.*) Hard labour	281	5,140
11. (*b.*) Industrial employment . .	256	4,766
12. (*c.*) Light labour	242	4,520
13. Mean of English, Scotch, Welsh, and Irish } farm labourers (E. Smith) . . }	300	6,478
14. English farm labourers, lowest of the four } (E. Smith) . . . . . }	228	5,810
15. Low-fed operatives average (E. Smith) .	214	4,881
16. Bare sustenance diet (E. Smith) . .	200	4,300
17. ,, ,, (Letheby) . . .	181	3,888
18. ,, ,, (Playfair) . . .	161	3,103

Notes to Table IV.

1. For a male European adult of average height and weight (5 feet 6 inches to 5 feet 10 inches, and 140 to 160 lbs.), in moderate work.

2. Average weight (154 lbs., Church) and moderate work.

3. Mean calculated from researches of various physiologists for adult males.

5. Soldiers during war.

6. Calculated from amount of food consumed by 495 men of the Royal Engineers at work at Chatham.

7. Mean of English, French, Austrian, and Prussian soldiers during peace.

16. Average representing the daily diet of an adult man during periods of idleness.

17. Mean calculated from researches of various physiologists, representing the amount required by an adult man during idleness.

18. Mean of diet of needle-women in London, certain prison dietaries, common dietary for convalescents, Edinburgh Infirmary, average diet during cotton famine of 1862 in Lancashire.

Three diet scales which are given (Tables V. to IX.) are calculated as follows:—

Diet Scale No. 1.—This is the Bombay House of Correction diet ([*a.*] Tables I. and III.) raised and lowered in proportion to weight. The average weight of the prisoners on admission into the House of Correction being

105 lbs., nitrogen 201·6 grains, carbon 4,011 grains (the value in nitrogen and carbon of the House of Correction diet) is placed opposite the weight, 105 lbs. For every 5 lbs. in weight over or under 105 lbs. $\frac{1}{21}$ of these quantities of nitrogen or carbon is added or deducted as the case may be. It will be observed that at weight 150 lbs., the quantities of nitrogen and carbon become respectively 288 and 5,730 grains. At 150 lbs., therefore, the nitrogen is very slightly above the nitrogen of the English convict hard labour diet (Table IV., 10), viz., 281 grains; the carbon, however, is considerably higher than the carbon of the English convict hard labour diet, viz., 5,730 as compared with 5,140 grains, or 11·47 per cent. higher. Letheby's mean estimate for ordinary labour (Table IV., 3), viz., nitrogen 307 grains, carbon, 5,688 grains, comes as regards carbon very near diet scale No. 1, at weight 150 lbs. The quantity of nitrogen in Letheby's estimate, however, is higher, viz., 307, as compared with 288 grains.

Diet Scale No. 2.—This is (diet scale No. 1) lowered in the same proportion as English convict light labour diet (Table IV., 12) is lower than English convict hard labour diet, i.e., as 281 is to 242 for the nitrogen, and as 5,140 is to 4,250 for the carbon. Lowered in this proportion, the quantities become—

At 105 lbs., nitrogen 173·6 grains, carbon 3,528 grains.
At 150 lbs., ,, 248·0 ,, ,, 5,039 ,,

At 105 lbs., therefore, diet scale No. 2 is very similar in value to the non-labour diet of the Common Jail, Bombay (Table III. [*d.*]), and somewhat better than the Oudh Jails non-labour diet (Table III. [*f.*]) at 150 lbs. Diet scale No. 2 is better than the average diet of low-fed English operatives, as estimated by Edwin Smith (Table IV., 15); it is, of course, also better than the light labour diet in English convict establishments in the same proportion that diet scale No. 1 is better than the hard labour diet at the same establishments.

Diet Scale No. 3.—This is calculated as follows:—Of the three estimates for bare sustenance diet the mean of the two highest (Edwin Smith's and Letheby's Table IV., 16 and 17) is nitrogen 190·5, carbon 4,094 grains; both these estimates are for average adult males. Playfair's estimate (Table IV., 18), which is considerably lower than the other two, is excluded, as it does not wholly refer to adult males. Raising this mean in the same proportion as diet scale No. 1 at 150 lbs. exceeds English convict hard labour diet, the figures become nitrogen 195·3 grains, carbon 4,564 grains. These quantities placed opposite weight 150 lbs. form the foundation of diet scale No. 3. For the other weights shown in the table, the quantities are proportionally reduced. Comparing diet scale No. 3 with Playfair's estimate for bare sustenance (Table IV., 18), it will be seen that the nitrogen of the scale does not run below Playfair's estimate until after weight 125 lbs. is reached, and, similarly, it is only when the weight runs below 105 lbs. that the amount of carbon becomes lower than that given in Playfair's estimate.

TABLE V.—SHOWING THE QUANTITY OF NITROGEN AND CARBON RE-
QUIRED DAILY ON EACH OF THREE SCALES, VIZ. :—

Scale 1.—A labour scale, the Bombay House of Correction diet raised and
lowered in proportion to weight.

Scale 2. A light labour scale, scale No. I reduced in the same proportion
that English convict light labour diet bears to English convict
hard labour diet.

Scale 3. A bare sustenance scale, scale No. 1 reduced in same proportion that
a mean bare sustenance estimate for Europeans (mean of 16 and
17, Table IV.) bears to English convict hard labour diet.

Weight—lbs.	SCALE NO. 1, DAILY		SCALE NO. 2, DAILY		SCALE NO. 3, DAILY	
	Nitrogen grains	Carbon grains	Nitrogen grains	Carbon grains	Nitrogen grains.	Carbon grains.
80 . .	153·6	3,065	132·3	2,688	104·2	2,434
85 . .	163·2	3,247	140·5	2,856	110·7	2,586
90 . .	172·8	3,438	148·8	3,024	117·2	2,739
95 . .	182·4	3,629	157·0	3,192	123·7	2,891
100 . .	192·0	3,820	165·3	3,360	130·2	3,043
105 . .	201·6	4,011	173·6	3,528	136·7	3,195
110 . .	211·2	4,202	181·9	3,696	143·2	3,347
115 . .	220·8	4,393	190·2	3,864	149·7	3,499
120 . .	230·4	4,584	198·4	4,032	156·3	3,652
125 . .	240·0	4,775	206·7	4,200	162·8	3,804
130 . .	249·6	4,966	210·9	4,368	169·3	3,956
135 . .	259·2	5,157	223·2	4,536	175·8	4,108
140 . .	268·8	5,348	231·5	4,704	182·3	4,260
145 . .	278·4	5,539	239·8	4,872	188·8	4,412
150 . .	288·0	5,730	248·0	5,039	195·3	4,564

TABLE VI.—SHOWING THE TOTAL QUANTITIES OF MIXED CEREALS
AND PULSE WHICH, PLUS HALF AN OUNCE OF FAT, ARE EQUIVA-
LENT TO THE QUANTITIES OF NITROGEN AND CARBON SHOWN IN
EACH OF THE THREE SCALES OF TABLE V.

Weight—lbs.	Scale No. 1, ounces daily	Scale No. 2, ounces daily	Scale No. 3, ounces daily
80	16·98	14·81	13·32
85	18·10	15·80	14·21
90	19·23	16·79	15·11
95	20·35	17·78	16·00
100	21·48	18·77	16·90
105	22·60	19·76	17·79
110	23·72	20·74	18·69
115	24·85	21·73	19·58
120	25·97	22·72	20·48
125	27·10	23·70	21·37
130	28·22	24·69	22·27
135	29·35	25·68	23·16
140	30·47	26·66	24·06
145	31·59	27·65	24·95
150	32·71	28·64	25·85

Three tables which followed, viz., Tables VII., VIII., and IX., show in what proportions each of the eight cereals—rice, barley, jowari, common millet, bajri, maize, oats, and wheat—must respectively be mixed with pulse in order to furnish the quantities of nitrogen and carbon shown on each of the three scales of Table V.

Dr. Cornish's reply to Mr. Lyon was in his best vein, and cannot be passed over in a summary of the controversy. The Sanitary Commissioner craved the permission of his Grace in Council briefly to state that, in his opinion, the data of Surgeon-Major Lyon's paper did not justify the conclusion which Sir Richard Temple had formed on it, viz., that ' a ration based on a pound of grain is sufficient for the sustenance of persons not performing severe labour.' He could not find any statement in Mr. Lyon's paper in which he expressed such an opinion in words, although a casual reader might perhaps draw some such conclusion from his figures.

' In all the scales of diet drawn by Surgeon-Major Lyon ' (Dr. Cornish continues) ' he has proceeded on the assumption that " there is no theoretical objection to the proposition that the quantity of food required by adults is proportionable to their weight, provided of course always that the quantity of work expected from them is likewise proportioned to their weight." This method of procedure is in my opinion extremely fallacious, and I shall briefly show why any scale of diet drawn up in furtherance of this view must be received with the greatest caution.

' Surgeon-Major Lyon argues that a human being requires food in exact proportion to his weight, and he has furnished tables showing, according to this theory, the quantity of nitrogenous and carboniferous food necessary for the sustenance of persons weighing from 80 to 150 lbs. under the different conditions of hard labour, light labour, and complete rest.

' If there was any relation between the weight of an individual and his capacity for assimilating food and effecting work requiring expenditure of force, there might be some show of reason for laying down a principle that men require food in proportion to their weight. But we know as a fact that there is no such correspondence—that in a very considerable number of persons the power to work diminishes as the body increases in weight, notably in those who with increasing years tend to develop fat instead of muscle.

'The every-day experience of the most superficial observer must afford instances of persons of large appetite who never get fat, and of persons who are not large eaters who lay on an amount of flesh that becomes a serious burden and inconvenience to them; and with regard to these persons it is apparently seriously proposed by the chemical analyser to the Government of Bombay that they should be fed, the thin and the stout alike, in proportion to their weight. The mere statement of the proposition in this form is sufficient to show that, without being hedged in by important qualifications, the theory cannot be applied in practical dietetics.[1]

'The theory that work can be performed in proportion to weight is still more wide of the field of practical observation. According to this theory "The Claimant," who weighed 22 stone on going to jail, was then more fit to endure hard labour than he was six months after, when he had lost one-fourth of his weight; and athletes, instead of striving to keep their weight down, ought according to this theory to take means to lay on extra flesh. There is in fact no relation between the ability and capacity for labour and mere weight of body, as Mr. Lyon would seem to suggest.

'There are so many things more important than weight of body

[1] The physiological needs of men whose tendency it is to clothe themselves with flesh, and of those who remain thin and spare in spite of all the food they consume, are essentially different. The two types and their personal characteristics have been well defined by Shakespeare, who makes Julius Cæsar say to Mark Antony:

> *Cæs.* Let me have men about me that are fat;
> Sleek-headed men, and such as sleep o' nights.
> Yond' Cassius has a lean and hungry look,
> He thinks too much; such men are dangerous.
> *Ant.* Fear him not Cæsar, he's not dangerous!
> * * * *
> *Cæs.* Would he were fatter! * *
> I do not know the man I should avoid
> So soon as that spare Cassius. He reads much;
> He is a great observer, and he looks
> Quite through the deeds of men: he loves no plays
> As thou dost, Antony! he hears no music!
> Seldom he smiles, and smiles in such a sort,
> As if he mocked himself, and scorned his spirit
> That could be moved to smile at anything.
> Such men as he be never at heart's ease,
> Whiles they behold a greater than themselves,
> And therefore are they very dangerous.

—W. R. C.

bearing on the necessity for food that it is surprising to find a chemist in these days laying so much stress on *weight* as the principal factor in determining the quantities of food necessary for health and strength. One might think that questions connected with the idiosyncrasies of the individual, his age, race, temperament, habit of body, slowness or rapidity of vital changes, were to be set aside as of no value in comparison with a theory that the body needs sustenance in proportion to its bulk. I suppose Mr. Lyon would admit that a very different amount of nutriment is needed for a spare man of large frame and without fat and another of equal weight, but whose size depended on an abnormal deposition of fat in his tissues; yet this weight-theory makes no distinction between the requirements of the two.

'Mr. Lyon has taken 150 lbs. as the average weight of male Europeans, and 105 lbs. as the average weight of natives of India. According to Sir R. Christison's experiments in Perthshire, the average weight of Scotchmen was 140 lbs., and from some experimental measurements and weighings made of various castes by Dr. John Shortt in Madras some years ago, he found that the average weight of male adults of the fishermen, Boyas, and other labouring castes, was about 120 lbs., and of certain other castes from 114 to 118 lbs. It would seem, therefore, that as regards the classes of persons suffering from famine in this part of India, there is not that great difference in weight and bulk of the people as a whole which would justify a very marked reduction of food in comparison with European diets.

'The argument in regard to food and average weight and bulk of the body must not be pushed too far. With certain limitations it must be admitted as useful in the construction of dietaries, but after all the facts of most importance are (1) the habits of the people themselves in the choice of food, its nature and amount; and (2) the daily waste which the body suffers from vital changes. Observations on the former head are sufficiently accurate, but in India we have never had any scientific determination of the daily waste of the body under strictly defined conditions of diet and labour. The subject is so important that I hope some of our scientific officers who have leisure and means of observation will take it up, and let us know if there be any truth in Sir Richard Temple's surmise that natives of India excrete less nitrogen in proportion to weight, food, and exercise than the European races do.

'I observe that Surgeon-Major Lyon bases his table of diets on the experience of the Bombay House of Correction, where it is stated that the prisoners on hard labour gained in weight on the average 1 lb. 10¼ oz. each while existing on the scale of food for labouring prisoners. I admit that the increase or decrease in weight of the people subjected to a dietary with certain reservations and limitations affords indications of value regarding the sufficiency of the food, but the weight record alone is only a portion of the evidence necessary. Surgeon-Major Lyon says nothing about the sickness and mortality of the prisoners in the Bombay House of Correction. It would be essential to know to what extent they suffered from bowel-disorders, anæmia, scurvy, and other diseases of innutrition, as well as the general rate of mortality, before coming to the conclusion that the hard labour scale of diet was actually sufficient to keep the people in ordinary health. As regards the proposed diets, for those on light labour and those doing nothing at all, there appears to be no practical evidence whatever to prove their sufficiency or insufficiency ; and all that can be said of such scales is that they are based on a theory which in some respects has been shown to be fallacious.

'As a matter of fact, and excluding all theory whatever, we have ascertained in certain Madras jails that where punishment by restrictions in food, so as to reduce the daily amount of nitrogen to much less than 200 grains, has been persevered in for any length of time, there has been loss of strength, loss of· health, and sacrifice of life, and this knowledge would make me very sceptical as to the sufficiency of a "bare subsistence" diet, containing only 136·7 grains of nitrogen, such as Mr. Lyon now proposes. In his table of "Food Equivalents,' published a few years ago, I observe that Mr. Lyon was more liberal in his views, for he there speaks of 200 grains of nitrogen and 3,070 grains of carbon as "almost a starvation diet." Certainly without the most cautious experimental tests, a dietary like the No. 3 Scale of Mr. Lyon would never commend itself to those practically acquainted with the subject of the connection of food with vital force, and based as it is on mere theory, I think it is to be regretted that a subsistence ration, ranging in nitrogen from 104·2 to 195·3 grains according to the weight of the individual was ever seriously put forward as a practical guide for those dealing with famine relief.

'There is one other point requiring a cursory notice. Mr. Lyon proposes to eke out the deficient nitrogen of various cereal grains by the addition of pulse, so as to make the total nitrogen of the food equivalent to the needs of the body, as reckoned by the weight theory. To take for instance the case of an obese native merchant, accustomed to feed on rice, and sentenced to hard labour. His daily diet would be made up of 21 ounces of rice and 9·55 oz. of gram or dhall. In all probability he would be unused to the latter food, and certainly under no circumstances could he digest and assimilate the nutriment contained in 9·55 ounces of that grain in the course of 24 hours. If he failed to digest the dhall, the nitrogenous principles of it could in no way assist in the nutrition of the body. In these proposed dietaries Mr. Lyon has in fact omitted the very necessary caution enjoined in his former paper on "Food Equivalents." "Regard should always be paid to the relative proportions in which, by custom or habit, articles of food are consumed by a population. This often indicates a limit of digestibility which ought not to be greatly exceeded."

'The present period of famine is presenting many opportunities for the study of those conditions of the body induced by privation of food; and the more this subject is considered, the more important does it become that we should follow only sound and true principles in dealing with questions connected with the food of a community.

'A careful study of the condition of the people who have been subjected to slow starvation shows that there is a point in the downward progress of such cases from which there is no possible return to health and strength. Food of the most nutritious character, and in the greatest profusion, is then powerless to save life. Chemical theories as to the composition of food do not in the least help us to explain why people should die with an abundance of nutritious food within reach; but if we carefully examine the bodies of those who have died of this form of starvation, we shall find that the delicate structures engaged in the assimilation of nutriment from food have wasted (owing probably to insufficient use) and undergone degenerative changes, so as to unfit them for their peculiar office. It has been my painful duty to observe not one or two but many thousands of such cases within the last few months, and I need not say that the contemplation of the causes leading to these slow but almost certainly fatal changes in the assimilative structures of the human body lead me to look with very grave suspicion upon all proposals for "bare subsistence" dietaries, and especially when such proposals are known to be out of harmony with the natural habits and customs of the people to whom they are proposed to be applied.

'This is not the time nor the occasion to review the practical effects of Sir Richard Temple's experiment in reducing the famine-wages of the people to the basis of one pound of grain; but this much may be stated, that the recent experience of nearly every famine officer who has observed the practical effects of the reduced wages has led him to believe and publicly record his opinion that the subsistence scale of wages was perilously low; while as regards our destitute poor in relief-camps we have had too abundant evidence of the fact that a more liberal scale of food than that purchasable for a famine relief wage is inadequate to restore health or to arrest decay.'

All the evidence summarised in the foregoing pages, and much more of a similar kind, was before the Madras Government. Public opinion had expressed itself very strongly against a continuance of the lower ration; the Government of India had decided to leave the matter in the hands of the local authorities, the Secretary of State telegraphed approval of whatever action they might take, and eventually, on May 22, it was decided to issue the following order:—

'The attention of Government having been closely given to the subject of the sufficiency of the scale of wages established by G. O. of January 31, 1877, No. 329, Financial Department, and the weight of the direct evidence being decidedly adverse to the continued maintenance of the lower rate which evidently has only very limited operation in Bombay, if any, and which the Mysore authorities have never introduced, his Grace the Governor in Council resolves to direct that the No. 1 rate of wage in the above scale be made of general application to all famine works, the task to be exacted being not less than 50 per cent. of a full task estimated according to the physical capacity of the individual labourer in his normal condition, and with reference to the circumstances of the work, such as nature and condition of the soil, proximity of water both for work and drinking purposes, accessibility of site from lodging place, &c.

'The Government consider that labourers who are unable to perform this amount of task should not be in the labour gangs at all, but should be on specially light work or in a relief-camp until strong enough for effective labour.

'All nursing mothers employed on works will be paid as adult males, and all working boys and girls above 12 years of age will be classed as adults.

'All children of labourers under 7 years of age will be excluded from works, but allowed a quarter anna daily subsistence allowance.

'The full rate of wage will be paid for Sunday, but no task will be exacted for that day.

'Wages should be disbursed not less frequently than once in three days.

'Piece-work at ordinary district rates and petty contract work, when the labourers associate themselves in family or village gangs under proper and, as far as possible, under professional supervision, should be encouraged as much as possible ; but the system of large contracts by outsiders for famine works is disapproved.

'The Governor in Council relies on the collectors to give the fullest and most speedy publication to these orders, so as to allow of their being brought into operation with the least possible delay. They will be telegraphed in abstract to all collectors.'

In August the Bombay Government had before it a mass of evidence directly contrary to that furnished by the officials in Madras. It was as follows:—

Camp Dhond, July 7, 1877.

In reply to your No. 4,664, dated July 6, I have the honour to report on the working of the civil agency rates in the Ahmednagar district.

When they came into force last January, I was co-operating with Mr. Spry, and made the first civil agency payment on the Nagar-Sheogaon road. The immediate result was great discontent, some violent talking, and a very general desertion of the work. There was a similar result in Rahuri taluk about the beginning of February.

I have since seen the working of civil agency rates on the railway and in the Shrigonda taluk. The civil agency gang on the railway, which was under me for a long time, was composed of those really unable to do hard work : they got on very fairly, and I did not observe any deterioration in their condition.

On the Mandavgaon road the coolies kept very well on civil agency rates, but they did very little work. Where the better class of people engaged in work, such as cleaning out of wells, I found civil agency rates had the effect of clearing them off very quickly.

I am of opinion that the introduction of civil agency rates in contradistinction to public works rates has been most beneficial, and has saved Government a large sum of money, for civil agency rates afford only a bare subsistence, while public works rates allow a small margin ; hence idlers, who came on the works to make money, found their hopes frustrated by the payment of civil agency rates.—R. E. CANDY, *First Assistant Collector.*

Ahmednagar, July 12, 1877.

In reply to your No. 4,664, of the 6th instant, I have the honour to state that the labourers under civil agency in the taluks under my charge have continued in good health and condition on the lower rate of wages, and that they appeared to get sufficient to eat.

I think it, however, very probable that the majority of them either had some small private means, or received additional help from their co-villagers. Women with small children were certainly better off than those who had none, for the additional quarter anna per head was more than sufficient for the cost of their food.

I think the reduction in the rate of wages was felt most by individual men and women without families, though beyond doubt large numbers of such individuals have managed to keep their health and perform a little work.—T. S. HAMILTON, *Second Assistant Collector.*

About the working of the civil agency rates :—During the time that the rates have been in force, I have had to go from one taluk to another so often that I could not inspect any particular work at frequent intervals, so that it was difficult to say from personal observation whether individual labourers were or were not falling off in condition. However, the people generally on these works have kept in fair condition, and I may safely say that those who were thin, who consisted principally of old people and young children, did not fall off in condition after coming to work, and that the thin children improved. Extra pay was given to emaciated children and others.

A considerable number of people were able-bodied. Some of these were women, who had no male relatives who could take them to the railway. Others were admitted with aged or feeble-bodied parents, under the rule not to separate members of a family. Some had been improperly admitted. At my last inspection I turned off two or three able-bodied people from the Jamkhed work, and about twenty-five from the Karjat work.

The people on the works were mostly from the surrounding villages. In my last inspection I found women and children at work, who had parents or relatives at home. These were turned off, as they evidently had some means of subsistence at home. This was especially the case on the Kargat to Ghogargaon road. On inspecting this work about a week ago, I found a large number of new people who had joined from neighbouring villages since the work came near them. Some of these had relatives at home sowing their fields. I reported yesterday the number turned off.

There were also of course on both works a number of people who had been on the works since they were opened. They appear to be the people who are most in want.—A. F. WOODBURN, *Supernumerary Assistant Collector.*

Camp Kolhar, July 7, 1877.

In reply to your letter No. 4,664, of yesterday's date, I have the honour of reporting as follows, on the working of the civil agency rates in the taluks under my charge.

When these rates were first introduced, there was a certain outcry among the people regarding their insufficiency. The rule was to accept all who applied for work in the first instance, and to reduce their numbers afterwards, by drafting the able-bodied to works under professional supervision. When this rule was enforced, it appeared that the very people who had been vigorously protesting against the reduced wages were very unwilling to leave, and to proceed to where they would receive the full rates. This unwillingness was not confined to any one work, but was universal in the taluks under my charge. It was found that wherever these works were opened the great majority, in some cases almost all the applicants, were inhabitants of adjoining villages. They usually refused to go to the larger works, openly avowing that they preferred lighter tasks near their homes to the greater labour and discomfort on the works under professional supervision.

The reason of this independence can, I think, be demonstrated. The people received per man from one anna one pie to one anna three pies on the civil agency works. Roughly, the difference between the rates on the two classes of work was six pies per diem, or about one rupee per mensem. Thus, a man with a capital, or the power of raising it, of eight rupees, could have to spend, while on civil agency works, as much as his fellow on the other, or enough to keep him at the higher rate from November till June. It may be supposed that a goodly number of the people possessed property in ornaments or utensils sufficient to raise this amount or more. It was remarked that the ornaments worn by women on the works were of but little value, and for the most part this was true ; but it should be remembered that silver to the value of one rupee would, as above, raise a labourer's wages to the higher rate for one month, if sold.

As regards the sufficiency of the food which could be bought with the daily ration on civil agency works to keep a labourer in health, I can only give the result of my own observations among people who were undoubtedly badly off. My experience is that there were few, if any, who could be called unhealthy from lack of food, and there were no cases of severe distress. This was especially apparent among women who were deserted by their husbands, of whom the number has been large, and among widows. Both these and the nursing mothers with their infants have been all along in excellent health. Weakness of voice, the most certain sign of starvation, has not in any case been a characteristic of these people.

Altogether, I am of opinion that, whatever the cause may be, whether that the people all had supplementary resources, or that the rates sufficed, they were enabled to keep up their health and strength, and to remain singularly free from disease on the rate of pay under civil agency.—A. B. FFORDE, *on Special Duty.*

Ahmednagar First Assistant Collector's Office, July 9, 1877.

In reply to your letter No. 4,664, dated the 6th instant, I have the honour to report that I have been only in charge of the first assistant collector's taluks for two months, and am unable to give any decisive opinion as to how the civil agency rates were working, but from what I saw lately of the labourers employed on the works in Nagar and Newase taluks, I always found them in good condition and health.

I don't mean to say that the bare allowance (value of one pound plus 1 pice and 2 pies) would have enabled them to preserve so good a health as they have been enjoying, but calculating this, together with the charity of 3 pies to each child under seven years of age, they make up their wages to the standard of 2 annas to the male and $1\frac{1}{2}$ anna to the female, and nothing to the children.—APAJI RAOJI, *Extra District Deputy Collector*.

Poona, August 9, 1877.

I have the honour to submit the general report on the working of the civil agency rates in the southern division, called for in Government memorandum No. 1,193 F., dated 3rd ultimo. Before doing so I wished to obtain the opinions of the collectors and their assistants on the subject, and I accordingly addressed the collectors on the 4th idem. I have now received all their replies, with the exception of that of the collector of Ratnagiri, Mr. Crawford, but I deem it unnecessary further to await his reply.

Mr. Percival, Collector of Sholapur, has replied briefly as follows:—

'Before reporting, I sent the following questions to my assistants, as, although I know their opinions generally, I wished to obtain as definite answers as possible :—

'1. Have people who came on civil agency works improved or not?

'2. Have people on any civil works fallen out of condition to such an extent that they have been obliged to give up the work and come on charitable relief?

'3. What has been the effect of the rates on the children?

'The answers to these questions are—

'1. Doubtful, or not improved much.

'2. No such cases known.

'3. Good everywhere.'

Mr. Percival observes that Mr. Davidson, who has watched the effect of the civil rates most carefully, sums up thus :

' As a whole, I think the civil rates, modified by grants of extra allowance to nursing mothers, and with a little straining the point as to when boys and girls should be counted as men and women, and with payment as charity through the village officers to work-people temporarily unfit for work through illness, have proved quite sufficient to keep the people alive and in health, though not to fully satisfy their appetites, or to keep their strength up to its normal point in an ordinary year.'

3. Mr. Percival adds :—

' Soon after I came here, I noticed that growing boys particularly complained of the low rates, and I advised the taluk officers to take a liberal view of such cases, which has been, I think, generally done in this district. It is difficult to fix the exact age at which a boy is to be considered to be an adult, and on civil agency works this must be left to the relief officers to decide, as cases arise.

' With this exception, I think that the civil rates have proved sufficient for all persons on light work, and that the distinction between civil and public works rates should be kept up on relief works.

' In order to watch the work-people and give such extra relief as is indicated by Mr. Davidson, civil relief works should not be scattered. One or two works in each taluk should, if possible, be chosen of sufficient size to employ all those needing relief who are unfit for Public Works Department labour.

' Such minute supervision is necessary in receiving people in low condition, sending them away when fit for public works tasks, arranging about families and sick people, that it does not seem advisable to place the incapable under the Public Works Department, to whom they would be a constant trouble, and with the regularity of whose work they would interfere.'

4. The collector of Satara, Mr. Moore, states that from the opinions which his assistants have expressed on the subject, and from his own observation, it appears to him that the civil agency rates are sufficient to maintain persons employed on light labour, such as is exacted on civil agency works, in good health and condition. The diet allowed to prisoners in jails, *not* on hard labour, is given by him as below ; and he observes it will be found on comparison to be almost equal to the civil agency rates. Whatever appears extra in this scale as compared with our relief wages can, he states, be purchased with the money allowance of half an anna which the prisoners do not receive, but the civil agency labourers do. He adds that it is a well-known fact that, as a rule, prisoners gain in weight during their confinement

in the gaol, and this only confirms him in the conclusion he has come
to as to the sufficiency of the civil agency rates.

	lb.	oz.
Bajri, wheat, jowari, nagli flour	1	3
Dal—tur, chunna, mug, masur, math	0	3
Salt	0	$\frac{3}{8}$
Fresh vegetables	0	6
Curry stuff—onions, red-pepper, turmeric, coriander . .	0	$\frac{1}{2}$
Kokam or tamarind	0	$\frac{1}{2}$
Oil, or its equivalent of ghee, in money value . . .	0	$\frac{1}{2}$
Fuel	1	0

5. Mr. Jacomb, collector of Ahmednagar, in forwarding the reports of his assistants as below, which I beg to submit in original for
the perusal of Government, observes as follows :—

‘ In my previous reports on the subject of the civil agency rates
I recommended a slight increase, as I considered that the rate
was sufficient only for a bare maintenance; but I am inclined to
think *now*, from the way in which the labourers on civil agency
works have kept in condition, that the addition of 3 pies which I
once thought necessary as a margin for accidents and off-days,
was not, *as a rule*, indispensable for the sustenance of people on
work.   In many cases this extra allowance was necessary, and
has in reality been provided under the exceptional treatment
plan, and I still think that though no harm has come of the
reduction of wages, the cost of extras, of village inspection, of
feeding weakly wanderers at the relief-houses, of allowances to
children under seven years of age, and of lower-power labour,
will about counterbalance the saving that may have been effected
under the change of wages.’

Mr. Candy’s No. 455, dated July 7, 1877.
Mr. Hamilton’s No. 385, dated July 12, 1877.
Mr. Woodburn’s, dated July 7, 1877.
Mr. Fforde’s No. 113, dated July 7, 1877.
Mr. Apaji Raoji’s No. 594, dated July 9, 1877.

6. Mr. Norman, collector of Poona, after consulting his assistants,
has little to add to the reports he has already forwarded on this
subject.   He observes that—

‘ It seems to be the general impression, in which he concurs,
that civil agency rates have proved sufficient for the maintenance
of the old and infirm, and such persons as are incapable of performing a fair day’s work.

'On the other hand, it must be remembered that the orders of Government, under which special allowances could be granted to all persons in need of such assistance, have been freely made use of.

'It is also as well to note that task work on civil agency works has never been rigidly exacted, partly for want of adequate establishment, but chiefly because the people, being in very poor condition, could not be turned off even if unable to perform the tasks allotted.'

7. It will be seen from the above that all the officers in this division, who have now had no inconsiderable practical experience, are of opinion that the civil agency rates are sufficient to maintain those receiving them in fair condition. I concur fully in this opinion. It must, however, be noticed, that all lay no inconsiderable stress on the fact that much of the success attending these rates is due to the exceptional treatment which has been sanctioned by Government in certain cases. In Sholapur they have found it necessary to deal liberally when deciding whether young lads should be rated as boys or as men. The aid given to young children and nursing mothers has been also a great boon, as the civil agency rates were not calculated for these exceptional cases.

8. I desire to remark that officers have been most careful to keep strict watch over the cases treated exceptionally, and, to prove that not many irregularities can have occurred, I may notice the very great zeal and activity of the famine officers, who from the returns submitted to me have day after day, and in all weathers, personally examined works, and on an average visited from four to five villages daily, personally examining the registers and the people. The zeal and devotion of the officers to their duty is beyond all praise, and I feel confident that Government may rely on the opinions expressed by them, and feel certain that had they found the rates insufficient, they would at once have clearly and strongly represented such to be the case.

E. P. ROBERTSON, *Revenue Commissioner, S.D.*

The Bombay Government passed the following resolution on the foregoing order:—' The views expressed by the officers of the southern division in the reports now submitted are confirmed by the recorded opinions of the sanitary commissioner to the same effect, and also by the opinions of experienced officers in the Kanarese districts, especially in Kaladgi, the worst of all the districts in the famine area ; and Government have therefore every reason for feeling satisfied that the wages all through the famine districts, both on civil agency and on Public Works Department rates, when paid under the adjustment of the sliding scale, and for six days only, are safe and sufficient, provided there be a proper and efficient organisation to pick up and deal with special cases of weakly persons.'

CHAPTER IV.

THE QUESTION STILL TO BE SETTLED.

IN spite of all that has passed on the subject, the question of the sufficiency of one pound of food, plus one anna for condiments, as the ration of a full-grown man engaged in moderate work, is not decided. Two opinions are held upon it with great tenacity. Dr. Cornish, with the medical profession in Madras—from the surgeons-general to the apothecaries,—and non-professional opinion in the Presidency, are unanimous in thinking the allowance too small. In Bombay, on the other hand, Sir Richard Temple, in his final report on the famine, says that there are not two opinions upon the question of the sufficiency of the ration. The question is one that should be settled. With the data already in existence the Famine Commission could make further investigation, and put the matter on a definite footing once for all. Much collateral evidence has been furnished by the experience of the famine, which it would be useful to have collected once for all, and the reasonable deductions to be drawn therefrom formulated for future guidance. Among other isolated facts to be found in large quantity if search be made, is the following interesting account of what has been done at Belgaum. The Poor Fund Committee at Belgaum provided during the famine, 31,144 meals, very ample meals, it is said, which could not in all cases be consumed at a sitting—and the cost was $9\frac{3}{4}$ pies per meal, rather more than three quarters of an anna.[1] Mr. Shaw, the judge, superintended the distribution of the meals daily, and he was aided by native gentlemen of the locality. The sanitary commissioner of Bombay, Dr. Hewlett, saw the distribution, and he stated that the recipients appeared to be quite satisfied with the quantity and quality of the food supplied to them. It is of course a moot point whether each meal could be procured for $9\frac{3}{4}$ pies, if the recipient had to purchase and cook the materials for himself; the Poor Fund naturally made its purchases wholesale, and was able to economise in fuel, &c. Still, if it be the case that substantial meals can be provided in thousands at so trifling an outlay, there is good ground for believing that the claims of hunger and of economy are not after all quite irreconcileable.[2]

The considerations which enter into the question are manifold. The chief argument urged during the controversy was on economic grounds, the formula being, ' A good day's work for a good day's wage,' and it was urged that works of permanent public utility had better be performed by those who could do good work for adequate pay, than be carried on by people who merely played with employment. Even if the first cost were greater, which it is not certain it would be, the country would be the gainer in the end. A favourite parallel with some writers at the time, was shifting the scene to England, and asking what would be done under like circumstances there. One contributor to the Madras press put the matter thus :—' Say we are landed proprietors in England, and have a bad season on our estates. We have people who cultivate the land either as small farmers or farm-labourers ; we want

---

[1] The drawback in this cited case is that weighings and mortality rates are not given.

[2] *Times of India.*

them to tide over the bad season. We have roads very much neglected, which, in fact, we had not time to attend to before. We must employ our people ; we, therefore, mend these roads when all other work is slack. Then, are we, like the Indian Government, to say, "We won't give you ordinary wages. No, not even if you do extra work. But when screwing you down, we don't intend that any one is to die of starvation. So the bailiff has orders to visit all the cottages, and see what food you have in each, and, according to his discretion, dole out some gratuitous relief. At first we intended that all the non-workers were to go to the poor-house. Now, we see that it would be wrong to separate the mother from her young children, and that they can be fed at home, and besides, there are the old people past work. Well, they need not go to the poor-house, but here is the money we have cut from the wages." Fancy the "blessings" which would accompany this mode of dispensing relief in an English county! To slightly vary and to take over the observations of an English labourer, Hodge may be supposed to say, "Why, they wouldn't let me earn my wage, and now they come to my house and examine my wife and parents, and leave their tuppenny pieces here ! What I says is this, give I a proper wage, and none of that 'ere gammon." Ramasawmy, when his wage is cut down, grumbles too ; he would prefer taking proper wages home, and having his family meal in peace, without the intrusion of the village monegar, or beat constable. He prefers to have as little to do with these gentry as possible ; the monegar is perhaps no friend of his, because he would not sell the cow that the monegar had set his heart upon—or there might be numerous other reasons to cause unpleasant feelings ; and the peasant, it is well known, does not, as a rule, like the policeman. What we have alluded to is what naturally comes of attempting too much. It is true, that by the simple mode of paying the people proper wages for their work, there will be adequate relief, in the mode most agreeable to their feelings ; but then, again, there will not be the opportunity for interminable "narratives," wearisome iterations (*not* to use a stronger word), volumes the bulk of which acts as a deterrent to perusal, those " exhaustive" reports which now accompany administration. Work will go on, as in ordinary times, only more people will get work, and the result will be that the work will be well chosen, and a lasting benefit to the country. But what *kudos* is to be gained by simply recording that " I made, or repaired, a few hundred miles of roads at a cheap rate, allowing of grain traffic in carts to every village, I reduced the wear and tear and expense of cartage 50 per cent., I cleared out silted channels, neglected or inefficiently repaired for generations. The people were well off and managed to pull through." '[1]

Another point in favour of sufficient wage is the necessity for keeping the people alive, an object to be urged from the economic point of view. In India a ryot represents revenue. A large proportion of the revenue of the country—two-fifths—comes from the land. If the people die, the land lies waste, and no kist is paid. In the Madras Presidency in the latter half of 1877 two and a half million acres less than the average were uncultivated. This, at a moderate estimate, means the loss of nearly a million sterling in land-revenue—not for one year only, but for a long series of years. Then, village tradespeople, the weavers, the shoemakers, the watchmen, who depend upon a share in the produce as the reward of their services, also do not get what they should and therefore die. Their absence, as well

[1] Contribution in *Madras Times*, March, 1877.

as that of the ryots and coolies, is felt by the State in a diminished salt-tax return. Above all, and comprising all, is the general backwardness into which the country is thrown, by one individual out of every four, as in many Madras districts was the case, being removed by death in one season. It seems reasonable to argue that whilst the State in India is virtually landlord of a large estate, it must care for the people under its charge more paternally than other countries, where different relations exist, would think of doing. If possible, arrangements should be preventive rather than palliative. The people should be taken in hand before they are too far reduced for recovery. This is a practical question in famine administration, for though there can be no question that at some period, if the British remain lords of the continent, famine will be as impossible in India as it is in Europe, that time is far distant, and frequent famines will meanwhile have to be faced. Sir Bartle Frere said at the Society of Arts, in 1873 : ' There is one more fact which you will find noted in all accurate descriptions of famine, which should be borne in mind as of importance to right conclusions. It is that men are death-stricken by famine long before they die. The effects of insufficient food, long continued, may shorten life after a period of some years, or it may be of months, or days. But invariably there is a point which is often reached long before death actually ensues, when not even the tenderest care and most scientific nursing can restore a sufficiency of vital energy to enable the sufferer to regain even apparent temporary health and strength.' How to find out when this period is reached, and how to avert the consequences, is not the least of the problems which the Famine Commission should set itself to determine. A famine can scarcely be said to be adequately controlled which leaves one-fourth of the people dead. This was the effect of the Madras and Mysore famines of 1876–78 in the worst-affected districts.[1]

[1] 'The Census recently taken in this (Salem) zillah shows, I hear, that the population is about *one fourth less* than in 1871. Of course, there should have been a natural increase since last census, and if this properly-expected increase be added to the returns of 1871, and if the present figures be compared with what *ought* to be the present state of things, I think I shall be right in concluding that Salem has, perhaps, lost one-third of its population by the last famine; and that the loss is certain to be not less than twenty-five per cent. If the figures are correct, this will give about half a million of famine deaths in this one zillah alone. How many thousands of lives were saved by the untiring efforts of the over-worked officials, and by the Mansion House Fund, will never be known. Most certainly, the very lowest estimate would give a number equal to that of the deaths; and if those who have laboured night and day beyond their strength, for more than a year past, can feel that half a million lives have been saved by their labours, who will grudge them the pleasure and satisfaction of the thought? And who will not give grateful thanks for the funds which came in time to save so many lives?'—Salem Correspondent of the *Madras Times*.

APPENDIX A.

A CONTRIBUTION of value on the point dealt with in this section was furnished to the discussion by an article in the *Times of India*, of December 13, 1877, from which the following passages are taken :—

When, then, the bare subsistence allowance of one pound of grain was condemned by experts here and at home as miserably insufficient, and had to be actually abolished in Madras, the Bombay Government determined to justify their own policy, which latterly has happily been chiefly theoretical, by making experiments on the prisoners in the Presidency gaols ; thus endeavouring to show that the prisoners had received too much food, rather than that the labourer on the civil agency relief works had ever received too little. At the same time, no real effort was made to test the question thoroughly by giving the prisoners the exact quantity of food that had been allotted to relief labourers. The prisoners now receive less than they received before last July, that is all, and the allowance, as we shall see, is still something very different from the 1 lb. ration for only six out of seven days, which proved the one signal flaw in the otherwise admirable administration of the Bombay famine.

Though the Bombay Government could not well venture to put the question to a practical test by adopting the 1-lb. ration, pure and simple, in all the Presidency gaols, and recording averages of death, sickness, and questions as to increase or falling off in weight, working-power, and so forth, they are now, in the introduction of a reduced dietary scale, endeavouring to prove that the dietary scale for prisoners, which was dragged into the famine controversy, was excessive, and that Dr. Lyon's views are sounder than Dr. Cornish's outspoken opinions. In Dr. Lyon, our Government undoubtedly has the ablest scientific supporter in this Presidency, but in allowing his delicate theories to be put to a practical test, of which the records are preserved and should be available, they have supplied Dr. Cornish and those who think with him, most valuable material.

The experiment, as we said, has only been attempted in a modified manner, and has lasted but six months ; yet the results are simply disastrous. The prison yards now contain many of the painful features of the very earliest relief camps. An important minority of the prisoners have still the strange famine look on their faces, or, perhaps, rather they have never been able to lose it, for some of them are famine wallahs sent to prison for stealing grain, &c. They appeal throughout the day, after meals as before, to any passing official for something to eat. They are unable to execute their task properly after a few weeks' trial of the new ration. More than double the average number of patients have to be accommodated in the hospitals, and the death-rate has increased to something like five times its ordinary standard. This state of things is openly acknowledged by the officials, who, indeed—gaolers, doctors, and regulation visitors alike—are almost as loud in complaint as the unhappy prisoners themselves.

The scale previously in force for prisoners sentenced to hard labour was as follows :—

24 oz. of their own country grain daily.
5 „ of meat, including bones, &c., made into a kind of broth on Wednesdays and Saturdays only.
5 „ dhall 5 times weekly.
1 „ linseed oil daily.
8 „ vegetables such as pumpkins, vegetables, onions, and radishes.
6 dr. salt.
4 „ curry stuff.

This was a very different thing from the 1-lb. grain ration of the civil relief works. But even the new scale introduced last July, and still in force as an experiment, can give us nothing more than an idea of the insufficiency of that unfortunate food standard. The new scale for hard labour is :—

20 oz. of their own country grain daily.
4 „ of meat on Wednesdays and Saturdays only.
4 „ of dhall 5 times weekly.
¼ „ of linseed oil daily.
6 „ of vegetables.
6 dr. salt.
4 „ curry stuff.

The scale has thus been reduced by 4 oz. grain, 1 oz. meat, 1 oz. dhall, ¾ oz. linseed oil, and 2 oz. vegetables. But the mutton, which is weighed whole before it is hashed up into a kind of soup, necessarily contains a large quantity of bone. Prisoners on hard labour for three months, and all non-labour prisoners, women and boys, receive a still smaller allowance :—

19 oz. of their own country grain.
3 „ dhall.
6 „ vegetables.
6 dr. salt.
4 „ curry stuff.
4 „ oil.

This last is the dietary scale to which the present state of things is in great proportion due. The reduced rations have very different effects upon the hard labour and non-labour prisoners. The women, a few of whom cook in every gaol, while the great majority have nothing but light work to do, have been affected less than any. The males committed without hard labour have not yet suffered very severely, but when we come to the men undergoing hard labour for three months on this reduced ration we see the cruellest result of the experiment. But sickness, languor, and inability to execute a due share of taskwork, are to be found in both classes whenever hard labour is required. Experts in the gaols tell us that the reduced rations might perhaps suffice—though even here they are doubtful—for people who had absolutely nothing to do, but that the reduction begins to tell immediately they are put to a task. This, too, was the experience of those who managed the relief camps and relief works. In the gaols, as we said, the effect of the change has been disastrous. During the year 1876 the rate of mortality in the Bombay House of Correction was only 19·5 per mille. But with the introduction of the new scale the rate of mortality in one of the great gaols in our Presidency, has recently been upwards of 96 per mille. In the Bombay House of Correction the daily average sick from all diseases in 1876 was only 4·6 per cent. The present daily average sick in one of the Presidency gaols is more than 9 per cent., with an additional 4½ per cent. of convalescents. In the hospitals food is given liberally, and even as much as 4 oz. of alcohol is daily administered if required. The prisoners take their turn here to be recruited, and, but for these periods of comparative luxury, the mortality, large enough already, would have been far greater. At the same time they are not admitted until in some sort of danger, and the cost of restoring them cannot have been far short of the saving effected in their diet. The gaols are unusually full now, the extra prisoners being due to thefts and misdemeanours connected with the famine. Many of the famine prisoners were in a very weak state of health on admission, and the time chosen to change the diet experimentally, was, to say the least of it, unfortunate. In the course of our inquiries we heard of one wretched man in the famine districts who was driven by hunger to commit suicide. He was discovered in time, and punished by a term of imprisonment on rations which are slowly doing for him what he wickedly attempted himself. We also heard that the prisoners who grind the grain have now to be specially prevented from snatching and eating it raw. In bringing the matter before the public we are anxious that those who have had practical experience of the way the experiment has failed, should be invited or permitted to lay their opinions before

Government. The gaolers, the gaol surgeons, and the official visitors are thoroughly convinced of the necessity of an immediate inquiry. Scientific men may tell us that carbo-hydrates, albuminates, and fats mixed in a proper proportion constitute the ideal ration, and a set of tables may teach us the chemical value of every food under the Indian sun. But when we learn that half a pound of pulse contains 142 grains of the essential nitrogen, half a pound of bajri 56 grains, and half a pound of rice only 40 grains, we begin to see that the cooking of a day's meal, to contain exactly 201·6 grains of nitrogen, and 400·1 grains of carbon, requires as much scientific knowledge and care as the concoction of a doctor's prescription, or the performance of a chemical experiment. A pound of grain food, nicely assorted from various cereals in a chemist's laboratory, must be a very different thing from a pound of bajri or rice served out to hundreds or thousands of men in a gaol or a relief camp. But the failure of a scale of diet which, at worst, was almost twice as good as the famous 1-lb. ration should prevent any repetition of the one mistake made in the treatment of the late famine. If all the questions connected with the famine are, as we hear, to be submitted to a Parliamentary Committee, the evidence as to the working of this new scale of diet in the Presidency gaols will be of the greatest importance.

APPENDIX B.

No. 568.   OFFICE OF SANITARY COMMISSIONER,
                              Madras, May 24, 1877.
From

        The Sanitary Commissioner, Madras.

To

        The Additional Secretary to Government.

Sir,—With reference to the discussion in regard to the amount of food necessary for the maintenance of health of natives of India, I have the honour to state for the information of His Grace in Council, that feeling strongly the importance of the subject, I forwarded to Professor Sir Robert Christison, Bart., of Edinburgh, a copy of Proceedings of Government, No. 757, of March 1, containing my letter, No. 115, of February 13, and requested Sir Robert Christison to be good enough to advise me whether my protest against the reduction of the famine relief wage to the basis of one pound of cereal grain a day, was or was not justified by scientific and practical observation, in regard to dietaries. I have now to submit for the information of Government a copy of Sir Robert Christison's reply.

2. Sir Robert Christison was not aware of the special inquiry made in India in 1863, regarding the nature and amount of food consumed by the free population, and by prisoners in gaols. The results of this inquiry went to show that in the South of India, at least, the people were not so entirely dependent on grain diet as superficial writers have frequently asserted. It was shown that the so-called vegetarian castes used milk, curds, and butter, to a large extent, in their food, while the great bulk of the labouring poor used animal food and pulses rich in nitrogen whenever they could get them, and that their staple food grains were richer than rice in albuminous constituents. It was a direct consequence of this inquiry that the gaol diets in this Presidency were revised in 1867, and the effect of this change was, as already pointed out, a reduction of mortality from more than 10 per cent. to an average for the last nine years of about 2½ per cent.

3. As this subject is one of great public interest, I would suggest that Sir Robert Christison's opinion may be placed at the disposal of the press.

I have the honour to be, Sir,

Your most obedient servant,

(Signed)   W. R. CORNISH, F.R.C.S.,

Sanitary Commissioner.

(*Enclosure.*)

Edinburgh, April 18, 1877.

Dear Dr. Cornish,—I received your letter a week ago, and the folio print yesterday.

1. Mere practical experience is a very dangerous guide to a dietary for a body of men. The fact is, in this matter, what is called practical experience is nothing else than loose observation. I could mention many striking instances from practical men trusting to their practical experience. But perhaps Sir Richard Temple will be satisfied with the history of the victualling of our troops for the Crimean war. The authorities at the Horse Guards provided the men with a dietary which proved to contain less real nutriment than their food in barracks or garrison at home, and not above one half of what was required for the labour and hardships which they had to undergo. Their hardships accounted of course in part for the sad result. But a sufficient dietary would have enabled them to resist these hardships, as had been found before with our Navy seamen exposed to equal labour, and quite as great hardships of a different kind.

Sir Richard Temple will find the facts I mention in the Crimean

Report of Sir John McNeill and Colonel Tulloch. But I may add that when Sir John on his return asked at the Horse Guards how they had fallen into such an error, he was told that they were not aware that there was any other way of valuing a dietary except practical observation. Nevertheless the analytical method was at that time well known to scientific men, had been taught by myself for twenty-two years to large classes, and would have pointed out the error in five minutes.

2. But neither should scientific analysis be trusted to singly. It must be tested by practical observation, and the two methods together will supply trustworthy results.

3. Caution should be observed in applying the results of scientific inquiry in Europe to India. In all my investigations my subjects have been bodies of men of British race.

Now there is something in the constitution of the grain-eating Indian races which seems in the course of ages to have adapted it to a very different dietary from that found most suitable here. There can be no doubt whatever that men of British race do not thrive so well, and are incapable of much labour, unless their dietary contains a fair proportion either of the mixed albuminoid principles of meat or of albumen itself, animal or vegetable, or lastly of caseine, in the shape of milk; but the long habit of ages seems to have rendered the Indian grain-eaters independent of any of these powerful aliments. Therefore you will see that a special inquiry is required for ascertaining the dietary of these people suitable for them in the various circumstances of life.

I am not aware of any such inquiry in India but one; and that is a report by Dr. G. C. Sutherland in 1871, on the prisons of Oude.

4. Dr. Sutherland, on entering on duty as Inspector-General, found the health of the prisoners very bad, the mortality being ten per cent. In two years he reduced it to two per cent. This was brought about by various changes, and among these by increasing somewhat and varying their food. I am very sorry that I have been unable to lay my hands on my notes on this interesting subject.

Of course they will all be found in Dr. Sutherland's report. I now send, however, a copy of his table for prisoners undergoing hard labour. I cannot at present sustain this strain of computing the nutriment, but it may be seen at a glance that the nitrogenous food constitutes a large proportion of the whole. Of course you know nothing is more certain than that the nutriment in a dietary must increase with the amount of labour.

5. In practically observing the effect of any experimental dietary the main test is to weigh the men every 14 days. If there is a progressive diminution in a large proportion of them the dietary is faulty,

and will ere long cause serious consequences. Dr. Sutherland found that under his improved scales of diet the men went out one pound heavier than on admission.

6. In applying European observations to India, account should be taken of the inferior bulk of the men. The average weight of about 1,500 Oude prisoners was 106 pounds, without clothes. The average weight of the adult prisoners in the General Prison at Perth is 140 pounds. It is plain, therefore, that men so different in bulk must require a material difference of food.

7. The last point which occurs to me is that a very meagre fare will serve for prisoners and the destitute poor for short terms of a week or a fortnight, but that it would be a grievous error to suppose that the same fare will answer for long terms of several months.

This fact has been substantiated by careful observations expressly made here a few years ago.

I am, yours truly,

(Signed)   R. CHRISTISON.

P.S.—On the principles already explained, it is my opinion that the dietary proposed by Sir Richard Temple is both insufficient in quantity, and ill chosen.

DIETARY OF THE PRISONERS IN OUDE ON HARD LABOUR, AS REFORMED BY DR. SUTHERLAND, 1871.

I. *Daily*: 1. Wheat flour coarsely sifted and made into cakes. Taken with I. chtk.[1] grs.   oz.
       or II.   .   .   . 10   0 = 20·25

  2. Grain, parched (eaten dry)   .   .   . 2   0 =   4·50 *Cicer arietinum.*
  3. Salt   .   .   . 0 100 =   0·23
  4. Pepper or Chillies   . 0   36 =   0·08 *Capsicum annuum.*

II. *Four days weekly*: 1. Dhall   . 2   0 =   4·50 *From various peas.*
  2. Ghee boiled with pepper and salt into thick pea-soup   . 0   36 =   0·08 *Clarified butter.*

III. *Three days weekly*: 1. Fresh vegetables   .   . 6   0 = 12·15 *Spinach.*
  2. Oil boiled with pepper and salt into thick soup   .   .   . 0   38 =   0·03 *Mustard Oil usually*

---

[1] 1 chittack = 2 ounces, a standard of weight in the North-West Provinces.

Notandum.—'For some months after the autumn harvest; maize and various sorts of millet, Penicillaria spicata, Sorghum vulgare gns. are substituted for wheat, being cheaper. But in consequence of their inferior nutritive value the daily allowance is increased to 24·70 ounces.'

Feb. 8, 1871.　　　　　　　　　(Signed) G. C. SUTHERLAND, M.D.

　　　　　True copy,　　　　　　　(Signed) W. R. CORNISH, F.R.C.S.,
　　　　　　　　　　　　　　　　　　Sanitary Commissioner for Madras.

THE RAILWAYS

THE RAILWAYS.

In the narrative of famine administration for Madras, particulars are given of the extraordinary activity which was manifested by the mercantile community in importing grain. The quantity imported by sea with its value will be found in the following table :—

	Average of 3 previous years		Actuals. 1877.	
	Quantity	Value	Quantity	Value
	Tons Cwt	Rs	Tons Cwt	Rs
6 Months. July to December 1876 .	*"*	*"*	154,740 1	145,00,252
January 1877 . .	4,301 13	2,53,457	75,969 16	91,35,738
February . . .	5,913 14	3,53,965	69,057 12	72,67,354
March . . .	5,062 5	3,18,015	48,397 19	49,16,848
April . . .	3,881 19	2,33,544	41,780 15	39,26,697
May	3,171 14	1,81,413	37,806 2	39,76,550
June . . .	5,965 15	2,83,672	26,891 16	28,74,755
July	9,202 18	4,85,790	57,028 8	75,02,374
August . . .	8,820 13	4,71,265	75,092 1	97,96,130
September . .	—		—	
October . .	8,691 0	6,82,067	56,270 15	65,02,542
November . .	14,609 15	15,65,393	13,453 9	13,87,576
December . . .	20,689 3	22,83,725	9,001 3	9,07,943
January 1878 . .	30,097 1	33,70,160	11,547 10	12,50,976

Under any circumstances, with an open sea-board and with the enterprise which characterises the mercantile community of Madras, it was clear that imports would be large : the difficulty was to decide how the grain could be conveyed to the distressed districts. The railways solved the question. Sir Andrew Clarke, from his place in the Legislative Council in Calcutta, in December 1877, said:—' The railways have proved the saviour of Southern India.' To this remark there can be no denial. By the Madras railways alone, 800,000 tons of grain were carried into the interior and distributed through the districts. As soon as the difficulty was seen, efforts were made to meet the increased traffic. Passenger trains were cancelled, and the carriage of grain was given the preference over all other descriptions of traffic. The line from Madras to Arconum was doubled to facilitate the conduct of traffic. One of the chief objects to which Sir Richard Temple directed his attention whilst in Southern India was that of increasing the carrying power of the railways, and with Captain Bisset, R.E., spent much time in consideration of this subject; he penned a large number of minutes, which had some effect in relieving great pressure at particular junctions, and in simplifying arrangements. The capabilities of the railways was a subject in which the Duke of Buckingham and Chandos, once chairman of the London and North-Western Railway in England, took particular interest, and over which his Grace spent much time. The Governor was ably assisted by the railway officials—particularly Mr. R. B. Elwin, the agent and manager, and Mr. Herbert Church, the traffic manager. Arrangements made by his Grace, when it was found that the railway was unable to carry off all the grain imported, caused much dissatisfaction among merchants. Railway trucks were registered in advance, not according to the largeness of the trade of the importer, but according to order of application. The consequence was that two or three trucks on a particular day would be reserved for a firm which had chartered three or four steamers, one or two of which were at the time unloading, and a whole

truck to Parthasarathy Chettiar, who never imported on
his own account, but bought a few hundred bags of rice
for transit up country, or it might be who had no grain
of his own whatever, and was merely making a profit in
selling the trucks allotted to him to others. Many representations were made to Government, but no improved
system was introduced. A merchant in the south of
the Presidency, writing to the author, says:—

The Government scheme for granting available trucks to all
registered applicants attracted some 1,200 to 1,400 men belonging to
Tuticorin and the district, with the certainty of drawing an occasional
prize. Many of the successful applicants sold their trucks to importers, others taking advantage of the stocks held by importers, and
their inability to move them along the line of rail or to promise
carriage to customers, bought importers' grain at their own prices,
that is at prices dictated to importers not by consumers, but by the
Governor's order. The consequence was that petty dealers who would
have otherwise bought grain along the line, and cartmen who would
have worked out rice, thus supplementing the railway power, were
drawn to Tuticorin, and in combination with their friends in the
district, virtually held the markets in the face of the importers, who
had to incur the long risk and supply the capital. It may be asked
why, under such circumstances, did not importers engage in the cart
trade alluded to. The reply is simple. Importers had no facilities in
knowing the demand of every isolated village, and would have been
imposed upon at every turn. Besides, the order opened a very wide
door for bribing railway officials. Natives who recognised the order
as unjust applied the only antidote they knew of.

The Governor's order was defective and actually injurious, without, as far as I can discover, any redeeming virtue.

(1) Because it disturbed the action of many petty dealers and
cartmen, who were in the habit of resorting to Tuticorin to purchase
and take away grain in carts.

(2) Because it discouraged importers, who frequently lost in
their imports for the sole benefit of truck dealers.

(3) Because it increased the price to consumers of the interior,
giving truck dealers the command of the market here and in the
interior, raising up middlemen who were pernicious.

(4) Because it fostered bribery amongst native railway employés.

In a country stricken by famine I conceive the ruling power
should seek to attract early imports, and strain every nerve to sustain

them at the highest possible level. This can be best done in a steady and effective way by letting importers pocket every available pie per bag that consumers are out of pocket. It becomes a struggle between the two. The grand object must be to keep on terms with importers, and secure to consumers the lowest possible rates *that importers will go on at.* Stimulate the importer to import his bags for one, and the true policy is achieved. Help the importer to consider 8 as. profit on two bags of grain as equal to a rupee on one bag, and though truck dealers may object, the consumer will reap the benefit. Such a policy would have been an intelligent policy, and under such a policy profits would have been held at a minimum for the benefit of consumers, instead of being turned into a loss for the benefit of truck dealers.

The Governor of Madras had it in his power to say to importers, ' The railway carriage is insufficient to supply the country with the food required, but as you find the capital and run the risk, neither of which the Government will undertake and guarantee, a fair distribution will be made of all available carriage on a *pro ratâ* footing, according to the capital invested and the risk undertaken.' On the other hand he had it in his power to say, ' Importers may import as much as they like, but the carrying power of the country shall be given to the non-importer in equal proportion with that given to importers, and as there will be fifty non-importers against every importer, the importer shall be kept at a distance from the consumer, and from the monopoly of the carrying power in the non-importer's hands. Importers must submit to their values without reference to the consumer's price.'

It is almost incredible that the Governor chose the latter, and persisted in it in the face of representations and expostulations from all the commercial circles of the Presidency. Though I have seen fifty reasons against his policy, I have never seen one in its favour that would bear investigation.

My experience is that my imports would have gone into consumers' hands *at least* 8 annas per bag cheaper, and my imports and profits would have been larger, if the Governor had adopted the first line of action. Presuming this to be the experience of other importers, the upshot is, that on the imports, say 13,000,000 of bags, a sum more than equal to the Mansion House Relief Fund has been forced out of consumers' pockets for the benefit of middlemen, and to the injury of importers.

What was expected from the Madras Railway at the period of the Viceroy's visit will appear from the following passages occurring in a despatch from Lord

Lytton to the Marquis of Salisbury. Lord Lytton said:—

Much discussion has taken place during the past week on the working and the requirements of the Madras Railway. Seventeen additional engines and 100 waggons have, during August, been borrowed from other lines and sent to Madras: 100 more waggons will shortly arrive from the Baroda line; the Madras Railway is receiving from England six to eight new powerful engines per month; 200-metre-gauge waggons are on their way (some have actually arrived) from State lines for work on the South Indian Railway. The double line from Madras to Arconum has been opened for traffic. The despatches of grain from the Madras terminus are reaching 1,800 tons a day, while the despatches inland from Negapatam and Beypore are keeping up to the mark. I anticipate that the several Madras railways will, if grain be consigned in sufficient quantities, despatch inland the full quantity required daily, namely:—

		Tons
From Madras terminus by the Madras Railway .	.	1,800
„ Beypore	.	400
„ Raichore	.	900
By the South Indian Railway .	. . .	800
„ canal and road from Madras.	. . .	600
Total .	. . . .	4,500

Under these circumstances the Government of India have for the present refrained from compelling other guaranteed lines, by forced Government requisition, to lend more rolling stock than they can willingly spare to the Madras Railway; and we are the more anxious not to make requisitions, if it can possibly be helped, because the other railways have loyally obeyed our request for loans of rolling stock as far as they possibly could, and because we do not know what urgent need may spring up for grain transport in other parts of the Empire which are threatened with scarcity.

Though the Madras railways, by working full power, can thus almost meet the necessities of the case, yet it is by no means certain that they can continue to do so, or that they will be prepared for new demands which may arise if the north-east monsoon fails. Some of their engine and waggon stock is very old, and may become unserviceable before the crisis is over; the northern railways may, if difficulty comes in Upper India, have to reclaim the engines they have lent. In order therefore to provide against possible difficulties, we have telegraphed to your Lordship supporting the Madras Government in their indent of August 17 for 20 more engines, 600 waggons, and 40 brake-vans; and we have asked for 20 more engines in addition to the Madras indent. You have informed us by telegraph that 500 of these waggons will reach India within ten weeks' time. We hope that this additional stock, together with 30 new heavy engines now arriving, will enable the Madras railways to meet all emergencies. We have asked that the 40 new engines should, for reasons explained in my colleagues' railway letter, quoted in paragraph 10 of the present letter, form part of the State reserve of engines.

It has been mentioned that the railways will carry the required amount of grain, if only it is consigned by the trade. And upon the question whether private trade will send into the famine country all the grain that is required, the safety of the people depends. It cannot be said that the trade sends all the country can take, for the dear prices ruling in so many districts would show that more grain would be readily bought, if sent. But this much is certain; private trade is still consigning to the famine country much more grain than the railways can carry into the interior. In previous letters we have reported that more than 100,000 tons of grain are awaiting despatch at or near the railway stations in the Central Provinces. The Bengal exportable surplus, if the crop now in the ground turns out well, will not fall short of 350,000 tons. Already 100,000 tons of freight, chiefly steamer freight, has been taken up for despatch of grain from Calcutta to Madras ports during the present month. The actual despatches of rice from Bengal to Madras were 53,225 tons, or an average of 3,800 tons daily, during the fortnight ending August 29. The despatches from Burmah to Madras were only 400 tons during the same period ; so that there would seem to be truth in the opinion, generally expressed by merchants, that the Burmah rice ports have no more grain to send till next crop comes to market in December. From Saigon it was reported that 150,000 tons were ready for export, but that most of this would go to China, where also there is a large famine demand. But a telegram from the Governor of the Straits Settlements, dated September 1, has told us that the Siamese Government has prohibited the export of rice from Bankok until September 30, on account of the threatened dearth in those territories. At the same time the Persian Government has prohibited grain exportation from Bushire. It would seem therefore that, for the present, India cannot expect food supplies from further Asia, but must send the surplus of the north to supply the deficiency of the south. For the present, and so far as we can foresee, any grain imported by Government would occupy railway waggons to the exclusion of private despatches, and would paralyse trade to an indefinite extent.

The work actually performed by the various railways converging upon and running through the Madras Presidency will be found in the following series of tables, kindly prepared at the author's request by the Railway Department :—

A.

STATEMENT SHOWING THE QUANTITY OF GRAIN FORWARDED FROM THE UNDERMENTIONED STATIONS FROM AUGUST 1876 TO NOVEMBER 1877.

Periods	Madras	S. I. Ry.	Beypore	G. I. P. Ry.	Total	Earnings
1876	Tons	Tons	Tons	Tons	Tons	Rs. As P
August . .	3,098	1,573	113	4,039	8,823	75,822 15 9
September .	6,390	2,030	223	5,163	13,806	98,429 12 0
October .	10,958	5,124	1,121	4,921	22,124	206,638 3 0
November .	13,208	2,432	1,952	7,951	25,543	248,096 10 0
December .	30,745	1,337	5,570	12,281	49,933	392,101 14 0
1877						
January .	27,185	1,151	10,275	7,872	46,483	397,133 1 0
February .	20,113	481	8,982	10,665	40,241	330,630 1 0
March . .	37,405	1,835	6,161	9,138	54,539	423,361 10 0
April . .	34,272	1,168	9,072	8,617	53,129	418,881 6 0
May . .	33,696	2,398	11,069	10,599	58,362	411,479 9 0
June . .	35,800	2,519	8,418	11,487	58,224	437,204 5 0
July . .	43,784	3,467	9,495	13,683	70,429	483,047 2 0
August . .	47,865	3,683	10,663	11,755	73,966	544,684 4 0
September .	39,070	3,391	12,253	16,142	70,856	482,042 4 0
October .	28,160	920	7,216	4,411	40,707	293,050 11 0
November .	28,089	1,667	6,597	821	37,174	204,344 4 0
Total	439,838	35,178	109,780	139,545	724,339	5,536,947 15 9

B. Madras Railway.

Items	1876				1877					
	August	September	October	December	February	April	June	August	October	November
1. Rolling Stock Available.										
Total mileage	248,368	250,278	292,399	376,262	343,400	390,385	395,007	430,635	384,795	
Number of engines on hire.	—	—	—	4	10	21	21	21	35	15
" new	30	31	27	23	24	31	2	10	16	16
" under repair.	98	97	101	108	106	117	29	31	38	41
" in steam daily							119	125	139	122
vehicles constructed, new	—	—	—	4	—	100	—	12	6	
" on hire.	—	—	—	—	—	—	300	300	220	8
" under repair at the end of the month	114	183	241	152	181	186	243	197	123	278

Altogether 40 engines have been hired from time to time.   Altogether 500 vehicles have been hired from time to time,

Items	1876				1877					
	August	September	October	December	February	April	June	August	October	November
2. Number of Extra Hands Employed.										
Total enginemen and firemen	334	329	320	345	374	398	414	470	488	
" of all artificers	1703	1890	1861	1901	2120	2177	2257	2383	2450	
" coolies	1019	1051	1264	1432	1607	1708	1788	2030	2019	
" superintendence, clerks, etc.	105	104	106	106	109	113	116	120	122	
Total	3251	3374	3551	3784	4210	4396	4575	5003	5079	
3. Number of trains run out of various stations	No available record in the Locomotive Department.									
4. Number of Locomotives and Waggons that broke down	Cannot well be answered in this form. *Vide av-rage number under repair.*									
5. Average of Work done and Pay received by each employé in excess of what is usual.										
Total overtime per month.	Rs. 5155	Rs. 5301	Rs. 8498	Rs. 13,288	Rs. 11,873	Rs. 11,516	Rs. 15,377	Rs. 16,456	—	

Does not include anything chargeable to capital.

B. MADRAS RAILWAY—continued.

Statement showing the Waggon Rolling Stock in use month by month from September 1876 to September 1877.

Stock	1876				1877								
	Sept.	Oct.	Nov.	Dec.	Jan.	Feb.	March	April	May	June	July	Aug.	Sept.
Madras Railway	2659	2659	2659	2659	2659	2659	2659	2659	2659	2659	2659	2659	2659
Hired											300	300	300
Total	2659	2659	2659	2659	2659	2659	2659	2659	2659	2659	2959	2959	2959

Passenger trains discontinued.

The local passenger trains between Madras and Vellore, and between Arconum and Triputty, were discontinued on February 4, 1877.

The cooly class trains between Madras and Jollarpet, between Jollarpet and Erode, between Arconum and Cuddapah, and between Jollarpet and Bangalore, were discontinued on August 1, 1877.

C.

Statement showing additional Staff employed in the Traffic Department month by month during the Famine over and above the Staff employed in August 1876, on the Madras Railway.

Items	1876				1877										
	Sept.	Oct.	Nov.	Dec.	Jan.	Feb.	March	April	May	June	July	August	Sept.	Oct.	Nov.
Office establishment	—	—	—	No. 2	No. 1	No. 6	No. 2	No. 5	No. 9	No. 12	No. 11	No. 24	No. 25	No. 30	No. 35
Station staff	43	139	244	270	284	336	364	379	369	426	424	476	484	492	
Train staff	3	10	20	40	43	42	38	39	38	40	53	54	66	66	61
Overtime allowance	rs. 3 9 1	—	215 11 8	295 15 6	297 2 6	173 9 6	113 9 6	167 0 0	—	103 6 2	177 13 2	239 12 9	208 3 4	125 8 2	70 9 6
Telegraph department	—	—	—	—	—	1	4	1	—	—	—	—	—	—	—

Railway extension forms an important feature in the famine policy of the future, as described in Sir John Strachey's speech in the Legislative Council in December 1877. The value of railways and good roads connected with them, without which their full usefulness cannot be developed, is very great indeed. Their effect on prices also, irrespective of the actual carriage of the grain, is an element to be considered. The knowledge that in a few days at most, large supplies can be imported, keeps down excessive prices, which an increased demand is likely to produce. The impossibility of forming a correct estimate of the quantity of stored grain—the knowledge, if it exists, being confined to the class who deal in the produce—renders the grain trade to outsiders one of great risk. Grain dealers naturally wish to make the maximum of profit, and the stores are withheld until competition is roused. A famine or scarcity is the grain-dealer's opportunity, and he cannot, more than any other trader, be blamed for making the most of his opportunity. While railways afford the quickest mode of transit and equalise supply, they are not alone the saviour of the people. Grain may be poured into a district, but the poor and the destitute must be enabled to purchase it. Thousands may starve in the midst of plenty, as can be seen in every metropolis, even in the greatest of the world. In the Irish famine there were ships and ports, and means of transport, but the people had to be helped to purchase.

'FREE' TRADE IN FAMINE TIMES

'FREE' TRADE IN FAMINE TIMES.

ELSEWHERE the story has been told of the dispute between the Governments of India and Madras regarding purchase of grain ; the policy of the former has been vindicated. A few considerations, apart from the actual circumstances which caused so much and such angry feelings, may be of interest. The expression ' free ' as regards trade applies more properly to an unrestricted or unburdened trade than to one in which Government is directly concerned. Taking the expression, however, in the latter sense, which is now meant, it may be well to examine the condition of things in former famines, and weigh the result of non-intervention and the result of intervention. In the Orissa famine more than a million of people died of starvation, the result of non-intervention. This was justly considered a blot on British administration, and action likely to have a similar result was studiously avoided in the subsequent Bengal famine. But if the causes of the Orissa famine be enquired into and the cost of the Government transport of grain be calculated, it will be found that grain was not imported into Orissa from causes which equally prevented Government aid and also private trade from taking adequate action. The coast was shut by the monsoon, and there were no roads. A railway to Orissa from Calcutta would have prevented the loss of life, but without such means of communication neither Government nor private trade could help the people.

The carriage of grain from a dear to a cheap place is evidently not an economical remedy; it is a question of carrying facilities. In the Bengal famine, on the other hand, there were no such conditions as existed in Orissa. There was not a tempestuous sea-coast, nor an isolated territory. Roads existed; they were not cut to pieces by the abnormal traffic, Government and private grain passing and repassing on the same roads. Such was the result, most disastrous to the revenue, of Government interference in 1874, and so strong was the impression it left on the Government of India, that strict non-interference with private trade has now become a recognised policy. In a distressed district, where prices are higher than elsewhere, trade seeks that district as a matter of course. Government, however, have still to aid the distressed. In the Bellary district in the Madras Presidency in 1866, when prices were abnormal on account of distress, trade never ceased. The district had prospered in former years by good cotton prices. The harvests had been scanty, but wages had kept up, and grain poured into the district for months before the crisis of distress. There was no railway then, and want of water and fodder made trade very difficult; nevertheless traffic kept on.

An attempt was made to import some tons of grain for the use of the destitute. The grain was given gratis by Government at Bangalore. It was carried half-way to Bellary for nothing, but the double cost of carriage the other half-way to Bellary made the grain as dear as it was in the worst time of distress. Moreover, the carriage broke down, the contractors failed, the bullocks died of famine and the drivers of cholera. There was, therefore, no effectual competition with native transport or prices.

It is not in the least to be supposed that there can

be a saving of money by Government carriage rather than by native carriage. Government always pays extra, and its agents have not the stimulus of private profit. Personal interest produces the greatest effect all over the world, and Government support is only claimed by schemes not sufficiently remunerative. To buy dear and sell cheap is not an uncommon occurrence in Government operations; but this, though not affecting Government, would soon terminate the career of a merchant.

When means of communication are open to a district free trade enters, and all Government competition with that trade is only and wholly evil. Private traders can make much better bargains as regards carriage than Government. Their distribution is more economical, and self-interest is admitted to be the greatest factor in all such transactions. The argument, therefore, that Government can intervene with advantage when private trade cannot, is unsound when the subject is fully investigated. Government has a function to perform, it has to save the lives of its subjects; but it does so most effectually when it constructs roads and thus facilitates trade, and when by giving wages to the destitute it enables them to buy food and live. A case occurred in the time of the famine of 1866, in a district next to Orissa, which was overflowed by the destitute from that province. Grain was sent by a mercantile firm from Madras, and had to be sold for less than prime cost; it had to compete with Government grain sent there, and yet the famine was not stopped by the comparative cheapness of grain in the distressed district. The real relief would have been to have enabled the distressed to buy the grain; to have employed the poor at liberal wages. When wages are good trade is active, and the converse holds good.

Trade follows profit. It may, of course, be argued that it would be cheaper for Government to pay wages with grain, but there are many difficulties and drawbacks in payment with so bulky a commodity—transport, storage, distribution, the liability to damage and to peculation. But whenever Government, with its indifference to loss, deals in grain, it paralyses private trade, which cannot make head against so formidable a competitor. In the anxiety to save life conditions of trade are overlooked. Wherever, on the contrary, there are open communications, private trade has been found equal to the emergency, only Government has its part still to play in enabling the destitute to purchase food.

The question is wholly one of open communications. As regards relief when communications are open, Government has a choice; it may attract destitute persons from a distressed district by offering work and wages out of the distressed locality, or it may open remunerative public works, if such are feasible, in the locality. It is a question of comparative economy; it may be more economical to carry the man to the work than to carry the work to the man. When people starve in the midst of cheap prices, their destitution must be great.

RELIEF CAMPS

RELIEF CAMPS.

IN respect to administration each district, in the Madras Presidency at least, was, during the famine period, an *imperium in imperio*. The mode and order of relief adopted may, therefore, be fairly understood if the procedure of one district is given. The district of Coimbatore is, perhaps, above the average in careful famine administration, its collector having had experience in Bellary in a similar disaster in 1866. It may, however, be useful to cite it for the purpose of illustration. In this district the Government relief was originally confined to public works organised by the collector and his division officers. A forecast of the results of the failure of the north-east monsoon in 1876 had been made about the latter end of November. In December a plan of works was prepared, tools procured, gangs organised, and work began wherever the need arose. No stoppage or hitch of any kind occurred. The repair of the neglected village road was first taken in hand, and cart tracks, indeed fair roads, leading to villages substituted for the narrow, cactus-overgrown, stony ravines, to which want of funds and neglect had reduced these tracks. The storage of metal for the trunk roads, in which, for want of maintenance funds, they had always been deficient, was carried on to an enormous extent. Stones were collected and broken, and arranged in neatly measured piles along the lines of the main road. The storage was effected, never above, but often below, the ordinary rates. Neglected irrigation channels were cleared of silt, a work well suited for the unskilled labourer. The irrigational capacity of the district could not be increased: every river had been laid under contribution, and there was more land fitted for irrigation than water, even in good seasons, but in a year like that of the famine the rivers were very low, and their supply failed to reach the lower channels. Much sanitary improvement of villages was carried out. In Erode, Caroor, and Dharapuram, the *glacis* of the forts was levelled and ditches filled up, and obstructions to ventilation removed. At Coimbatore town valuable work was carried out by the reclamation of a swamp close to the town which was caused by the ebb and flow of an irrigation tank. The silt in the bed was excavated and carried to the shallow swampy part, which was raised above high water level, thereby adding thirty or forty acres of valuable land which was immediately utilised as a plantation. The water space was contracted and deepened, so that there was less surface evaporation, and the salubrity of the town, which used to suffer from fever and cholera, greatly improved. The cost of this work was about 500 rs. an acre, and the mean depth of silt removed about 4½ feet.

The superintendence of all famine works fell on the revenue officers from January till October, when the professional department relieved them of this onerous task.

For the destitute and suffering private charity was at first organised, then supplemented by State funds, and, finally, wholly superseded by them when the increasing distress put it out of the power of former contributors to continue their subscriptions. Room, however, was again found for relief funds when British munificence was made available, and in no district was that charity better disbursed.

The first mode of relief adopted was the distribution of cooked food to persons with tickets; the next was large camps with sleeping accommodation for the houseless, and daily task-work. The final arrangement was that of closed camps, where the inmates were shut up as a condition of relief. This mode of relief, even though modified to suit the various castes, was abhorrent to the habits and feelings of the people, and induced a great reduction of numbers who preferred liberty and the chance of alms to confinement. Ranges of leaf huts, within inclosures, with sanitary appliances, were constructed. The accommodation was comfortable and the food good, but still the confinement was unpopular, and thousands elected to return to their villages rather than remain in a closed camp. The worst feature in this was that the parents took away their children with them, and these were those who mostly profited in condition by the food given in camps. To each large camp was attached an hospital—much needed, as famine diseases of dysentery, diarrhœa, and dropsy were frequent. The hospitals, with their wards, dispensaries, and all needful accommodation, were also constructed of cocoanut leaves ; raised platforms were constructed for the patients, and mats and clothing provided. The great difficulty, when many people are congregated in a certain space, is sanitation. The Coimbatore camps were inspected by the Viceroy on his visit to Southern India, and his Excellency recorded his approval of them, but thought the expenditure rather extravagant. The constant supervision of camps, without which great evil would have resulted, was a severe tax on the collector and his assistants. In fact, the supervision of work for nine months, and camps for fifteen, involving incessant travelling, physical toil, and continuous mental anxiety, was a strain on the strongest constitutions. This was also all extra work. In October, when the famine began to ebb, additional officers were sent from the Bengal Presidency, but their ignorance of the language and their taking up the time of the superior native officials who had to attend on them and interpret for them, were considerable drawbacks to their usefulness. In fact, it seems doubtful whether more good would not have resulted from employing a less number of local officers acquainted with the people and their language.

So far the experience of one district in its general relief operations. Particulars may follow of the practice adopted for relief of paupers generally, which was only decided upon after much consideration and accepted as containing in it the teaching of much experience.

The first principle of gratuitous relief was that the aid should be given in the shape of cooked food. There might be various modes of fraud connected with the purchase of grain, its issue and the accounting for the same ; but when relief houses were well supervised, the food reached the people, and the children especially showed its beneficial effect. When a man does not supervise the issue of grain to his horses, from want of time or other cause, he has one test in their condition ; and when condition steadily improved among the young, the relief was shown to be efficacious.

There was, however, another theory started, viz., the food for man, woman, and children being alike in quality and only differing in quantity, it was suggested, and the local Government adopted the suggestion, that a dole of money should be substituted for cooked food. The mother it was argued would purchase with the money milk and appropriate diet for her child. Milk,

however, after the cows had died, was not procurable
to the ordinary purchaser.   Only the better classes had
been able to preserve their cows during the period
of drought, and although they might, as a favour, sell
the same to the collector for use in a famine camp,
they would not part with it to outside applicants.

It was found, as a knowledge of native character
might have predicted, that though the mother had an
animal affection for her child, yet in very many cases
she loved tobacco and betel nut more.   Paupers were
found lying starved on the roads with tobacco in their
possession and some small coins.   They had indulged
in these luxuries in preference to the necessaries of life.
Infant life could not safely be left to the tender mercies
of an ignorant parent.   In some districts the cooked
food relief which was first approved by Government
was never changed for a more dubious charity.

As regards the recipient of State relief the degradation of appearing at the relief house was some test in
preventing the better classes from partaking of the
charity of Government until dire hunger compelled
them to do so.   In the towns, large sheds were built of
bamboos and cocoanut leaves, gigantic caldrons allowed
of rice being cooked in bagsfull, people were made to sit
in order, and the attendants carried round the food
generally and gave the recipient the contents of a tin
measure of rice ; next followed another attendant, who
distributed a savoury mess of tamarind and pepper with
an ounce or so of dhall and salt which gave a flavour to
the otherwise insipid rice.   In some districts work of a
light nature was given to those who partook of the food,
but it was optional to all to stay during the night in
sheds or obtain other shelter.   In one district the
children were for their own good, and to provide them
with occupation, taught their letters.

One argument in favour of the district camp system was that it introduced order. The inmates were, by the fence surounding, debarred from going away. In spite of this, however, they climbed walls, squeezed through barricade hedges of prickly pear, and frequently would be afterwards found dying on the roads. This sort of imprisonment was, as has been already said, most offensive to the character of the people. And it must be admitted that the large concourse of people which prevented the possibility of separate accommodation for each family was repugnant to those who wished to preserve self-respect. They would come early in the morning, work the whole day for their meals, and go home or anywhere at night, but they would not endure being shut up at nights, as in a gaol, with inferior food and house-accommodation. Be the idea of the natives right or wrong, their repugnance to closed camps was unmistakable.

The next system adopted was the money dole, supposed to be given on house-to-house visitation. When a famine is sore in the land, and ten to twenty per cent. of the population have to be relieved, and the number of relieving officers is necessarily few, there is no help but to entrust to some degree the head of the village with the distribution of money dole. The immemorial practice of India, and perhaps other countries, is to pay a percentage on favour bestowed by subordinate official influence. Those who were convicted of the offence of receiving part of the money dole were punished, but the evil was universal, and even those who were paid from the hand of an unimpeachable distributor voluntarily contributed a percentage to the village official who had enrolled their names as proper objects of relief. House-to-house visitation, the preparation of correct lists, may be feasible in a small country, and with a sufficient staff of honest controllers, but where recipients counted by thousands, over thousands of square miles, it is a gigantic operation, and one not likely to be properly controlled. There are limits to human power. The story is told of one collector, on the receipt of a list of alleged proper recipients for the money dole, which had been forwarded by the village officer, inspected and certified by the inspector, and perused by the tahsildar, who, not being satisfied with the list, deputed a European officer to make enquiry. This officer paraded the proposed recipients, and found not one in real need of relief.

The relief camp is intended to provide temporarily for those who are able to work,[1] and permanently (that is as long as they require it) for those who are sick and unable to do any considerable amount of work through old age and infirmity. The temporary cases are those where applicants come for labour and the relief officer is not able at the time to provide them with labour; he must not turn them away, but must relieve them in the camp and work them there till he can draft them on to a relief work. The relief camp may also be used as a rest house for gangs on their way to a relief work who come with an order from the relief officer entitling them to food and shelter for the night. There is further the case of the emigrants' rest house which will be treated separately.

The permanent cases are those who are not so decrepit and bedridden as to require village relief, but who are not fit to be sent on to a relief work, or to look after themselves and cook for themselves. They are the least efficient portion of those who are not fit to be put into Class II. They include those who are in

[1] The description is from Mr. C. A. Elliott's Famine Code.

bad health but not ill enough to be put into hospital, and those who are convalescents and have just left hospital.

Nothing but cooked food is given at relief camps, the ration being one pound of rice or of ragi flour plus three pies' worth of condiments for an adult, and half the quantity for a child over seven, plus two pies. A chapter in the Code on special treatment applies equally to special cases in relief camps. No raw rations are permitted. The daily food is given in two meals, morning and evening, at about 7 A.M. and 5 P.M.

The two conditions on which food is given at a relief camp are residence and work. For this reason the camp must be enclosed and admission or exit only be possible by a gate at which a guard is constantly posted. Sufficient accommodation must be provided inside for the usual population of the camp, with a margin over for any exceptional influx. Every person in the camp must be put to some work, however slight, except those who are actually sick. The feeblest old woman can spin a little thread, and others can carry a light basket of sand to throw on the floor, or card cotton, or pick wool, and those who are a little stronger can collect and break stones. For the sake of their health and spirits and self-respect, it is better they should do this than that they should sit idle all day.

The establishment should consist of paupers as far as possible. The only paid officials should be the superintendent, the accountant, and the hospital assistant; but one rupee per month may be paid to the overseers and to the head cook in addition to food. Carpenters and blacksmiths if required may be called in and paid in cash. But all other servants of the camp should be paid in food, or in raw grain if their caste requires it, and should as far as possible be appointed from among the paupers themselves, not from outside.

The duty of the superintendent is general supervision. He is responsible for examining the supply of grain received from the contractor, testing its quantity and quality, and entering it in the stock register, also for seeing that it is securely kept in a safe chamber under a good lock or sufficient guard. He is bound to be always present at feeding time, to see that the food is well cooked and the amount of it correct, to see that the paupers are properly organised into gangs and parties, are set to work at labour suitable to their capacities and do a sufficient quantity of the work; and that all members of the establishment do their duty punctually and thoroughly. He will muster the establishment every day and record their attendance in a register. He will also receive daily from the taluk relief officer all new admissions, will assort them into gangs, and see that their names are entered by the overseer on his muster roll.

The gangs are to be organised according to their capacity for work, and also, where necessary, according to their caste, provided they are not thereby split up into too small numbers. If the numbers are small, persons of good caste can be allowed to sit a little apart in working and eating from other members of the gang, and can have a portion of the shed walled off for them while still continuing to be numbered in the gang. The number of a gang should usually be about 40 or 50; when the work is sedentary, like spinning or stone-breaking, it may be more; when the labourers are scattered over a large space, as on stone-collecting, it should be less. The gangsman or head cooly should ordinarily be a respectable illiterate resident of the taluk in distressed circumstances, who is glad to accept the post for the wages of a ration half as large again as the ordinary one, *i.e.* 1½ lbs. of grain, which may be given raw. The organisation of the gangs should be kept as uniform as possible, so that people may know their work and their place and each other; they should sleep in the same shed, eat meals in the same place, and after meals go together to the same work in the same place, as nearly as possible.

This establishment, which consists of cooks, water-carriers, rice cleaners or grinders, guards, and sweepers, should be kept down to a moderate strength, and should as far as possible be recruited from the paupers of the kitchen, or from respectable people of the taluk who are in distressed circumstances. As a rule they should be paid in grain, which may be given raw if desired, at the rate of 1½ lbs., or for the most onerous tasks 2 lbs. a day; but where the numbers are large, the head cook may in addition receive 1 r. per mensem. The number of each class of servants should be arranged on a sliding scale in proportion to the number of paupers to be attended to. The number of cooks should probably be about 1 per cent., but more may be required where rice is cooked than where ragi, and where the resident population is very feeble, more persons must be entertained to carry and distribute the cooked food than where there are able-bodied paupers who can be so employed. The number of water-women and of sweepers should be about the same as the cooks. B it for the sick in hospital probably one sweeper will be required for 25 patients. The occupation of rice-cleaning or ragi-grinding is one that can be suitably given to women of respectable castes ; two women in good health should easily grind thirty seers of ragi a day, or enough for sixty adults ; but if they are enfeebled, then two relays of two women each should be allowed for each mill. It is not intended in these rules to tie officers down to a too rigid uniformity, but every superintendent and taluk relief officer is expected to do all in his power to combine efficiency with economy.

The orphans and children deserted by their parents should be formed into a separate gang, or if necessary two gangs of boys and girls separately, and clothed in a distinct uniform. As soon as preparations can be made to receive them, they should all be sent in to the relief camp at the district head-quarters, and not kept in outlying camps. The disposal of these orphans is in the hands of Government, and no officer is entitled to make any of them over to any society or private person without the special sanction of the Famine Commissioner.

For want of sufficient and efficient European supervision some of the camps were grossly mismanaged, and large sums of money were spent which ought never to have been expended; instead of helping those in need, the funds supplied were squandered in ministering to village officials and their friends. A non-official gentleman who, at great personal inconvenience and solely with a desire to benefit the people, secured order where before there was chaos, and who managed, at no cost to the State, a large camp for several months, has yielded to the request of the author of this work and has written a description of his experience. It is most valuable and interesting. He says :—

'The daily allowance prescribed by Government for relief camps was to "ordinary diet paupers" about twenty-four ounces, and to "special diet paupers" about thirty-five ounces of uncooked solid food, and there is no doubt that it was enough to sustain life well.

Dr. Dalton, the eminent physiologist, says : " The quantity of solid food required during twenty-four hours by a man in full health and taking free exercise in the open air, is rather less than 2½ lbs.—that is, less than forty ounces." The daily allowance of the United States soldier[1] during the American Civil War was thirty-five ounces of solid food, though it is said that many of the greatest marches of that war were executed when the troops did not receive over two-thirds of that amount—sometimes less than that proportion. It appears, therefore, that the rations prescribed for relief paupers were not much inferior to those of soldiers on active duty, and they were certainly liberal. Moreover, when it was borne in mind that one or more relief camps existed as a rule in each taluk, responsibility for the frightful mortality in many parts can hardly be set to the account of district officials commissioned with the execution of the Government orders.

' Perhaps a few days' experience in a relief camp— believed not to be wholly an exceptional one—may cast a ray of light on this subject.

' The camp was large enough to permit the feeding of several thousand people at once. It was furnished with kitchen, store-shed and hospital-sheds, and was in general well-arranged. Twenty cooks, a sufficient number of scavengers, peons, carts, &c., constituted the working force of the camp ; all being under the management of three gumastahs and a superintendent. The salaries of the establishment aggregated about two hundred rupees a month, an expenditure sufficient to warrant expectation of good results.

---

[1] The writer of this narrative of camp life served with the Federal troops in the American war, and was with Sherman in his march through Georgia, which accounts for the source whence the illustration is drawn.

'Yet the number of destitute persons to be seen wandering in the streets and around the camp, the late hours for issuing food, and especially the frequency with which dead bodies were found lying in out-of-the-way places, all indicated, to say the least, a want of efficient use of means at hand for relieving distress.

'Thinking that perhaps something could be done to render the camp more efficient, the writer offered to supervise it during the severest months of 1877. The proposition was accepted, and the native officer at the head of the taluk gave over charge to me. He at the same time informed me that the camp was in good working condition, and that to guard against the admission of unworthy persons, all applicants for relief were first examined at the taluk kachcheri. Those deemed worthy were furnished with tickets stamped with his own private seal, and only such ticket-holders were allowed in the camp.

'On repairing to the camp in the evening to observe its work preparatory to assuming charge next day, I found a crowd said to number fourteen hundred in the enclosure. They were all arranged in divisions according to castes—Sudras, Mussalmans, Pariahs, and Chucklers—though many of those called Chucklers were in fact Christians and should have been so classed. Some eighty or more persons reported sick and on special diet were in a shed by themselves, and some twenty small-pox patients were in another shed at a little distance from the camp. There were, probably, five hundred outside crying for admission, many of whom were, to use the medical officer's words, "in the last stages of destitution," while a glance at the ticket-holders would have led any intelligent man to suspect that many of those gratuitously fed were well

able to earn wages on relief works. Especially noticeable was the number of young women who were either
not accompanied at all by children, as was required, in
order to entitle them to gratuitous relief, or had with
them children whose extremely emaciated condition
was in marked contrast with the physical appearance
of their alleged mothers.

'There were also many persons of both sexes who
appeared to be well enough in other respects but seemed
to be blind or lame, or crippled in arms, or had swollen
joints wrapped in enormous rolls of leaves. These
matters were noted for enquiry at a future time.

'One of the first things that attracted attention after
entering the camp was a group of gumastahs (overseers)
seated on a mat enrolling new paupers ; one taking
names, another writing tickets, and a third stamping
the tickets with the tahsildar's private seal—all this a
half-mile from the taluk kachcheri.

'When I asked to have the officers and servants
pointed out to me, it was found that there were a
number of fellows running here and there, apparently
very busy guarding gates, keeping order, &c., whose
names could not be found on the rolls. As they could
not therefore receive cash payment for services, their
presence was a source of some surprise.

'Constables on guard could be seen at one minute
several paces outside of the enclosure, making most
energetic efforts to drive back the crowd, and at the
next would be as far within, shouting and scolding.
While thus engaged in faithful discharge of their duty,
numbers of persons availed themselves of the opportunity afforded to glide in behind the guards and find
seats in the crowd inside.

'Supplies for the camp were purchased through one
of the village merchants with whom a regular account

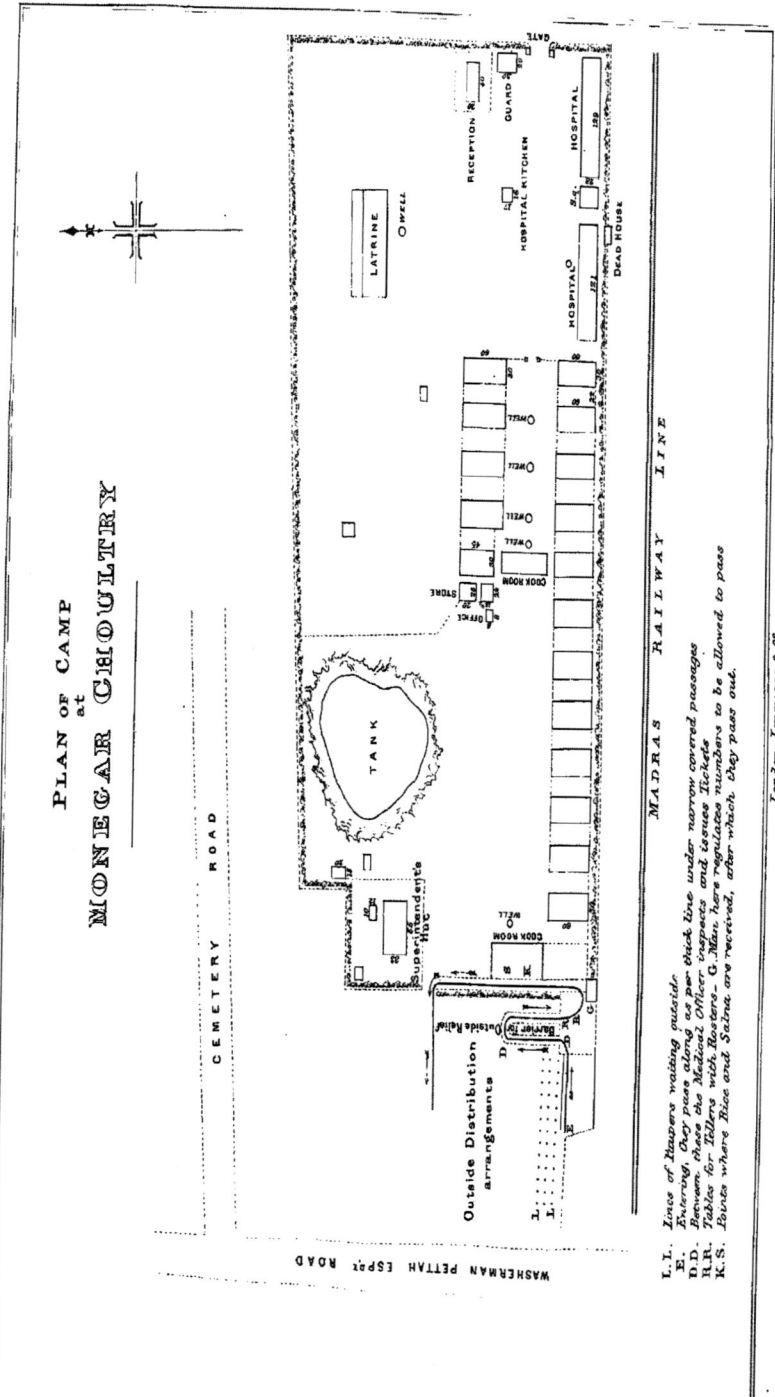

PLAN OF CAMP
at
MONEGAR CHOULTRY

CEMETERY ROAD

WASHERMAN PETTAH ESPer ROAD

TANK

LATRINE

RECEPTION

GUARD

HOSPITAL KITCHEN

HOSPITAL

DEAD HOUSE

HOSPITAL

COOK ROOM

STORE

OFFICE

Superintendent's Hut

COOK ROOM

MADRAS RAILWAY LINE

Outside Distribution
arrangements

L.L. Lines of Paupers waiting outside.
E. Entering. They pass along as per thick line under narrow covered passages.
D.D. Between, these the Medical Officer inspects and issues Tickets
R.R. Tables for Tillers with Rosters. — G. Main, here regulates numbers to be allowed to pass
K.S. Booths where Rice and Salava are received, after which, they pass out.

London, Longmans & Co.

E. Weller, litho

was kept. Orders for supplies were sent daily, and the supplies were generally obtained in the bazaar by this merchant. No examination of grain bags was made to determine the quality of their contents, nor were any consignments tested to see whether the quantity returned was equal to that ordered and paid for by the Government. Persons accustomed to do business in an Indian bazaar need not be told what possibilities of fraud there were under such a *régime*, where the transactions amounted sometimes to hundreds of rupees daily.

'This merchant's bills were presented weekly, endorsed by the superintendent, and paid at the taluk kachcheri, the only possible check on fraud being simply to see that the number of paupers "reported" justified the amount of supplies returned in bills.

'One item of these daily orders was a sum of ready cash, varying from ten to fifteen or more rupees for sundry expenses. The only trace made of the use of this money was found in the indefinite entries :—" Paid wood," " Paid vegetables," &c.

'Food was not ready for distribution till nearly dark, and had to be issued by torch-light. As the force of cooks was not sufficient to permit the organisation of more than two distributing parties, work was necessarily continued till a late hour in order to properly feed all. I learned, indeed, that work was regularly thus prolonged until eight or nine o'clock, and that the exhaustion of the lamp oil, or any one of several occurrences, was regarded sufficient cause for closing the camp, even though but a part of the people had been fed.

'The Sudras were fed first, then the Mussulmans, and afterwards the Pariahs, Chucklers, and Christians, and lastly the sick. It happened this evening—it was said to be a thing of frequent occurrence—that the supply of cooked food fell short, and the last-named class were dismissed with half-rations. Moreover, there is good reason to believe that at least part of the sick were not fed at all, and as many of them were quite helpless, they were without food or drink for thirty hours. As the above order was regularly followed, losses from whatever cause always fell on these most needy classes.

'I noticed, too, that a rich curry prescribed by Government for special diet paupers, was issued to the Sudras, while the sick, for whom it was intended, received pepperwater only on their food.

'On assuming charge of the camp next day, as a beginning of better work, orders were given that no bill presented for payment at the kachcheri on account of the camp should be paid unless it bore my endorsement, and arrangements were entered into to supply the required fuel from certain stores of Government wood then offered for sale. With this arrangement ceased the daily order for ready cash, and with the cash ceased the supply of buttermilk with which the gumastah and visiting friends were wont to regale themselves. Separate lists of the christians were made out, and orders issued that the sick should have warm conjee two or three times a day in addition to regular meals, and water to drink when desired.

'On going to the camp in the evening at the appointed time it was found that food would not be ready till five o'clock, though strict orders had been given to have everything ready by three o'clock. It seemed as if the servants had an understanding among themselves that food should be distributed after dark.

'Seeing that it would be quite impossible to feed the

people within reasonable hours, I called up a party of mussulmans and another of christians, placed each under a brahmin gumastah, and prepared to distribute food by four parties instead of two as formerly.

'To guard against violation of caste rules, the sudra cooks were directed to bring out food from the kitchen and pour it into distributing vessels. The mussulmans were then sent to feed the mussulmans and christians. But some one whispered that the chucklers had touched the food; and though this all took place in presence of the camp, and was in perfect accordance with rules to which all classes were accustomed, yet the sudras and mussulmans rose in a body and left the camp, refusing to take the food. Five minutes later the cooks bolted and confusion reigned. Rumours say the superintendent stationed men along the roads and warned all caste people of the outrage, thus spreading the reports. The village was soon in an uproar, which was not hushed till a late hour.

'Thus ended the first day: bad for the caste people, but the rest had full rations for once; the sick received their curry, and seemed well pleased with the change.

'Next morning the discontented paupers were at the camp early, but were evidently hungry and disposed to be quiet. Deeming the vessels defiled, the cooks refused to go to work. Orders were therefore given to clear out the kitchen, new vessels were bought, and a brahmin priest was allowed to purify the ground according to their own rites, whereupon the servants all resumed duty.

'The acting tahsildar was present, heard my statement of caste troubles just as here given, heard the above-mentioned orders issued, and saw work resumed. Yet knowing all this, he sat down an hour later and wrote to Government an account of the difficulties as he had heard them in the streets the night before, without a word of the facts, or so much as an intimation that the difficulty was at an end.

' The same day the telegraph flashed the story to Madras and brought a message from his Grace the Governor on the subject. But, unfortunately, before the despatch reached the camp the plans of the previous evening had again been acted upon, with the difference that hunger had brought people to their senses. All castes ate their food quietly, the sick were cared for, and the camp closed before dark. It may be added that this plan was not changed so long as it was necessary to use an increased force.

' A little enquiry by competent authority resulted in the superintendent's sudden departure from the camp. The acting tahsildar availed himself of a short sick-leave and visited friends in a neighbouring taluk.

' Some of the special diet paupers were so helpless that it was necessary to lift them about, and even to put food into their mouth or allow them to die of hunger in the camp. As caste gumastahs would not do such work, an intelligent young christian man was appointed gumastah and assigned to this duty. Many persons of all castes owe their lives to this young man's kind and faithful care. Yet the camp servants were so angry at his appointment that only after the summary dismissal of one or two of the most insolent could they be brought to treat him with respect. Even then he lived several months in constant fear that he would be drawn into some trap set for him and brought to trouble.

' On the third day I determined to make a careful examination of the paupers to ascertain the cause of certain matters noted on my first visit. The better to do this the people were admitted to camp one caste at a time and inspected as they came.

'The strong young women were there, indeed, with little children, and passed in regularly. But a half-hour later an inspection of the lines revealed the same state of affairs as at first and solved the mystery. The babies had been borrowed for the occasion and returned to their mothers as soon as the gates were safely passed. Emaciated mothers being admitted on their own merits, loaned their poor little babies to stranger women that they too might have an apparent excuse for resorting to the camp. A vigorous pull often straightened a crooked arm or hand; a sudden pass with the hand proved many of the blind to be cheats. Many a swollen knee or ankle when stripped of its bandages of rags and leaves proved to be of normal size, and lame men became as antelopes when startled by sudden fear. In a word, it was quite evident that more than half of the people that were gratuitously fed were able to do a good day's labour.

'Breaking up of certain relief works about this time sent many persons wandering around the country, and in a few days over three thousand were at the camp. With increased numbers came greater difficulties and confusion.

'Lingering in the camp till dark one evening I discovered a sudden increase in the crowd outside. This was caused by the village ryots, coolies, and masons flocking in after their day's work was done. As many of them were personally known to me it is certain that this was the class of people referred to. I soon discovered that they were creeping through the fence in all directions. At my approach a dozen sprang from a single hiding place and ran away.

'Having gained access to the camps, they would sit

down in the various lines. Some would crouch down and cover their heads with their cloths, others would half hide themselves behind other persons, and in this way they would wait their turns to receive food as the servants passed along. Having succeeded, a quick movement into another line, or a sudden leap over a fence into the next caste, would enable them to secure a second allowance ; and so they went on. An active man could easily obtain several portions. One of the village officials was caught with a considerable quantity of food in his cloth. In justification of his conduct he asserted that he had only been drawing for his family, and presented seven tickets, all duly stamped, in proof of his statement. Three months in the Zillah gaol probably convinced him of the irregularity. I was troubled to account for the fact that no grain or cooked food was ever to be found in the morning, though there was a balance over on several occasions, and that new vessels had to be bought every day. Desiring to ascertain the cause, I one evening left the camp at an earlier hour than usual, but rode back again at about eight o'clock. Dismounting and walking quietly into the camp, I found a number of the cooks still at work, but the officers were gone. A crowd of at least one hundred men, mostly large strong ryots from the village, had gained access to the camp, and was gathered in the vicinity of the godown and kitchen. Among them were the fellows I noticed the first day acting as volunteer gate-keepers, &c. Presently two cooks, followed by a column of ryots, entered the camp, all carrying pots of water on their heads, and marched straight into the kitchen. The case was plain enough now. These fellows intended to enter the kitchen by this *ruse*, when each would have set down his water pot, taken up a pot of food or curry, and pass off to his house. Others would have helped themselves to vessels, filled them with dry grain, and gone away. But where were the two constables on duty at night? In the farther corner of the camp, of course, carefully watching the stones piled up there when the camp was cleared, lest some one should steal them!

' This night's rounds firmly convinced me that it was a matter well understood between the cooks and ryots, and perhaps with full knowledge of some of the officers, that work was to be continued till after dark, and that lamp-oil was purposely short every night, allowing darkness to cover the premeditated loot.

' It thus became evident that nothing short of a complete revolution would reach the centre of the trouble. The distressed poor were starving in sight of plenty, while a demoralisation almost as much to be dreaded as famine was fast seizing the able-bodied of all castes. Even when sent off in companies under escort of constables, who were ordered to conduct them straight to relief works, they would not go. An hour later they would be wandering in the streets, and in the evening would be again crowding around the camp.

' The full state of affairs being clearly brought before the proper officers, a complete reorganisation of the camp was decided upon, and was made under the supervision of the authorities. It could hardly be otherwise than that some worthy of gratuitous relief should have been sent off with the crowds that were dismissed to work. But by this radical stroke the camp was put into a manageable condition, and those in charge had the satisfaction of knowing that a very large proportion of the persons retained ultimately recovered strength and returned to their villages.

' One more fact deserves mention, as it indicates that there is an important element which should enter into

any correct solution of the problem of famine expense
and loss, but which is likely to be overlooked. I one
day received a note from the acting tahsildar, asking
what arrangements had been made for burial of dead
bodies from the relief camp, and also stating that the
mortality was rapidly on the increase, for he had the
day before paid for burial of *thirty* corpses at half a
rupee each.

'This information was somewhat of a surprise to me,
for on the day referred to I had been in the camp all
day, and had seen every dead body found in or around
the camp. The number was just *seven*, nearly all
deaths from cholera and small-pox. Moreover, these
seven bodies had been buried by coolies under my direction, and had been paid for by me, the total cost being
one and a half rupees. The thirty reported were
returned by village officials as deaths in the camp,
when not one had been so buried. I cannot account
for the strange report except in this way. When I
assumed charge of the camp, village vetyans were
engaged to bury the dead, but I noticed that they were
rarely more than half an hour disposing of a body. As
the ground was almost as hard as a stone, proper burial
was, of course, out of the question at such a time. My
belief is, that they simply threw the bodies into holes
or ditches, or into the prickly pear, and reported them
buried. Another party of village vetyans would happen
to pass that way by previous arrangement, and take the
corpses to the village officials as those of persons dead
by the wayside. The burial receipt being obtained,
another ditch or bunch of prickly pear would serve as a
place where a third party could find them, repeat the
rites, and so on at will. But would not the trick be
detected? No, not necessarily. The karnum would
be debarred by his caste from a close inspection, and a

handful of dust would effectually prevent recognition from a distance. Besides, two annas out of each burial fee would suffice to forestall any inspection. I do not say this plan was followed, but in what other possible way this number could be made out I do not see. One thing is certain, not a single burial took place from the camp that day, where thirty were reported and paid for, and it is exceedingly improbable that so many unknown and unclaimed bodies would ever be found in any day in a small town.'

Perhaps it may be thought that this camp was exceptional in its condition. An illustration may be in point. A special famine relief officer in charge of a neighbouring taluk told the writer that the number reported in the camp where he was on duty was only about half as great on the day of his arrival as it had been the day before. On asking why this difference existed, he was told by the officers that an inspection of the camp the previous day had resulted in half of the paupers being sent to their villages. The fact probably is, that Government had been paying the cost of feeding two hundred persons who were never in the camp.

The source of all this trouble appeared to be in the want of honest efficient supervision. The few European officers in each district could not personally visit the camp except for a day or two at a time, and at long intervals. A European officer at the head of each taluk would have saved untold sums to the Government. An honest intelligent corporal would probably make sad work of handling a well-drilled battalion. What would be expected if an ignorant, inexperienced, and probably dishonest recruit were placed in command of two thousand raw militiamen as ignorant and dishonest as he?

The question of the quantity of food to be given in the camps was the subject of much discussion. Regarding the Monegar Choultry camp near Madras— probably the best managed camp in the Presidency— Dr. Cornish on April 9 said, ' I have just completed an inspection of the Monegar camp, and I regret to state that I do not find the condition of the people to be at all satisfactory. While a great many of the inmates have put on flesh of some sort, they appear to me to be, as a rule, in a very poor condition of health. Their muscles are soft and flabby, and they are decidedly anæmic. I fear there are very few of those who have been fed some months really fit to do a day's work. But the most marked feature in the people of this camp is a peculiar condition of the tongue. In many cases the tongue is quite denuded of its usual coating, and is preternaturally clean, while the lining membrane of the mouth is unusually red and tender. In others there is a redness of the tongue at the edges, and cracks and fissures on the fur on it, denoting an irritable condition of the mucous membrane throughout the intestinal tract. I observe, too, that a considerable number in the camp have spongy and discoloured gums, indicative of approaching scurvy, and of some deficiency in the diet. The young children in the nursery are nearly all dropsical, and most of the old people are in the same state. The mortality amongst these is still very high, and likely to continue high, so far as I can see. If an epidemic of cholera broke out in the camp just now, I believe the mortality would be very serious indeed.' The Sanitary Commissioner suggested that the opinions of independent medical officers should be obtained, and the Government appointed the surgeons-general of the British and Indian medical services—Dr. George Smith, and Dr. C. A. Gordon, C.B.—to inspect the paupers at the Monegar Choultry and Red Hill camps, and to report, with as little delay as possible, their opinion of their condition and whether the diet they were then receiving was sufficient to keep them in health.

A most valuable and interesting report was prepared by Drs. Gordon and Smith, of which more cannot be given here than the conclusions arrived at as to whether the diet the paupers were then receiving was sufficient to maintain them in health. The inspectors said :—

(a) We consider that with respect to paupers admitted into the relief camp during the early part of the existing famine the particular ration of food sanctioned has so far enabled a number of them to hold their own. Even with this class, however, we doubt whether the state of health in which they now are is likely to continue much longer under existing conditions of diet, &c.

(b) In the cases of persons presenting the deranged state of the tongue, gums, and general health already detailed, we consider the present scale of diet altogether insufficient; this insufficiency in our opinion being partly in its quantity and partly in the nature of its constituents.

(c) With regard to paupers more recently admitted, and who have been for a considerable time previous exposed to the severity of the famine, we consider the present ration to be insufficient to maintain health. In the cases of such persons the natural reserve of power possessed in greater or less degree by all men had been diminished to an extent varying with the severity with which the scarcity or want had affected them; a considerable number of them have become affected with the characteristic derangement of the digestive organs indicated by the signs already noted, and the functions of digestion and assimilation in them are proportionally impaired.

(d) For the women who are now nursing infants at the breast, the present scale of diet is insufficient to maintain them in health. In their particular case it is insufficient even to a greater degree than in that of men ; with the former not only does it become necessary to support the physical powers of the individual as with the latter, but over and above this, material has to be supplied for transformation into food on which growth and health on the part of the nursling infant are dependent.

It is an important question in laying down a diet scale what are the purposes to be filled by it in respect to the person partaking of it, that is, whether he shall be maintained only at a point of mere existence without a reserve of tissue and power to enable him when the time comes to undertake ordinary labour, or whether he shall be preserved in a condition sufficient to maintain this reserve and physique to resume hereafter his ordinary occupations.

For the first-mentioned purpose the scale now in use seems to be sufficient in respect to those who have only suffered from the effects of ordinary poverty or scarcity.[1] For such, however, as have been lowered by the pressure of want and famine, it is deemed to be altogether insufficient. Our opinion is that, in order to maintain the health of all according to the standard we have indicated, a rate of diet considerably above the present is necessary.[2]

In respect to all classes now in camp, we consider the scale laid down for ordinary non-labouring prisoners to be the most suitable, with a few trivial modifications as noted below, viz. :—

	lbs.	oz.	drs.
Rice	1	8	0
Vegetables	0	4	0
Dholl	0	2	0
Mutton, excluding bone, or equivalent in fish (three times per week)	0	3	0
Salt	0	1	0
Tamarind	0	0	8
Ghee (clarified butter) or oil	0	0	8
Curry powder	0	0	7
Onions	0	0	8
Garlic	0	0	4

Surgeon-General Smith recommends on non-meat days six ounces of buttermilk.

The Madras Government, when these papers were laid before them, directed that the scale of diet recommended by Surgeons-General Gordon and Smith in their report on the Monegar Choultry camp 'be adopted at all relief camps, and that the apparent result of the alteration now ordered be reported every fortnight.'

In March Sir Richard Temple thought it necessary

---

[1] *Note by Surgeon-General Smith.*—Add, although the dietary is defective as regards certain necessary elements of food.

[2] *Note by Surgeon-General Smith.*—We deem it also necessary that the dietary indicated shall avoid sameness, and be constructed so that existing pathological tendencies in the pauper population of the camp be, if possible, checked.

for officers in charge of relief camps to make their camps 'somewhat more popular than they are now.' 'After consulting various native gentlemen of experience' he says, 'I think that some concession might be made in relief camps to the caste feelings of the people. For very poor classes, who in this Presidency are often said to belong to no caste, the present system of public cooks in the camps might suffice. But for those who have grown up with caste feeling some relaxation of the present arrangements might be permitted. Inmates might be allowed to cook their own food, either for themselves or for self-arranged gangs, and they might be allowed to eat their meals apart and free from observation. In most of the camps there would be ample space for the enjoyment of such concessions. Then again, the sheds might be set apart for the principal castes; the casteless or very low caste people would in such cases have sufficient shed accommodation for themselves. In most cases it would be possible to make these not very great (but still to natives acceptable) concessions without any considerable increase of expenditure. If such concessions could be given, the relief camps would certainly become more efficient as safeguards against dangerous distress.'

There is no wonder that the camps were regarded with suspicion by the people. The death-rate in them was appalling. As this very high death-rate was one of the features of the famine—a fact that attracted very great attention in England, and has been the subject of questions asked in the House of Commons—it may be desirable to quote fully a report upon the camps in several districts, and likewise to give a few tables showing the terrible nature of the mortality. Writing on June 11, 1877, Dr. Cornish said:—

The mortality occurring in the famine relief camps of this

x 2

Presidency is one of the subjects that have been engaging my attention for some time past, and I have now the honour to submit, for the information of his Grace in Council, the results of my enquiries up to the end of May.

As it did not seem at all clear to me that the deaths occurring in newly-established camps would be registered by the village officials, I addressed collectors of districts on the subject, and requested that a weekly return of strength and mortality, according to a form circulated, might be sent to my office. This request has been very generally responded to, and for the month of May the information has been received in a tolerably complete form. The figures for the period previous to April 28 are not so complete, but will serve to indicate, in some degree, the rate of mortality in the camps for the periods they were severally in working. There are, I imagine, many small relief-houses in the several districts which do not furnish any returns to me, but which are noticed in the returns of the Board of Revenue.

I propose to show the mortality. in relief camps for irregular periods prior to April 28, and distinctly for the month of May. As the camps had been in operation for various periods of time, the annual ratio of deaths to average strength has been calculated on the number of weeks each camp was in existence.

Madras Camps.—The relief camps under the administration of the commissioner of police only are included in the return. For the period of fourteen weeks up to April 28 the average strength was 11,815 and the total deaths 2,511, the annual death ratio being 787·8 per mille. For the four weeks ending May 26 the strength was 16,970 and the deaths 615, or in the ratio of 471·1 per mille.

This shows an apparent improvement in the death-rate of the Madras camps in May, but in my opinion it is attributable mainly to the reception and accumulation in these camps of able-bodied persons who were taken in because they were emigrants, and not because they were in that state of physical destitution which required immediate relief. Great efforts have recently been made to reduce the numbers of those who are in a condition to work, and I hope by sending them back to their villages and districts, or to working gangs, it will be possible to find room for the numerous starving people from the provinces who are now either on out-door relief, or picking up a precarious living by begging in the streets. I am quite certain that the town of Madras has never been fuller of really destitute wanderers than it is at this moment.

Salem District.—I have received returns from eleven camps in Salem district. These on the average had been eleven weeks in existence on April 28, and in that time the strength of the inmates averaged 5,393, and the actual deaths were 1,075, giving an annual ratio of 935·3 per mille. In the month of May the average strength of the camp population was 7,000, and the total deaths in the four weeks was 746, or in the annual ratio of 1,388 per mille. The heaviest mortality of all has occurred in the Dharampury camp, where, since January 2 to May 26, 646 deaths occurred out of a weekly strength of about 1,120. Some deaths from cholera occurred in this camp, but the great bulk of the casualties here and elsewhere in the district were due to famine diseases. It is worthy of notice that the ratio of mortality to strength in the camps of the Salem district was higher in May than in the previous period, proving, I think, the severity of the famine and the extreme destitution of those who are now coming into the camps for relief.

North Arcot.—From the North Arcot district I have received returns only from five camps. There is a relief camp at Chittoor which, I believe, has lately been opened, but no returns have been furnished. Up to April 28 the average strength of the destitute in camps for an average period of eight weeks was 1,870, and 340 deaths were recorded, giving an annual ratio of 1167·9 deaths to 1,000 living. For the month of May I observed that the average number under camp relief was 4,202, and the total deaths 471, or in the proportion of 1,457 per mille of the strength. The mortality has been very high in the Vellore camp, and also in Punganoor and Palmanair, though in the latter camp the numbers were but few. In Punganoor the great mortality of the camp inmates shows how much destitution there has been in that zemindari. It must be borne in mind also, with regard to the North Arcot district, that many thousands of destitute and starved people have wandered away to Madras and other districts. Whether the centres of camp relief in this district are sufficiently numerous may, I think, be considered doubtful.

Cuddapah.—The returns for this district show some of the mortality in April up to certain weeks in May included in May, and are otherwise not as accurate as I should wish. Up to April 28 there are returns only for two camps, Voilpaud and Peelair, in the Voilpaud taluk. These show a weekly strength of 681 for five weeks, and 224 deaths. The May return, which for Cuddapah, Royachoti, and Madanapalli includes deaths occurring in March and April, shows an average strength of 6,465 and 925 deaths in fourteen camps. Adding the 224 deaths in Voilpaud taluk in April, the Cuddapah camps have had altogether 1,149 deaths since they were formed. And in regard to Royachoti, Madanapalli, &c., many deaths occurred while the people were being fed, and before the regular camps for their reception were ready. Of these deaths no special record was kept. Owing to the way in which the information has been given, it is not possible to determine the ratio of mortality to strength for the month of May, but I am afraid it has been so heavy as to indicate very severe pressure and distress amongst the destitute classes in Cuddapah.

Bellary.—Returns have been received only from nine relief camps in the Bellary district, and these in some cases do not show the dates on which the camps were established. Up to the end of April there appear to have been five camps, with an average strength of 4,926, and 248 deaths. In May nine camps return a strength of 6,419, with 585 deaths, but the returns for the Madakasira camp for April are brought into the May account, and thus add to the actual mortality of the month. The deaths in the Bellary camp (147) indicate in May a very high ratio of mortality.

Nellore.—The number of camps of which I have received returns is eight, and these only for the month of May. Of a strength of 3,801, there are returned 337 deaths, but some of these deaths appear to have occurred in April in Sooloorpett camp.

Chingleput.—There have been only four relief camps instituted in this district; of these, two, one at Palaveram and another at Poonamallee, have been in work ever since the beginning of the year, while the camps at the Cortelliar and Chingleput are of recent origin. The strength of the Palaveram camp, I believe, includes the relief workers as well as the destitute. All that is necessary to record of these camps at present is that they show 331 deaths up to May 26, and that the weekly strength furnishing this mortality remains to be adjusted when corrected returns are received.

Kurnool.—The system pursued in the Kurnool district has been mainly one of village relief, but a camp was established at Khaderbagh on April 11, since which time, out of an average weekly strength of 835, there have been 205 deaths. This indicates a very high rate of mortality, and probably of advanced destitution in the inmates.

Returns have been received of relief camps in Madura, Tinnevelly, and South Arcot, but the comparatively low ratio of mortality in the camp inmates would appear to show that the privation and distress in these districts have been nothing out of the ordinary way. No returns of relief camps have been received from the Coimbatore district.

To sum up the results as regards the eight famine districts : the returns prior to April 28 show an average strength of 26,980 receiving relief in camps, and 4,576 deaths, while the returns for May how 50,284 on relief, and 4,037 deaths.

In the weekly reports sent to me the causes of death are generally given. In two or three camps there have been a few deaths put down to cholera or small-pox, but more than nine-tenths of the whole are specified as famine diseases—dysentery, dropsy, diarrhœa, and debility.

The accompanying abstract return will show the registered mortality of each camp. I trust to be able to have more complete figures on this subject for the following months.

From my own observation of relief-camps in Bellary, Cuddapah, Chingleput, and Madras, I do not think that the assembly of the people in the centres of relief has had any bad effect on their health. Our camps have on the whole been very free of epidemics, notwithstanding the general prevalence of small-pox and cholera in the districts. In these camps the poor have had shelter, food, and generally medical supervision, all of which might have failed to reach them under a system of village relief away from direct observation of the district officials. The great mortality I attribute to the hopelessness of the cases from the time they came under relief, and not to causes connected with the aggregation of sick and feeble, or insanitary conditions arising therefrom.

The only peculiar feature of the mortality in relief camps is the frequency of diseased conditions of the bowels. In slow starvation, from which the great majority of the people have suffered before they seek relief, there is a diseased condition of the organs (lacteals) by means of which the nutriment of certain kinds of food is conveyed into the blood, and where this diseased condition exists to any great extent there is very little prospect of recovery. The use of nutritious food fails to restore such persons because the organs which assimilate nutriment have lost their functions. But besides this special condition of the organs of assimilation, it frequently happens that life is cut short in the famine-stricken by dysentery, or diarrhœa, or secondary inflammation of the lungs. Infants at the breast and young children up to the seventh year and old people appear to succumb in the greatest numbers to the famine. Cholera and small-pox especially find their victims ready at hand in those who have been impoverished by bad food.

It is worthy of note that not in one single instance has there been any reason to suspect that the victims of famine have died of what is called 'relapsing' or 'famine' fever in Europe. This disease, which is a variety of typhus fever, was recently supposed to have made its appearance in Bombay, but I believe that further enquiry has elicited the fact that the supposed relapsing fever was nothing more than the ordinary malarious fever always present in Bombay.

Our famine people in Madras have not shown symptoms of fever of any kind. Their temperature, in fact, in the simple wasting of famine, is always lower than normal. In looking back for historical evidence of the diseases accompanying famine, I find that in Guzerat, in 1812, there was a very virulent epidemic of *small-pox* prevailing with famine, just as we have now in this Presidency. It is curious to note that while a variety of typhus is the usual accompanying disease of famine in Europe, here in India small-pox, another contagious malady, should take the place of relapsing fever.

Sufficient has been stated to show that chronic starvation (by which term I mean irregular and inadequate supplies of daily food continued for weeks or months) is a very deadly disease. So deadly is it, in fact, that when degenerative changes of the assimilative organs have set in, recovery is almost hopeless. In acute starvation, such as in the instance of men immured in a coal-pit for five or six days without food, there is not time for the destructive changes to occur in the bowel, and food judiciously administered will restore such persons to health. This is not the case in regard to persons who by a long course of privation have been forced to seek the shelter of relief camps, and wherever these people may be, in camps or in their own villages, the deaths must be appallingly high. In camps we can take cognizance of the mortality, but the village registration will, I fear, show it but imperfectly.

Terrible as was the general experience of camps, ludicrous incidents occurred now and again, one of which may be given.

The superintendent of the famine relief camp at Yerrakancherry reported to Colonel Drever, the commissioner of police, the following incident. On January 19 a man named Vencatagadoo, aged about 55 years, by caste a Yeanadi, of Chittor taluk, was admitted into the hospital suffering from diarrhœa, and after a few hours he was to all appearance dead. His body was ordered by the medical subordinate to be carried away and put into the dead-house. The vettyan, or grave-digger, belonging to the camp was sent for and directed to remove the body of the supposed dead man. Whilst the body was being wrapped in a date mat, the man arose and wanted to know what they were doing with him. The grave-digger and his assistant ran away from the dead-house in great terror and repaired to the quarters of the medical subordinate, and reported that the man whom he had a few minutes ago removed from hospital as a corpse had come to life. Vencatagadoo was then removed to the hospital, where, on arrival, he said he felt hungry and wanted something to eat. Some rice and mutton broth were then given to him, but he refused to eat the food unless a glass of liquor was supplied. Humouring the patient's whim some liquor was obtained. He then ate a hearty meal and began singing songs. He appeared very pleasant and went through a number of antics, dancing in an erect position for some time. He then sat down and moved his hands and legs in different positions, keeping time to the songs he continued to sing. This merriment continued for a couple of hours, and towards evening he again wanted something to eat and drink. His wants were supplied and he slept soundly that night, and awoke apparently in perfect health. But about 9 A.M. the following day he was really dead and was removed to the dead-house, where he was wrapped up in a date mat for the second time and subsequently taken away to the graveyard and buried. The body was watched closely for several hours after the 'second death' by the medical officer, who was quite satisfied the man was really dead this time.

Similar cases to the one above reported have been heard of by medical men after a patient has been suffering from cholera ; it is simply a bright flicker for a few hours before the light of life goes out finally.

Mortality in Camps.

DISTRICTS — Place at which relief camp was opened	Date on which camp was opened	No. of weeks up to April 28	Deaths up to week ending April 28			Deaths in May up to week ending May 26		
			Average strength	Total deaths	Ratio per 1,000 of strength per annum	Average strength	Total deaths	Ratio per 1,000 of strength per annum
MADRAS								
Vencatasawmi, Naick's Market, Triplicane (Royapetta)		14	232	160	2560·3	359	95	3367·6
Salt Cotar		14	1,639	453	1020·8	1,519	30	250·7
Monegar Choultry and Tondiarpett		14	4,276	709	615·7	7,173	214	387·8
Yerkencherry		14	1,089	260	907·2	1,627	45	359·5
Red Hills		14	4,579	923	748·6	6,292	231	477·2
Total			11,815	2,511	787·8	16,970	615	471·1
SALEM								
Gangaleri	February 10, 1877	11	299	48	759·2	396	28	919·2
Namkal	December 21, 1876	18	284	68	690·1	562	75	1734·8
Darampuri	February 1, 1877	13	1,129	424	502·2	1,140	222	2531·5
Ditto Pennagaram	March 28, „	4	.	.	.	604	77	1657·2
Ornagaram	April 1, „	4	510	33	841·2	575	5	1140·4
Ahtur	February 1, „	12	80	13	700·0	115	15	1695·6
Tripatur	January 28, „	13	515	149	1157·2	835	55	856·2
Sunkerrydroog	„ 16, „	15	335	108	1116·4	647	51	12120·6
Oossoor	February 6, „	12	529	98	803·4	943	64	1203·9
Uttengeri	March 1, „	8	1,100	18	106·4	503	79	1137·3
Ditto Haroor	February 6, „	12	632	116	795·8	680	75	1433·8
Total		11	5,393	1,075	9·353	7,000	746	1388·4

	Date							
NORTH ARGOT								
Vellore	February 5, 1877	12	847	179	910·1	1,212	148	1563·0
Ranipett	,, 23, ,,	9	906	159	1014·3	1,347	03	807·5
Palnanair	April 1, ,,	4	117	2	222·2	199	27	1763·8
Punganoor	,, 22, ,,	1				916	168	1873·3
Trichinoor	,, 4, ,,	3				528	37	490·5
Total		8	1,870	340	1197·9	4,202	471	1457·1
CUDDAPAH								
Goondalore at Cheyar Embankment	March 31, 1877	4				108	16	092·9
Budwail	April 30, ,,					288	13	586·8
Sidhout	,, 24, ,,					140	13	1207·1
Proddatur	May 2, ,,					613	21	445·3
Royachoti	April 17, ,,	6				1,040	172	2150·0
Pullampett	May 2, ,,	5				213	11	6710·3
Cuddapah	March 15, ,,					441	137	1014·5
Pulivendalla	,, 22, ,,					333	44	762·7
Pournanilla	April 21, ,,	2				533	84	2048·7
Chitwail	May 7, ,,	6				143	5	454·5
Madanapalli	April 9, ,,	5				1,452	179	3265·9
Kadri	March 12, ,,	6				446	42	488·8
Voilpaud	,, 23, ,,		374	40	1006·2	343	81	3060·9
Peelair, Voilpaud taluk	,, 18, ,,		307	184	5020·6	399	105	3418·5
Total		5	681	224	2350·7	6,465	925	1835·2
BELLARY								
Adoni	March 17, 1877		65	2		365	6	213·7
Sundoor	,, 11, ,,	6	368	1	244·4	467	10	278·3
Bellary		7	3,226	131	3036·6	1,175	147	1626·3
Callianadroogam						486	32	856·0
Hindupur			725	57		805	26	559·9
Pennakondah			542	57		1,287	56	565·6
Madaksira						890	287	5589·1
Anantapur						405	14	898·7
Dharmaveran						539	7	2251
Total			4,926	248	2617·9	6,419	585	11847

Mortality in Camps—continued.

Districts / Place at which relief camp was opened	Date on which camp was opened	No. of weeks up to April 28	Deaths up to week ending April 28			Deaths in May up to week ending May 26		
			Average strength	Total deaths	Ratio per 1,000 of strength per annum	Average strength	Total deaths	Ratio per 1,000 of strength per annum
NELLORE								
Kundukur	February 29, 1877	8	...	...	...	243	5	86·4
Ohundi	March 11, „	7	...	...	...	76	.	.
Gudur	January 1, „	17	...	...	...	735	28	78·7
Vencatagherry	November 26, 1876	22	...	...	...	930	180	279·5
Kaligherry	May 2, 1877	...	...	...	...	628	24	496·8
Soolloorpet	„ 6, „	...	...	...	...	810	144	2294·1
Ongole		...	...	...	...	373	6	836·4
Total			...	...	...	3,801	337	1152·5
CHINGLEPUT								
Cortelliar	April 25, 1877	1	1,694	65	110·8	2,045	79	502·2
Palaveram	December 20, 1876	18	...	...	...	1,806	29	208·7
Poonamallee	„ 16, „	19	601	113	2754·3	807	43	692·7
Chingleput	May 15, 1877 .	...	...	...	...	366	2	281·4
Total			2,295	178	212·2	4,592	153	433·1
KURNOOL								
Kadherbagh	April 11, 1877	2	...	...	...	835	205	2127·7
Grand Total			26,980	4,576	...	50,284	4,037	.

VILLAGE RELIEF AND
VILLAGE AGENCY

VILLAGE RELIEF AND VILLAGE AGENCY.

—+—

Unfortunately, one of the greatest difficulties we have to contend
with in the present emergency is the wily scheming of the
village authorities, who, it is feared, in many instances are
taking advantage of the prevailing distress, and of the
inadequate supervision as yet supplied, to feather their nests
at the expense alike of Government and of their fellow-
countrymen in distress.'—R. DAVIDSON, *Collector of Kurnool.*

ONE of the chief features in the policy being carried out
in Madras when Lord Lytton arrived there at the end
of August 1877, was the system of village relief,
whereby, according to the official returns, more than
one million persons were being supported gratuitously,
a proportion receiving a money dole at their own homes.
The distributors of this relief were village officials,
whose position and influence have been described in
earlier pages of this work. It is putting the matter
mildly to say that Indian village officials are not above
suspicion, and, in cases where money is to be distributed, only to be trusted where there is close scrutiny
and efficient European control. This control was not
possible over the vast area of the Madras Presidency ;
European officers were too few, and great abuses were
the consequence. Hindus themselves do not hesitate
to say that their countrymen made vast sums of money
in an illegal way, whilst the testimony of special relief

officers, and the experience of others who endeavoured to prosecute, and, in some cases succeeded in prosecuting such criminals, was unanimous in describing defalcations as very numerous, but at the same time as exceedingly hard to prove.[1]

[1] A correspondent of the *Indian Daily News*, a special relief officer engaged in Madras, describes the frauds as follows :—' The variety and the intricacy of the means employed to defraud the Government have been granted. Both the givers and the receivers of the charity have been duped. But it must be said that those for whom relief was intended have given proofs of the most criminal duplicity.

' Suicide by violent means, when the cause of it is despair, excited no astonishment. But what can we think of those persons who have tamely submitted to a slow process of starvation, through fear of annoyance hereafter at the hands of the munsif, should they expose his misdeeds and his cruelty towards them. This has actually been the case. When persons, who were being starved because the munsif chose to misappropriate the funds entrusted to him were questioned, they told the most deliberate lies to exonerate their unscrupulous headman. Those who received nothing, or perhaps a handful of grain twice or three times a week, positively asserted that they received relief regularly, and the full amount—a miserable lie— to which, among other evidences, their broken-down condition gave the most emphatic denial.

' Abject creatures have been paraded before European officers. They have been bribed, threatened, cowed into saying that all was right, and they have said what they were bid. They have deceived those who came to relieve their sufferings, and when any of them had the courage to speak out before the " special relief officer," it availed them nothing, for that officer was as harmless as a lamb. He would, however, report! Imagine reporting that a number of people are on the point of death, and that, as you are powerless to remove the oppressor, even for an hour, or to check his powers of mischief, you expect early orders, that is early famine orders. The worst of it is that prosecutions will not stand in these fraud cases. On one side would be a few wretched creatures, whose very destitution and misery would be their safeguard against persecution hereafter at the hands of a vindictive village magistrate, and who would not fear to face even that dreaded official, and accuse him of malpractices, and perhaps of crime. On the other hand, there would be a host of timid and demoralised persons, whom trifling bribes or lengthy threats would induce to give evidence exonerating their tyrants, and this evidence would be backed up by the statements of respectable inhabitants, who perhaps had during a long period received their share of the plunder. This sometimes represents a considerable sum. Wealthy villagers have often obtained the munsif's connivance and sanction to their drawing from six to ten rations daily. Taking six as the more common number, and valuing each ration or dole at one anna, the amount would be in six months something over sixty-seven rupees. Only the more respectable inhabitants could command sufficient interest to secure a large number of

In their first order on the subject, issued on February 1, 1877, the Madras Government feared that 'abuse' would follow a system of village relief owing to the paucity of inspectors. When the inevitable consequences of the practice were pointed out the authorities admitted that the system was open to the objections stated, 'but the village relief is a necessary complement to the camp relief. The orders of Government must be carried out in their entirety, the officers of Government exercising the closest supervision possible.' Sir Richard Temple also strongly insisted upon and urged house-to-house inspection in villages, so that those physically incapacitated should not be altogether overlooked.

A great many reports were sent to Government, indicating fraud and the impossibility of checking it. One or two may be given. Mr. Davidson, collector of Kurnool, wrote :—

In paragraphs 5, 6, and 7 of my letter to the Board, dated February 17, 1877, No. 4, Extra, I had the honour to point out the difficulties we should probably have to contend with in introducing the village relief system owing, among other things, to the wily scheming of the village headmen.

2. Knowing the class of men I had to deal with, I thought I had adopted every precaution to give full effect to the orders of Government, and at the same time minimise the chances of peculation and abuse, by circulating printed instructions to all heads of villages and devising a system of checks.

3. I enclose copies of the marginally-noted papers,[1] and I shall

---

shares. It would take a vast amount of labour to find out where the evil began and where it ended. Moral conviction based on proofs acceptable to common sense as conclusive, are not evidence in a legal sense.'

[1] (1) Copy of this Office Circular, No. 8, of 1877. (2) Copy of this Office Circular, No. 9, of 1877. (3) Printed Takeeds to Reddies. (4) Revenue Inspector's Diary. (5) Reddies' Application for Funds. (6) Return of Persons fed in each week. (7) Translation of Cumbum Tahsildar's Report. (8) Nominal Roll. (9) Copy of this Office Circular, No. 17, of 1877. (10) Copy of Takeed to Tahsildars.

feel greatly obliged if the Board will do me the kindness to suggest improvements or modifications in them, as I find that they have been inoperative to prevent what would seem to be an unnecessarily lavish expenditure of State funds.

4. It would appear from the relief-returns for the week ending April 14, that in 407 out of the 787 villages in the district relief was afforded by the headmen, and that 13,794 persons were being fed daily at an aggregate cost of 7,141 rs. per week. The weekly average cost in each village was thus over 17 rs. 8 as.

The Board of Revenue, on receiving the above, stated that they had anticipated that considerable frauds would result from the village relief system, and ' the abuses which appear to have prevailed in Kurnool are so great that nothing short of the stoppage of the relief and the substitution of more numerous and well-managed camps on the system the trial of which was authorised in G. O. dated April 21, 1877, will, in the Board's opinion, suffice. The village relief should, if continued, be confined to providing temporary relief for persons who are to be sent to the camps, or are willing to go there, or who are in immediate danger of starvation. The collector might try the system of village relief in force in Salem, viz., granting permanent tickets, entitling the holder to receive a daily subsistence allowance, to such persons as by reason of caste, age, or infirmity cannot be put into relief-camps. G. O. March 26, 1877, will be communicated to the collector. One anna a day would probably be sufficient to allow for adults.' The Government simply ordered the collector's letter and the Board's remarks to be ' recorded,' which is equivalent to shunting a subject into a siding, whence it may never be removed.

Another case is given by Mr. Ross, acting head assistant to the collector of Bellary, who, morally certain of the guilt of the parties, could not obtain proofs sufficient for conviction in a court of justice. Writing to the collector on the case, he says :—

The recipients who at first informed me that they usually got only half rations (the village officers appropriating the other half of the grain accounted for), almost immediately retracted their statements, and I could get nothing out of persons whose only chance of getting any food at all would have been lost if they had 'peached' either on this point or on the curious fact that hundreds did not appear for relief just on the day of my inspection. As, however, the names and descriptions of the recipients were not written down (this practice having been quietly dropped after a short time), I could get no proof positive of fictitious entries, and there was then left only the evidence obtained by a check of the accounts which showed daily so many seers for so many persons fed. Here I found, from variations in the number of seers used on different days for the same number of persons, that there had been evidently cooking of the accounts and no attempt at counting or recording the real numbers of those fed. I judged, however, that it would be useless to put the village officers on their trial on the evidence I was able to obtain, which was clearly insufficient for conviction in a court of law. I therefore punished them departmentally.

The acting collector of South Arcot (Mr. F. R. H. Sharp) asked for instructions on certain points in one of the Government Orders relating to the subject, and remarked :—

With reference to clause C, I take the liberty of asking sanction for continuing the system of village relief in the form of distribution of cooked food rather than ready money, for the following reasons :— Where difficulty of supply of grain arises, it is far more likely that the poor will suffer from this difficulty in making their trifling retail purchases than the munsif who has to buy comparatively large quantities, and has the prestige of his position, and of the fact that he is buying for charitable distribution on a large scale to help him. The having to wait some time for the food and to eat it in the appointed place (where this salutary provision is enforced) has a good effect in deterring those not really in want or who can get a day's work from applying. If a money dole is given, all the well-to-do labourers of the place, including servants of ryots, all professional beggars, and others of this class, will doubtless besiege the munsif for money, and even amongst families requiring relief there is no guarantee that the money received will not be spent in 'liquor' or 'betel' for the adults, instead of on food for the children. Even maternal instincts cannot be trusted in this matter; from personal observations I have

reason to believe that mothers recognise in a half-starved infant a potent
pass for relief, and are glad to have their babies' skeletons to secure
their own interests. The munsif is much more likely to cheat in
the matter of distribution of money than in that of food; and, if
called on to account for the extreme emaciation, or perhaps death by
starvation, of any of the people (especially the very young or very
old) of his village, he can easily reply—' What can I do, Sir? I have
given the little (deceased) girl's father or the blind old (deceased)
man's son the prescribed money-payment for the past three weeks,
but I could not compel the father (or son) to spend the money properly.' Relief by means of distribution of cooked food must be a
longer process, and there is a far better opportunity for inspecting
officers suddenly visiting a village to inspect this process, than that of
giving the money-dole. Of course the system of money dole would
be still reserved for gosha females and other exceptional classes.

The reply to this was: ' Government do not
recognise the force of the collector's objections to the
money dole. With careful scrutiny of the village
registers by the relief inspectors and weeding of
persons who should not be on them, there should not be
much room for fraud by village heads.' To the opinion
in favour of money doles the Madras Government
tenaciously adhered. Towards the end of August,
when H. E. the Viceroy was on his way to Madras
from Simla, it was stated:—' This (Madras) Government decided on the adoption of the " money dole "
system for the relief of necessitous residents in villages as being on the whole less open to abuse, more
advantageous to recipients than relief in the form of
cooked food, and not more costly to the State. It was
adopted after long and careful consideration of the
results of other systems, and as likely, by enabling the
poor to remain in their villages, to have a material
effect in checking that tendency to wandering which
has been, and is, one of the causes chiefly conducing to
the great mortality which is prevalent, and which 'it is
most important but very difficult to arrest. Nor is the
advantage arising from the circulation of money which

results from the system to be overlooked ; for in the several villages that circulation will act as a stimulus to trade which is much needed, and which, indeed, it is necessary to keep alive.' After further explanations the letter concluded as follows :—' On reconsideration of the question, his Grace in Council sees no reason to modify his views as to the advisability of maintaining the money dole system.'

This letter reached the Viceroy whilst his Excellency was at Poona, and the consequence was close examination of the subject with a view to its discussion at Madras in conference with the local authorities. It was found that the first mention of this form of village relief was in the 'Proceedings' of the Madras Government, No. 1830, of May 28, 1877. It was therein laid down that, inasmuch as people dislike removal to relief camps, and inasmuch as the unsatisfactory organisation of relief camps induces wandering and unhomely habits among the people, and inasmuch as his Grace was not prepared to concentrate people on large public works, the collectors were authorised to relieve in their respective villages any distressed persons who might be fit objects for transmission to relief camps, but who were reluctant to leave their homes. The relief was to be given in the shape of a daily dole of money, to be fixed in the first instance at 1 anna 2 pies for each adult and 6 pies or $\frac{1}{2}$ anna for each child. The amount was to be paid daily by the village headman on the authority of a certificate given by the village inspector, who was to examine the register and check abuses. The village inspector, if the circumstances of Bellary may be taken as a general guide, was an officer paid about 20 rs. a month, and he was subordinate first to the famine inspector and then to the tahsildar, or taluk officer ; his jurisdiction was something like twenty villages on an average.

The returns issued in July showed that in each village in which such relief was given, the average number of recipients was only twenty-four persons ; but doubtless, as the system was then in its infancy, and had not been fully developed by drafting to village relief the surplus numbers from relief camps and kitchens, the numbers greatly increased.

The numbers receiving the money dole in the villages were not more than the village inspector, if honest and kept under due control, could properly supervise ; but it may be observed that in the same despatch which gives the average number relieved in each village to which the system had then extended as only twenty-four, the Madras Government once more throw doubts on the honesty of these men. They say the mortality of people receiving village relief was un- doubtedly understated, because it was the direct interest of the village headmen not to report deaths among those on whose account rations could be drawn,[1] and in

[1] The correspondent of the *Indian Daily News*, who has been already quoted in this chapter, says :—The following is a list of some of the means employed by dishonest village magistrates to defraud the Government and to better their friends' and relatives' condition, as well as their own :—

1. The names of the friends and relatives of the munsif and other influential residents were entered as paupers.

2. Distinct from the above was the reckless distribution of money to well-to-do brahmins.

3. Names of deceased persons were entered in the books ; and

4. When people died, their names were not struck off.

5. Deserters' names were also entered.

6. People residing in other villages ; and

7. Fictitious persons were shown as receiving relief.

8. Several sets of accounts were kept, and a false account was shown to the inspecting officer, in which the numbers given were small as compared with the accounts submitted at treasuries.

9. The fragmentary state of accounts ; and sometimes

10. Their total absence, proved the most thorough and complete check, where village magistrates had sufficient resolution to adopt this method of open and defiant opposition.

11. The same persons' names were entered several times.

12. When grain was given instead of money, the people were of course easily defrauded ; and when money was given,

fact, unless human nature in Madras was very different from what it was elsewhere, it was obvious that the class of men from whom village inspectors are drawn would find it to their interest to support the headmen in swindling the Government and in keeping up fictitious registers, rather than in reducing the numbers on the register, and the amount of money dole, down to the lowest possible figure. Nor could such men be expected to realise the necessity for drafting from village relief on to public works all those who might be fit to give to Government, in the shape of work, some return for their subsistence. It is clear that in such an organisation local and personal prejudices would come into play, and it will be gathered from the instances already cited that the superior officers were, as a rule, not sufficiently numerous fully to control and check their subordinates. The direction in which the Viceroy looked for a remedy was in strengthening the supervising agency from outside. In the Bengal famine, where at first the authorities had precisely the same difficulty to cope with (though, owing to the absence of any indigenous village agency, it took in Bengal an exaggerated form), the remedy applied was the introduction of outsiders as circle officers. These

---

13. A heavy percentage was deducted. Any opposition or remonstrance was met occasionally with the complete stoppage of relief, and the sum payable to the offender was drawn by the munsif, who of course,

14. Did not remove the name from the list.

15. Payments were made from four times to once a week, but this kind of brutality was not extensively practised—the usual thing being to retain one day's ration in the week.

16. Occasionally a lump sum, say a rupee, was given to a pauper with instructions to give no trouble, and not to come again for assistance. The name, however, being kept on the list for months, the rupee thus invested gave handsome returns. The misappropriation of money is in itself bad enough when carried out by trusted and responsible servants of Government; but when it is necessary to starve human beings to accomplish an iniquitous object, the crime becomes serious beyond words. Yet this has been done.

were to some extent Europeans, but the supply was mainly sought for among the tahsildars and sub-tahsildars of the North-West Provinces. There was some friction in introducing them. The Bengal officers prophesied that, from their ignorance of the language and the revenue system, and from their contempt for Bengalis generally, they would prove a failure ; but the result, it is said, was very different. They worked admirably for Government ; the absence of local sympathies prevented their hiding or conniving at malversation, and, on the other hand, the people had no hesitation in complaining against them.

In regard to the money dole system itself, there was no objection to it, provided (1) that it were rigorously confined to the aged; infirm, and people who could not do any work, and who would otherwise inevitably perish ; and (2) that there was a sufficiently brisk private trade to keep the villages in which it was in force well supplied with grain. The first condition is based on the obvious consideration which stands good for all famine crises, viz., that Government is bound not to spend more money than is absolutely necessary to keep people alive ; but as long as there is Government money available, the distribution of which is left to village officers, it will be almost impossible strictly to enforce this condition, and people who might support themselves, or be supported by their relations, will infallibly, from caste and local feelings, be allowed improperly to draw the Government dole, involving not only an unnecessary burthen on taxpayers generally, but also a real and wide-spread demoralisation from which it will take much time and labour to recover the people themselves.

The second condition is one which was put forward at the time, but which scarcely needs explanation. It was argued that if Government has to bring grain to the villages and store it there, because private trade has ceased to do so, it is manifestly foolish to give people money with the right hand, in order that the same person may give grain in exchange for it with the left. If village doles are to be given at all, experienced administrators would prefer to have them given in grain and not in cash ; but obviously a money dole is incompatible with the local storing and distribution of grain by Government officers, and the two systems should not go on side by side.

Under the system inaugurated by the order of September 24 the money-dole was modified and strictly confined to the bedridden and the helpless, and a more rigorous carrying out of the relegation to works was adopted. Meanwhile great mischief had been done, and not a little demoralisation caused, by the money dole system in villages.

MISCELLANEOUS

MISCELLANEOUS.

(1) EMIGRATION.

WHEN the distress in Madras had fully manifested itself in 1877, one of the first thoughts which presented itself to interested onlookers in Great Britain and in India was that something akin to blood-letting in plethoric patients might be done to give ease to the country. 'Cannot you cause your surplus population to emigrate to neighbouring lands or to parts of India where famine is not present?' This question was asked many times and was answered according to the ideas or idiosyncrasies of the person addressed—by no means according to special knowledge. Among other suggestions made in England was one by Sir Julius Vogel, K.C.M.G., who, in a letter to the *Times*, pointed out the field which existed for tropical labour on public works in Northern Australia. The Marquis of Salisbury, then Secretary of State for India, speaking at Bradford in the autumn of 1877, seemed to think Indian emigration was a famine panacea, but wisely refrained from giving reasons for his opinions. In India itself much faith was not put in emigration. The immobility of the people, the vast numbers affected,[1] the absolutely

---

[1] The *Pioneer*, writing in April, 1878, said:—'The recent discussion between the Secretary of State and the Government of India about the encouragement of emigration from India to the British colonies, has shown the unimportance of the question as regards the general well-being of India. The colonies at the most do not need more than 20,000 emigrants annually, and this would have absolutely no effect on the increase of a population of 200 millions, adding to itself between two and three millions a year.'

ineffectual relief such a movement would afford, all conspired to prevent attention needed for remedial measures on the spot being turned to what after all was but speculative and Utopian. Not that the subject altogether escaped the attention of the Madras authorities. Moreover, as population in India represents revenue, and proof of the land being overcrowded not being forthcoming, Indian governments were not over-anxious to lose their people.

British Burma is a land not unsuited to the Madras agriculturist, and thitherwards the eyes of some administrators were turned early in 1877. On March 3, Mr. Rivers Thompson, chief commissioner of British Burma, addressed the Revenue Secretary of the Government of India upon the subject, and on the 21st of the same month received a reply. In consequence of that he telegraphed, on April 3, to the Chief Secretary to the Madras Government as follows:—' Please say whether you are in a position to promote emigration from the famine-stricken districts of your Presidency to Rangoon; if so, how many emigrants can you send, and when would the emigration commence? It would be desirable to send healthy men with their families, and as early as possible. Detailed particulars will be sent by letter, but information is required generally on these points by telegraph, to enable this Administration to decide upon the necessary preliminary arrangements to be made here.' To this the Government of Madras replied that they were ready to promote emigration by giving every publicity through distressed districts to Mr. Rivers Thompson's proposals. At the same time they said they were not aware of any number of emigrants being available at present. The telegrams were communicated to the Collectors of Bellary, Kurnool, Cuddapah, Nellore,

North Arcot, Salem, and Chingleput, who were instructed to report how far, in their opinion, the measures contemplated by the chief commissioner of British Burma were likely to produce any effect. The telegram from Rangoon was followed by a letter from Major W. C. Street, secretary to the chief commissioner, to the Madras Government, dated April 7, in which the advantages of emigration were set forth in detail. It was as follows:—

I am directed by the chief commissioner to invite the attention of his Grace in Council to the proposals submitted by this administration for the encouragement of emigration from the famine districts of the Madras Presidency to British Burma. These proposals have met with the approval of the Government of India, and sanction has been given for a liberal expenditure for carrying them into effect. It is understood that a copy of the correspondence on the subject has already been forwarded to the Government of Madras, but, for ready reference, a second copy is enclosed. It remains to consider the necessary arrangements for commencing the emigration as soon as possible, and, with this view, the chief commissioner has been authorised to communicate directly with the Government of Madras.

The great need of population in Burma, and the facilities which exist for settling immigrants, with their families, throughout this province, lead the chief commissioner to hope that, in the present severe pressure in Madras, large bodies of the labouring classes from the famine districts may, with very little inducement, avail themselves of the opportunities which now offer; and he trusts to the good offices of the Madras Government for the promotion of the measure.

As regards the arrangements for the reception of emigrants on arrival here, I am to observe that there is a depôt in Rangoon capable of holding 1,000 persons, and available for immediate occupation. It is under the charge of the superintendent of immigration, assisted by an efficient establishment, already accustomed to deal with emigrants. Further arrangements are under consideration for providing shelter, at places to be selected, principally along the line of railway from Rangoon to Prome, where opportunities of employment at good wages will be afforded, and where waste land is available, near the line, for those wishing to cultivate.

It will be seen, then, that as far as this administration is concerned everything is either ready or in course of preparation for the reception of intending immigrants; but it will be necessary to decide at once on the rules under which the details of the scheme are to be carried out. The law which at present regulates the transportation of native labourers to British Burma, and their employment therein, is contained in the Enactment No. III. of 1876. It provides for the establishment of depôts at ports of embarkation, the appointment of agents and medical inspectors, and the method under which recruiting shall be licensed and carried on. It permits, further, the engagement by written contracts for service in British Burma, with specific obligations as regards work and wages. It seems to the chief commissioner that, while in the present pressure the strict enforcement of all these details will involve very undesirable delay, the necessity for their enforcement is to a great extent obviated by the emergency which has given rise to the proposals under consideration, and by the nature of these proposals themselves. The measure is undertaken for the relief of those suffering from famine, and also with the object of inducing persons to settle in British Burma. Under it advances will be made to all emigrants, to be repaid by small instalments; grants of land, for purpose of rice or garden cultivation, will be given to those desiring them, and which will be exempted from payment of revenue for periods varying from one to twelve years; whilst labour on public works at high rates of wages will be available for those who do not wish to clear and cultivate land. None of these matters are provided for in the Act, and, under the circumstances, the chief commissioner would venture to suggest that the provisions of the Act might, in a measure, be dispensed with, and that with a few simple rules for the guidance of medical officers, depôt agents, and district officers, all that is necessary in the matter of forwarding intending emigrants to the ports of embarkation, and of despatching them to Burma, might be secured. In this view the intermediate agency of recruiters could be abandoned, and the negotiation of contracts (which is entirely permissive) avoided; while district officers might be placed in direct communication with the agents appointed at such depôts on the coasts (in addition to Cocanada, already established) as his Grace the Governor in Council might consider favourably situated for the promotion of emigration.

I am to point out the urgent necessity of a careful medical examination of all those wishing to avail themselves of this scheme. The season at which they would arrive, the commencement of the rains, is not always a healthy one, whilst the voyage, the change of climate and of mode of living, will be trying to all who are not in a thoroughly healthy condition. Any great mortality would seriously affect the success not only of the present arrangements, but of any emigration from the Madras side for the future. The chief commissioner would also ask that every endeavour may be made to induce as many married men as possible to emigrate, accompanied by their families. Single men would probably return to their villages after making a little money, as experience shows to be the practice with the great majority of labourers who come over yearly from the Madras coast, and the main object aimed at in the present undertaking is the permanent settlement of extensive tracts of fertile country, where population is much needed.

In conclusion, I am to ask that when matters have so far progressed that some idea can be formed of the number and class of persons likely to avail themselves of the terms offered, early information may be given, so as to enable this administration to complete the arrangements which are now in progress.

Enclosure No. 1.

From Major C. W. STREET, M.S.C., Secretary to the Chief Commissioner of British Burma (Immigration), to the Secretary to the Government of India, Department of Revenue, Agriculture, and Commerce, dated Rangoon, March 3, 1877.

I am directed by the chief commissioner to submit, for the consideration of the Government of India, whether, in view of the prevalence of very widespread famine in the Presidency of Madras, an impulse could not be given, by special arrangements, for a more extended emigration of labourers from the distressed tracts to British Burma, partly as a measure of relief from the famine, and partly in promotion of the settlement of population in this province.

The British Burma Labour Law, for regulating the transport of native labourers to this country, was passed in 1876, and came into force in January of that year. Many preliminaries, however, had to be arranged before the law could come into operation; and the following details have now been settled. The chief commissioner, after reference to the Local Government (Madras), and the Government of India, has, under section 4, appointed an emigration agent at the Port of Cocanada, the most favourable, under ordinary circumstances, as a port of embarkation. Similarly, a medical inspector of emigrants has been appointed at the same place; and the detailed rules required to be prepared by the chief commissioner, under section 87 of the Act, for the general security, protection, and well-being of immigrants after their arrival in this province, have been published. It is necessary to await the action of the Madras Government, as regards the preparation of the rules required by section 86; and the attention of his Grace in Council has been called to the urgency of the matter. As soon as these rules are notified, the measures necessary to give effect to the law will be completed.

It is impossible to say, beforehand, to what extent the Act will succeed in promoting emigration to Burma. Possibly, the special condition of the Madras Presidency may, of itself, stimulate emigration from the distressed districts during this year ; but ordinarily it may be noticed, there is a large number of labourers who come over from Madras to British Burma during the busy season of the rice operations ; and lately, every vessel which has arrived from the Madras ports has brought from 600 to 900 Madras coolies, eager to obtain employment in the mills. This is without any intervention of Act III. of 1876. The emigrants are volunteers who make their own arrangements with contractors for the labour market here ; and experience shows that the great mass of such labourers who annually visit Burma return to their homes enriched with the gains of high labour rates prevalent in Rangoon, as soon as the season in which the mills are at work is passed. The object of legislation on the subject was, primarily, to regulate this system of emigration. In the hands of the contractors, it was thought to be open to many abuses, and the coolies, probably, in all cases did not come by their full rights. It was also, perhaps, anticipated that under formal contracts and a well-organised system for regular employment at high wages, the people would be induced to settle in the country, and, by taking up lands, promote the cultivation of wastes, and thus benefit the province. The result of this has yet to be seen. As long as there is no legal prohibition against the contractor system, it will not cease to compete with the Government arrangements under the Act of 1876 ; and, as hitherto there have been large employers of labour in Burma, beyond those who need workmen for the limited season of the rice operations, the chief commissioner has doubts whether much will be gained by the Act as regards the settlement of emigrants in this province, in the absence of special measures to promote that object. The coolies from Madras will still come for the high wages which they receive as mill hands ; but they will probably return to Madras when that work ceases.

It seems to the chief commissioner that the present opportunity is a favourable one for considering the practicability of giving a more permanent character to the emigration which the Act gives us the power of carrying out in detail. We need population here in every district for agricultural purposes, and in every branch of the Public Works Department. If the large railway works are to be continued, either by the extension of the Prome line to the frontier (for which application has been sent in), or for the construction of the new line to Toungoo (for which the estimates will shortly be submitted), a large number of labourers might be engaged at once, under contract for the full period of the three years which the law allows. Similar dispositions would be of advantage for the completion of the embankments which are still in progress, while, for people wishing to settle as agriculturists, lands are widely available behind the embankments in the Henzada, Bassein, and Thonkwa Districts, and culturable wastes ready to be occupied and cleared in most districts of the province under liberal rules of five years' exemption from payment of any rent.

It would appear from the papers that there are now a million of people suffering from the famine, receiving relief at the Government expense in the Madras Presidency. It is estimated that the relief measures in Madras and Bombay will involve an outlay of six and a-half millions sterling. It can be in a very small way at best that British Burma can help to alleviate distress of such wide proportions by offering work and lands in this province; and even the measure of its aid in these respects would depend upon the extent to which the Government of India would favour the scheme, and promote it by a special allotment for the purpose. Assuming, however, that in their present calamity the Madras labouring population would show a greater willingness to emigrate, and that the Government of India would divert a portion of the large unavoidable expenditure imposed on it by the famine in furtherance of this project, the chief commissioner would be prepared to receive 20,000 persons within the next three months, and find them occupation, or lands upon which they could settle. If either of the large railway works before referred to receive early sanction, it would facilitate the immediate employment of the emigrants and reduce the expenditure which would be necessary to maintain them on their first arrival.

Mr. Rivers Thompson is aware that, in the famine in Bengal in 1874, a scheme of a similar nature was approved and carried out with only partial success, under a system of State emigration. He is of opinion, however, that in face of special difficulties and drawbacks, the general outcome of those arrangements was of benefit to British Burma, with a corresponding relief, probably, to the famine-stricken districts from which the emigrants came; and that, if any similar scheme was favourably entertained now, we should commence operations under better securities for success. In the first place, the Bengalee has never amalgamated with the people here in the same way as the Madrassee. The latter is always in much greater demand as a labourer, and the people from Madras in this province are already so numerous as to impart to every new comer a stronger home feeling, and a greater readiness to remain than the Bengalee emigrant ever experienced, coming among a people alien in habits, language, and religion. Again, in giving effect to the measure of 1874, the chief commissioner had not the aid of a law to regulate emigration from the continent of India. The provisions in this respect are now ready at hand, and can be put in operation at any port in the Madras Presidency, from which labourers could be most easily embarked. So, on debarkation, the depôt arrangements in Rangoon are complete and ready for immediate use, while the opening of the railway to Prome will facilitate most advantageously the transport of immigrants with their families to many districts in the interior.

It will be, of course, in the cost of carrying out the project that the greatest difficulties will present themselves. The emigrants, coming from a part of the country in which severe famine prevails, to establish homes in a new country, will not be in a position to settle or maintain themselves for one year at least after their arrival : and some system of advances would have to be devised and sanctioned before the measure could be attempted. In the inquiries upon this subject which were made in 1874, it was ascertained and generally accepted that an advance of 150 rs. would be required for each family —man, wife, and say, two young children—to start them in this province. The calculation was made out as follows :—

	Rs.
The construction of a house	20
One pair of bullocks	80
Thirty baskets of paddy for consumption and seed . .	30
Salt and condiments	5
Ploughs and other agricultural implements	15
Total	150

The cost of rice would be cheaper now than then, and in some other details a reduction might be feasible ; but, probably, it would involve an outlay of not less than 140 rs. for each family, as above constituted, to give effect to the measure. It would be of immense advantage, as tending directly to the permanency of settlement, if the men could be sent over with their families ; but, perhaps, taking the figure of 20,000 as the total number who would be induced to emigrate, not more than one-fourth of these would be accompanied by their families, and in the case of single men the preliminary expenses would be considerably less, perhaps not exceeding 80 rs. per head. Upon these calculations, the expenses to be incurred in the way of advances would amount to a sum of nineteen lakhs of rupees, viz., 5,000 × 140 = 7,00,000, and 15,000 × 80 = 1,200,000 rs.

As on the previous occasion, an emigration account would have to be established, supervised by the officer in charge of the department at the head-quarters depôt, in which a separate entry would be kept of each family or individual emigrant received in the province. As these get settled in different districts, the deputy commissioner of each district would maintain a corresponding register of the settlers in his district, the lands assigned to them, the moneys advanced to them, and the re-payments on account of such advances as gradually adjusted. The rate of re-payment, which could not be enforced till the end of the first year, would be fixed at 3 rs. per month in liquidation of the debt to Government.

The almost daily representations which are made to the chief commissioner on the difficulties which embarrass every branch of industry in this province from the want of labour, and the pressure from similar causes felt in departments of the public service, must be his excuse for bringing the subject thus prominently to the notice of his Excellency in Council, and expressing a hope of its favourable reception. An investment, if so it may be termed, of nineteen lakhs of rupees in an undertaking of the nature proposed, would not, in the chief commissioner's opinion, end in failure, even financially; and if the Imperial Government is involved in an expenditure which is counted by millions for the alleviation of famine, the assignment of 190,000l. as a relief measure to Madras, when it would benefit Burma so incalculably at the same time, does not seem extravagant. Already, with the prospect of the opening of the railway, an impulse has been given to arrangements, for some time in contemplation, for working earth-oil mines, establishing sugar refineries, and extending the cultivation of jute and tea in various parts of the Pegu Division; and any project for the importation of labour into the country would be hailed by the gentlemen who would introduce these industries with great satisfaction. The scarcity of population is practically the one want which has hindered hitherto the application of capital to all enterprises of this nature, and if it can be overcome in any measure, even the large initiative outlay which the proposal under consideration involves would be soon repaid by the rapid development of the resources, and, through them, of the revenues of British Burma.

Enclosure No. 2.

From the Officiating Secretary to the Government of India, Department of Revenue, Agriculture, and Commerce, to the Chief Commissioner of British Burma, dated March 21, 1877.

I am directed to acknowledge the receipt of your secretary's letter, No. 368–1, dated the 3rd instant, in which it is proposed that in view to benefiting British Burma, and at the same time affording relief to the famine-stricken districts of the Madras Presidency, immediate encouragement should be given to the emigration of labourers from those districts to British Burma, by introducing a system of advances.

In reply I am to say that the Governor-General in Council approves of the proposal, and, subject to the condition that the emigrants are to be exclusively selected from the famine-stricken districts, has sanctioned the allotment of nineteen lakhs of rupees to meet the expenses to be incurred in making advances to the emigrants in question.

A copy of this correspondence has been forwarded to the Government of Madras, with whom you are authorised to enter into direct communication with a view to arrangements being made for commencing the emigration without delay.

From the foregoing correspondence the project seemed a most hopeful and tempting scheme. On one shore of the Bay of Bengal great enterprises were languishing for want of labourers; on the other millions of people were being supported gratuitously and employed on public works, many of the works being merely put in hand to find occupation for the distressed. Closer examination of the subject, however, revealed difficulties which proved insuperable. The Madras Government, from the first, feared this would be the case. On May 9, Major Street was informed that his Grace the Governor in Council had considered the chief commissioner's proposals, and had referred them to the collectors of the famine districts for an expression of their opinions as to the probability of their having any effect in inducing persons to emigrate to British Burma. The replies of all had not been received, but the collectors of two of the most distressed districts gave very decided opinions that the scheme as propounded would have no effect. His Grace in Council desired, however, to do all that lay in his power to make the chief commissioner's proposals fully known, but thought it essential that they be set forth more definitely.

The points on which further information was required were:—

1. Will any advance be made to the emigrants before they embark?
2. What extent of land is to constitute a grant?
3. What are the conditions of the land grant?
4. What assessment will the lands bear which are to be exempted from land-tax for periods varying from one to twelve years, when they are assessed?
5. How are the expenses of recruiting, examining by medical officers, feeding, transporting to depôts, &c., to be met?
6. What are the rates of labour and prices of food-grain in British Burma?
7. What public works are in progress of such a permanent character as to induce a man to go with his family to Burma to live by the wages he could earn.

His Grace in Council further observed that, while the chief commissioner laid some stress on the emigration being undertaken for the relief of those suffering from famine, he was evidently anxious that none but thoroughly healthy and able-bodied emigrants should be sent to him—a class of people not likely to be found among famine-relief labourers in any numbers. They would consequently require to be recruited, and to that end recruiters would be necessary, as it was out of the question that the district officers, who were overburdened with work, could find time either to look for emigrants or to act as emigration agents in their respective districts, and pass on such as might offer to emigrate.

Meanwhile the following telegram had been sent to Rangoon:—' Of what size are the grants of land to be given to intending emigrants?' The reply was:— ' Ordinary grants vary from five to twenty acres. No particular limit to area of grants. Depends chiefly on amount of land available and means of applicant to reclaim land.'

The seven questions asked in the letter from the Government of Madras were replied to on June 14. It was said:—

1. Necessity of making advances to emigrants before embarking was not contemplated in the scheme submitted to the Government of India, but I am to observe that if such advances are absolutely necessary the cost can be met from the allotment sanctioned by the Government of India for that purpose.

2. There is no special limit to the extent of land which constitutes a grant. Under the rules in force a deputy commissioner of a district has power to make grants of land for the purposes of cultivation to an extent not exceeding 100 acres. The larger number of grants, however, are made by Thoogyees or heads of circles, and do not exceed five acres for rice cultivation; in the case of garden land they are, as a rule, somewhat smaller, varying from one to three acres. The sizes of grants vary very much according to the kind of jungle to be cleared, and the means of the applicant to bring it into cultivation. The case of immigrant settlers would be favourably considered.

3. There are no special conditions attached to grants further than those under which exemption from payment of revenue for a term of years is permitted. All immigrants are exempted from the capitation tax for five years. I am to forward, however, a copy of the revenue rules at present in force in the province, and of those formed under the Burma Land and Revenue Act of 1876. These have not yet received the sanction of the Government of India. They contain all the information that you may require in regard to the terms on which land is held in this province.

4. The assessment varies according to the fertility of the soil, the situation of the land, and facility for intercourse with markets. On rice lands the rate varies from 8 annas to 2-8 rs. per acre, and in the case of garden land from 1 r. to 3 rs. per acre.

5. The necessary expenses for the objects referred to in your fifth question can be met either from the allotment specially sanctioned by the Government of India or from the provision made for the expenses likely to be incurred on account of general emigration under the Burma Labour Law.

6. The rates of labour and prices of food-grains will be found in the list attached. The price of rice will gradually rise during the rainy season, and fall again when the new crops commence to come in about the close of December.

7. The more important public works in progress in British

Burma are the Prome Railway, which, though open for traffic, still provides for employment to a large number of labourers. The prospect of an early sanction to an extension of this line to the frontier, a distance of 40 miles, will give regular employment to immigrants settled along the line for at least two years. The construction of a large canal connecting the Pegu and Sittang rivers requires a constant supply of labour, and in this direction there are wide areas capable of cultivation, and in need of population. In addition to these there are works of various kinds being carried on in nearly every district in the province, such as roads, bunds, tanks, &c., for which labour is much required. The improvement, too, of the larger towns under municipalities will give ample employment to a large number of labourers. During the harvest season in every district extraneous aid has to be sought to reap the crops.

This communication reached Government at an unpropitious time. The south-west monsoon was seen to have failed, and all energies were turned to meet the new and aggravated crisis. Nevertheless, the chief commissioner's letter, together with the list of prices current of food-grains in Burma which accompanied it, was communicated to the collectors of the Bellary, Kurnool, Cuddapah, Nellore, North Arcot, Salem, and Chingleput districts, and as soon as the draft rules under the Burma Land and Revenue Act of 1876 had been approved by the Governor-General in Council, they were to be communicated to the collectors above named, in view to their being translated into the vernaculars of their respective districts and widely promulgated throughout them.

With this intimation ends the episode of emigration to British Burma.

As will have been noticed in the narrative of the Madras famine, emigration in one direction had served to greatly lessen the distress. Sir Richard Temple observed again and again that emigration to Ceylon had been no small boon to the Madura and contiguous districts. Ceylon is to the labourer of certain districts in Southern India what England during harvest-time in pre-reaping machine days used to be to Irish labourers—and more. The coffee plantations on the hills in the interior of Ceylon depend entirely on imported labour, and about 300,000 persons are regularly employed upon them. A perfectly free system of emigration, fostered by the Government in the provision of hospitals, &c., *en route*, is in existence, and suffices for all needs. It has never failed the planters when left to itself, but has occasionally hampered them when the island Government has injudiciously interfered to 'protect' it. A bad season in Southern India means a plethora of labour for Ceylon, and when, towards the end of 1876, the harvest had proved a failure, immense numbers of people flocked to the narrow straits between peninsula and island, over which they were conveyed in vessels maintained by the Ceylon Government. It is reported that the number of persons who left for Ceylon at Paumben between November 1 and 23, 1876, alone was nearly 10,000, or four times the usual number, and it is known that large numbers had gone to Tuticorin and there embarked. The emigrants were the able-bodied; and their weakly ones, both young and old, were as a rule left behind them. Those who found work sent money-order remittances to the connections they had left behind them, but where that was not the case the relief camp was the only resource for those who stayed at home. In March 1877, 1,101 villages, with an approximate population of 150,000, were inspected by the collector of Madura. From these villages about 23,600, or 17 per cent., had emigrated to Ceylon. The stream of emigration continued in force for many months, and the feeble and sickly followed the example of the robust. Cholera broke out among them, and many died long before they could reach the plantations. In Ceylon the planters, mindful of their great dependence upon the Tamil people for labour, did their utmost to support the people who came to them, and in the town of Kandy a relief house was opened to supply those who could not find work with food. The Ceylon Government also provided public works for employment, but would not take up railway earth-works, which they were urgently requested to do.

Mr. J. Lee-Warner, special assistant-collector, Ramnad, writing in August 1877, on the subject of coolies proceeding to Ceylon, said:—

I inspected a large number of coolies waiting for passage to Ceylon, and I am sorry to have to report that the average physique of these persons was far below what I have noticed on the two previous occasions that I have visited this port. I observed among the crowd several young men and women whose personal appearance would have justified their admission into any relief camp were they willing to apply. Altogether there were about 4,000 persons then waiting for their passage, and I am informed that several hundreds more may be expected to arrive each day. From the registers I saw that they came mainly from Pulni, Dindigul, Tiroopoovanam, Puducottah, the northern taluks of Ramnad, and a certain number from Trichinopoly. The arrivals from Salem are diminishing; whether they embark from other parts or that emigration thence is satisfied, Mr. Reidy is very anxious about the fate of these poor people. From his knowledge of the island he has satisfied himself that he has already imported at least 40,000 more than are needed or than the planters can find employment for. It is no use telling the people this, as the Kanganies are interested in getting them across. Once there, they have little care what becomes of them, as they have pocketed their commission and can prepare to return for another batch. It seems from some correspondence that I have seen in the Ceylon papers, as well as other information received, that the planters have determined to dispute the right of their Government to limit or check the influx of coolies. The Government on the other hand is perfectly aware that the stock of grain in Ceylon is desperately low, and that the planters, in their anxiety to cheapen the labour market, are threatening to swamp the island with paupers, the burden of whose support will eventually fall upon the Government, who shun having any conflict with the planters. It is difficult on this account to predict what will be done. At present the only orders given to the superintendent of immigration at Devipatam has been to do all he can to get the Madras officials to stop coolies engaging themselves to Kanganies. This agrees with Mr. Elliott's recent and very abortive mission, and makes me think that the Government of Ceylon is afraid of the planters, and would prefer that any action involving a direct check upon the present excessive immigration should originate with this Government or their own superintendent, Mr. Reidy, whose conduct the planters are now attacking, as it seems to me, most unfairly. I have always supposed that Mr. Reidy knows what he is talking about when he insists that the continued supply of coolies exceeds the demand, and his anxiety in the matter is directed distinctly by humane motives. A crisis is evidently at hand when the Ceylon Government must declare its intentions, and two of the ferry-boats seriously want repair, which will diminish their carrying power by one-half. In these circumstances I request early information how to act in case of the Ceylon Government telegraphing to Mr. Reidy to stop further immigration by his ships. There will be from three to six thousand persons suddenly told that they must return to their villages. Many of them are entirely destitute; nearly all have to travel a long distance to their homes. I propose that I should be allowed to pick out the poor and half-starved and put into their hands a small advance of grain or money on the condition of their starting the same evening to return to their villages, and not waiting about Devipatam, which is already a seed-bed of cholera. I need hardly add that I will do all in my power to distinguish the right cases for this assistance; but, if immigration is going to be stopped, help should be given in all parts of the district by public notification what the intentions of the Ceylon Government really are, and this information can only be obtained from the fountain-head. Mr. Reidy writes that he may require large assistance by the 18th, and there is not much time to be lost.

The Ceylon Government subsequently made formal application for emigration to be stopped. They said it was of great importance that some check should, if possible, be given by the Madras Government to the enormous influx of famine-stricken coolies *viâ* Devipatam. If the emigration was allowed to continue at the

Statement showing the Number of Emigrants to Ceylon, &c., during the Ten Months ending 31st July 1877.

Districts.	Number of Emigrants during the Ten Months ending 31st July 1877.								Average Number during the Corresponding Period of Previous Three Years.							
	Ceylon.	Burma.	Straits Settlements.	Mauritius.	Réunion.	West Indies.	Natal.	Total.	Ceylon.	Burma.	Straits Settlements.	Mauritius.	Réunion.	West Indies.	Natal.	Total.
Ganjam								3,099								2,036
Vizagapatam	1	1,971						1,972		1,690						1,690
Godavery		1,735						1,735		1,958						1,958
Kistna								—								—
Nellore					1,560	1,199		2,759								—
Madras	26							26	16			791	983	1,132		2,906
South Arcot			2,506					2,506			118					134
Tanjore	156,973							156,973			1,776					1,776
Madura	38,693							38,693	66,744							66,744
Tinnevelly								—	20,872							20,872
South Canara								—								—
Malabar								—								—
Total	195,693	3,706	2,506	—	1,560	1,199	—	204,664	87,632	3,648	1,894	791	983	1,132	—	96,080
								3,099								2,036
								207,763								98,116

rate then noted, there was great danger of the supply of water along the roads falling short, which, in addition to the destitution prevalent amongst the immigrants, would lead to much suffering and hardship. Certain correspondence, relative to assertions that people had died of starvation, was also enclosed. The Madras Government, in reply, said they were taking all the measures in their power to relieve those in need in their several districts, but had no legal authority to prohibit emigration to Ceylon, the management of which was principally under the control of the Ceylon Government and influenced by the action of recruiters sent by planters in the island to the mainland. It is a good thing for the labour supply of the island that the injudicious suggestion of the Ceylon Government was not heeded by the Presidency authorities. With this the correspondence ceased. (See table p. 349.)

No other proposals for emigration were laid before the Madras Government, and, save that the regular recruiting for Mauritius and Natal was brisker than usual, the distressed districts received no other alleviation by this so-called panacea for famine.

(2) WEAVERS.

A famine in India means total ruin to ryots, who depend upon agriculture for their means of existence; but these are not the only classes who suffer by the calamity. All who are in petty trade and depend upon agriculturists for employment, feel the visitation even more severely than the ryots. Such workmen as weavers and chucklers (shoemakers, &c.) are the first to suffer and the last to recover. In the Madras Presidency, according to the last census, there were nearly 600,000 weavers exclusive of families. Their condition speedily became very bad; all custom was gone and there were literally no means before them of obtaining a livelihood. In December, 1876, the matter was brought before the Madras Government, but no decisive action was taken. In March 1877, his Grace the Governor in Council again had the condition of weavers in distressed districts under his consideration, and, being satisfied that their case was different from that of other handicraftsmen, resolved to authorise the collectors of all distressed districts to make advances of materials to them for the prosecution of their trade, paying them in addition, in the first instance, a sufficient allowance to maintain their families until the materials advanced were worked up, when the manufactured articles were to be bought at their usual market price, on account of Government, and their value adjusted against the advances made. The balance in favour of the weavers it was thought would then probably enable them to keep their looms at work so long as they were sure of the Government purchasing their manufactures. At Adoni, where weavers are numerous, the task of starting the system was entrusted to an experienced officer.

Under this order the following advances were made from time to time :—

	Rs.
Nellore	44,263
Cuddapah	40,038
Bellary	2,01,406
Chingleput	3,908
North Arcot	4,050
South Arcot	3,681
Madura	43,649
Coimbatore	94,744
Salem	6,95,969
Total	Rs. 11,32,208

The relief of weavers was, from time to time, pressed on the attention of the Executive Committee, Famine Relief Fund ; but several circumstances combined to render the task an undesirable one to undertake with the contributions of the charitable people of Great and Greater Britain. The most complete scheme laid before the committee was one by Mr. Seshiah Sastri, C.S.I., which was in the following terms:—

Trichinopoly: December 20, 1877.

I have the honour to inform you that at a special meeting held yesterday it was resolved unanimously to address the Executive Committee, Madras, for an allotment to our Committee of a lakh of rupees for the special relief of distressed weavers in this district.

Observing from the published proceedings of the Executive Committee, Madras, that advances out of the relief fund for *setting up weavers in their trade* were generally discountenanced, probably for the reasons (1) that it would interfere with the natural course of industry, (2) and that the object in view was itself *subordinate* to the *primary* one for which the fund was intended, viz., the support of life, we had made it our *rule* to appropriate no portion of the money entrusted to us for such a purpose as yet. Of course the *distressed weavers* received, and continue to receive, relief like *distressed* people of any other profession.

But the distress among them is of a kind and character that threatens to be of longer duration and of greater severity than may be experienced by other classes of the population.

The information which we gathered at our yesterday's meeting—information furnished by members (some of them Tahsildars) who are engaged in the distribution of relief as the Committee's agents—went to prove clearly that many weavers who left their homes are unable to return to them, and that many still clinging to their villages are in utter destitution and distress, and that, guessing most favourably, scarcely half of them have looms at work, the remainder of the looms being either out of work, or mortgaged for a few rupees for subsistence, or sold outright for trifling sums, not exceeding 10 rs., the full price of a loom.

There is yet three months more before the harvest will be in, when it is *hoped* prices will fall, and place food more within the reach of the poor than it now is. The *reaping* of the harvest will no doubt give employment to a large number of the poor of the strictly agricultural population, who are from childhood accustomed to reap, bind (sheaves), thresh, and stack; and the entrance of the harvested grain *itself* into the market might *reduce* the prices, to what extent (if any at all) cannot now be safely calculated on. But what are the weavers to do meanwhile? and what help will the coming harvest bring to them? They cannot get work from it, and few landlords would engage *their* services for work which they do not know. Even if *agricultural* prosperity returned so soon, the looms are not likely to find immediate employment, while the weavers are still beggars, without capital, and utterly prostrated.

It occurred to us that to a class so situated nothing could bring *substantial* relief which did not enable them to start their looms once more and *to live*, till the produce of the looms could be brought to market and made to yield a *subsistence*, to say nothing of a profit. It is impossible to hope that the richer class of weavers would come to their relief, they themselves having suffered in their degree from the famine and been able, perhaps, just to keep their heads above water, nor is it at all likely that capitalists, who deal in cloth, would venture to make *advances* to *undoubted paupers* who have not even their *looms* in many cases to weave with.

The only chance then for the poor weavers is, if they could get sums of *money* from the Relief Fund to live with, and small quantities of cotton twist, purchased and supplied from the same source, to set their looms going. Their after-chances we need not concern ourselves much about. We shall have done much if we succeed in bringing them back to their looms and setting the looms going.

We calculated at the meeting, from the census returns, that the weaver population of all castes was about 18,000, comprised in about 4,500 families, scattered over 50 villages in all the taluks of the district. That 1,500 families (one-third) might be assumed to be well off. That 3,500 might safely be considered as already utterly pauperised or on the very verge of pauperism. That to give these subsistence and twist, for four or five weeks' work, would require, at 20 rs. per family, 70,000 rs. That another sum of 25,000 rs. may be required for the poorest of the *silk-weavers* chiefly in the town of Trichinopoly, and that 1,00,000 rs. might thus be found sufficient to ameliorate in a substantial manner 3,500 families, consisting of 14,000 souls, who must otherwise wander abroad beggars *for years* or fall victims to starvation and disease.

If the Executive Committee, on a consideration of these facts, are of opinion that relief of the kind is desirable, and have the funds in their power at this late hour of our application, our committee will feel thankful for a special grant of the sum named, viz., a lakh, and will take every precaution for our plan being carried out in a faithful and successful manner.

One of the agencies employed in the distribution of relief funds largely employed this—the best, where practicable—means of dispensing charity. The Rev. A. D. Rowe, of the Krishna district, thus describes his work:—

In addition to the work for weavers and shoemakers, since my last report work has been given to a great number of poor women— including Mahomedans and Sudras, as well as the lower castes ; the employment furnished is *spinning*. There being no cotton found here, I had a bandy load brought from Guntúr, had it weighed out into 1¼ lb. bundles and distributed, giving 2 annas cooly in advance, 2 annas more as the work advances, and 4 annas more when the thread is done. Though spinning in the country is at all times very poorly paying work, the cotton is being taken most eagerly and joyfully by these people at present. It gives employment to those members of the family who have for a long time not been able to get any work.

About Inkole (22 miles north of- Ongole) the condition of the people is still very pitiable. In most of the *palems* about one half of the houses are in ruins, *i.e.*, the timbers and roof have been sold, the owners have deserted them, and the walls are crumbling down. One good effect of our relief is to attract the people to their homes and villages again, and to inspire confidence. I have never seen such utter despair as is manifested by the poorer people here.

As I should not be able to control the giving of gratuitous relief properly, I have hitherto not given any except in a few cases of great want among old and helpless people. To those who are at all able to work, our present plan commends itself, and it is my opinion that it does them more real and lasting good than the same amount given gratuitously would do. Many of those who are taking the work have expressed the same opinion.

I shall, however, have made out, or rather make out myself, a list of very needy persons whose houses have been consumed by the famine, and present it to you by and by.

If any of the gentlemen who are on deputation for the committee should happen to come as far north as Ongole and should have another day to spare, I should be very happy indeed to meet one of them at the Inkole Bungalow. With the exception of such local help as I can get from police officers and village officials, I am working alone on this ' committee,' not from choice but necessity.

A. Laksmidas Garu, municipal manager of Guntúr, who is well acquainted in this section, has promised to accompany me during the Christmas holidays. But whether working alone or otherwise, I shall do the best I possibly can for the relief of these people with the money you have kindly placed at my disposal.

Inkole (22 miles north of Ongole), December 28, 1877.

I beg to state that the work of giving relief which your committee have kindly entrusted to me has enlarged greatly beyond what I had expected. There is still no work in the fields, and prices of grain are higher than they were a month ago. Though I give only the ordinary rates for work, *i.e.*, 8 pies a yard for weaving, and from 8 annas to 14 annas for a pair of shoes, and a *rupee a viss* for spinning cotton, the poor people are most eager to get the work. In ordinary times neither spinning nor weaving at these rates is considered *paying* work. This in itself is an indication of the great want still existing here. People come from villages as far as sixteen miles to the west, *i.e.*, from the south-eastern corner of Narasapet taluk.

Up to this time we have given work to about fifty villages (list enclosed), but in scarcely any case do we give all asked for, thinking that if we get this work the remaining portion will be able to get along by doing what work may be found about the village.

The employment which seems to reach the most helpless class of all is the *spinning*. The cotton is bought in Guntúr, brought here and given out in bunches of 1½lbs. ; 4 annas cooly is given in advance, and 4 annas more when the thread is returned. Until the *varega* crop is harvested, in about a month, there will be no other work for these people.

To continue the work of relief as begun for a month longer I shall need (above the receipts for the goods sold) about 1,000 rs. As our cloths sell readily at 60 per cent. of cost, and the shoes at 50 per cent., we received a considerable income now which will appear in my next financial statement. (N.B.—We do not sell to merchants, but only to *poor people*, else we could sell for a little more.)

In a former letter I stated that I should apply for some money to aid people about Inkole to repair their houses, such as were actually consumed by the famine. Last week in a village five miles from here, sixteen houses were consumed by fire. They were thatched houses of poor people, and they lost their spinning wheels, looms, and in some cases their clothing. They applied to me for some help to re-build ; they are very badly off indeed, and I shall ask you for a small grant for them. After a somewhat careful calculation of what will be needed I respectfully ask for the following :—

	Rs.
To continue the work among the weavers and shoemakers, and to give spinning to poor women of all classes who may apply up to January 31	1,000
For the repair of 150 houses consumed by the famine, giving 5 rs. each	750
For the repair of 16 houses consumed by fire in Idipallipadu on December 16, giving to each 5 rs. . . .	80
Total	1,830

If your committee have granted the 1,000 rs. applied for for the eastern section of Bapatla taluk it will not affect this calculation. I have not heard anything about it yet.

I again ask that you will kindly send a telegram for me to Guntúr as soon as this action is taken. Thanking you for your kind attention to my former letter and reports.

Villages in which employment is given at present.

Palaparru, Anavarum, Torlepoder, Rozapalem, Timapurum, Jaggapurum, Yedlapudi, Gintunapalum, Uppurlapadadu, Yelluru, Kopperti, Sudepudi, Parchoor, Nagulapallem, Timaragapalem, Gottipadu, Jagalamudi, Uppurturu, Vernapalem, Jujanipilly, Kunkalanurti, Tonamudunapalen, Peddavernapalem, Vonkayzelapalem, Pusapodu, Idipallipadu, Nutalapodu, Dogupodu, Kondrupodu, Yenamadalu, Nimagudipalen, Viragani, Naudipadu, Yurjala, Ganapura, Vidavorapadu, Tanivuderapalem, Posapodu, Adipudi; Bordada, Abiniguntapalem, Tikkiredipalem, Vinagalu, Sirimanundla, Tumulupadi, Cousara, Goddipadu, Inkole.

As I write new applicants are coming for work from villages in the Ongole taluk of Nellore district.

Assisting weavers by advances was one of the modes of relief which Sir Richard Temple strongly pressed upon the Madras Government. Writing on March 12 the delegate said:—

I desire to invite attention to the advisability of establishing some light labour test for the many thousands of weavers and spinners who are now coming upon the hands of Government in several of the famine districts of the Madras Presidency. It was proposed, as I understand some months ago, by some of the Madras authorities, that Government should advance money to enable destitute weavers to buy material and carry on their trade. For several reasons it was then thought the plan might be deferred. But I submit that the time has come when this proposal might, with such modification as may be required by local circumstances, be resuscitated and carried into effect.

Near Bangalore, on a tank, I saw a special gang of poor weavers, who were allowed a higher rate for their piece-work than ordinary relief labourers, because their habits and the condition of their hands and fingers prevented their doing a full day's work. Some similar arrangements are, I believe, carried out in several places in the Madras Presidency also. And such arrangements may suffice for those weavers who make the coarser fabrics at Adoni, at Bellary. and other places.

But there are many weavers who work in silk, or who do the finer kinds of cotton weaving; and such people might, if put upon tank or road work, become physically unfitted, for a time at any rate, to return to their usual employment after the end of the famine. Yet many of these poor people are undoubtedly in great straits; they can get no market for their products, and they can get no credit wherewith to buy materials. Yet there are many of them quite ready to work to the best of their power, in return for such relief as the State may give them. At Salem, for instance, I learnt that the silk weavers had reduced themselves to some extremity sooner than go on relief works, and at present they are subsisting on an organised private charity. Similar instances will ere long occur in Nellore, even if they are not already occurring.

In parts of Bengal (Burdwan and other places), during the famine of 1874, advances were made to weavers, and their manufactures were taken over by Government officers in return for the advances and for their support. At some of the relief houses, also, weavers were employed in making cotton and silk fabrics.

(3) Seed-Grain.

The papers quoted below will show the spirit in which the Government were disposed to help the people by granting them advances of seed-grain when the growing season came round:—

In their official memorandum above quoted the Board of Revenue called upon all collectors of distressed districts to submit with the least possible delay a statement of the cultivation in June talukwar as compared with the average of the last three years, together with such general information regarding the progress and prospects of cultivation as they might be in a position to afford to enable the Board to judge how far it might be necessary to inaugurate a system of money advances for the purchase of seed-grain, with reference to the considerations set forth in their proceedings recorded in G. O., dated June 12 1877.

2. Only five replies have been received as yet, but the Board do not consider it necessary to await the remainder, as each district must be treated separately with reference to its condition and prospects. The marginally noted figures extracted from the returns show that in

| | Cultivation in June, 1877 | | Average of the Cultivation | |
| | Dry | Wet | In June | In past 3 years |
			Dry	Wet
	acres	acres	acres	acres
Cuddapah	29,586	7,138	22,800	2,931
Chingleput	5,763*		5,157	
Trichinopoly	51,204	10,772	17,566	3,749
Madura	15,431	21,429	8,082	9,058
Salem	72,443*		156,380	

* Dry and wet not distinguished.

Madura, Trichinopoly, and Cuddapah, there has been a very considerable increase in the area brought under cultivation, as compared with the corresponding month in previous years in Chingleput. There is a slight increase in the month of June itself, but a decrease in the extent of cultivation up to the end of the month, whilst in Salem the total is less than the average by more than a half, and in one taluk, Uttengeri, the cultivation was *nil*. This state of things is ascribed to the extreme poverty of the ryots and loss of their cattle. The matter of seed-grain is not noticed by any of the collectors, except Mr. MacQuhae, who states that ' there is nothing that the Government can do at present; the ryots are ready with their seed and cattle, and nothing is wanted but a favourable season.' In some villages in Pulni and in Ramnad, however, he apprehends a difficulty about seed. The Board observes that provision for advances to the extent of 5,000 rs. has been made in the Ramnad estate budget for the current fasli.

3. The Board consider that the returns for the first four districts show that any general aid for the purchase of seed-grain was quite unnecessary, and as regards Salem it is doubtful whether any assistance in this direction would have had much effect. It may perhaps be necessary to afford assistance in some districts at a later date, but it is much to be feared that a large proportion of the early-sown dry crops will perish, and that seed and labour will have been lost. In order, however, that the ryots may be enabled to take immediate advantage of any favourable change in the seasons, the Board think that collectors should be authorised to make advances for the purchase

of seed-grain within reasonable limits, say 10,000 rs., without previous sanction, when such a course is rendered absolutely necessary by the poverty of the ryots. If assistance of this nature is to be of any service, it must be afforded directly the necessity arises, and it is desirable to obviate the delay entailed by a reference to the Board ; further, such advances being recoverable as arrears of revenue, the risk is materially reduced. The Board will always be able to negative extravagant proposals, and they think that within a certain limit collectors should be empowered to take action directly the necessity manifests itself, bearing in mind that lavish expenditure is not contemplated.

(True copies and extract.)

(Signed)   C. A. GALTON,
Acting Secretary.

Proceedings of the Board of Revenue, dated Aug. 1, 1877.
Read the following letter from R. W. Barlow, Esq., Collector of the Chingleput District, to C. A. Galton, Esq., Acting Secretary to the Board of Revenue, dated Madurantakam, July 27, 1877 :—

Adverting to G. O., No. 2,260-A, of the 9th instant, and Board's proceedings thereon, No. 3,249, dated the 11th idem, I have the honour to report that I fear it will be absolutely necessary in this district to give advances of seed-grain for wet crops if the ryots are ever to cultivate again. That the bulk of ryots here are exceptionally poor is well known to the Board, and just now their condition, in addition to want, is almost one of despair.

2. All the tahsildars, before being consulted, have expressed their opinion that such advances are necessary, and a circular has been issued asking them what amounts they require, and the figures will duly be submitted to the Board for approval.

3. Seed-grain, however, will not be procurable in the district. The wealthy ryots of this district are not numerous, and a good number of them live in Madras, and the remainder certainly cannot provide the wants of the needy as they might in other districts,[1] and I wish to know whether the Board will be able to procure it for me. Of course I should not desire to distribute any seed until good rain falls, and this, I fear, will not now be till October. The time for utilising seed-grain for dry crops affected by the south-west monsoon has passed except for varagu.

---

[1] Vide paragraphs 2 and 3, Board's Proceedings, dated June 6, 1877, No 2,636, in G.O., June 12, 1877, No. 1,972-A.

The collector is authorised to make advances for the purchase of seed-grain to all who may really need it.

4. The Board are of opinion that the advances should be made in money, as the purchase of grain by Government officers is likely to cause confusion. There are many different kinds of seed, and ryots are the best judges of what will suit them.

(True copy and extract.)

(Signed)   C. A. GALTON,
Acting Secretary.

Proceedings of the Board of Revenue, dated Aug. 14, 1877.

Read G. O., dated July 28, 1877.

The Government enquire what the Board are doing, and what they propose to do, in the matter of advances for seed-grain. As regards the first point the Board beg to refer to the correspondence marginally noted.[1] A confidential circular was addressed to collectors by Government in February last, the replies to which showed that district officers were almost unanimously of opinion that there was a sufficient stock in the hands of the richer ryots, who would supply their poorer brethren, and that Government interference was not called for. The commissioner of the Nilgiris having, however, applied for sanction to advance a small sum for this purpose, the Board were vested with authority to deal with such applications and to direct the necessary disbursements. A grant of 3,000 rs. was accordingly placed at his disposal as requested. Subsequently the collector of Bellary applied for a grant of 5 lakhs, and suggested that divisional officers should be authorised to make advances for the purchase of cattle, as well as for

[1] G.O., April 5, 1877, No. 1,336.
„   June 12, „   „ 1,972-A.
„   July 3, „   „ 2,202.
„   „   9, „   „ 2,260-A.
„   June 21, „   „ 2,071-A.
Board's Proceedings, dated July 11, 1877, No. 3,249.
„   „   „   „ 30, „   „ 3,541.
„   „   „   „ 1, „   „ 3,584.
Circular Official Memorandum, July 3, 1877, No. 1,131.
Board's Proceedings, dated July 31, 1877, No. 3,561.
Circular Telegram, Miscellaneous No. 10,945.
Replies to do.
Telegram to Collector of Bellary, dated July 30, 1877, Miscellaneous No. 10,553.

the purchase of seed, at their discretion. The Board thereupon laid their views on the whole question fully before Government,[1] stating the reasons which led them to the conclusion that advances for the purchase of seed and cattle were of doubtful necessity and expediency, and that at any rate the time for any action in that direction had not then arrived. The Government concurred in these views, but desired that this important matter should be borne in mind.

2. This expression of the wishes of Government was communicated to all collectors of distressed districts (Proceedings, dated July 11, No. 3,249), and the Board signified their readiness to grant such assistance as might be required, but up to date only two applications have been received, namely, that disposed of in Board's proceedings dated August 1, No. 3,584, wherein the collector of Chingleput was authorised to make advances for the purchase of seed-grain to all who may need it, and one from the collector of North Arcot, just received, which will be dealt with in a similar manner. Similar instructions were issued to the collector of Bellary by telegram, reports of a deficiency of seed-grain in the western taluks having reached the Board, and the collector of Kurnool was directed in Board's proceedings, dated July 26, 1877, No. 3,511, to watch the condition of the head assistant collector's division in this respect. The Board also called for a return of the area under crops in June as compared with the average of the three preceding years, with the view of ascertaining whether the cultivation returns afforded any indication of inability on the part of the ryots to till their lands. A few replies only have been received, and these show with one exception a considerable excess over the average of past years; the Board, however, deemed it advisable without waiting for complete information from all districts to recommend that collectors should be vested with authority to grant advances for purchase of seed-grain within a certain limit, as they must be the best judges of the necessity for the measure; the Board can only act on the recommendations made by district officers, and a reference entails delay. No orders have as yet reached the Board.

3. The accompanying statement of cultivation up to June (A), as compared with the average of the previous five years in the nine most distressed districts, shows that in all except Bellary, Coimbatore, and Salem the breadth of cultivation under both heads ' dry ' and ' wet ' has considerably exceeded the average, so that cultivation has not so far been retarded by a want of seed-grain as far as two-thirds of them are concerned : whether this had anything to do with the falling off in the other three there is nothing to show, but from the collector's

---

[1] Proceedings, June 6, 1877, No. 2,636.

telegram it appears that in Salem, at any rate, the local supply is believed to be sufficient. The collectors concerned were again addressed by telegram on the 7th instant, and requested to state whether a sufficient quantity of seed-grain is procurable locally, and if not to specify their requirements, in order that the Board might arrange for a supply. Replies have been received from the districts marginally noted.[1] Mr. Grose believes that if money be advanced grain will be forthcoming, though at exorbitant rates ; Mr. Price considers that local stocks will suffice, and strongly deprecates State interference ; in the other districts also no difficulty is anticipated.

4. As to what the Board propose they are of opinion that, as a general principle when aid is considered necessary, as it certainly often will be for the purchase of grain, it should be afforded in the shape of a money advance, the intervention of Government for the purchase and distribution of seed-grain being neither generally expedient nor in fact feasible. But collectors will be invited, if they consider seed supplies indispensable from any particular causes, to make their recommendations to the Board, whereupon the Board will be prepared to do their utmost to arrange for supplies being obtained. The necessity may occur, but it is earnestly to be hoped it will not, for undoubtedly the practical difficulties in meeting it efficiently will be enormous, and apart from the obstacles in the way of the transportation, storage, and distribution of several hundreds of tons of grain, the ryots have their predilections and would probably object to make experiments with seed to which they are unaccustomed. As already proposed in the proceedings now before Government it should be left to the discretion of collectors, who are in a position to obtain the most trustworthy information as to existing stocks and can best judge when and where State help is needed, to decide whether advances should be given, and to make disbursements within a certain liberal limit, for exceeding which sanction should be obtained. The Board concur with the collector of Nellore in thinking that if money is furnished grain will be forthcoming and that deficient stocks will be supplemented by importation : the state of the stocks must be far better known to the leading ryots and native merchants in each district than to Government and their officers, and private trade may be relied upon to supply what is needful.

5. The Board would not lay down any hard and fast rules as to the amounts to be advanced, the period of recovery, &c. Such advances are recoverable as arrears of revenue, and such conditions with regard to security as are provided in the Mysore rules appear unneces-

---

[1] Nellore, Cuddapah, Kurnool, Tanjore, Trichinopoly, Salem, Madura.

sary; the fewer formalities the better; the solvency and capacity to cultivate of the applicant should be ascertained by inquiry through the village officers; the registered holder only should be eligible to receive an advance; the amount should be proportioned to the means and extent of land owned by the applicant, and a simple receipt for the money is all that need be required. There must in any case be considerable risk in any system of advances to impoverished ryots which is not likely to be materially diminished by requiring personal sureties. The principle of the 4th rule is, in the Board's opinion, erroneous; the class most needing assistance is to be found amongst ryots paying more than 20 rs. annually in assessment, and efforts should be directed towards enabling them to tide over the crisis; the smaller ryots must in many cases sink for the present to the grade of agricultural labourers, and it will serve no good purpose to try to avert this fate. The Mysore rules may work in a small province but are not suited to the circumstances of this Presidency, nor should advances be allowed for the purchase of ploughing cattle; the arguments advanced by the Board at paragraph 5 of their Proceedings of June 6 last are, it is submitted, conclusive as to the inutility of any such scheme.

6. At the suggestion of Sir William Robinson, K.C.S.I., some statistics are furnished which may serve as a rough guide to the expenditure which the Government must be prepared to incur in the event of their determining upon any measures for the provision of seed-grain or funds for the purchase of it. The average area cultivated under the north-east monsoon (October to March) during the five years ending 1875–76 is 4,481,618 acres in the nine districts principally affected by the famine; the proportions of cholum and ragi required may be estimated with reference to the areas sown with those crops, the two principal dry food-grains, as shown in the crop statement for Fasli 1284,[1] a favourable season, on the assumption that one ton of seed-grain will suffice for 80 acres of punjah and 30 acres of nunjah land; valuing the grain at the prices ruling in Madras on July 31, according to the collectors' returns the result is that it will cost approximately nine lakhs of rupees to furnish seed-grain for one-tenth of the area likely to be brought under cultivation. From these data the sum involved in providing seed-grain or the means of purchasing it for any given proportions of the cultivated area can be readily ascertained; but any attempt to extend aid of this nature to all those

---

[1] Paddy, 10·08 seers of 80 tolahs per rupee.
  Cholum, 8·05   „   „
  Ragi, 7·9.

who may from a consideration of the amount of the assessment paid by them be presumed to stand in need of assistance must entail a vast outlay as the last quinquennial returns show that nearly half the land assessment is paid by ryots holding puttahs for less than 50 rs.—*Vide* the marginal extract from paragraph 33, Board's Proceedings, embodied in G.O., dated February 11, 1874, No. 184 :—

	Number	Amount
		rs.
Ryots paying less than 10 rupees . .	1,252,000	45,63,000
„ 10 to 30 rupees . . .	455,000	77,26,000
„ 30 to 50 „ . . .	122,000	45,20,000
	1,829,000	1,68,09,000
Above 50 rupees	118,000	1,32,12,000
	1,947,000	3,00,21,000

(Signed) C. A. GALTON,

Acting Secretary.

ENCLOSURE No. 1.

A.—*Statement showing the Area under Cultivation in* 1877–8 *up to June, compared with the Average of five years ending* 1875–6 *during the same period.*

Districts	1877–78			Average		
	Dry	Wet	Total	Dry	Wet	Total
1. Nellore .	15,549	15,445	30,994	3,626	2,797	6,423
2. Cuddapah .	37,680	11,237	48,917	21,691	4,221	25,912
3. Bellary .	31,470	6,727	38,197	70,712	11,165	81,877
4. Kurnool .	2,528	381	2,909	—	6	6
5. Chingleput .	13,772	8,615	22,387	4,350	6,790	11,140
6. North Arcot	92,099	26,453	118,552	50,243	14,246	64,489
7. Madura .	18,018	29,866	47,884	13,218	17,581	30,799
8. Coimbatore	150,391	4,065	154,456	272,971	5,020	277,991
9. Salem .	100,501	16,153	116,654	180,871	22,947	203,818
Total .	462,008	118,942	580,950	617,682	84,773	702,455

(Signed) C. A. GALTON,

Acting Secretary.

ENCLOSURE No. 2.

B.—*Average Cultivation during the five years ending 1875-6, under the North-east Monsoon (October to March) and Estimate[1] of quantity of Seed required for 10 per cent. thereof.*

Districts	Acres Cultivated			Seed required for one-tenth area		
	Dry	Wet	Total	Jonna	Raggy	Paddy
	Acres	Acres	Acres	Tons	Tons	Tons
1. Cuddapah .	402,131	40,408	442,539	392·6	110·0	134·6
2. Bellary .	848,821	35,954	884,775	981·4	79·6	119·8
3. Kurnool .	374,712	6,877	381,580	450·8	8·5	22·9
4. Nellore .	405,227	93,770	498,997	463·2	43·2	312·6
5. Chingleput	109,830	165,819	275,649	19·8	117·4	552·7
6. North Arcot	125,245	79,470	204,715	29·1	127·4	264·9
7. Madura .	340,783	86,513	427,296	266·7	159·3	288·4
8. Coimbatore	1,011,002	35,100	1,046,111	945·6	318·2	117·0
9. Salem .	294,490	25,457	319,947	59·8	308·3	84·8
Total .	3,912,241	560,377	4,481,618	3,618·0	1,271·9	1,897·7

Price

Rs.   Rs.   Rs.
5,03,000 | 1,78,000 | 2,11,000
or nine lakhs nearly.

[1] *Note.*—Seed required for ' Dry ' has been assumed at 1 ton for 80 acres, and for 'Wet' at 1 ton for 30 acres.   (Signed)   G. A. GALTON.
Acting Secretary.

APPENDIX TO STATEMENT B.

Statement showing Proportion of Cholum, Raggy and other Dry Crops cultivated according to Crop Returns for Fasli 1284

Districts	Cholum	Raggy	Other Dry Crops	Total Dry Crops	Percentage of			
					Cholum to Total Dry	Raggy to Total Dry	Other Dry to Total Dry	Total
	Acres	Acres	Acres	Acres				
Nellore .	362,000	34,000	323,000	719,000	50·3	4·7	45·0	100
Cuddapah .	468,000	132,000	754,000	1,354,000	34·6	9·7	55·7	100
Bellary .	1,240,000	102,000	1,452,000	2,794,000	44·4	3·6	52·0	100
Kurnool .	905,000	18,000	760,000	1,683,000	53·8	1·0	45·2	100
Chingleput .	7,000	42,000	80,000	129,000	5·5	32·5	62·0	100
North Arcot	20,000	87,000	231,000	338,000	5·9	25·8	68·3	100
Madura .	101,000	114,000	408,600	713,000	26·8	16·0	57·2	100
Coimbatore	652,000	219,000	1,180,000	2,051,000	31·8	10·7	57·5	100
Salem. .	71,000	369,000	751,000	1,191,000	6·0	30·9	63·1	100

(Signed)   C. A. GALTON,
Acting Secretary.

ENCLOSURE No. 3.

Miscellaneous No. 10,553.

Telegram to Collector of Bellary, dated July 30, 1877.

'GIVE advances for seed-grain wherever necessary; said to be wanted in western taluks.'

Miscellaneous No. 10,945.

Telegram to Collectors of distressed Districts, dated August 7, 1877.

'Is sufficient seed-grain procurable locally? if not, state whether Board should arrange for supply, specifying description and quantity?'

(True Copies.)

(Signed)   C. A. GALTON,

Acting Secretary.

ENCLOSURE No. 4.

Telegram from the Collector of Nellore, dated August 8, 1877.

'CANNOT ascertain stocks seed-grain.' Believe ryots having money can get, but price exorbitant. Supply by Board unadvisable. Best to encourage importation by letting people know taccavy may be granted (*vide* my letter on subject, paragraph 14).'

Telegram from the Collector of Kurnool, dated August 8, 1877.,

'IT is generally believed that sufficient seed-grain of sorts is procurable in the canal taluks. Further inquiries are being made.'

Telegram from the Collector of Tanjore, dated August 8, 1877.

'SUFFICIENT seed-grain procurable locally.'

Letter from the Acting Collector of Cuddapah, dated August 9, 1877, No. 416.

IN reference to your telegram of the 2nd instant, I have the honour to state that, as far as I can learn from personal observation and inquiry, made from time to time, seed-grain is procurable locally.

2. I do not think that for the present any supply is needed. I would most strongly advocate leaving the matter of seed and cattle alone, as, if a beginning as regards either is made, there is no knowing where it will end and to what cost it will not put the State.

3. Some ryots, I dare say, are without seed, but they are men of the poorest class; they have no cattle, and would only eat the grain if given to them.

Telegram from the Collector of Trichinopoly, dated August 9, 1877.

'No difficulty in seed-grain now.'

Letter from the Collector of Madura, dated August 9, 1877, *No.* 522.

In reply to the Board's telegram of the 7th instant, I have the honour to point out that it is useless to answer the question asked now as the drought is such that no cultivation can be commenced in any of the Government taluks or in Ramnad. A considerable area of punjah land was sown in some of the taluks when rain fell in May and the beginning of June, and before this second period of drought set in. Some of this crop is dead, and the question now is whether showers will come in time to save the rest. If a change of season occurs within a reasonable time I would not recommend the Board to interfere in any way for the supply of seed, but supposing this drought to last till the end of October, as it probably may, I think there will be great difficulty about seed, and, if the north-east monsoon rain fails also, I cannot see how Government is to prevent large tracts of country from being temporarily depopulated. South Ramnad has now been depopulated for more than seven months, but I have no doubt the people will come back and the country will recover if a favourable change occurs within a reasonable time. At present I can only say that I am assured by leading merchants that they and many others have sufficient seed in store; that some of it has been in store for more than a year; and that they are ready to give it to the ryots as soon as rain falls. I trust that rain will fall before this seed is spoilt, for it will not be good for more than eighteen months.

Telegram from the Collector of Salem, dated August 11, 1877.

' Your telegram eighth. Supply of seed-grain sufficient locally.'

(True copy.)

(Signed) C. A. GALTON,

       Acting Secretary.

No. 294-D. ORDER THEREON, August 21, 1877, No. 2,547-A.

1. The Government concur with the Board as to the necessity of authorising collectors to make advances of money for the purchase of seed-grain only, and empower the Board to authorise them accordingly within such limits as the Board may deem it expedient to fix in each case.

2. The Board will keep the Government continuously informed of their action in th's matter and of the necessity, should such arise, for further measures. .

(True extract.)

(Signed) J. H. GARSTIN,

    Additional Secretary to Government.

The total amounts granted by the Board of Revenue under this head to March 30, 1878, will be gathered from the following table:—

	Rs.
Nellore	29,628
Bellary	97,865
Kurnool	2,862
Chingleput	22,714
North Arcot	23,210
South Arcot	23,779
Madura	30,000
Tinnevelly	13,894
Coimbatore	73,380
Salem	71,478
Total	3,89,219

A large proportion of the sum subscribed by the people of Great Britain and the Colonies was disbursed for the purchase of seed-grain and plough bullocks; but aid in this direction was only given to cultivators too far reduced to afford any security which would enable them to receive advances from Government.

(4) Prickly-pear as Food for Cattle.

When fodder failed in the famine districts for want of rain, great anxiety was experienced as to means whereby the cattle might be kept alive. In Bombay and some districts of the Madras Presidency the only plan adopted was to drive the cattle to grazing lands on the higher hills, which was generally Government reserve. In Madras, thanks to an enterprising firm at Bellary—Messrs. Harvey & Sabaputhy—something more was done. At the very beginning of the distress these gentlemen wrote to Mr. Thornhill, C.S.I., who was on special duty in the Bellary district, a letter, in which the following passages appear:—

'Owing to the famine prevailing throughout the Presidency, especially in the Bellary district, large numbers of cattle, on which the ryots depend principally, are reported to be dying through starvation, and are also being sold for nominal prices, less even than the value of their hides, to butchers. To relieve this distress as much as is in our power, and to impress upon the ryots the necessity of following our example, we have adopted the system of feeding our own cattle, twenty-five in number, with the leaves of the "prickly-pear;" although the feeding of cattle in this way has been made known both through official and private sources, the ryots did not adopt it on account of the great trouble and inconvenience connected therewith, in the absence of proper instruments to enable them to do so with ease. This difficulty we have surmounted by means of three instruments, samples of which we send herewith for your inspection, viz., a pair of tongs to catch the leaf, a pair of pincers to remove the prickles, and a knife to cut away the leaf. After gathering the leaves as described above, it is necessary to wash each one in water, with a brush, a piece of "gunny," or the root of the cholum stalk, to prevent injury to the fingers, and to take away all the stray and loose thorns adhering to the gummy matter. Of course the cattle require to be taught to eat this fodder for the first three or four days by putting the leaf folded or in pieces into their mouths, and afterwards they will eat it as greedily as boiled grain. By this simple process we are now keeping all our cattle in good condition. Our experience has taught us that this fodder is as good and as nourishing as green cholum stalks both for bullocks, milch cows, and buffaloes.

'The ryots are so conservative that we had great difficulty in impressing upon them the advantages of this system until we sent a couple of our bullocks with a basket of this fodder into the market, where more than 200 bullocks were being exposed for sale last Friday, and there set them to eat, and at the same time showing the owners the method and instruments necessary, and offering to sell them at a nominal price of two annas. This had such a wonderful effect that many took home their cattle resolved to adopt the system. So far as the town of Bellary is concerned, many of the ryots and others have taken our example, and purchased instruments from us.

'We need hardly mention that bullocks are the main support of the ryots and also the means by which the whole traffic of the country is carried on where railways have not yet penetrated, but they also form the means by which they earn not only their livelihood, but the revenues payable to Government. Under these circumstances, it would be very impolitic on the part of the Government at any cost not to take immediate steps to preserve these useful animals from starvation and death, as the eventual loss to Government, the owners, traders, in fact to all, would be inestimable.

'We therefore propose that at all places where tahsildars and deputy tahsildars are located, sheds be erected, or shady places be selected, where the cattle of all who are unable to support them be collected, and a gang of coolies out of those at present employed on the relief works comparatively of little use be set apart to collect prickly-pear, and therewith to feed all the cattle presented. Our experience has been that one only can gather enough to support a couple of bullocks. By this means we feel sure that all the cattle which would otherwise perish would be saved to the advantage of all concerned.

'Notices might be sent to all the villages to the effect that the bullocks of all who are unable to feed them would be received at these sheds and taken care of in the above manner until such time as rain falls, and they are able themselves to procure fodder. By these simple and inexpensive means (as the coolies in any case have to be employed and paid) the property of the ryot, who is the principal pecuniary support to Government, may be preserved.

'If it is considered that this system is in any way impracticable, we are prepared to undertake to carry out the business in Bellary, Adone, and Tadputri where our works and agencies are established, provided that Government grants us a sufficient number of coolies, say at the rate of one for each couple of bullocks, if desired, of course under supervision of the Government officials. In the event of the bullocks being lost to the ryot, it will take many years for him to regain his former position. We trust that you will be good enough to give this suggestion your early attention, as even a day is of great importance.'

A copy of this letter was forwarded to the Board of Revenue with samples of the instruments. The Board remarked:—'A similar proposal was made by Mr. Thomas, the present Collector of Tanjore, in 1866, and to a limited extent the plant was used as fodder in that year. The Board observe that the instruments sent are somewhat similar to those designed by Mr. Thomas, but of far cheaper construction. The suggestion appears to the Board to be worthy of further trial in the present necessity, and the letter will be communicated to collectors of distressed districts.'

In February, Mr. Harvey furnished the Madras Government with two reports by Veterinary Surgeon Cox, of Bellary, on cattle fed on prickly-pear, and trusted that Government officers would take the trouble to make them public amongst the ryots. The healthy animal was slaughtered for *post-mortem* examination at the instance of the Aide-de-camp to Sir Richard Temple, who strongly recommended the support of cattle in the Bellary district on that useful though despised plant.

The reports were in the following terms :—

ENCLOSURE No. 1.

At your request the cow fed on prickly-pear was destroyed on February 13 (Tuesday).

Post-mortem examination revealed the whole of the internal viscera healthy; the stomach and intestines contained large masses of prickly-pear in various stages of digestion and assimilation; the function of the different organs seemed to be properly performed, and reparation of tissues generally carried on in a satisfactory manner.

ENCLOSURE No. 2.

In answer to your letter, I beg to state that I examined the cattle at your establishment fed on prickly-pear ; they seemed to be in good health, although in poor condition.

At my request prickly-pear was given them with a little meal scattered over it; they ate ravenously, and seemed to enjoy it. From information received, it appears that each animal gets a daily allowance of 40 lbs. with 1 lb. of rice straw.

So far I see no reason why cattle should not be able to subsist on prickly-pear, if it is properly prepared and administered whilst they are in a condition to stand the change. If they are allowed to become very much emaciated an addition of a small quantity of grass or grain might be necessary. Their not liking it at first is due, probably, to its peculiar taste; this may be easily overcome by a little patience and judicious management.

As you have so kindly placed one or two animals at my disposal for experiment, I purpose visiting your establishment again for further inquiries.

This report was communicated to collectors of all distressed districts; and it was impressed upon officers that every endeavour should be made to spread the knowledge of the utility of the plant as fodder.

A large number of most interesting reports were, in August 1877, sent to the Board of Revenue, and were summarised for the Government of India. After describing the circumstances under which Messrs. Harvey and Sabaputhy initiated the effort, the Additional Secretary to Government goes on to say:—' On the 18th of January, the collector of Cuddapah informed the Board of Revenue that he saw no way of keeping the cattle alive, except by making the feeding of them with prickly-pear a famine work; and he asked that he should be allowed to form depôts for feeding the cattle, and to supply tho labour and instruments, which cost only a couple of annas, gratis. In their proceedings of the 24th January, the Board approved of the experiment to the extent of an outlay of 500 rupees, the result to be reported after a month. This Government being disposed to give the experiment a more extended trial, authorised the Board to instruct all collectors of districts, where fodder for cattle was not procurable, to try the experiment within the limit laid down by the Board for Cuddapah. In the case of Madura only was the purchase of animals on which to try the experiment sanctioned. Some, however, were also purchased in Coimbatore.

' With their proceedings of the 24th May, the Board submit the reports called for from the collectors. Reports have been received from the districts as shown in the margin.[1] Of these fourteen districts the collectors of Trichinopoly, Tanjore, and Kistna report that, as

[1] 1. Kistna. 2. Nellore. 3. Cuddapah. 4. Kurnool. 5. North Arcot. 6. Tanjore. 7. Trichinopoly. 8. Madura. 9. Tinnevelly. 10. Salem. 11. Malabar. 12. Bellary. 13. Chingleput. 14. Coimbatore.

other fodder was available and was not likely to fail, the experiment was not made by them. From North Arcot the collector reports that the experiment could not be tried owing to press of other work. In Tinnevelly and Malabar there is no prickly-pear. No particulars of the experiments as to cost, numbers fed, etc. are given for the districts of Nellore, Bellary, Salem, Chingleput and Coimbatore. In all these districts, however, sufficient data on which to form a general conclusion have been obtained.

'The unanimous opinion of the collectors may be stated to be that, if gradually accustomed to this food, cattle will eat the cactus with relish, and will thrive on it after a little time. Owing, however, to the great labour and consequent cost involved in its preparation, together with the extremely disagreeable nature of the labour itself, it is never likely to be largely, or indeed at all, resorted to except in times of great pressure and want of forage. The cultivators generally are much adverse to its use on the ground that it causes diarrhœa and dysentery, but without sufficient ground apparently, according to the reports. In many instances, however, some impression has been made on their prejudices, though it is expected to pass away quickly.

'The experiments have been carefully and systematically carried out and reported only in three districts, and the results are tabulated below:—

Districts	No. of feeding depots	Average number of cattle fed daily	Average number of days for which fed	Entire cost of experiment, including feeding instruments	Daily cost per head fed
				rs.	as.
Cuddapah . . .	5	114	32	248 11 2	1·10
Kurnool	1	37	98	460 14 11	[1]2·00
Madura	2	13	42	[2]212 11 9	1·20

[1] Cost high, as hill grass was expensive. The cactus had to be brought a long way. [2] Of this sum, Rs. 171 12 0 was paid for the cattle.

' From these figures it will be seen that the cost per head daily, which represents almost entirely the cost of the labour necessary for the preparation of the plant, is so great as to preclude its introduction as fodder generally. In Mr. Robertson's Farm report for 1876 (pages 57 to 60) it is similarly shown that the fodder is costly, and its use suited to times of extraordinary pressure only.

' The ration given in Cuddapah was at first 20 to 25 lbs. of the cactus per head. This it was subsequently found necessary to increase to 40 lbs. per head. In Kurnool the ration seems throughout to have been from 20 to 22 lbs. of the cactus and 4 lbs. of hill grass. In Madura the ration is not distinctly stated, but two men are said to be able to prepare enough cactus for 8 beasts. It does not, however, seem to have been the only fodder used. Where cattle are fed on the cactus alone a ration amounting to 40 lbs. per head must be given. The quantity which a man can prepare daily is stated at 60 lbs.

' Two methods of preparing the plant were tried. Under the first the thorns were removed by roasting, but this mode of preparation proved a failure in the Chingleput and Coimbatore districts, where alone it was tried. The second method is removing the thorns with pincers, and cutting the leaves into pieces, about an inch square, with a knife made for the purpose. The leaf should be given half sun-dried, or else should be carefully wiped. It should not be much handled as, if it is so, a glutinous substance exudes which is distateful to the cattle, and to it is ascribed slight dysentery or diarrhœa which prevailed in one camp. The leaf has, at first, in many instances, to be forcibly introduced into the animal's mouth, and has in all cases to be mixed with salt and bran or oil-cake or some such other bait before it will eat it voluntarily.'

In Mysore the experience gained was satisfactory. The Deputy-Commissioner of Chittaldroog said:—

'The Pavagada Taluk Amildar has been most successful in his attempts; several animals he began to feed on December 12 are now reported to be quite fat, and that the owners of some of them have removed them.

'My own experiments have been more limited, but, on the whole, successful. I have found that, if the prickly-pear is burnt sufficiently to remove all thorns and well washed, animals eat it with greediness. I have tried the experiment on my own animals, and also upon a Government Amrut Mahal bull—the latter has been entirely fed upon it for the last three months, and, although not in such good condition as grass or straw fed cattle, he has thrived hitherto remarkably well. This animal has been under my own observation, and in my own compound.

'It may be interesting to remark that, in a village in the Doderi taluk, a small portion of this plant was set on fire by some villagers, the thorns only being burnt up, but, as soon as this had been done, some six or eight head of cattle made a rush at it and ate it up. I only regret that the supply is so scarce, as there is no other plant that appears to answer the purposes of fodder.'

For exceptional seasons, and for these only, the cactus known as prickly-pear would seem to be of great service.

THE MORTALITY ARISING
FROM THE FAMINE

THE MORTALITY ARISING FROM THE FAMINE.

WHILST the proofs of this work are passing through the press enquiries are in progress regarding the mortality in the famine districts. It will be some time before all the evidence which has been obtained can be collected and trustworthy results deduced. Meanwhile, the Government of India have courteously placed at the disposal of the author certain documents, upon which a judgment may be founded. They are quoted below.

NOTE ON THE BOMBAY TEST CENSUS.
BY COL. MERRIMAN, R.E.

The census was taken on the 19th of January 1878. The general census of 1872 was taken on the 21st of February. The times of year selected on the two occasions correspond sufficiently to prevent any ordinary annual movement among the population from vitiating a comparison between the results of the two censuses.

Nine Collectorates were affected more or less severely by the famine, but it was not considered necessary to take a census in all of these. The five districts in which, according to returns received from the Sanitary Commissioner, the mortality had, during the nine months ending with September 1877, been highest, were chosen. These were, in order according to the height of the rate of mortality in each, Kaladgi, Dharwar, Belgaum, Satara, Sholapur.

The period of nine months mentioned above was taken, as January 1877 was considered to be the first month in which the death-rate could possibly have been affected by the scarcity, and as September was the last month for which returns were available. Had a selection of the five worst districts been made not on the basis of the mortuary returns but on the general information in the hands of Government, the only difference would have been that Poona would have been substituted for Satara.

Within the five districts, taluks were selected in this wise : in order to know the worst, the taluk in which the death-rate appeared to have been highest was chosen, and in order to have an estimate of the effect of the famine on the whole population of the district, that taluk was chosen in which the death-rate had been most nearly identical with the death-rate of the district. The taluks in which the death-rate was shown as the highest in each district were, Sangola in Sholapur, Man in Satara, Bagalkot in Kaladgi, Athni in Belgaum, and Ron in Dharwar. And the taluks in which the rate of mortality most nearly agreed with that of the district were, Madha in Sholapur, Khatau in Satara, Badami in Kaladgi, Sampgaon in Belgaum, and Kod in Dharwar.

Of these ten taluks accordingly a census has been taken. And the method of selection having been as above described, it follows that it would be meaningless to combine, in the way of aggregation, the results pertaining to the first group of five taluks with those of the second group, or indeed to take the aggregate of the results belonging to the first five taluks at all. The returns of each of these taluks must be looked at individually : their purpose is to show how far the population of each district has been affected by the famine in that sub-division in which, as was conjectured, the effect of the famine was greatest—though, as is explained below, they cannot in all cases be accepted as indicating this. On the other hand, the second group of taluks having been selected each as the average representative of its district, the results in their case, it was expected, might have been combined to furnish an estimate of the effect of the famine on the whole population of the five districts. But though at the time of selecting the worst and the mean taluks it was thought best to be guided by the mortuary returns, the results of the census tend to show that those returns did not furnish the very best guide. In the cases of Sholapur and Kaladgi the taluks selected as average ones appear from the census to have suffered much more than those supposed to be the worst. But it is to be noticed that in these two cases the selection of worst taluks made on the basis of the mortuary returns is not the same as would have been made if the recorded accounts of the condition of the taluks only had been considered, while in those cases in which the mortuary returns correspond with the general accounts of the taluks, the census returns also are found to agree. Thus in the districts of Satara, Belgaum and Dharwar, the taluks of Man, Athni and Ron respectively are indicted as the worst as well by the accounts received of the failure of crops, &c., as by the mortuary returns. But in Sholapur it is the very taluk (Madha) selected by the mortuary returns, as an average one, that the reports at the close of 1876 showed to be the worst of all. Madha was the. only taluk in Sholapur in which the outturn of both kharif and rabi crops was estimated as nothing. Of the taluks of Kaladgi worse accounts were given of three others than of either Bagalkot or Badami. The returns of the taluks of the second group therefore must be taken, like those of the first, each by itself. And in judging of the returns of the ten taluks it can safely be assumed only in the case of Man, Athni and Ron that the taluk in question is the worst of its district, though that is probably true also in the case of Madha. Of the other taluks Sangola may be taken as one of the worst three in Sholapur, Khatau as one of the worst four in Satara; Bagalkot was a little below the average, and Badami—except in the matter of prices—one of the best in Kaladgi; the accounts of Sampgaon are conflicting, as its crops were estimated to be among the best in the district, while as regards rainfall and prices it was amongst the worst; Kod was one of the best districts in Dharwar.

The purpose of the census being merely to ascertain to what extent the growth of the population had been checked by the famine, it was deemed unnecessary to make the census meet all the requirements of the elaborate returns called for on the occasion of the general census. Other reasons of simplifying the work as much as possible were the long and trying labours the district officers and their subordinates had just undergone and the wish to obtain the results of the census while famine and famine policy were still prominent objects in the deliberations of the Indian Governments. Accordingly those of the statements prescribed for the general census of 1872 which are not addressed to matters liable to be immediately influenced by famine have been on this occasion omitted, and no classifications of the population have been made except those according to (1) sex, (2) age, (3) religion in so far as the divisions connote race, (4) condition as judged from the style of house dwelt in, and (5) occupation in so far as it is agricultural or not. As regards the classification according to ages, the same divisions of age have been observed as in 1872. As regards religion, the numbers of Buddhists and Christians in the districts in question were too small for it to be worth while to maintain them as separate classes—indeed it was only on account of the numbers of these classes in Burma and Madras that they were so distinguished in 1872—so only Hindus and Muhammadans have been shown separately and the few others remaining counted together.

The results of the census now taken are set forth in certain tables, and, to facilitate comparison, the corresponding figures of the census of 1872 are set out in parallel lines throughout the tables, the difference in each case being shown in a third line below. In some points—but fortunately points of less importance—no comparison is practicable, as different standards have been adopted or some of the instructions differently interpreted on the two occasions, and indeed in different districts and different taluks of the same district on the same occasion. Thus a comparison of the number of enclosures with the number of houses shows that the definition of enclosure has in some cases been misunderstood. A comparison of the number of houses of the better sort in 1872 with the number in 1878 shows that in some cases a different standard of quality has been taken. Again in both taluks of Belgaum and in Madha of Sholapur some classes not counted as Hindus in 1872 have obviously been counted as such in 1878. And lastly the number given as the total agricultural population is, in many instances in the returns of 1872 and in the case of Kaladgi in 1878, obviously too small in comparison with the number of male agriculturists above 20 years of age. But these discrepancies do not interfere with the more important objects of the census. The salient points indicated by the different tables are considered in the following paragraphs.

The first table shows that with the exception of the taluk of Kod in Dharwar where there is a slight increase, there has been a diminution in the population of every taluk since 1872. Of the population recorded in 1872 the percentage of diminution for each taluk is given below :—

Sangola	3	per cent.
Madha	19	„
Man	12	„
Khatau	10	„
Bagalkot	11	„
Badami	20	„
Athni	13	„
Sampgaon	4	„
Ron	7	„

In Kod an increase of 1·7 is shown on the population of 1872.

This is briefly the result of the census just taken, but an examination of the detailed returns is necessary to a proper understanding of its significance.

In the second table the people are classified (1) according as they live in houses of the better or of inferior sort, (2) according to sex, and (3) according as they are Hindus, Muhammadans or of some other denomination.

That the poorer people should suffer from the scarcity more than those in better condition is axiomatic, but the table furnishes no means of comparing the ratios of diminution of the two divisions, as the classification of houses has not been regular.

An examination of columns 7 and 8 of this table discloses that the number of males has diminished a great deal more than the number of females. This is true of every taluk except Kod, where there has been no diminution, and where such increase as there has been is more among males than females. The exception is important as indicating, so far as it goes, that the difference in the rates of diminution of males and females is really due to a cause relating to famine—the cause being found to bear its result in every taluk except that in which the influence of the famine was least. The percentage of diminution in the numbers of each sex in each of the nine other taluks is shown below :—

DISTRICT	TALUK	PERCENTAGE OF DIMINUTION OF THE POPULATION OF 1872	
		Males	Females
Sholapur	Sangola	4	2
	Madha	21	18
Satara	Man	13	10
	Khatau	11	9
Kaladgi	Bagalkot	13	10
	Badami	22	18
Belgaum	Athni	14	11
Dharwar	Sampgaon	5	3
	Ron	9	5

As there is no known reason why the male population should decrease much, if at all, faster than the female, whereas it is probable that men go further in search of occupation than women, the deduction to be drawn appears to be that part of the diminution of population the census shows in this respect is due to migration only.

The third table shows, separately for males and females, the population divided into nine classes according to age. Comparing the results with those of the census of 1872 it will be seen that there is a very great diminution in the numbers of very young children, an increase in the numbers of older children and persons up to 20 years of age, a slight diminution in those between 20 and 40 years of age, a more considerable diminution of those above 40, and a great diminution in those above 60 years of age. Or, stating the results in greater detail, the diminution in the number of infants under one year of age varies from 23 per cent. in Kod to 73 per cent. in Badami; that in the children between one and six years of age from 13 per cent. in Man to 41 per cent in Bagalkot. The number of childreᴜ between 6 and 12 has increased in seven out of the ten taluks. So also the persons between 12 and 20 years of age have increased in seven out of the ten taluks. But those between 20 and 30 are fewer in eight taluks; those between 30 and 40 fewer in seven taluks; those between 40 and 50 fewer in nine taluks, the percentage of diminution rising to 21 per cent. in Man; those between 50 and 60 are fewer in eight taluks, the percentage rising to 28 per cent. in Badami; and those above 60 years of age are fewer in eight out of the ten taluks, the percentage of diminution amounting to 57 per cent. in the Man taluk.

Now, it is well known that in ordinary years the diminution among the very young and the very old is very much more than among those of intermediate ages; and in a year of famine, such diminution would be even much more marked than in ordinary years. The registration during 1877, the records of which are now complete, fully bears this out.

In 1872 it was computed that the death-rate amounted to 3·557 per cent. of the whole population of the Presidency of Bombay, whereas in 1877 it amounted to 3·876 per cent., and in the nine affected districts to 5·447 per cent. of the population of those districts, indicating large mortality; but, even assuming a death-rate based upon the loss of very young children, which is the most unfavourable view of the case, the census of 1878 most distinctly indicates very large migration from Madha and Badami, a fact borne out by the reports of the District Officers, considerable migration from Man, Khatau, Bagalkot and Athni and some migration into Kod.

It is impossible to state precisely what proportion of the loss exhibited by the census of 1878 is due to excess deaths from 1872 to 1876, to excess deaths during 1877, and to migration out of the distressed districts, but an examination of the calculations and speculations given in the appendix to this note will tend to throw some light, at any rate, upon the subject.

APPENDIX TO COLONEL MERRIMAN'S NOTE.

The death-rate for the whole Presidency was in 1877=38·76 per 1,000 of population.

The death-rate of each class was during the same year—

Infants under 1 . . .	149·43	per 1,000
Children from 1 to 12 . .	28·75	,, ,,
Adults ,, 12 to 50 . .	25·64	,, ,,
Old people above 50 . . .	125·72	,, ,,

Taking the ratio of increase as 1 per cent. per annum, the population at the beginning of 1878 ought to have been 6·15 per cent. greater than shown by the census of 1872.

One Table (F) shows the loss per 1,000 of each class in each taluk, and the question comes what proportion of this loss, if any, is due to migration. It may be reasonably supposed that whatever portion of the loss is due to death, in such portion the respective losses of each class would approximate to that shown above, and that the special conditions giving rise to increased mortality in 1877 would tend rather to raise than to lower the loss of infants and old people, as compared with the loss of children and adults.

Another Table (G) is obtained by dividing the loss per 1,000 of each class by the figures given above. Where the figures under the columns children and adults exceed the figures under the columns infants and old people, we must either suppose that the special conditions above referred to caused increased mortality among children and adults as compared with infants and old people, or, what is more reasonable, that a portion of the loss was due to migration of children and adults, and the greater the difference between the figures the greater such migration. Referring to this table, it will be seen that the figures under children and adults exceed those under infants and old people in greatest proportion in the taluks of Bádámi and Mádha, indicating that a large portion of the loss of population of these two taluks was due to migration. Bádámi shows the highest loss rate for children and nearly the highest loss rate for old people, indicating a large mortality as well as much migration. More or less migration is also indicated *from* the following taluks:—Mán, Khatau, Bágalkot, and Athni. No migration is indicated from Sángola; here the loss is probably due to mortality, what proportion in 1877 and what in previous years it is impossible to say. The same remarks apply to Ron. On the other hand, the figures indicate migration into Kod; hence the indications are—

Large migration from Bádámi and Mádha.
Less migration from Mán, Khatau, Bágalkot, and Athni.
No migration indicated from Sángola and Ron.
Migration into Kod.

If the taluks are placed in order of their loss-rate, we have—

1st.—Bádámi 254·11, Mádha 245·15.
2nd.—Athni 187·10, Mán 171·72, Bágalkot 169·29, Khatau 153·14.
3rd.—Ron 127·64, Sampgaon 98·78, Sángola 92·66.
4th.—Kod 41·58.

As a speculation, as to the amount of migration from each taluk, we may proceed as follows:

Assuming that the loss-rate of children and adults, in excess of that for infants and old people, represents migration, we find that in the six taluks named this amounted to

Mádha	.	12,091 individuals = loss per 1,000 of population of the taluk	. . . .	110·95
Bádámi	.	10,081	„ „	83·09
Bágalkot	.	8,351	„ „	71·39
Khatau	.	4,211	„ „	48·40
Athni	.	5,010	„ _„	41·15
Mán	.	1,785	,· „	26·71

These figures are obtained by taking the highest of the two figures under infants and old people, i.e., the figure under infants in every taluk except Khatau, and deducting it from the figures under children and adults; the remainders multiplied by 28·75 and 25·34 respectively give loss per 1,000 of children and adults due to migration, and these, calculated on the numbers of each class, give the loss of individuals.

But it is fair to suppose that the actual migration was higher than the numbers shown above for the following reasons:—

1st.—The migration rate is calculated above on the presumption that the special causes prevailing in 1877 caused increased mortality of all classes alike. Now table G. shows that in every taluk except one (Khatau) and one (·Mán) where the losses are equal, the loss of old people was less than that of infants, from which it may be presumed, that of the two classes (infants and old people) likely to suffer most, the infants suffered in greater proportion than the old people.

2nd.—Migration of children and adults would, in all probability, be accompanied by migration of infants and old people, of which no notice has been taken in the calculation.

We may attempt to eliminate the error from the first of these two causes by repeating the calculation just made, employing the mean of the figures in Table G. under infants and old people in place of the highest of the two figures; modifying the calculation in this way, we get the following migration rates:—

Mádha	.	14,802 individuals = loss per 1,000	.		134·10
Bádámi	.	12,952	„	„	.	106·76
Bágalkot	.	13,696	„ .	„	.	117·09
Khatau	.	8,131	„	„	.	93·46
Athni	.	8,261	„	„	.	67·86
Mán	.	1,785	„	„	.	26·71
Sampgaon	.	4,921	„	„	.	35·25

The recorded death-rate during 1877 in the nine affected districts was 54·77 per 1,000, and the death-rate of each class in the same districts was—

Infants under 1	173·16	per 1,000
Children 1 to 12 . . .	42·91	„ „
Adults 12 to 50 . . .	35·85	„ „
Old people over 50 . . .	176·16	„ „

Repeating the last calculation, employing these figures instead of the figures for the whole Presidency, we get the following migration rates :—

Mádha, loss per 1,000	122·79
Bádámi „	91·82
Bágalkot „	115·82
Khatau „	95·46
Athni ,;	56·67
Mán „	22·76
Sampgaon · „	27·98

It will be noticed that in two cases, Bágalkot and Sampgaon, these estimated migration rates, if deducted from the total loss-rate, give figures below the recorded death-rate in the taluk. But the migration rates deducted from the loss-rates only give the excess loss which has taken place in each taluk during the six years ending January 1878, over and above that due to the loss by average mortality during the same period ; three causes may have been in operation to produce this excess loss.

1st.—Migration of infants and old people accompanying migrating children and adults, of which, in the previous calculations, no notice has been taken.

2nd.—Excess mortality during the five years ending January 1877.

3rd.—Excess mortality during the year ending January 1878.

What proportion of the excess loss is attributable to each of these heads it is not possible to say.

The conclusions come to by the Bombay Government is that this new and partial census leaves the question of mortality from famine very much in the same doubtful state as before, but that, so far as the Governor in Council can judge, the following conclusions may be formed :—

1st.—That the new census taken in the taluks or tracts of country selected as the worst or most distressed by the famine does seem to show a diminution of the population.

2nd.—That this diminution is in a considerable degree apparent only, as arising from migration, and partly real, as arising from mortality.

3rd.—That the mortality arose partly from sickness other than famine—sickness extending not only throughout the year 1877, that is, the year of famine, but also throughout the two previous years 1876 and 1875, which were not years of famine—and partly also from famine.

4th.—That the mortality arising from famine itself cannot be exactly estimated, but probably it was not considerable, or was rather comparatively inconsiderable.

MADRAS.

The partial census in the famine districts of Madras was taken, on the 15th March, 1878, in one taluk out of each of the six severely stricken districts of Bellary, Kurnool, Cuddapah, Nellore, Coimbatore, and Chingleput, and in all the nine taluks which constitute the district of Salem; a census was also taken in one taluk out of each of the districts of Kistna, Trichinopoly, and Tinnevelly, in parts of which some distress was felt, but in parts of which the crops were saved by irrigation, and in one taluk of Tanjore, throughout almost the whole of which the crops were saved by irrigation from the Cauvery river. The results of the census were as follows :—

In the	Population as per Census of		Difference.	Percentage of difference on original population.
	November, 1871.	March, 1878.		
Six taluks of the six very distressed districts - - -	859,132	739,989	−119,143	minus 13
Nine taluks of the Salem district - -	1,977,034	1,559,896	−417,138	„ 21
Three taluks of the three slightly distressed districts - - -	496,702	528,574	+ 31,872	plus 6
One taluk of the Tanjore district - -	221,749	242,999	+ 21,250	„ 9

No review of these figures had been received from the Madras Government early in July, when these pages left India; but Sir Michael Kennedy had furnished the Government of India with remarks upon the results of the partial census. He considers that the diminution of the population must be due to the effect of migration, of increased mortality, of diminished births; or to a combination of all these three causes. No figures, even approximate, are available to show the extent to which emigration has taken place from the famine districts. The number of emigrants by sea from the Madras Presidency to Burma, Ceylon, and elsewhere is shown by the returns from sea-ports to have been 287,482 during the 14 months of famine, as compared with 156,143, the average number for a corresponding period in ordinary times; that is to say, the emigration by sea nearly doubled during the famine. But there is nothing to show how many of these emigrants came from the famine districts, or from the particular taluks in which the recent census was taken. Again, there is no available information regarding the great exodus of population from the famine districts to the neighbouring tracts in Malabar, Tanjore, Ganjam, and parts of Tinnevelly and Kistna, where drought had comparatively little effect. The figures of the recent census show that the diminution among the males of ten years old and upwards has been considerably greater than among women of the same age. Sir Michael Kennedy points out that there was no reason why men should have died from famine more rapidly than women, while it is quite probable that men would migrate more readily than women. He considers that this excess diminution among men tends to show that the total number of persons migrating from the famine tracts must have been very large, and that a part at any rate of the decrease of population must be due to emigration. He shows that a part of the diminution must be due to the decrease in births; for the returns (confessedly imperfect as yet) of births for the 15 famine taluks, in which the census has now been taken, give a decrease of 32,054 births as compared with the average of ordinary years. Further he shows that, according to the monthly returns of mortality, a great part of the loss of population was due to unusual epidemics of cholera, small-pox, and fever, which swept off in these 15 taluks 149,053 persons, compared with an average mortality of 32,909 from these diseases as returned during the years 1870–75.

The table, given later on, regarding the results of the partial census in Madras, takes the normal increment of the population to be 1½ per cent. per annum. And some of the subsidiary statements forwarded by the Government of Bombay assume the normal increase of the population to be one per cent. per annum. If it be assumed that any such increase really occurred during the years 1872–75, before the distress began, then the actual loss of population attributable to famine will be proportionately larger. Sir Michael Kennedy in his memorandum [1] shows that the excess of registered births over registered deaths, according to the returns published by the Madras Government, gave a normal increase of population at the rate of ·2 per cent. per annum in the 15 taluks during the period of 1872–76; and he considers that there is no sufficient ground for the assumption that the population of the Madras Presidency increases at the rate of 1½ per cent. per annum. It appears to the Government of India that no absolute certainty has yet been attained regarding the normal increase of population in India. The Madras Census Report of December 1873 shows (pp. 11–13) that, according to four censuses taken from 1851 to 1871, the annual rate of increase ranged from 0·74 per cent. during the earliest to 3·02 per cent. during the latest period. But the writer of the report (Dr. Cornish) rejects these deduced rates of increase, and holds that the figures merely prove the earlier censuses to have been imperfect. In the North-Western Provinces a detailed census has been taken on scientific principles more often than in other parts of India. The report of the 1871 census for the North-Western Provinces shows (page 2 of vol. i. of the report) the annual increase of population to have been 0·52 per cent., as compared with an increase in Great Britain of 0·56 during the ten years 1851–1861. The Census Report of the Bombay Presi-

---

[1] Sir Michael Kennedy's conclusions have been formulated thus:—

(1.) That looking to general considerations, to the records of births and deaths, and to the census results as to the number of existing houses, there has not been an increase of population since 1871 at the rate of 1½ per cent. per annum; that, in all probability, any increase that may have taken place does not exceed ·2 per cent. per annum; and that there may possibly have been a decrease of numbers.

(2.) That a large portion of the apparent loss of population shown by the last census is due to migration. What the number of absentee migrants actually was, it is not practicable to determine; but that, on a consideration of the actual number of resident males and females over 10 years of age, found in the districts, the number may fairly be assumed to be about 350,000.

(3.) That cholera, small-pox, and fever account for nearly ⅔rds of the excess mortality during the period between the latter part of 1876 and the and of February 1878.

(4.) That the loss of population, not thus accounted for, amounts to about 68,290, or to less than 2½ per cent.; some, but not all, of which loss may be attributable to the distress that has prevailed

dency of January, 1874 (pp. 72–74 and 236–247), shows the deduced rate of increase in the population to be 0·54 per cent. per annum. Probably, until the information on this subject is more complete, the normal increase of an Indian population might be taken at between 0·5 and 0·6 per cent. At this rate the population would double itself within 130 years. As pointed out by the Bombay Government, parts of the country were afflicted by epidemic diseases during 1875 and 1876, and during those years the supposed normal rate of increase may not have been maintained. But during the years 1872–1875, or four years, some increase of the population must, it may be believed, have occurred. And the apparent, as well as the actual loss of population, during these two sad years of famine, must be proportionately increased above the figures shown or suggested in the foregoing paragraphs.

There is still much uncertainty as to the numbers who have migrated, and who may return to their homes. The figures for the several taluks, both in the Bombay and in the Madras Presidency, show remarkable differences between the percentages of apparent loss of population; and it is not possible to say over what proportion of the famine country the higher, the medium, or the lower percentages of decrease in the population extend.

The statement alluded to will be found in the tables appended.

Upon the figures given in these tables the Madras correspondent of the *Times* wrote to that journal in May last, as follows :—

The census operations were completed on the night of March 14, and were of a simple character, but, of course, involved a preliminary numbering of the houses and people, leaving the correction of the house schedules for the night of March 14. The results were sent down to Madras for tabulation, and this work has just been completed by Mr. Kalyana Sondara Chettiar, a gentleman who acquired his experience of census tabulation in 1871, when the last Madras census was taken. On this occasion every village in a district was separately numbered, and the district tables show the particulars of population for every one of the 55,000 villages of the Presidency. In this way it was easy for the tabulator of the famine census to show the loss or gain of population in each village, and this practice was followed in the tables, which will hereafter take a prominent place in the history of the famine. I should only weary you if I attempted to give particulars. The main facts brought out by this statistical

Statement showing the number of ploughing cattle in Government villages according to the Census of 1878, in the selected taluks given below.

Districts	Taluks	Number of ploughing cattle as per Census of 1878	Number of ploughing cattle as per quinquennial returns for Fasli 1281 (1871-72)	Percentage of increase or decrease	Number of houses in 1878	Average number of ploughing cattle per house in 1878
1	2	3	4	5	6	7
Salem	Salem	46,258	64,858	− 28·6	51,357	0·9
	Athur	25,946	27,128	− 4·3	26,025	0·9
	Namkal	19,514	16,902	+ 15·4	28,174	0·6
	Trichengode	22,285	87,082	− 39·8	37,570	0·5
	Oossoor	17,430	25,842	− 32·5	25,841	0·7
	Kistnagiri	15,208	10,788	− 9·0	20,929	0·7
	Darampuri	16,795	21,694	− 22·6	26,644	0·7
	Tripatore	15,371	19,239	− 20·1	16,970	0·9
	Uttengiri	17,464	21,420	− 18·4	26,296	0·6
	Total	196,331	250,909	− 21·7	259,806	0·7
Bellary	Gooty	22,544	24,157	− 6·6	23,400	0·9
Kurnool	Nundikotkur	14,019	15,870	− 11·6	19,676	0·7
Cuddapah	Madanapalli	28,783	26,304	+ 9·4	28,518	1·0
Nellore	Gudur	19,736	21,970	− 10·2	17,730	1·1
Coimbatore	Palladam	41,494	54,370	− 23·6	59,307	0·7
Chingleput	Ponneri	16,034	15,143	+ 5·8	11,170	1·4
Kistna	Gudivada	28,565	29,656	− 3·7	18,781	1·5
Trichinopoly	Museri	44,187	38,444	+ 14·9	44,074	1·0
Tanjore	Mayaveram	39,000	38,630	+ 0·9	41,127	0·9
Tinnevelly	Ambasamudram	20,259	29,776	− 31·9	30,584	0·5

Statement showing the results of the partial Census of 1878 in the undermentioned selected taluks, as compared with the Census of 1871, plus an increment of 1½ per cent, per annum, during the 5 years, from 1872 to 1878, and after deducting necessary additions and deductions have been made (on account of the transfer of certain villages from one taluk to another) in order to render the comparison correct.

Districts	Taluks	NUMBER OF VILLAGES			NUMBER OF HOUSES				POPULATION ACCORDING TO CENSUS OF 1878								POPULATION OF 1871 PLUS THE INCREMENT						
		Inhabited	Uninhabited	Total	According to Census of 1878	According to Census of 1871	Difference Increase or Decrease 6 and 7	Percentage of Increase or Decrease	MALES			FEMALES			Total			Population according to Census of 1871	Increment of 1½ per cent, per annum from 1872 to 1876	Total	Difference between 16 and 19	Percentage of increase	Percentage of decrease	Difference between column 15 and 19	Percentage of increase	Percentage of decrease
									Above 16 years of age	16 years of age and under	Total	Above 16 years of age	16 years of age and under	Total	Males	Females	Total									
1	2	3	4	5	6	7	8	9	10	11	12	13	14	15	16	17	18	19	20	21	22	23

enquiry are that the death registration, as all along contended by the Sanitary Commissioner, did not represent the real mortality of the famine. According to the estimated population at the end of 1876, the losses in the famine year have been as follows :—Bellary, 21 per cent.; Kurnool, 27 per cent.; Cuddapah, 26 per cent.; Nellore, 21 per cent.; Coimbatore, 17 per cent.; Chingleput, 10 per cent. The Salem district, as I have already said, was numbered throughout. Its estimated population in 1876 was 2,129,850. The actual population on March 14, 1878, was 1,559,876—that is, there were 569,956 souls in this one district, or nearly 27 per cent. of the people, unaccounted for. And I wish you to remember that in this Salem district the famine distress is not yet over, nor will it be for some months; so that the half a million and odd of the two millions of population does not represent the whole of the fearful life-waste of the famine.

But I have said that a trial census was also made in some districts in which there had been no actual famine, and the results are of the highest value in corroboration of the figures of the worst famine districts. For instance, in the following districts there was an increase over the estimated population, as follows :—Kistna, 5·1 per cent.; Tanjore, 1·7 per cent.; and in the subjoined districts there was a very slight decrease :—Trichinopoly, 2·9 per cent.; Tinnevelly, 1 ? per cent. But in all these four districts the population of 1878 was above that of 1871, though in two of them not quite equal to the 'estimated' population. It has been assumed throughout that an Indian population grows normally at the rate of 1½ per cent. per annum, and this proportion is within the mark in ordinary times; but we have now the most convincing testimony that the death-rate indications throughout the famine were right, and that no Government can in future afford to neglect the warnings afforded by such testimony. The Government of India must already be aware that any famine policy which allows one-fourth of the population to die can hardly be put forth as a policy to be followed on future occasions. In all my letters on the famine during last year, you will remember that I never ceased to dwell upon the gravity of the crisis as regarded the vitality and energy of the people, and the census figures now tabulated show how completely my forebodings were justified by actual facts. We have probably lost not less than three millions out of the twenty millions of population severely affected by the famine, and if we add the mortality in Mysore and Bombay, the total losses of the population in South India will not be far short of six millions.

These results are obtained by applying to the districts respectively the experience obtained from an examination of one taluk, it being held that the whole numbering of the people in Salem justified this course. These conclusions, however, are considered doubtful, and the subject is still (July 1878) being discussed between the Government of India and the Madras authorities.

As matters stand when these pages are sent to press, the evidence available is not sufficient to justify an estimate of the famine mortality of 1876–78 being made.

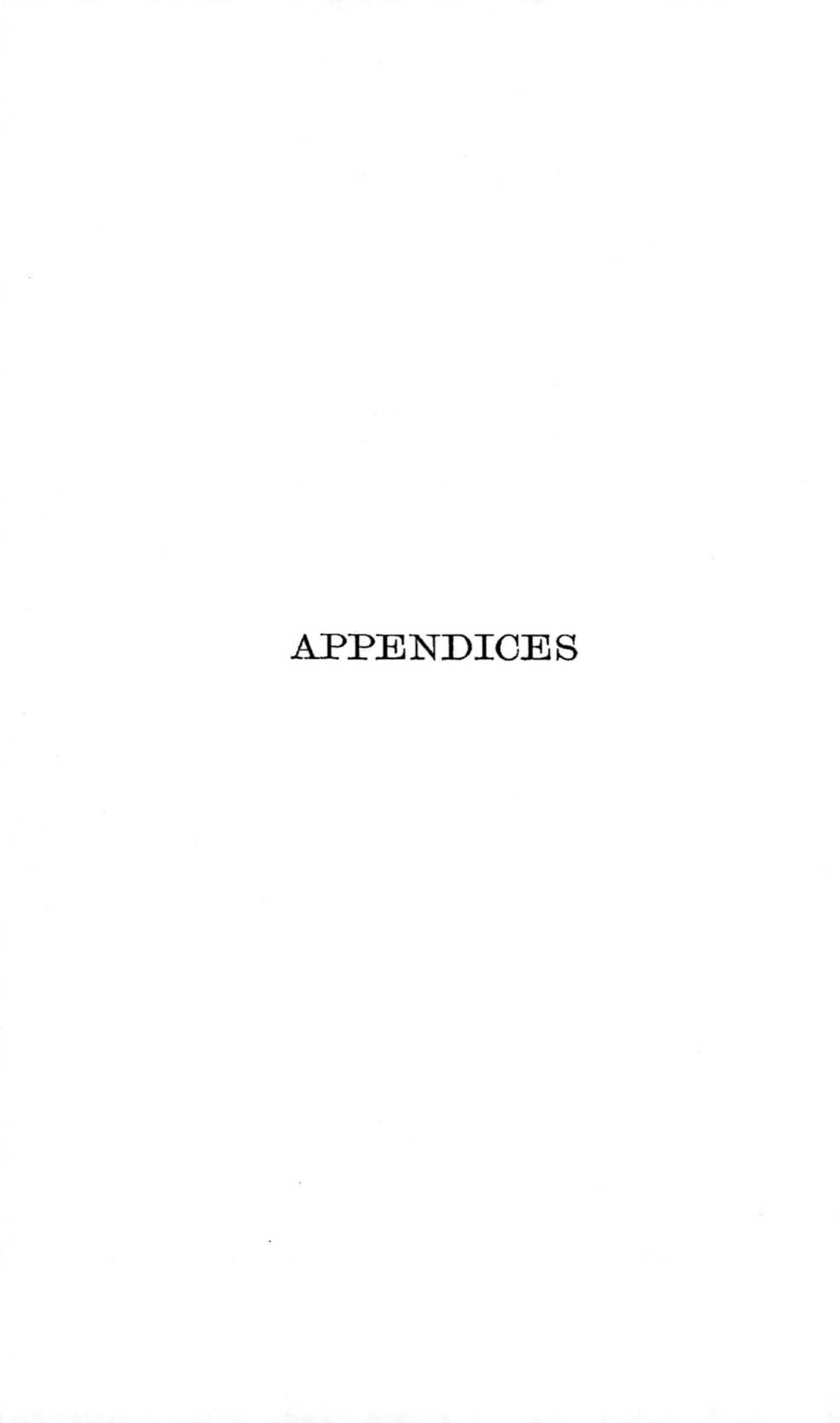

APPENDICES

APPENDICES.

APPENDIX A.

INSTRUCTIONS TO SIR RICHARD TEMPLE, BART., G.C.S.I. AS FAMINE DELEGATE.

From the Secretary to the Government of India to the Hon. Sir Richard Temple, Bart., K.C.S.I., Lieutenant-Governor of Bengal (on a special mission).

Calcutta, January 16, 1877.

His Excellency the Governor-General in Council having been pleased to depute you on a special mission for the purpose of inspecting the districts suffering from scarcity in the Presidencies of Madras and Bombay, and conferring personally with the Governments of those Presidencies regarding the measures which are being carried out, and which will have to be carried out, for the relief of distress, I am directed to communicate to you the following observations, indicating the general views of the Government of India on some of the more important questions with which you will have to deal.

2. I am to observe in the first place, that while it is the desire of the Government of India that every effort should be made, so far as the resources of the State admit, for the prevention of deaths from famine, it is essential in the present state of the finances that the most severe economy should be practised. The distress is so widespread, extending over 21 districts in the two Presidencies, and more or less affecting a population of 27,000,000, and threatens to be protracted for so many months, that the utmost care is necessary to restrict the expenditure to the absolute requirements of the case. Even, however, if financial considerations were less overpoweringly strong, it would still be true that a Government has no better right in times of scarcity than in other times to attempt the task of preventing all suffering, and of giving general relief to the poorer classes of the community. False and mischievous ideas on this subject have

become so prevalent, that the Government runs some risk of being charged with inhumanity when it declares that these are the principles by which it intends to be guided. The Governor-General in Council will not be deterred by such considerations as these from a course of action which he knows to be right. Everyone admits the evils of indiscriminate private charity, but the indiscriminate charity of a Government is far worse. The Government of India is resolved to spare no efforts which may be necessary and practicable, with reference to the means at its disposal, to save the population of the distressed districts from starvation, or from an extremity of suffering dangerous to life; but it will not sanction a course of action which must tend to demoralise the people themselves, who are passing through a time of temporary trial, and inevitably lead to the imposition of heavy and permanent burdens on the industry of the country. Even for an object of such paramount importance as the preservation of life, it is obvious that there are limits which are imposed upon us by the facts with which we have to deal. If the estimates of the local Governments are to be accepted, the relief of the existing scarcity in the Madras and Bombay Presidencies, including loss of revenue, will not cost less than six and a half millions sterling. Considering that the revenues are barely sufficient to meet the ordinary expenditure of the Empire, and that heavy additional taxation is both financially and politically impracticable, we must plainly admit that the task of saving life, irrespective of the cost, is one which it is beyond our power to undertake. The simple fact is this, that the recurrence of a few famines, such as that from which the country is now suffering, or such as that which occurred three years ago in Behar, would, if measures of relief were carried on upon that principle, go far to render the future government of India impossible. The embarrassment of debt, and the weight of taxation, consequent on the expenditure thereby involved, would soon become more fatal to the country than famine itself. Happily, however, the Government are not placed in any such dilemma. They believe that from the history of past famines, rules of action may be learnt which will enable them in the future to provide efficient assistance for the suffering people without incurring disastrous expenditure.

3. One of the first points which should engage your attention is the extent to which relief is given, and the principles on which it is afforded.[1] The numbers on the relief works are so great, that the

[1] Madras—

On relief works	. . . . . .	1,125,117
Fed gratuitously	. . . . .	119,363
Bombay—		————1,244,480
On relief works	. . . .	287,000
		1,531,480

Government of India see reason to apprehend that many persons must be employed to whom such relief is not absolutely essential, and who without it would have been able to maintain themselves, at all events for some time to come. The Governor General in Council does not for a moment doubt the reality of the calamity that has fallen upon the country, a calamity which unhappily threatens to become ere long still more disastrous. But it is necessary to remember that the mere collection of enormous numbers of people on relief works in seasons of scarcity is in itself no sufficient proof of serious actual suffering. If relief works are carried on upon wrong principles; if labour is not strictly exacted from all who are physically able to work; if proper supervision is wanting, and people find that they can obtain, almost for the asking, and in return for next to no work at all, wages in money or in grain, there is hardly any limit to the numbers who even in prosperous times may be attracted to them. 'When,' as Sir George Campbell has observed, 'a lax system is established, and every-one down to the merest child gets paid for the merest pretence of work, with probably a good many abuses besides, the thing becomes too attractive, the whole country tends to come on the works, the numbers threaten to be absolutely overwhelming. The people, too, become demoralised; works where real work is exacted are deserted, and many evils follow.' A good illustration of this may be found in the official narrative of the scarcity of 1873–74 in the North-Western Provinces. 'In a season of considerable pressure, but not of absolute famine, the relief works in Gorakhpur and Basti were for some weeks daily thronged by more than 200,000 men, women, and children, who found an attraction in the light work, in the liberty of going at night to their houses after attending a sort of vast pic-nic during the day, and in the wages earned at a time when ordinarily they had no em-ployment in the fields, and had to live on their harvest savings. But when the wages were cut down to a mere subsistence allowance, when a full day's labour was insisted on, and when the liberty of living at their homes was threatened, these immense crowds melted away as rapidly as they had collected, and it was found that there was hardly anyone who really stood in need of relief.' The Governor-General in Council does not assert that a similar condition of things now exists in any of the districts of Madras or Bombay, but the matter is one which requires the most careful observation.

4. The general principles on which operations for the relief of famine in India should be conducted, have been established beyond question by past experience. When, as may easily happen at the commencement of a period of distress, it is a matter of doubt whether serious scarcity is actually threatening a tract of country, it may be

desirable, in the first instance, to open, as a tentative measure, small and well-supervised local works. The Government may thus avoid the risk of finding itself committed to serious expenditure on large public works which there was no immediate necessity for undertaking. It was for reasons of this kind that the Government of India, at the commencement of the present scarcity, and while still in doubt regarding the extent to which relief operations might ultimately become necessary, thought it right, both in the Madras and Bombay Presidencies, to encourage, in the first instance, the organisation of works of a local character in preference to those of greater magnitude. But when it becomes no longer a matter of doubt that serious scarcity is impending, and that relief will have to be provided upon an extensive scale, the great difficulty of insuring adequate supervision for numerous scattered works renders it necessary to resort to large works on which large gangs of labourers can be employed, and on which adequate labour tests can be exacted. As soon, therefore, as it is clear that the Government will have to undertake serious measures for the relief of scarcity, no time should be lost in giving to the people, to the greatest extent practicable, the means of employment on large public works. Such works supply the means of subsistence to the able-bodied poor ; they prevent, instead of merely relieving, distress.

5. In choosing such works it is obviously of great importance that those selected shall be of a permanently useful and remunerative character; for it is in the last degree unsatisfactory that when the necessity for employing great multitudes of people is forced upon the Government, their labour, which might have been devoted to works which would have conferred lasting benefit on the country, should be thrown away. The works should also be such as are calculated to absorb, in comparison with their entire cost, a sufficient proportion of labour during the anticipated period of famine. They need not always be in the distressed districts, or near the homes of the people who require relief. When railways or other thoroughly good means of communication are available, it may sometimes be easier and wiser to carry the people to the works and to their food, than to carry the food to the people. Temporary migration from their homes has always, in times of scarcity, been the natural and one of the best remedies to which the people have had recourse, and the organisation of public works in places where food is plentiful, and to which access is not difficult from the distressed districts, may in some cases be more useful than works at places where the supply of food is already insufficient. No apprehension need be felt that the people will not return to their homes when the period of distress has passed away. It will be for you to consider how far these principles are being acted on, and

if necessary to recommend to the local Governments the discontinuance of any works, or system of works, which, in your opinion, cannot be usefully proceeded with.

6. When, by undertaking large public works, employment has been provided for the able-bodied poor, it may still be necessary, even before the pressure of famine has become extreme, to afford means of support to persons who are physically unable to give a full amount of labour in return for the wages they receive. These must either be employed in poor-houses or on roads and other easy work, every effort being made to prevent relief being given to anyone who does not really require it. It has often been found a most useful test of actual distress to insist, when charitable relief is necessary, that it shall ordinarily be given in the shape of cooked food.

7. It should be added that when distress becomes extreme, and a state of absolute famine has been reached, that large public works may become insufficient to afford relief to the numbers of people in need of it. At such a time the Government may be driven to set up relief works near the homes of the people on a scale inconsistent with careful supervision or searching tests. Such measures as may be practicable must then be adopted for reducing to a minimum the inevitable evils that will then arise. The Governor General in Council leaves it to you to communicate to the local Governments the results of your own experience in regard to this very difficult part of the question.

8. A very satisfactory feature in the course taken by the Bombay Government in dealing with the present famine is their adherence to the principle of non-interference with private trade, which up to the present time they have acted on with marked success. In Madras a different policy has been observed. At an early stage in the scarcity, the Government of Madras contracted through a local firm for a supply of 30,000 tons of grain, to be used as a reserve to meet deficiencies in the local markets. Applications for authority to make further similar purchases have since been received, but have not been sanctioned, the Government of India being of opinion that such purchases are seriously calculated to discourage the operations of private trade, and to increase, instead of diminishing, the difficulty of procuring the supplies which will be necessary to augment the deficient food supply of the Presidency. Enquiry has been made whether this objection would apply to the Government advertising for tenders for the supply and delivery of grain in the immediate neighbourhood of certain works on which gangs of labourers are employed at a distance from all local markets. The answer must of course be in the negative. There is no more objection to such purchases than there is to the Government

making purchases through the commissariat for the troops. The objection is to the Government entering into transactions which may excite apprehensions on the part of traders, that the Government are about to take their place, and so to disarrange the bases on which they found their calculations of profit. This objection is especially applicable to purchases of a secret character. In such cases the fact that the Government are in the market is almost certain to become known, and thereupon doubts are raised as to the nature and extent of the transaction, and private trade is paralysed. In regard not only to this but all other matters connected with the management of famines, the general rule should be that the operations of the Government, and the reasons on which those operations are based, shall receive full and complete explanation and publicity.

9. One of your most important duties in connection with the present state of things in the Madras Presidency will be to ascertain how far private trade, if left perfectly unfettered, may be counted on to supply the wants of that Presidency. As at present informed, the Governor General in Council entertains a strong opinion that the supply of that Presidency from foreign sources, such as Burma, Bengal, &c., should be left altogether to private trade, and that the intention of the Government so to act should be widely made known, together with full and frequent information regarding the prices of food grains and other articles of consumption in the distressed and other districts. It is possible, however, that in certain localities at a distance from the lines of railway and from large markets, it may be requisite for the Government to intervene by making purchases at the nearest local depôt to which the trade will convey the grain. In such cases, where the local trade, from whatever cause, is not active, the direct intervention of the Government may probably tend rather to facilitate than to discourage the importation of grain, by affording confidence to the trade that importations will find a certain purchaser. Finally, it must not be overlooked that there is a great advantage in paying labourers on relief works in money, wherever and so long as this mode of relief is practicable.

10. The Governor General in Council would have hoped that it was hardly necessary to impress upon local officers the importance of exercising no interference of any kind with the object of reducing the price of food; but cases have come to his notice which show that a warning on this point may not be uncalled for. It is obvious that, especially in a time of scarcity, nothing could be more mischievous than such interference, and that high prices, by reducing consumption and encouraging the importation of fresh supplies of food, are not only necessary but highly beneficial.

11. Another matter of importance is the question of transport of grain, both on the railways and to parts of the country with which the existing means of communication are insufficient, as well as of providing additional facilities for landing it at the ports. These matters, the Government of India have reason to believe, have not been at all overlooked by the local Governments, but it is probable that your experience will enable you to offer valuable suggestions on the subject.

12. There is one other subject to which the Governor General in Council thinks it desirable to refer, not because it is one with which you will have at present in any way to deal, but because he wishes to place you generally in possession of the views which are held by the Government of India on all the more serious questions connected with the treatment of Indian famines.

You will observe that his Excellency in Council, in my letter to the Government of Bombay, No. 5 A., dated the 5th instant, has laid down the principle that if any great irrigation works or other works of local and provincial importance, involving heavy future responsibilities for their completion and maintenance, be undertaken, certain rules will be held applicable, which will hereafter be prescribed, in regard to the enforcement of provincial responsibility for meeting the charges for extraordinary public works. This is not a convenient time for entering into a full discussion of these questions, but his Excellency in Council desires to take the present opportunity of declaring his opinion not only that the main portion of the charges incurred on public works which protect the people against famine, and which add greatly to their wealth, should be borne by the people protected and benefited, and not by the general taxpayer, but also that every province ought, so far as may be practicable, to be held responsible for meeting the cost of the famines from which it may suffer. The Governor General in Council believes that until these principles are enforced, the only real security for wise and economical management will be wanting. When local Governments and local officers understand that the inevitable consequence of unnecessary expenditure will be the imposition of heavy burdens upon their own people, and not upon those of other provinces, a powerful and most useful check upon extravagance will have been established. On this subject the opinions of Her Majesty's Secretary of State for India have been expressed in a passage which may properly be quoted here : [1]—

[1] Despatch from Secretary of State to Government of India, No. 59 (Revenue), dated November 25, 1875.

'There is a further point, though not one to fall within the scope of such an enquiry as that which you have directed to be made, which should, in my opinion, be carefully considered by your Excellency's Government before the questions that arise in connection with the occurrences of 1873–74 can be regarded as fairly met. I refer to the proper incidence of the charges that are necessarily incurred in providing for the requirements of the population of a district in a period of drought. However plain may be the primary obligation on the State to do all that is requisite and possible towards preserving the lives of the people under such circumstances, it would be most unwise to overlook the great danger of tacitly accepting, if not the doctrine, at least the practice, of making the general revenues bear the whole burden of meeting all local difficulties or of relieving all local distress, and of supplying the needful funds by borrowing in a shape that establishes a permanent charge on the general revenues for all future time. In Bengal, where (as the Lieutenant Governor observes in reference to the objections of the Government in relation to emigration) the beneficial interest of the Government in the land is limited by the permanent settlement, these considerations are of special and more pressing application.

' The question which is thus raised, of how to make local resources aid in meeting local wants, is no doubt one of great difficulty and complexity, particularly in a country like India. But the difficulty of providing any satisfactory solution of it should not be allowed to obscure the perception of its vital importance to the future well-being of the country, as well as of the troubles to the Government and the demoralisation of the people which must necessarily result from postponing too long the introduction of some system under which shall be suitably recognised the undoubted responsibility which rests on the people themselves to provide for their own support and well-being. The duty of the State does not extend further than to see that the needful means are supplied for giving effect to this principle, and for distributing the local burdens arising from its practical application in the manner which shall be most equitable and least onerous to those who have to bear them.'

The manner in which these principles shall be carried into practical effect is under the consideration of the Government. It is sufficient at present to say that the Governor General in Council is of opinion that they ought to be kept in view in connection with the present scarcity, and that a considerable portion, if not the whole, of the permanent charges which relief operations now in progress may entail ought to be borne by the Presidencies in which the expenditure is being incurred.

13. The above are the only observations that the Government of India deem it at present necessary to place on record in connection with the onerous and delicate duty which you have undertaken : and they have been made, not so much with the view of advising you on a subject which you have probably studied more thoroughly than any other public officer in India, as for the purpose of furnishing you with a statement of the views of the Government of India, to which you can refer in your communications with the local Governments. I am directed, in conclusion, to convey to you the cordial thanks of the Governor General in Council for the promptitude with which on this, as on other occasions, you have responded to the call made upon you.

APPENDIX B.

MINUTE BY HIS EXCELLENCY THE VICEROY.

1. The summer rains of June and July have now failed, more or less, over many of the districts in Southern India, where the rainfall of 1876 was lamentably deficient. The severity of the situation is increased by the scantiness of the rainfall in western and northern India during the past six weeks. I desire to place on record my appreciation of the probable effect of these unanticipated circumstances on the condition of the people and the prospects of the Government. In so doing, I will endeavour to indicate my general views as to some of the measures required to prepare for a second year of famine if unhappily so terrible a calamity should overtake any large tract of Southern India.

2. The time has not come for the Government of India to review the famine operations of the year 1876–77 for the famine is still almost at its worst. But a short notice of the failure of last year's harvest, of the misfortunes thereby caused, and of the relief operations undertaken, is necessary to a proper understanding of the extreme gravity of the present situation.

3. The summer rains (south-west monsoon) of 1876 were extremely scanty over tracts belonging to the Presidencies of Madras and Bombay, to the State of Hyderabad, and to the Province of Mysore. Over these tracts, which contain a population of about twenty-six millions,

the summer rains yield the main rainfall of the year; they fill the irrigation tanks, and on them depends the safety of the main food crops. In the above-mentioned districts, therefore, the chief food crops of 1876 failed by reason of the shortness of the summer rains. But in the rest of the Madras country the main rainfall comes with the October rains (north-east monsoon); these rains were also very deficient, and so the irrigation tanks of the Madras districts remained dry, and the chief food crops failed. The fate of the Madras crops was thus partially in doubt until the middle of November.

4. The failure of the crops of a single year might not have caused a famine, if it had been confined to only one province, or to a few districts; for inter-communication, by railway and by road, is easy and cheap all over Southern India, and the surplus of one province would have supplied the deficiency of another. But last year the area of failure was so vast that famine prices were inevitable ; and by the month of December 1876, food grains in the markets of Southern India were three times as dear as in ordinary years. The calamity pressed with special weight on some of the stricken districts (notably Bellary, Sholapur, parts of the Carnatic, and of Mysore), because the crops of one, or even two, preceding years had been short. In such districts food stocks were lower than usual, and the people had less money to buy food brought from a distance. In Bengal, Burma, Central and Northern India, the crops were happily good ; food stocks were large ; and there was plenty of grain to supply the stricken districts, if it could be carried thither, and if the people could afford to pay for it.

5. The policy of the Government of India, as declared after previous famines, was to give all possible facilities for the transport of grain to distressed districts; to abstain from interference with the grain trade, so long as that trade was active ; to give relief wages to the destitute who would labour on useful public works; to relieve, gratuitously, under trustworthy supervision, the helpless poor, when the pressure of famine became extreme ; and to avert death from starvation by the employment of all means practically open to the resources of the State and the exertions of its officers ; but to discharge this duty at the lowest cost compatible with the preservation of human life from wholesale destruction. In the autumn of 1876, no general instructions were issued by the Government of India for the management of serious and widespread famine; nor until November was it certain, from the reports received by the Supreme Government, that positive famine was impending in the Madras districts.

6. From the month of September 1876 a large importation of grain from Northern India and Bengal into the distressed tracts began ; and this traffic rapidly increased till, in the month of Decem-

ber, grain was landed by sea at Madras; and was also consigned by railway, from the west, through Raichore (the westernmost limit of the Madras Railway), in much larger quantities than the railways could distribute, to the districts of the Madras Presidency, and of the Mysore province. From December up to the present time of writing private traders have kept consigning, month by month, into the interior of the famine districts, more grain than the railways from Madras, Beypore, Negapatam, and Raichore have been able to carry. This grain has come from Bengal, Burma, the Punjab, the North-Western Provinces, Central India, and Scinde. Government has done much to facilitate the traffic; and on one occasion only have Government operations interfered with private trade, namely, when 30,000 tons of grain were bought by the Madras Government at the beginning of the famine, and were carried into the interior of the country. To this extent the railway and cart power of the country was temporarily occupied by Government to the exclusion of private trade. These proceedings of the Madras Government were disapproved by the Government of India. Prices have been very dear, but from nowhere, until July 23, have we received reports that food cannot be had in the bazaars by those who can afford to pay for it. In some of the worst districts the imported food has sufficed for the needs of about one-third of the total population. The remaining two-thirds in such districts, and a much larger proportion in the less severely afflicted tracts, have subsisted on old stocks and on the yield of the petty crops that have been harvested even during this year of famine. The importation of grain by railway into the interior has not yet exceeded an average of about

2,200 tons a day into the interior of Madras and Mysore;
1,000 „ „ „ the Bombay Presidency.

These figures do not include the large quantities of grain distributed into the interior by road or canal, from the port of Madras, and from the lesser ports on the Coromandel, Malabar, and Southern Mahratta coasts. There are in Central and Northern India and in Bengal large stocks of food, ready to go forward to the famine districts as soon as the railways can carry them.

7. At the outset of the famine operations there was general failure to employ the destitute poor on properly managed and useful public works. During November and December hundreds of thousands of people sought and obtained relief wages on works which were not of the highest utility, and on which there was no adequate professional supervision. For this result I fear that the orders of the Government of India, enjoining the employment of the people on petty works

near their homes, were in some degree responsible. In the Government despatch, conveying instructions for Sir Richard Temple's mission to the famine country, it was mentioned that small and well-supervised local relief works might properly be opened at the beginning of a period of distress, so long as there was doubt regarding the extent of scarcity ; but that, when measures of relief on a large scale became clearly necessary, great public works of a permanently useful type should be opened for the employment of relief labourers. The experience of the present famine—the friction, distress, and loss caused by the transfer of labourers from small to large works during February in the Bombay Presidency—and the difficulty of moving to large useful works any considerable proportion of the relief labourers in Madras has since convinced me of the impolicy of opening petty local relief works during the early stages of a scarcity. The orders directing the opening of small local works were modified in December, and it was subsequently laid down that relief labourers should be employed to the utmost extent possible on large useful works, under the direction of competent engineers. Meanwhile, before those orders had reached the local officers,

> 1,050,000 persons in the Madras districts,
> 266,000 „ „ Bombay districts,

were, n the beginning of January, receiving relief wages for labour that was generally inadequate on works that were often of little value.

8. During the month of January the manner of employing relief labourers changed greatly for the better in the Bombay districts, where the local Government utilised to the full its staff of engineers, and possessed a number of excellent irrigation schemes and other projects. During the same month Sir Richard Temple was deputed by the Government of India to visit the famine districts and to confer with the local Governments and their officers as to the best means of enforcing economy and system in relief operations. The admirable services rendered by Sir Richard Temple have already been acknowledged by the Government of India. It was found that vast numbers were in receipt of relief who, for a time at any rate, could support themselves. The relief wage rate was lowered, the number of petty relief works was reduced, and the supervision of relief labour was increased. In consequence of these measures the numbers of people on the relief works were at the end of April

> In Madras districts . . . 716,000 persons
> In Mysore „ . . . 62,000 „

In Bombay, at the same time, the numbers had risen to 287,000. In Madras 11 per cent. of these labourers were employed on useful works under professional supervision. In Bombay 90 per cent. were so employed. In Mysore 47 per cent. were on useful public works; but in Mysore the numbers on relief works were, in a way that has not been explained, reduced as the pressure of the famine increased; and large sums are now being spent on infructuous alms, instead of being devoted to improving by relief labour the many irrigation works of the province.

It is not supposed that the relief works managed by revenue officers are absolutely useless, or are wholly unsupervised; but I fear that much of the roadwork done under revenue officers can be of no lasting value, while its cost is from twice to twenty times the ordinary rates; whereas, on the other hand, the irrigation and railway works executed under professional supervision will be of permanent good in improving the country and averting future famines, while some of these works (so far as imperfect information has reached the Government of India) are being executed at only from 20 to 50 per cent. above ordinary rates. At the present time of writing the proportion of relief labourers employed under professional supervision on large works in Madras has risen by the latest returns to about 21 per cent. on the total number of workpeople.

10. Gratuitous relief on a large scale began early in the present famine. By the end of December there were in receipt of gratuitous relief

110,000 persons in the Madras districts
  3,000   „   „   Bombay   „
 30,000   „   „   Mysore   „

These numbers were somewhat reduced in January and February, but since the end of February they have increased enormously, and have risen by the end of July to

839,000 in the Madras districts
160,000   „   Bombay   „
151,000   „   Mysore   „

In Mysore the number of persons in receipt of gratuitous relief is more than three times higher than the number of the relief labourers; and it appears that in this province relief works have not been properly managed. The persons on gratuitous relief in Madras and Bombay belong to three categories, thus:—

	Children of labourers on the relief works.	Persons fed at relief houses and relief camps.	Persons relieved at their homes through village agencies.
Madras (according to the latest detailed return for the beginning of July) .	149,000	207,000	218,000
Bombay	93,000	66,000	

The Mysore returns do not distinguish the several classes of charitable relief. So long as relief wages are kept at subsistence rates, the small allowance of 3 pies ($\frac{3}{8}$ of a penny) per diem must be continued to the infant children of relief labourers. The inmates of relief camps, and the daily recipients of food at relief houses are ordinarily fit subjects for charity, provided that able-bodied people are drafted to relief works as soon as they are strong enough to labour. Relief through village agencies may become unavoidable where famine presses severely; but its administration must be carefully supervised in order that the needy may be really relieved, and that there may be as little fraud as possible. In Bombay, the numbers so relieved in each district vary according to the pressure of distress and the numbers on the relief works. But the figures for Madras lead to a belief that different systems are pursued in different districts : for instance, in Kurnool, where severe distress afflicted the whole district, only 5,519 persons were receiving village relief at the beginning of July ; whereas in Salem, a part only of which district was severely distressed, 88,020 persons were on village relief.

11. In regard to the main object of relief operations, viz., the saving of human life, much, but not complete, success has been attained. In some tracts relief operations began too late; at centres of population like Madras and Bangalore, and on some of the roads leading to such centres, starvation deaths have occurred. The death-rate from cholera, dysentery, and such-like diseases has greatly increased over large areas. But, on the whole, the worst evils of famine have, so far, been successfully averted over the vast tracts visited by failure of crops. According to the standard of mortality during the Orissa famine, from three to five millions of people (instead of only half a million) must have died of famine in Southern India during the year 1877, if the guaranteed railways had not existed, and if Government had incurred no outlay on relief operations. Nothing of this sort has occurred, and on this result the Governments and the local officers, who have exerted themselves admirably, deserve the acknowledgments of the Government of India. I fear, however, it may hereafter be found that over large tracts relief operations were, for considerable periods, conducted without sufficient system, and without due regard to economy.

12. Regarding what is past, I have been obliged to say this much, because it is only after a consideration of the past that we can frame improved plans for the future. During the spring and early summer of 1877, it was hoped that the season might be favourable, that spring showers might bring forward some small extent of early food crop in June, that bountiful summer rains (south-west monsoon) would enable

the people to secure a large food harvest during August and September, and that favourable October rains (north-east monsoon) would fill the irrigation tanks, and restore plenty to the districts of the Madras Presidency. The October rains are not yet due ; but our spring and summer hopes have been disappointed. Had they been fulfilled, there would have been no present need for special aid from the Government of India ; some millions sterling would have been spent, there would have been some waste, but in the main the great object of all this expenditure would have been obtained, the difficulty would have been over, and the Government of India would, at the proper time, have placed on record for future guidance the lesson taught by the famine of 1877.

13. But, so far as the season has gone, our hopes have not been fulfilled; the spring showers came not; the summer rains have, until the last week of July, been very scanty and irregular ; the main food crops of part of the black soil country in the Deccan are still in great jeopardy ; it is feared that the unirrigated food crops of Madras and Mysore must be lost unless the good rain of the past week continues during August. The local officers report that already an unascertained but large proportion of these crops is dried up; the irrigation tanks of the Mysore country are still dry ; and no fresh food crops can be reaped on any large scale in Southern India before December next. If there are favourable rains in August and September, and if the October rainfall (north-east monsoon) is full, then plenty may, perhaps, be restored by January 1878, though the people will feel the effects of the famine for some years to come. But even under the most favourable circumstances, the pressure of famine in many districts of Madras and Mysore cannot abate greatly before January 1878; at the best, the tension in Bombay may lessen in September, and may cease altogether in December. But unless the rainfall of August and September is unusually heavy, there must be another year of famine in parts of Bombay, of the Deccan, and over a great part of Mysore; for in none [1] of these tracts can a heavy downpour be expected in October.

[1] The rainfall statistics for parts of Southern India are not very complete. So far as they go, the meteorological returns give—

	Average rainfall in inches during the months of		
	June to September	October to December	The whole year
Poona	22½	6	31
Belgaum	36½	5	47½
Secunderabad	20	3	30
Bellary	11⅓	3	17
Bangalore	19	7¾	34½
Mean of eight districts in Mysore	17	8	--

A great part of Bellary and Kurnool also, where the October rains are scanty, must suffer another famine if the summer rains are not plentiful during August and September; while, if the October rains, the main rainfall of the Madras littoral, should be scanty, there must be another year of famine over a great part of the Madras Presidency.

14. Thus, the present situation in Southern India is that, at the end of a season of famine, one of the great food crops of the present season is everywhere in jeopardy, and in some parts is almost irretrievably lost. Prices of food over the famine country are higher than ever—four or five times the ordinary rate. 2,500,000 people are being directly supported by State charity, of whom barely 450,000 are performing work that will have useful results. The present pressure of famine, and the present rate of expenditure (considerably above half a million sterling per month) cannot, at the best, be greatly lessened before December next; whereas, if the season turns out unfavourably in any part of the famine country, that tract, with its stocks already depleted, must suffer from a second year of famine more severe and more difficult than the year through which it is now passing.

15. The position in Southern India, grievous as it is, becomes much aggravated by the fact that the summer rains have hitherto been extremely scanty in the North-Western Provinces and the Punjab. Vast areas of these provinces are protected by irrigation; the surplus food in stock from the bounteous harvests of the last few

	Average rainfall in inches during the months of		
	June to September	October to December	The whole year
Madras City	15	29	48½
Salem	17	8¾	34¾
Coimbatore	6	8½	21
Negapatam	9	24¼	35¼
Trichinopoly	12½	11½	29½
Madura	15	14½	26

It seems, therefore, that in the Deccan, and in the Ceded districts of Madras, the summer rainfall (south-west monsoon) is the mainstay of the crops; that in Mysore the heavy rain which fills the tanks and saturates the soil comes with the summer monsoon, but that the October (north-east) monsoon also gives a considerable rainfall, especially in the south of the province; and that in the districts of the Madras littoral the October monsoon yields the main rainfall of the year.

Though the north-east monsoon may be merely the rebound of the rain clouds which travel up the Bay of Bengal with the south-west winds, still we need not fear that scanty summer rains in Madras must necessarily be followed by equally scanty October rains. For the cloud currents which have this year shed plentiful summer rains over Burma and Bengal may return with the north-east winds to water the Madras littoral.

years is said, in the Punjab at any rate, to be very great; the autumn crop in these provinces has not yet been lost; and the seed time of the main food crop is yet to come. There is no present ground for fearing actual famine in Northern India, although I fear there may be serious scarcity and suffering in some districts; but the surplus food available for export thence to the famine country will be greatly reduced. In Bengal, Burma, and Central India there is, according to present prospects, no reason to anticipate that the winter crops will not be full ones. But the main crops of Bengal and Burma can hardly be estimated before October, at earliest.

16. The prospect in Southern India, more especially in Madras and Mysore, is, therefore, as serious as it could possibly be. If a second famine has to be encountered over this large portion of the Empire, the duty of saving the lives of the people, and of utilising to the utmost the vast expenditure which must be incurred, will impose on both the Supreme and local Governments as arduous and gigantic a task as any Government could be called upon to undertake. Before entering on this task, it may be well to state shortly what are, in my opinion, the main principles which Government should follow on an occasion of this kind. Many of these principles were laid down by the Government of India in its instructions to Sir Richard Temple, but I think it desirable to repeat them.

17. In the first place, the Government of India, with the approval of Her Majesty's Government, and of the people of India and England, are resolved to avert death from starvation by the employment of all means practically open to the resources of the State, and to the exertions of its officers. Thus far, there can be no room for doubt or difference of opinion.

18. When harvests fail in an Indian province, considerable old stocks of food are left in the hands of the landholding and mercantile classes, but these stocks are often held back from sale. Markets have therefore to be supplied with grain imported from a distance. I consider that, except under most peculiar and exceptional circumstances, the function of supplying the demand for imported grain can be best and, indeed, alone discharged by private trade, and that private trade should be left to do its work in this respect with as little interference from Government as practicable. The Government and its officers should, however, give all possible information, and should give where necessary additional facilities to private trade. Early and correct information as to prices and means of carriage should be published. The carrying power of railways and canals leading into the famine tracts should be reinforced; tolls and other restraints on free intercommunication should be removed; roads into the interior should be

improved and kept in order ; rates of railway or other carriage might
be reduced ; and, in cases of extreme necessity, temporary railways or
tramways might be laid down from main railway lines into populous
tracts, whereto means of communication failed or were insufficient. These
will, indeed, be the most useful of all works if we have to meet another
year of famine.　Grain required by Government for alms to the helpless poor, or for labourers on relief works, or for any tract where supplies were deficient, should be obtained through the trade at or near
the local markets, and should not be imported from a distance by
Government itself.　Experience has shown that Government operations in the grain market disorganise and paralyse private trade to an
extent out of all proportion to the operations themselves.　Moreover,
where the carrying power of a country by rail, canal, or cart, is
limited and is fully utilised, Government grain importations must
necessarily displace a corresponding quantity of privately imported
grain.　My view, therefore, is that under no circumstances which are
likely to occur ought the Government itself to engage in the business
of importing grain.　Free and abundant private trade cannot co-exist
with Government importation.　Absolute non-interference with the
operations of private commercial enterprise must be the foundation of
our present famine policy.　Trade towards the famine country from
Bengal and Northern and Central India is at present active, and
there is every reason to believe that the Indian sources of supply are
still considerable.　But even if these should fail the interference of
the Government would be a ruinous error.　It could only have the
effect of decreasing the total amount of food available, and thus aggra-
vating the catastrophe.　I am confident that more food, whether from
abroad or elsewhere, will reach Madras if we leave private enterprise
to itself than if we paralyse it by Government competition.　These
remarks refer to the famine we are now dealing with.　I do not of
course intend to assert that famines cannot occur in which Government interference for the importation of food may not be absolutely
necessary.　Indeed, the Orissa famine was one of those cases.

19. Before scarcity of food deepens into famine, there is a large
and increasing section of the population who are out of work and
have no means of buying food at dear rates.　It is the policy of
Government to employ such people on relief works, and my view is
that relief employment at a subsistence rate of wage should be provided on large, fully supervised works, which will be of permanent
benefit to the country.　The advantage of large works of this kind
over petty local works is twofold.　Firstly, the obligation to do a full
day's work at a low rate of wage and to go some distance to work
keeps from seeking relief people who can support themselves other-

wise; and secondly, the money expended on such works bequeaths permanent benefits to the country.

20. On this point the following passages from Sir Richard Temple's excellent report of his recent mission to the distressed tracts of Southern India are very valuable. When discussing the lessons to be deduced from Indian famine experience, he writes :—

' It seems to me that from these events we forcibly and positively learn :—

' To determine beforehand, as soon as any forecast of the coming distress can be made, the large public works upon which relief labour can be employed and upon which task-work can be exacted or piece-work established under professional supervision.

' To notify generally, and to intimate to all concerned, especially to the civil officers, the particular public works to which the relief labourers in each distressed district are to be drafted.

' To organise an engineering staff in readiness for undertaking vigorously these particular public works when the time for active operation shall arrive, and to prepare for devoting to this purpose all the professional establishments which can be obtained.

' To prohibit absolutely, in the beginning of the distress, the opening of petty works under civil officers, or non-professional establishments, among the villages close to the homes of the people.

' To refuse relief to strong able-bodied persons of both sexes in any form, save employment on the large public works.

' To allow petty village works to be opened only when severe and wide-spread distress has declared itself at a comparatively advanced stage in any district, or part of a district, and even then to reject all, save those who cannot reasonably be expected to proceed to the large public works—in short, to reserve these petty works for the weakly, the sickly, the advanced in life, and for those who have any just claim for indulgence.

' To keep the wages on relief works at the lowest rate compatible with the health of the labourers; this being necessary, not only in the interests of economy, but also to prevent demoralisation of the people.'

I do not think it would be possible to define more clearly than is done in the foregoing extracts, those principles which seem to me the right ones for the organisation of famine relief works.

21. At the beginning of a famine there are some, and before the end of a famine there will be many, people who, from physical infirmity, or from social custom, or from some other reason, are unable

to earn wages on relief works, and who have no means of buying food. For persons of this class the State must, when the sources of private benevolence are dry, provide gratuitous relief, if it undertakes to provide for them at all; an undertaking which, if it assumes wide dimensions, must impose upon the State operations of peculiar difficulty and delicacy. For it is the inevitable tendency of all gratuitous relief afforded by the State, if it be not supervised and restricted with the most scrupulous exactitude, to intrude injuriously on the field of relief labour, and thus demoralise large masses of the population. Such relief may be given in the shape of grants-in-aid of private charity; in the shape of cooked or uncooked food, distributed at relief centres, at camps, or poor-houses, where the recipients of relief are housed and cared for; or (if complete means of supervision exist), in the shape of money alms distributed to paupers at their homes through village agencies. One or other, often more than one, of these forms of gratuitous relief must, sooner or later, be dispensed in every famine tract. At large centres of population relief camps are useful; for the inmates are prevented from wandering about the streets, and starving for want of miscellaneous alms. On great roads and lines of traffic, out-door relief centres are more suitable. Where a good indigenous village agency exists, it is advisable to register and relieve, at an early stage of a famine, the helpless paupers in their villages; so that they may be prevented from starving at home, or from wandering forth in quest of charity. But, in whatever shape gratuitous relief be given, the ordinary district organisation must be greatly strengthened to secure its due and honest administration. No other form of famine relief is more open to abuse and malversation. Every rupee spent in providing effective, trustworthy supervision, is saved over and over again, not only in preventing wasteful and unnecessary expenditure, but in securing that the relief given reaches the classes and persons for whom it is intended, without being turned aside into the pockets of people who can do without State aid.

22. The principles and the policy described in the four preceding paragraphs should, in my judgment, guide the operations of Government, not only at the beginning of a famine, but throughout its continuance. Disregard of these principles must assuredly, and indefinitely, aggravate the serious financial difficulties in which even a well-conducted campaign against a great famine involves the Government. If we have departed from these principles in parts of the famine-stricken country, then we should now strain every nerve to return to them as speedily as possible. Famine relief expenditure must, I fear, continue on á very large scale for some months to come. And it may be that we are on the threshold of another, and much

more terrible year of famine. It behoves us, therefore, to lose no time in reorganising and strengthening the forces with which Government hopes to contend against famine.

23. The amount of grain carried daily into Southern India will have to be greatly increased. The present estimate, founded on the figures of the local Governments is, that into the Madras, Mysore, and Hyderabad districts alone, from 4,500 to 5,090[1] tons of food may have to be carried daily; whereas 2,500 tons a day was the greatest quantity carried during the past season. I believe this full task, if it be required, can be accomplished. During the Bengal famine the railways, working from three directions, carried at times as much as 4,000 tons of food a day; and the railways into Madras and Mysore work from four different ports, besides the fifth line from the Bombay direction. No time should be lost in framing, in publishing to the trade generally, and in bringing into effect on the guaranteed railways, a scheme whereby 4,500 to 5,000 tons of food can, if consigned by the trade, be carried daily into the famine districts of Madras and Mysore. When the railway has brought the required supply of food into the country, the question will arise, whether the famine-stricken cattle can suffice for the task of distributing by cart the large quantities required in the interior of the districts. And the problem will have to be faced and decided at once, whether it will be best to lay down rough tramways for carriage of grain, or to bring the destitute poor to places near the railway lines, or to promote their emigration into other provinces.

24. Next, all the best engineering skill available in the many provinces of India should, I think, be lent to the Madras Government, so that a sufficient number of large public works may be opened in all parts of the Madras as well as of the Mysore famine country, at which the largest possible proportion of the two and half millions of people now supported by the State may be employed under proper supervision on works which will help to protect the country from future famines. The districts of Madras and Mysore are studded with irrigation tanks, and are traversed by rivers, many of which are already bridled and turned into irrigation channels. Much great work of this kind remains to be done. The projects and estimates for such works may not be everywhere ready in full detail; but it would be better for the people and for the country that the Government should accept a moderate proportion of failures in such works than not to attempt them at all. It would be wiser to lay out one million sterling on irrigation channels and reservoirs, which will store water for future

---

[1] This quantity would give subsistence to about ten millions of people.

needs, or on other works of lasting utility, than to spend half a million on petty works, which cannot be adequately supervised, and are of no permanent usefulness. Of the famine roads which in 1874 were undertaken in Bengal, about one-half had to be left unbridged and unfinished. These have since fallen into a condition of utter uselessness owing to the inability of local funds to complete and maintain them. I believe that it would be highly desirable to sanction for Madras a special chief engineer for famine works, as was done for Bengal in 1874. Nothing is more essential to successful administration in such a crisis as the present, than the concentration of authority in the hands of a single man of energy and judgment, who shall be responsible to the head of the local Government alone. I am satisfied that the great success which has attended the operations for the relief of the present famine in Bombay has been mainly due to the fact that this principle has been strictly acted on. The chief engineer, Major-General Kennedy, has been virtually responsible to no one but the Governor himself, and I believe that both the late and present Governors of Bombay have thus been able to carry out their orders with a vigour, promptitude, and success which would otherwise have been impossible. Of course, however, this arrangement might have been as injurious as it has proved beneficial, had the officer on whom the result of it depended been deficient in experience, judgment, or energy.

25. When the employment of relief labourers shall have been thus made over to professional agency, the civil officers will be able to give their time to organising and supervising gratuitous relief, and to saving the helpless poor from starvation.

26. The two main objects to which the best endeavours, and all the available power of the Government of India and the local Governments must now be directed, are,—firstly, the framing and working of a scheme whereby 4,500 to 5,000 tons of food may be carried daily into the famine country; and, secondly, the selection and commencement of large public works of lasting utility, on which all the able-bodied relief recipients of either sex and any age should at once be employed. If the rainy season, which has begun so badly, should happily end well, these special exertions on the part of the State, of the railways, and of public servants, may not be required beyond December next. If the season ends badly anywhere, then these exertions will have to be continued on behalf of such afflicted tracts until August 1878. In any case, the lives of millions, and the useful expenditure of large public funds, must depend, during the next five months, on the arrangements that may now be made. If matters are allowed to drift, there may be terrible loss of life; and there must be a wasteful expenditure of vast sums of public money, which might,

under proper arrangements, bequeath great and useful works to the district wherein it is incurred.

27. The beneficial effect of money expended on well-considered and well-organised public works will be felt in the future. But for the immediate relief of the present distress, the creation and supervision of new means of transport are urgently needed. I have every reason to believe that our reserve of grain is amply sufficient to meet the increasing demand, and that, even if it runs short, we may reckon with confidence on the enterprise of private trade to supply the deficiency. But the arrangements which must now be made for distributing over large tracts of country, where no sufficient means of transport yet exist, that quantity of grain which their population requires, and the trade is able to supply, will be as difficult and delicate as they are necessary.

28. I have not included the Bombay districts in the tracts where special joint effort by the Supreme and local Governments is at once required; because prospects in Bombay are not so bad as in the southeastern districts; and because the management of relief works and relief operations in Bombay has, during the past season, been such as to warrant confidence that famine there, if it comes, will be more easily met, and that relief labourers will be employed on well-organised works of permanent usefulness.

29. I am afraid that the situation in Mysore is, in proportion to its area and population, even more critical than in Madras. The Mysore demand for imported grain has, throughout the famine, been larger with reference to the distressed population than in the Madras Presidency. The fate of the crops now in the ground is more doubtful in parts of Mysore than anywhere else. The employment of the destitute poor on useful public works has, since April last, been quite inadequate to the occasion. At the present time the persons on gratuitous relief are three times as many as the relief labourers on public works. In Bombay, the numbers on gratuitous relief are now little more than half the total of relief labourers. In Madras the total number on gratuitous relief is somewhat less than the total on works. Reports have been received from more than one Madras district that people in the last stage of distress flock over from Mysore to British relief houses for help. It would seem that Mysore relief arrangements are at present neither efficient nor sufficient. In this province immediate steps must be taken for reorganising the relief administration.

30. As my colleagues are aware, it is my intention to visit Madras and Mysore immediately. Before starting on this journey, I have thought it desirable to place on record my reasons for undertaking it. These will be found in the foregoing general statement of the main facts of the present condition of the famine-stricken districts in Southern

India. I cannot contemplate such a condition of things without the most serious anxiety, and the deepest sympathy with all those local authorities who, after prolonged and arduous exertion, are now confronted with new administrative difficulties.

31. It is unnecessary, and indeed undesirable, to discuss in the present minute any of the particular measures which have been, or may have to be adopted for meeting those difficulties. The teachings of experience would be as barren as they are bitter, were it impossible to derive, from study not only of the phenomena of the late famine in Bengal, but also of the course of the present famine in Madras and Bombay, a clear apprehension of certain general principles of famine management. The soundness of these principles is, I think, established both by the beneficial results of their timely and intelligent application, and also by the disastrous consequences which have attended the disregard of them. I cannot doubt that they should everywhere guide our action. But it is obvious that the application of them must always be easier in some localities than in others. My object, therefore, in now proceeding to Madras is, not to urge upon the administrative authorities of that Presidency the adoption of any system of operations devised à priori, without due reference to local peculiarities, but to endeavour, by frank, unprejudiced personal conference with his Grace the Governor, to ascertain how far it may be practically in my power to place unreservedly at his disposal, for the furtherance of measures approved by his judgment and experience, all those resources which are commanded only by the Government of India.

32. Two or three such measures are, indeed, already foreshadowed by the Duke of Buckingham in an important and suggestive minute, which has only just reached me. In this minute his Grace has practically overruled the opinion of those who wanted to give extraordinary diet and comforts, costing several rupees a month per head, to all inmates of relief camps. He has also wisely decided that none who can work shall be relieved except on public works; and he has indicated some large public works, mainly of irrigation, which will supply labour for all applicants in six districts, and parts of two others.

33. Should it be found possible to develope yet further the salutary principles on which these decisions are based, by bringing the whole of that portion of the relieved population capable of work under a well-organised engineering supervision, one of the great dangers with which the Madras Presidency is now threatened will have been successfully averted. But, even to carry out with complete efficiency the wise measures already announced by his Grace, the local Public Works Department will, I should think, require some addition to the strength of its staff, and some relaxation of departmental rules. The Governor

of Madras has, no doubt, rightly preferred schemes for storing surplus water to projects for carrying it away; and the Madras engineers are, perhaps, the best hydraulic engineers in all India. It will be my earnest endeavour to afford the Government of Madras every encouragement and assistance in my power, for the prompt and bold development of large local public works of every useful kind. In the circumstances we have now to deal with, it is not absolutely necessary that such works should be remunerative in the ordinary sense. Since relief labour must now be employed, and employed on an enormous scale, it is, in my opinion, a matter of primary importance that it should be employed on works of the greatest possible permanent utility, even though such works be wanting in the remunerative conditions requisite to justify our sanction of them in ordinary times.

34. So long as we might reasonably hope that the worst difficulties and dangers of the Madras famine would by this time be passing over, I have purposely refrained from visiting that Presidency, lest my presence there should, however unintentionally, prove embarrassing, rather than helpful, to the efforts of the local Government.

35. But in face of the facts recorded and reviewed in the preceding paragraphs of this minute, I can no longer question the urgency of my own duty, and that of all concerned, under the pressure of a natural calamity greater than any which, so far as I know, has in modern times afflicted India. It is now clear that the humane efforts of the Madras Government have proved insufficient to diminish the intensity, or reduce the area of this calamity. The distress, which appears to be increasing with frightful rapidity, must, even under the most skilful, the most economical, and the most energetic management, strain to the utmost the administrative abilities of the local Government and the financial resources of the Empire. Therefore I cannot doubt that the Governor of Madras is entitled to receive from the Viceroy the unreserved assistance of all the technical skill and special experience this Empire can furnish, for the relief of the people and the revenue by a vigorous prosecution of the wisest measures that can be devised. In short, we are now fairly engaged in a terrible conflict with nature; our line of battle has been broken at Madras and Mysore, and it is, therefore, at these points we should now concentrate all our reserved force.

36. Nothing could be further from my intention than to interfere unduly with the local authorities, and the devoted officers, who have so long and zealously been combating the growth of a gigantic catastrophe. Although, up to the present moment, the result has not equalled the assiduity of their untiring efforts, yet the energy and devotion of the district officers throughout Madras, during the pro-

tracted and increasing strain upon their physical and mental faculties, cannot, I think, be too highly or gratefully appreciated. It is not to inadequate energy or intelligence, but to inadequate numbers and inadequate executive powers, that I attribute the incompleteness of their success.

37. My journey, therefore, to the famine-stricken districts of Southern India, and more especially my journey to Madras, is prompted by the hope that it may enable me to strengthen and augment the means on which his Grace the Governor of that Presidency is now dependent for the satisfactory solution of a problem as serious as any which has ever occupied the mind, or taxed the abilities, of an Indian statesman.

38. I think that the highest expert talent procurable from any part of India should now, at once, be placed unreservedly at the disposal of the Duke of Buckingham. His Grace will be able to supplement and direct the special knowledge of experts by the large generalisations of a varied experience. Such a combination can scarcely fail to ensure ultimately to the Government of his Grace an administrative success commensurate with the magnitude of those difficulties which nothing short of the coolest judgment and most resolute firmness can now overcome.

LYTTON.

Simla, August 12, 1877.

APPENDIX C.

THE RULES OF THE NEW SYSTEM IN MADRAS.

GOVERNMENT OF MADRAS.

REVENUE DEPARTMENT.

Famine Relief.

No. 497. Proceedings of Government, dated September 24, 1877, No. 2,847.

His Grace the Governor in Council is pleased to issue the following instructions for the guidance of all officers concerned in the administration of famine relief:—

1. Under the successive orders of the Madras Government, relief has been sanctioned to famine-stricken people—

    (1) In the form of wages for work done;

    (2) Gratuitously in camps, relief houses, and villages, to those unable to labour or temporarily incapacitated for work.

2. It has been determined that both relief by employment on works for the strong, and gratuitous relief to the infirm, shall be continued.

3. To enable employment on large public works to be more extensively and systematically carried on, the Government of India have agreed to lend a large additional force to the Public Works Department; and to enable collectors to duly watch the distribution of gratuitous relief, the Government of India have placed at the disposal of this Government a large number of European officers to supervise relief operations in the several taluks of the distressed districts.

4. In order that the wishes and instructions of his Grace the Governor in Council may be clearly understood, the conditions under which relief has been sanctioned, and is to be continued, are subjoined.

5. Collectors and civil officers are responsible for sending to relief works or for providing gratuitous relief, under the orders now issued, to all who have not adequate means of supporting life. The Public Works Department officers are responsible for providing a sufficiency of work in every distressed district for the employment of the persons who may be sent to them by the civil officers, and shall employ thereon all those so sent.

Relief Works.

6. The intention of his Grace the Governor in Council is that all relief shall be eventually given through relief works, closed camps, and village relief.

7. Relief works affording to indigent persons capable of some labour the opportunity of earning money with which to buy food constitute the backbone of the relief system.

8. These works are of two classes—

(*a*) Those under the supervision of the Public Works Department or other professional supervision which may, for the sake of brevity, be called professional agency works; Professional Agency Works.

(*b*) Those not requiring, to any great extent, professional supervision, and which may, for the sake of brevity, be called civil agency works. Civil Agency Works.
These works will be under the superintendence of the Public Works Department or of the Civil Department according to circumstances.

9. Every district engineer will prepare a list of works in his district which may be made available as relief works. These list should show approximately—

(*a*) The probable cost of each work;

(*b*) Roughly the proportion of the total cost required for earth-work;

(*c*) The number of persons who can be employed upon each, and for how long.

10. These lists will be submitted to Government through the chief engineer or the chief engineer for irrigation. His Grace the Governor in Council will sanction them provisionally either wholly or in part, and the works thus provisionally sanctioned may be taken up, from time to time, as need for affording relief arises, except large works, the commencement of which will be decided by his Grace the Governor in Council. The opinion of the collector should decide which of the works in the list so sanctioned shall be first proceeded with. Estimates to cover such works as may be approved by Government in these lists should be prepared and submitted for final sanction as soon as possible, but the commencement of no such work shall be delayed, where its commencement is necessary, for the reason that a plan and estimate have not been sanctioned. Lists of works which have been commenced, specifying the approximate number of persons who can be received thereon, will be furnished by the district engineer, from time to time, to the collector, who will send copies to every revenue, police, and famine officer. .

11. The very widest publicity of the locality of relief works must be given; the responsibility with regard to this point rests upon the collectors and their assistants.

Publicity of relief work.

12. The distinction between budgeted works and famine relief works is abolished in the following districts :—

Nellore.	South Arcot.
Cuddapah.	Trichinopoly.
Bellary.	Madura.
Kurnool.	Tinnevelly.
Chingleput.	Coimbatore.
North Arcot.	Salem.

And all works whatever therein (Imperial, provincial, or local, excepting only buildings) shall be considered famine relief works and shall be carried out under all the rules, tests, and restrictions applicable to famine relief works. Any relief works which may be necessary in any of the remaining districts will be carried out as special works under special arrangements.

13. All establishments at present employed under civil officers in supervision of, or in accounting in respect of, relief works, should be transferred, with the charge of the several works, to the Department of Public Works as soon as the district engineer is in a position to take them over.

14. All persons capable of labour, who are in fair health and condition, must be drafted to professional agency works, _{People to be drafted} and with them must also be drafted such members _{to Professional Agency} of their families as are willing to accompany them. _{Works.}

14. All persons capable of labour, who are in fair health and condition, must be drafted to professional agency works, and with them must also be drafted such members of their families as are willing to accompany them.

People to be drafted to Professional Agency Works.

15. Weaker people, who are nevertheless capable of some work, should be employed upon civil agency works, but should, as they recover strength, be drafted to professional agency works, the object being to employ the largest possible number of people to whom it may be necessary to afford relief upon works of this latter description.

People to be employed upon Civil Agency Works.

16. Work is to be exacted and musters taken for six days in every week; payment for the seventh day is, however, included, i.e., an increment to each working day's wage has been made in order to provide for the seventh day, in the following scale of wages.

Off-day.

17. The rates of pay to persons who perform their allotted tasks shall be for each working day :—

Upon Professional Agency Works.

		rs.	a.	p.
For a man the value of 1 lb. of grain . . Plus		0	1	6
For a woman „ „ . . „		0	1	0
For a child of 7 and upwards ½ lb. of grain . „		0	0	9

Upon Civil Agency Works.

For a man the value of 1 lb. of grain . . „		0	1	0
For a woman „ „ . . „		0	0	9
For a child of 7 and upwards ½ lb. of grain . „		0	0	6

18. By grain is meant grain of medium quality and of the description in ordinary use *at the time of payment* among the labourers upon the works. The price to be taken at the retail price of the grain ruling at the cusba of the taluk on the previous week.

Grain.

19. When work is interrupted by rain to such an extent that the tasks ordered cannot be exacted, professional agency labourers should be paid the civil agency rate and civil agency labourers should be paid the civil agency rate less two pies all round.

Interruption from rain.

20. No work is to be taken from children under seven years of age, nor are such children to be allowed to remain among the labourers while they are working. Such children, belonging to parents or natural guardians employed upon works, must be mustered at a convenient spot at some little distance from where

Children under seven.

the work is in progress, and placed under the charge of a sufficient number of the women drafted to the works who will be employed as nurses. At large works, and where working camps are established, kitchens must be provided, and these children supplied with rations of cooked food not exceeding ½ a lb. of grain per diem. The nurses must receive their full ration of cooked food, *i.e.*, 1 lb. of grain plus the money portion of the wage. On small works officers in charge must make suitable arrangements for effecting the same purpose.

21. To prevent relief works becoming unduly attractive, three tests are necessary, viz., 1st, *primâ facie* evidence that the individual really requires employment upon a relief work; 2nd, distance of the work from the home of the labourer; and, 3rd, tasks.

Tests.

22. The task to be exacted upon professional agency works is 75 per cent. of what the individual would be able to perform if he worked to the full extent of his ability; upon civil agency works 50 per cent. of what the individual would be able to perform if he worked to the full extent of his ability.

Tasks.

23. In settling and exacting these tasks it will be necessary for the officers concerned to use great judgment, discretion, and firmness, so as to avoid oppression of the people upon the one hand or encouragement to idleness and laxity on the other.

24. It may probably be expedient in many cases to take, as the unit for tasking, a gang composed of all the members of one family who are on the work, or a portion of the inhabitants of any one village; and it is the wish of his Grace the Governor in Council that, as far as possible, consistently with economy and discipline on the works, members of the same family should not be separated in their employment. But these points of detail, varying as they will with the size and nature of the work and other circumstances, must be left to the discretion of the executive officers acting under the general orders of Government.

25. The employment of contractors directly or indirectly is absolutely prohibited on relief works.

26. Masonry work requiring skilled labour, such as culverts, tunnels, sluices, calingulahs of tanks, and similar works found essential to the completion of relief works may be performed by contract in the ordinary way. In selecting works to be placed on the list, Public Works officers will bear in mind that the beneficial effect of the work as a relief measure is the principal object; therefore works of which a large proportion of the estimate is for masonry or compensation for land should generally be at once laid aside as unsuitable.

27. The distance test is necessarily, to a great extent, enforced by

concentrating relief labour upon a comparatively small number of large works, and, until further *Distance.* instructions, this test may be deemed to be complied with when the labourer goes to professional agency works and performs the tasks exacted there.

28. The question whether persons are fitting objects for employment upon relief works must be decided by the civil officers, who will refuse employment to all persons *Persons not destitute.* except those who are destitute.

29. The civil officers will despatch such applicants for employment as they consider eligible with written duplicate nominal rolls, and the production of such rolls will *Rolls for employment.* be the authority to the Public Works Department officers to employ the persons named in them. The rolls shall specify the name and father's name and village of each person, and shall be dated, and shall bear the signature of the despatching officer.

30. Where camps are necessary on works these camps will be under the charge of the Public Works officer directing the work, who will make arrangements, and *Sanitary Precautions.* enforce rules, for strict conservancy and sanitary measures, and select suitable persons from the relief coolies for the various duties of scavenging, water-drawing, &c.

31. In transferring people to works at a distance exceeding ten miles, it will be necessary, under some circumstances, to pay them batta. The amount and nature of this *Batta.* batta will vary with local circumstances, but it should never exceed 16 oz. of uncooked grain for each day's march.

32. There will probably frequently be exceptional cases, arising on works, requiring special treatment. It is obvious that what may be sufficient for the vast majority *Special cases.* may be unsuitable in quantity or quality in individual cases. Such cases, which will include also those of people arriving on the works worn out and in low condition must, as far as possible, be specially treated under medical advice ; and they may be fed in accordance with the scale laid down in G.O. No. 2,372, of July 24, 1877, for people under such treatment. The extra allowance must cease as soon as the person, in the opinion of the medical officer, regains strength.

33. Persons not permanently incapacitated for labour will probably regain health, as soon as convalescent, more rapidly upon a relief work than amidst the surroundings of a relief camp.

34. All labourers must be warned that they are liable to fine and dismissal from relief; but these punishments should be enforced with care and judgment. *Punishments.*

35. Short work from idleness should, in the first place, be met
Fine. with a small fine, and a repetition of the offence should be punished with greater severity. But, until further orders, the effect of the fine in the case of weakly people must never be to reduce the wages of an individual upon professional agency works below civil agency work rate, nor to reduce those of an individual upon civil agency works below the relief house scale.

36. Incorrigible idleness or insubordination on the part of persons
Dismissal. in fair physical condition should be met by immediate dismissal.

37. Payments upon relief works must be made at least twice a
Frequency of pay- week, and oftener if necessary. New arrivals should
ments. for the first few days be paid daily.

Charitable Relief.

38. All previous orders relating to gratuitous relief, so far as inconsistent with the following rules, are hereby cancelled.

39. Relief officers will be appointed to the charge of one or more taluks, or parts of taluks, according to size and local circumstances.

40. Their duties will be to supervise all relief operations within their charges except public works. Their especial duty is to see that the orders of Government are strictly carried out; that relief reaches all who need it; that waste, abuse, and fraud are prevented, and the utmost economy, consistent with due relief, enforced throughout.

41. They are expected to be constantly on the move, and to visit the several villages and relief camps as frequently as possible and at uncertain times.

42. They will furnish to the collector, every Saturday, information on the following points :—

(1) The number of cases in which relief has been granted, refused, or stopped.

(2) Any case of failure of duty, inattention, or inefficiency on the part of any officer or servant.

(3) The physical condition of the people generally on relief, whether failing, improving, or stationary.

(4) They will submit any general remarks.

43. Village relief shall be given either in the shape of cooked food or in money, according to the discretion of the collectors and local circumstances, and shall, subject to the provisions of paragraph 53, be confined to destitute resident villagers, who are house-ridden, or otherwise unfitted for, or incapable of, labour. This class will include such persons as are idiots, cripples, blind, or so old or decrepit that

they are not able to support themselves; or young children living with and wholly dependent on such persons; women in an advanced state of pregnancy, or who have been recently confined; and further, to qualify for this relief, these persons must be without well-to-do friends or relatives on the spot on whom their support would ordinarily and rightly devolve.

44. Immediately on the receipt of these orders, officers in charge of taluks shall cause each village to be inspected by an officer not below the rank of a village inspector, and after careful enquiry into the circumstances of each individual case, shall strike off the register any persons who, from condition and circumstances, do not come within the above description. The relief officer in charge of a taluk, or part of a taluk, shall visit each village as early as practicable, and satisfy himself that his instructions have been properly carried out. No fresh admissions to the register shall subsequently be made, except under the orders of the village inspector, who, whenever he may authorise any such admissions, shall, in his next weekly return, report them to the taluk relief officer, who shall transmit an abstract showing increase or decrease of numbers in each village of his charge to the collector weekly, for preparation of the weekly tabular statement for Government. The taluk officer shall take the earliest practical opportunity of inspecting the persons who have been newly admitted.

45. Persons, who under the operation of the above order are struck off the registers of village relief, shall at the same time, if capable of labour, be sent to work, and if temporarily incapacitated by illness or any other cause, shall be sent to the nearest relief camp, to be there maintained and treated until able to work or found permanently incapable.

46. All open camps, other than works camps, shall be abolished, and in their place such number of closed camps as may be necessary shall be established. On this point collectors should at once take such steps as may be needed.

47. Until further orders are published for the regulation and interior administration of closed relief camps, the arrangements now in force should continue; but it should be distinctly and clearly understood by the officers in charge that no person capable of labour should be received into a camp, and that, as soon as any inmate of such camp recovers strength and condition sufficient to enable him to undertake labour on professional agency works, he should at once be drafted off to such works, which should not be situated within ten miles of the village of which he is an inhabitant.

48. Officers in charge of camps will recollect that the primary object of the camp is that the strength of its residents should be

restored therein, and that they may be thus rendered fit for work. Food and shelter, but no money payment, will be given therein. Camp diet is prescribed in G. O., July 24, 1877, No. 2,372 ; but all camps must be so divided as to render it impossible for those not actually requiring it to obtain the special diet allowance sanctioned for those under medical treatment.   No person shall in any case be admitted to the higher scale of diet except under the written order of the medical officer of the camp.

49. Collectors will take care and watch carefully the effect of relief operations, and if it should appear that any camp has a tendency to draw to it those who should be relieved in their villages, or any undue tendency is observed on the part of those on works to seek camp relief, the diet must be so adjusted in accordance with the discretion given by the Government order referred to as to counteract such tendency.

50. No outside relief shall be given at any closed camp.

51. All able to work will at once be sent to a suitable relief work with a list as described in paragraph 29.   In carrying out these instructions, however, the officer will exercise a careful discretion in cases where husband or wife, mother or child, may be ill in camp, and should not enforce separation in such cases.   Any able-bodied person so retained temporarily in camp will be required to do suitable work in or about the camp.

52. The collector should keep superintendents of camps informed of all works in progress, and to what extent labour can be accommodated on each work, and the order of the superintendent of the camp to the officer in charge of the work shall be sufficient authority to the latter to receive the persons who may be sent from the camp.

53. Wanderers who present themselves at any village in a state of destitution shall be provided by the village head with one meal, i.e., 10 oz. grain, and he will be held strictly responsible that no person manifestly in need of assistance to prevent starvation shall remain unrelieved ; but such persons shall only receive one meal, and shall be passed on to the nearest relief camp where they shall receive support, or, if needed, medical treatment, or, if in a fit condition to support themselves by labour, be at once sent to suitable works.   In special cases, where necessary, village heads may incur such charge as may be needed to convey to the nearest relief camp destitute persons who cannot travel.   But whenever this is done an immediate report must be made to the village inspector.

54. In laying out relief camps, sanitary requirements, especially position of hospital, water supply, and latrines, should be carefully attended to.

55. With the exception of those in hospital, persons in relief camps are not to be allowed to remain idle; they must be employed in all the necessary duties of the camp, its conservancy, water supply, cookery, hospital attendance, &c., or in spinning, weaving, rope making, or other similar light work. No extra allowances are to be given for work performed in or about the camp.

56. This order, except as regards scales of diet, does not apply to the Nilgiris district, in which the commissioner's arrangements to meet the special circumstances will continue in force subject to further instructions.

(True extract.)

(Signed)   J. H. GARSTIN,

Additional Secretary to Government.

To the Board of Revenue.
    „   Financial Department.
    „   Public Works Department.
    „   Sanitary Commissioner.
    „   Surgeon-General, Indian Medical Department.
    „   Commissioner of Police.
    „   Inspector-General of Police.
To all Collectors.

APPENDIX D.

THE INDIAN FAMINE RELIEF FUND.

RECEIPTS.

Mansion House Fund.			£	s.	d.	£	s.	d.	Exchge.	Rs.	A.	P.	Rs.	A.	P.
1877.															
Aug. 28	By	1st remittance through Central Madras Bank .	25,000	0	0				1/9	2,85,714	4	6			
„ „	„	2nd „ „ „	20,000	0	0				$1/9\frac{1}{8}$	2,27,218	15	0			
Sept. 5	„	3rd „ „ „	20,000	0	0				—	2,27,218	15	0			
„ 19	„	4th „ „ „	15,000	0	0				$1/9\frac{1}{16}$	1,70,919	14	0			
„ 26	„	5th „ „ „	75,000	0	0				—	8,54,599	6	4			
„ „	„	6th „ „ „	45,000	0	0				$1/9\frac{1}{4}$	5,08,235	4	8			
Oct. 27	„	7th „ „ „	50,000	0	0				$1/9\frac{1}{2}$	5,57,267	0	1			
Nov. 27	„	8th „ „ „	55,000	0	0				$1/9\frac{5}{8}$ } $1/9\frac{1}{4}$ }	6,18,864	13	0			
Dec. 3	„	9th „ „ „	20,000	0	0				$1/9\frac{1}{4}$	2,25,882	5	8			
„ 11	„	10th „ „ „	25,000	0	0				$1/9\frac{3}{8}$	2,80,701	12	1			
„ 12	„	11th „ „ „	20,000	0	0				$1/9\frac{1}{8}$	2,27,218	15	0			
„ 18	„	12th „ „ „	25,000	0	0				$1/9\frac{3}{8}$	2,80,701	12	1			
„ „	„	13th „ „ „	10,000	0	0				$1/9\frac{1}{8}$	1,13,609	7	6			
„ „	„	14th „ „ „	25,000	0	0				$1/9\frac{1}{16}$	2,84,023	10	8			
1878.															
Jan. 2	„	15th „ „ „	25,000	0	0				—	2,84,023	10	8			
„ „	„	16th „ „ „	15,000	0	0				1/9	1,71,428	9	2			
„ 11	„	17th „ „ „	5,000	0	0				$1/8\frac{3}{4}$	57,831	5	2			
Feb. 11	„	18th „ „ „	15,000	0	0				—	1,73,493	15	7			
Mar. 11	„	19th „ „ „	10,000	0	0	500,000	0	0	$1/8\frac{7}{8}$	1,14,970	0	11	56,63,924	8	1

LANCASHIRE FUND.

Date			£	s.	d.	Rate	Amount		
Sept. 7	By 1st remittance from Manchester and Salford Indian Famine Fund		10,000	0	0	1/9	1,14,285	11	6
,, 22	,, 2nd ,,		5,000	0	0	—	57,142	13	9
,, 28	,, 3rd ,,		3,000	0	0	$1/9\frac{5}{16}$	33,882	5	9
Oct. 6	,, 4th ,,		3,000	0	0	$1/9\frac{3}{8}$	33,294	12	9
,, 12	,, 5th ,,		3,000	0	0	—	33,684	3	4
,, 19	,, 6th ,,		3,000	0	0	—	33,684	3	4
Dec. 21	,, 7th ,,		9,000	0	0	$1/9\frac{3}{16}$	1,01,946	14	6
Sept. 14	,, 1st ,, Blackburn		1,000	0	0	1/9	11,428	9	3
Oct. 10	,, 2nd ,, ,,		2,000	0	0	$1/9\frac{5}{8}$	22,196	8	6
1877. Nov. 10	,, 3rd ,, ,,		2,000	0	0	$1/9\frac{3}{8}$	22,456	2	3
1878. Mar. 25	,, 4th and final ,,		150	0	0	$1/8\frac{3}{16}$	1,782	0	7
1877. Sept. 15	,, 1st ,, Liverpool		13,000	0	0	$1/9\frac{7}{8}$	1,70,320	7	3
Oct. 3	,, 2nd ,, ,,		5,000	0	0	1/9	55,621.	7	4
,, 17	,, 3rd ,, ,,		7,000	0	0	$\left\{\begin{array}{c}1/9\frac{3}{16}\\1/9\frac{1}{16}\end{array}\right.$	78,670	13	0
Nov. 13	,, 4th ,, ,,		2,000	0	0	$1/9\frac{3}{32}$	22,693	7	10
Oct. 12	,, 1st ,, Oldham		1,000	0	0	$1/9\frac{3}{8}$	22,456	2	2
,, 20	,, 2nd ,, ,,		1,000	0	0	1/9			
Dec. 10	,, 3rd ,, ,,		900	0	0	1/9	10,285	11	5
Oct. 17	,, 1st ,, Bolton		2,000	0	0	$1/9\frac{1}{4}$	22,503	8	6
1878. Mar. 8	,, 2nd ,, ,,		1,500	0	0	$1/9\frac{7}{16}$	16,793	0	1

YORKSHIRE.

Date			£	s.	d.	Rate	Amount		
1877. Sept. 6	By 1st remittance from Bradford		2,000	0	0	$1/9\frac{7}{8}$	22,721	14	3
,, 7	,, 2nd ,,		1,200	0	0	—	13,633	2	2
Sept. 14	,, 3rd ,,		1,500	0	0	1/9	17,142	13	9
,, 26	,, 4th ,,		2,300	0	0	$1/9\frac{1}{4}$	25,976	7	6

Indian Famine Relief Fund—continued.

		£	s.	d.	£	s.	d.	Exchge.	Rs.	A.	P.	Rs.	A.	P.
	YORKSHIRE—*continued.*													
Nov. 17	„ 5th „ „	1,500	0	0				1/9⅜	16,842	1	8			
„ 6	„ 1st „ Widness	750	0	0				1/9½	8,372	1	6			
Dec. 31	„ 2nd „ „	275	0	0	86,075	0	0	—	3,200	7	0	9,73,023	12	4
	SCOTLAND.													
Oct. 13	By 1st remittance from Glasgow	10,000	0	0				1/9⅜	1,12,280	2	3			
Nov. 7	„ 2nd „ „	7,537	0	0				—	84,625	15	3			
Jan. 3	„ 3rd and final „	85	0	0				1/9	998	8	6			
Oct. 26	„ 1st, 2nd, & 3rd „ Edinburgh	11,000	0	0				1/9⅜	1,23,312	12	0			
Nov. 8	„ 4th „ „	4,000	0	0				—	44,912	4	5			
„ 15	„ 5th „ „	3,000	0	0				1/9 1/16	34,183	15	7			
Dec. 3	„ 6th „ „	2,000	0	0				1/8⅞	22,993	15	2			
Oct. 29	„ 1st & 2nd „ Greenock	1,500	0	0				1/9⅜	16,842	1	1			
Dec. 2	„ 3rd „ „	340	1	11				1/9¼	3,841	1	3			
Oct. 12	„ 1st „ „	200	0	0	39,662	1	11	1/9⅜	2,232	7	11	4,46,221	3	5
	AUSTRALIA.													
Oct. 12	By 1st remittance of Adelaide	2,000	0	0				1/9⅝	22,196	8	6			
Nov. 3	„ 2nd „ „	5,000	0	0				1/9 13/32	56,058	6	4			
Oct. 30	„ 1st „ Melbourne	6,000	0	0				1/9⅝	66,589	9	6			
Nov. 10	„ 2nd „ „	13,000	0	0				1/9⅜	1,45,964	14	8			
Dec. 20	„ 3rd „ „	5,000	0	0				1/8⅞	57,485	0	6			
Jan. 24	„ 4th „ „	3,500	0	0				1/8 27/32	40,271	5	8			
Feb. 22	„ 5th „ „	810	5	2				1/9 5/16	9,118	5	1			
Oct. 29	„ 1st „ Napier, N. Z.	300	0	0				1/9½	3,345	13	4			
Nov. 7	„ 2nd „ „	400	0	0				1/9⅝	4,436	4	10			
Jan. 24	„ 3rd „ „	700	0	0				1/8⅞	8,043	6	5			
Nov. 10	„ 1st „ Christ Church	1,500	0	0				1/9⅜	16,842	1	8			
„ 30	„ 2nd „ „	900	0	0				1/8 15/16	10,304	12	8			

Date				£	s.	d.	£	s.	d.	Rate	£	s.	d.	£	s.	d.
Dec. 20	,,	3rd	,,	2,500	0	0				1/8 7/8	28,742	8	3			
Nov. 30	,,	Subscriptions from Sir A. C. Wilson		100	0	0				2/0	999	4	0			
Dec. 18	,,	1st remittance from Hobarton		1,000	0	0				1/8 13/16	11,531	8	6			
,, Jan. 24	,,	1st ,, Launceston		700	0	0					8,072	1	2			
,,	,,	2nd ,,		505	11	0				1/8 27/32	5,821	0	5			
Dec. 20	,,	1st ,, South Australia		3,000	0	0				1/8 3/4	34,491	0	3			
Mar. 21	,,	2nd ,,		1,262	7	6				—	14,513	8	6			
Jan. 5	,,	1st ,, Brisbane		1,000	0	0				1/8 15/16	11,462	11	0			
Mar. 12	,,	2nd ,,		1,900	0	0	51,078	3	8	1/8 29/32	21,811	10	7	5,78,101	13	10
		OTHER COLONIES.														
		By Amount remitted by Mauritius									38,568	5	9			
Nov. 16		1st remittance from Gibraltar		400	0	0				1/9 1/16	4,551	12	10			
,, 29	,,	2nd ,,		136	19	0				1/9	1,564	10	0			
,, ,,	,,	3rd ,,		60	0	0				2/0	600	0	0			
Dec. 12	,,	1st ,, Natal		1,100	0	0	1,606	19	9	1/9 1/16	12,534	2	0	57,818	14	7
		INDIA.														
		By total amount received by Calcutta									85,000	0	0			
	,,	,, Rangoon									14,500	0	0			
	,,	Local and Indian Subscriptions									1,66,760	11	0	26,026	11	0
1878.																
Mar. 31		By total amount of Subscriptions received					678,612	5	4					79,79,350	15	3

The Mansion House Committee was composed as follows :—

President and Treasurer.

The Right Hon. the Lord Mayor (Sir Thomas White).

Committee.

The Right Hon the Earl of Northbrook, G.C.S.I.
Sir Nathaniel M. de Rothschild, M.P.
K. D. Hodgson Esq., M.P. }
E. C. Baring Esq. } (Baring Bros.)
Sir Charles H. Mills, Bart., M.P. (Messrs. Glyn, Mills & Co.).
Hugh M. Matheson, Esq. (Messrs. Matheson's).
The Baron de Stern (Messrs. Stern Brothers).
L. Huth Esq. (Messrs. F. Huth & Son).
C. G. Arbuthnot, Esq. (Messrs. Arbuthnot, Latham & Co.)
J. S. Morgan, Esq. (Messrs. J. S. Morgan & Co.).
John Fleming, Esq., C.S.I. (Smith, Fleming & Co.).
Francis W. Buxton, Esq. (Prescott, Grote & Co.).
Hon. Henry L. Bourke (Brunton, Bourke & Co.).
Henry Bayley, Esq. (P. & O. Company).
S. P. Low Esq., J.P. (Grindlays & Co.).
William Scott, Esq. (Binney & Co.).
M. Girod }
E. H. Hardcastle, Esq. } (Comptoir d'Escompte.)
John Sands, Esq. (Frith, Sands & Co.).
H. S. Cunningham, Esq., Advocate-General, Madras.
John Pender, Esq., M.P., Eastern Telegraph Co.
Samuel Morley Esq., M.P. (J. and R. Morley).
Charles Teede, Esq. (Teede & Bishop).
Mr. Alderman Sidney.
P. Macfayden Esq., Madras (Arbuthnot & Co.).
G. Parbury, Esq. (Messrs. W. Thacker & Co.).
Mr. Alderman and Sheriff Hadley.
Thomas Gray, Esq.
J. H. Crossman, Esq., J.P.
T. J. Reeves, Esq. (Dent, Palmer & Co.).
C. B. Dowden, Esq.
Arthur T. Hewitt, Esq.
George Arbuthnot, Esq.
George Smith, Esq. (Smith, Elder & Co.).
J. N. Bullen, Esq.
Alderman Sir W. A. Rose.
Alderman Sir R. W. Carden.
F. W. Heilgers, Esq.
General Sir Henry W. Norman, K.C.B.
W. R. Arbuthnot, Esq.
W. Mackinnon, Esq.
H. S. King, Esq., J.P.

Hon. Secretary.

William J. Soulsby, Esq., Private Secretary to the Lord Mayor.

Hon. Cashier.

G. J. W. Winzar Esq.

Bankers.

Messrs. Glyn, Mills, Currie & Co., Lombard Street.

APPENDIX E.

SOUTHERN INDIA'S GRATITUDE.

(*From the Madras Times, January* 29.)

THE good people of Madras will have to carry their memories very far back to recollect an occasion when a public meeting held in the Banqueting Hall was so numerously attended, so influentially represented, and accompanied by so much enthusiasm as that which took place last evening for the purpose of adopting resolutions conveying, on behalf of the people of Southern India, an expression of heartfelt gratitude for the sympathy and support nobly and generously accorded them by the people of Great Britain, her Colonies and India, in relief of the distress caused by the famine which has overshadowed the land throughout the last eighteen months. The meeting of yesterday evening was not only an assemblage of the people of Madras, but of the inhabitants of the whole of Southern India, the latter being represented by delegates from most of the districts which had felt the severity of the famine ; and another characteristic and highly interesting feature of the occasion was the pleasing fact that the hall was graced by the presence of a large number of ladies, the gentle influence of several of whom had in no small way helped in mitigating the severity caused by the period of scarcity. His Grace the Duke of Buckingham and Chandos received the delegates of the famine committees of the districts of Southern India and the province of Mysore at Government House, where they were introduced to his Grace, and, accompanied by them, came to the Banqueting Hall precisely at half-past four o'clock. The hall at this moment presented an animated and interesting spectacle. It was crowded almost to overflowing, and the assemblage represented members of every section of the public. On the dais were accommodated his Grace the Chairman, the Ladies Grenville, the Members of Council, the several speakers, and the delegates from the District Committees, including the Rajah of Vencatagherry, C.S.I., and Mr. Seshia Sastri, C.S.I. Among others present on the occasion were Lady Robinson, the Honourable D. F. Carmichael, Miss Carmichael, Colonel Michael, C.S.I., Mr. Tarrant, Mrs. Tarrant, the Rev. C. H. Dean, Mrs. Dean, Mrs. Digby, Mr. Thornhill, C.S.I., Mr. Ballard, Colonel Weldon, Mr. Campbell, the Honourable V. Ramiengar, C.S.I., Mr. Srinivasa Row, Mr. Runganadha Mudaliyar, Mr. Mahomed Yusuf Saib, and many others.

Mr. W. W. Munsie, the Sheriff, read the following notice convening the meeting :

' We, the undersigned inhabitants of Madras, request that you will be so good as to convene a Public Meeting at the Banqueting Hall, on Monday, January 28, at 4.30 P.M., for the purpose of expressing the gratitude of the people of Southern India for the sympathy and liberality exhibited towards the famine-stricken population of India by their fellow-subjects in all parts of the British dominions.

We have the honour to be, Sir, your obedient Servants,

(Signed)

C. R. Drury.	C. A. Ainslie.
Robert Stephenson.	J. W. Mellis.
T. E. Franck.	V. Krishnama Chariar.
H. R. Dawson.	J. Cramp.
Y. Vencatahramiah.	C. V. Cunniah Chetty.
Mahomed Yusuf.	G. Coopoosawmy Naidu.
J. Higginbotham.	L. R. Burrows.
S. Fennelly.	J. H. Taylor.
J. G. Coleman.	Robert B. Elwin.
G. Bidie, M.B.	Wm. Digby.
Robert Orr.	H. R. P. Carter.
T. Ramachendra Row.	P. Strinivasa Row.
T. Weldon.	P. Viziarungum Mudaliyar.
J. Colgan.	Mohideen Sheriff Khan Bahadur.
Ahmed Mohideen Khan Bahadur.	W. Walker.
C. A. Lawson.	Frederick T. Atkins.'

Mr. Munsie added that the meeting was held in pursuance of the above notice.

His Grace the CHAIRMAN said :—' The notice the Sheriff has read explains fully the cause of the present meeting—to thank the people of England, of the Colonies, to thank all parts of the British Empire for the aid which was so promptly and so liberally afforded to Southern India in her hour of distress. That dark cloud of famine which has so long overshadowed Southern India has broken and is dispersed. Much distress has been relieved, the condition of the people is vastly improved, and although in many districts yet there are still recurrences of distress, shadows of clouds still undispersed passing over, yet all the returns show from month to month that distress even in those districts is lightening, that the worst is passed, and that we may look forward to being relieved from the anxiety under which we have so long lived, we may look to that being very speedily and entirely dispersed. Although the famine is passed, yet,

as I said, much distress still remains, and good work remains to
be done with that remaining portion of the fund so liberally and
munificently afforded by England's charity. Those who are addressing you to-day, having taken an active part in the various districts
in the distribution of the fund, know well how great was the distress
they had to meet, how vast would have been the calamity if that help
had not been afforded to us throughout the length and breadth of the
land. Those purposes which I ventured to shadow forth at the meeting in August, as purposes which needed a large and liberal charity
to meet, to relieve those distresses that could not be brought under or
met by Government organisation or rule, have been found not less
than I anticipated they would be found, requiring the aid of the large
funds which have been given to this country for the purpose. I will
not detain the meeting with any details. Many in this room know
far better almost than Government the details of the distress which
they had to deal with in their towns and in their villages, and I will
not detain you longer than to call upon the Honorary Secretary, Mr.
Digby, to read a statement of the operations of the committee.
(Applause.)

Mr. DIGBY said that five and a-half months ago, when the appeal
went to England from that hall, the meeting which sent it was, necessarily, composed entirely of the citizens of Madras. There was not
time to make it other than a town's meeting. On the present occasion, the meeting was representative of the whole Presidency, indeed
of Southern India generally, for not only were there representatives
present from the various local committees, but also a deputation from
Mysore. Some local committees could not send delegates, but instead
had written expressing their gratitude. He held in his hand a list of
delegates and letters from committees. He would not read them to
the meeting, but the document would be handed to the press for publication. One or two letters, however, might be cited. After quoting
two or three of the letters, the following document was laid on the
table :—

*List of Delegates and Letters from Local Committees attending the
Public Meeting on January 28.*

Adoni.—No members able to attend, owing to business and other
engagements. Mr. Byramjee, Honorary Secretary, writes :—' The
committee here humbly request the general committee to excuse
them for their non-attendance, and at the same time beg leave to express many thanks for the kindness shown by the British public
towards their poor fellow-subjects of this country in their time of
distress.'

Arnee.—Iyaloo Naidu ; Akiland Aiyar.

Bellary.—Arthur Huson, Esq. ; Rev. E. Lewis; M. Abraham, Esq. ; A. Sabapathy Mudaliyar, Esq. ; Custoori Chetty, Esq., and A. Sadasiva Pillai.

Chingleput (and Saidapet) Central Committees.—Mr. Barlow writes :—' I greatly regret that my revenue arrangements will, probably, make it impossible for me to attend, as I am at present working away from any line of railway, for as collector—even more than as president of the Saidapet committee—I should have wished to express my thanks for British relief, especially as regards the allotments for agriculturists, which have enabled large numbers of petty holders to recommence cultivation, after eighteen months of famine, with something like a good heart.'

Saidapet sends the following gentlemen :—George Duncan, Esq. ; A. M. Jones, Esq. ; V. Ragava Charlu, Esq.

Chingleput.—C. N. Overbury, Esq. ; C. Soondarum Mudaliyar ; N. Ramakistna Aiyer ; M. Coopoosawmy Naidu ; P. Tharagaram Pillai ; P. Strinivassa Aiyengar.

Chitoor.—Thomas Stracey, Esq. ; V. Soondra Aiyer; T. S. Narasinga Rao.

Coimbatore.—No members able to attend, owing to business engagements.

Cuddalore.—O. B. Irvine, Esq. ; Vencoba Charriar ; Rajarutna Mudaliyar, and Sadasiva Pillay.

Dindigul.—We are reminded that this is the date for your great public meeting at Madras, for the purpose of expressing the gratitude of the people of Southern India for the very kind and munificent assistance they have received from kind friends in England in this time of famine and distress. We regret that our committee cannot be represented at this meeting, in the object of which we feel so hearty a sympathy. But they desire me to express for them their own gratitude, and that of the thousands and ten thousands in this district whose sufferings have been relieved by this most timely assistance. Words fail us in the attempt to express our appreciation of the kindness and love which have prompted this princely gift. It is hard to get an expression of feeling from this people, but they are not wholly insensible. This kindness astonishes them now, but for years to come it will be a lesson which cannot be lost upon them.

Dindigul.—The Rev. Louis St. Cyr, writing on January 24, says, 'Indeed England has given to the world the most splendid example of charity and generosity in the way she came to the assistance of the famine-stricken people in the Presidency of Madras. May God reward and bless her as she deserves ! I associate myself most cordially with the public meeting which is to be held in Madras the 28th instant, being unable to be present on the occasion.'

Erode.—Chinnamala Govindoo; Gopaulasamy Naidu; Abdul Kader Saib.

Kodi Kanal.—The Rev. J. T. Noyes, Honorary Secretary, writes: —'I am very glad to hear that there is to be a meeting in the Banqueting Hall to express thanks. Nothing could be more appropriate. It would give us great pleasure to attend. But I cannot, and I do not think any of our members can attend, unless Mr. Turner will go.'

Kurnool.—Feared no one can attend unless Mr. Latham, on his return from Coconado.

Ongole.—Rev. J. E. Loughridge.

Pulney.—The Honorary Secretary (Mr. Chandler) writes:— 'We received your telegram in regard to the public meeting to be held on the 28th instant, and at our meeting held on Saturday last, as no one volunteered to go, we decided to send an united expression of our thanks, which you will receive in a day or two.'

'Read and recorded telegram from Honorary Secretary, relief committee, Madras, requesting to know if any of the members of the Pulney relief committee would attend the meeting to be held at Madras on the 28th, for the purpose of drawing up an address thanking the people of England for their generous benefactions.

'Resolved,—That the Honorary Secretary be requested to inform the Madras committee that the members of this committee severally and jointly regret their inability to attend the meeting in question.

'Resolved also,—That an address be drawn up in the name of the people of Pulney taluk, thanking the people of England for their liberal charity in the time of great distress, and that the same be forwarded to the Madras committee for transmission to the promoters of the Mansion House fund.'

Pulney, January 26, 1878.

Your telegram in regard to the public meeting, to be held on the 28th, was received and read at the last meeting of our committee. No one has the leisure to accept the kind invitation. But though prevented by circumstances from being present in person, we must not fail to forward to you, and through you to the donors of the Mansion House fund, our sincere and most hearty thanks for the timely aid they have sent to the thousands of sorely distressed people of this taluk.

We thank you in behalf of more than two thousand landholders who have been able by your aid to bring their fields under cultivation during the recent rains, though in very many instances they had been compelled to consume their seed grain, using their farming utensils for fuel, and selling their ploughing cattle to keep themselves alive.

We thank you in behalf of the 12,000 poor, whom the pressure of famine and the severity of the rainy season had left roofless, and who are now able to secure some shelter.

We thank you on behalf of more than 4,000 persons, most of them women, who could almost literally say, ' We were naked and you have clothed us.'

We thank you in behalf of the little children, many of whom would have been in their graves but for the 16,000 meals of good wholesome food they have taken in our day nursery.

We thank you in behalf of more than 2,000 men, women, and children, who have been able to prolong their lives with the pittance given in the weekly money dole. And again we thank you in behalf of the 120 children of our orphanage who are thrown entirely upon our care. And we pray that the blessing of Him who is the God of the widows and of the fatherless children, and who has said, ' Inasmuch as ye have done it unto one of the least of these ye have done it unto Me,' may rest upon you, and abundantly reward you for your liberal, timely, and highly appreciated benefactions.

Ranipett.—H. W. Bliss, Esq., B.A. ; H. M. Scudder, Esq.,M.D.

Tripatore.—T. Misquita, Esq., District Munsif: Mr. Leonard, Police Inspector : M. R. Ry. Ananthram Aiyer; Annamaly Chettiar; Subba Row; Mr. C. Soondrum, Evangelist, L.M.S.

Tinnevelly.—Telegram, 'Our members regret cannot attend meeting.'

Madura.—No member can attend from any of the committees in this district, but Mr. Lee-Warner, C.S., writes, ' If it can be done by the president, on behalf of the whole area of country over which this grateful gift has been, and is being distributed, as president of the Ramnad relief committee, I venture to express the heartfelt thanks of the people of this estate.'

The secretary of Madura committee writes :—' I am desired to acknowledge the receipt through the collector of your telegram, dated 16th instant, to the president of this committee, and in reply to inform you that the committee much regret that they are unable to send any of their members to represent them on this interesting occasion; all find their time fully occupied ; and that their official and private avocations will not just now allow leisure for a visit to Madras. I am at the same time to express the committee's grateful acknowledgments of the ready and liberal consideration which the general committee has already given to their representation, and to assure you that, though unable to be present, they and this whole district will echo from the bottom of their hearts the resolutions in which your gratitude for the generous sympathy of the English people may find expression.'

Tindivanum.—Rev. W. H. Wyckoff.

Trichinopoly.—A. Seshia Sastri, Esq., C.S.I.; Periasami Mudaliyar; Syed Khan Saib.

Vellore.—Rev. J. Scudder, M.D.

Salem.—Rev. G. O. Newport; Dr. R. N. Manikum Mudaliyar.

Cuddapah.—This committee regrets that none of their members will be able to attend the public meeting at Madras, and therefore resolves that Messrs. N. Appa Row, C. Chengal Row, R. Raghavandra Row, T. N. Subba Reddy, Gouse Sahib, and Hussain Saib be requested to form a sub-committee, to draw up a note of thanks in Telugu, to be forwarded to the general committee, Madras.

Translation of Telugu Note.

To the General Committee of the Mansion House Fund, Madras.

Gentlemen,—We are much rejoiced at the notice sent to us by the Committee of the Mansion House fund, informing us that a meeting will be held on the 28th of this month at Madras, to convey thanks to the most exalted Englishmen who have liberally contributed funds towards the maintenance of the sufferers from the famine. We are all desirous to attend the meeting, but regret very much that our business engagements and other circumstances will not permit us to do so. The country has suffered severely from a great famine for nearly two years, but the funds liberally contributed by the British nation have greatly helped the poor in procuring food, clothing, seed grain, and cattle, and in relieving the sick and the emaciated. We, therefore, on behalf of our brethren who have benefited by the relief fund, beg that our most grateful and heartfelt thanks be conveyed to the subscribers to the Mansion House fund.

(Signed)   N. Appa Row.

           C. Chengal Row.

           R. Raghavandra Row.

           T. N. Subba Row.

           G. Gouse Sahib.

Tanjore.—A. Seshia Sastri, Esq., C.S.I. The president, writes :—
' You will have received a message that Mr. Seshia Sastri will represent
the Tanjore committee ; though we are in such excellent hands, we must
still regret that it is impossible that any member of our committee can
be present on Monday. Mr. Subrahmanya Ayyar, who will represent Tanjore, is in such poor health, I regret to say, that he feels
unequal to the journey. The vice-president (the sub-judge) and
myself are kept here by our heavy official work ; other members of
the committee have not quite finished their circles, or do not know
English. I much regret this, but trust that you will kindly explain,
if necessary, how matters stand. Allow me, personally, to thank
you for the ready answers you have always sent to my letters and
messages.'

(*Telegram from the Bishop of Coimbatore.*)—Unexpectedly prevented from attending meeting. Bishop, clergy, congregation thank
generous English people.

Bishop Fennelly wrote :—' The Vicar Apostolic of Pondicherry,
who regrets his inability to attend the meeting this evening, desires
me to assure you that he and his clergy and congregations unite
with the meeting in the expressions of heartfelt gratitude for the
sympathy and assistance accorded by the people of Great Britain and
other countries to the famine sufferers in Southern India.'

Mr. DIGBY continued by saying : I have the honour on behalf of
the general committee to lay the following statement before the
meeting :—

On August 4, a meeting was held in this hall to make an appeal
to English charity on behalf of the famine-stricken people of India, to
render such aid as it was beyond the province of Government to give.
A committee of gentlemen was appointed, from whom, two days
after, an executive committee was chosen ; an appeal was prepared
by this committee to be sent to England and elsewhere. By the
executive committee the work of distribution has mainly been
carried out.

The Lord Mayor of London, Alderman Sir Thomas White, at
once organised a committee and opened a subscription list at the
Mansion House ; meanwhile, the municipal bodies in Great Britain
were communicated with. Separate funds were opened in Lancashire,
Blackburn, Bradford, Edinburgh, Glasgow, and Greenock. In course
of time the movement spread, and, either directly to the committee at
Madras, or through the Mansion House, from all parts of the British
dominions, from Australia, New Zealand, Canada, Jamaica, and other
West India Islands, British Guiana, Mauritius, Ceylon, Gibraltar,

Hongkong, the Straits Settlements, from English residents in continental cities, Bengal and Burma—contributions flowed in, until, in November, the committee felt themselves in a position to say that the fund might be closed, as they had as much as they would be able to disburse. As soon as English feeling had been aroused, money flowed in very liberally, for two or three weeks; at the Mansion House alone, 10,000*l.* per diem was received. In the earlier days of the fund large sums, such as 500*l.* from the Queen Empress, 500 guineas from the Prince of Wales, 100*l.* from the Princess of Wales, several donations of 1,000*l.* each from the Bank of England and City houses were chiefly received, but later on, the large stream of charity was made up of multitudinous sums, chiefly collections from workmen, schools, churches and chapels. All sects and creeds contributed, and the money has been equally disbursed, irrespective of caste or creed. It is impossible to estimate the number of persons contributing to the fund, but, bearing in mind the small sums which characterised congregational and similar collections, the total must represent several millions of individuals. An analysis of the Mansion House list, the only one received in entirety, has not yet been made—there has not been time for this; but when it is done, it is believed that more than half, probably a good deal more, of the sum of 500,000*l.* sterling, will be found to have been contributed in amounts of 5*l.* and less. The sums received and promised from particular sources are as follows :—

	£
Mansion House, London and Bradford	500,000
Lancashire	75,932
Edinburgh	20,000
Glasgow	7,537
Greenock	1,840
Australia and New Zealand	100,000
Other colonies (Mauritius, Hongkong, British Guiana, &c.)	5,400
India generally (Madras included)	20,000
	731,209

Besides this a special fund was raised in the county of Buckingham, which has been entrusted specially to his Excellency the Governor, as Lord Lieutenant of that county.

Whilst the sum total of receipts at this stage (the various funds having closed) can be given with tolerable accuracy, only an approximate analysis can be prepared of expenditure to the end of the year. Although some committees are closing operations, none have yet actually ceased to give relief. As is well known, considerable difficulty was experienced in the months of August and September in obtaining efficient distributing agency throughout the Mofussil, but these were surmounted, partly owing to the services of Government officials being made available, and also to the success which attended the efforts of delegates sent by the executive to organise committees. Including local, sub, and taluk committees and individual agencies, more than 150 bodies were in existence in November, and over one thousand Europeans, Eurasians, and native gentlemen have been engaged in the work of relief. Their labours have been unremitting and most zealous, and the thanks of this meeting and of the English subscribers are due for their labour bestowed and energy expended by them. Among the most valued agents of the committee have been the missionaries of all creeds, who have been, in many cases, the only available means by which the suffering could be reached. In some cases several months have been devoted exclusively to this work, and missionary agents have lived for weeks together among the people, travelling from village to village, personally enquiring into cases of distress, and relieving wants with their own hands. This, in fact, has been a characteristic of all the committees, and it is but just to remark that the magnificent money gift has been worthily equalled by unselfish hard work on the part of distributors of the fund. The money has been disbursed as follows :—

To Madras city, for support and clothing, 1,69,000 rs. Many doles were given to caste and Gosha people who could not avail themselves of Government relief, and for partial aid to others not wholly destitute, in numbers varying from 5,940 on August 18 to 19,126 on November 12, the numbers decreasing a few thousands subsequently, until they are now 12,154 adults and 4,072 children. Cloths to these were given at a cost of 23,790 rs. The need for this aid still continues, rice being still as high as 4 measures per rupee, each measure being about 3 lbs. in weight, about two and a-half times its nominal rate. This relief was disbursed by nine divisional committees, superintended by the town central committee.

The district distributions are as follows :—

	Rs.
North Arcot	5,50,160
South Arcot	2,51,650
Bellary	5,73,000
Chingleput	4,25,000
Coimbatore	4,56,820
Cuddapah	3,56,000
Kistna	23,730
Kurnool	3,29,000
Madras, for Day Nurseries, Orphanages, Friend-in-Need Society, and Town Relief, &c.	2,41,988
Madura	3,70,450

	Rs.
Malabar	17,400
Neilgherry Hills	13,385
Nellore	4,49,159
Salem	6,29,650
Tinnevelly	1,80,000
Trichinopoly and Tanjore	3,63,900
Travancore	5,000
Vizagapatam	2,000

In addition to the above, and minor sums, 16½ lakhs have been sent to Mysore, and 80,000 rs. to Bombay, and some to Central India. At present particulars from these places which have been promised have not been received, and it is difficult to say how many persons have received relief and in what form. As regards our own committees we can give an approximate idea of what had been done with the money sent to them prior to the end of the year, but in quoting the following figures it must be remembered they are greatly within the mark, and founded on as yet incomplete examination of the voluminous returns received.

Relief has been afforded under seven heads, and to the number of people mentioned, viz. (the figures for Madras being already given, are not repeated here) :—

	Rs.
Food, money doles, out-door relief, &c., namely	10,00,000
Orphanages (about)	10,000
Day Nurseries	75,000
Clothing	1,14,413
Houses repaired or rebuilt	31,824
Agriculturists helped with seed grain, bullocks, &c.	1,39,650
Miscellaneous charity	17,936

Under the last heading is included substantial help to weavers and similar classes, who have been helped to redeem their looms, and to commence work. This, however, has only been done in an incidental way. Testimony from all quarters is unanimous as to the great good which has been done by the relief funds, and though here and there cases of peculation have been reported, compared with the vast sums disbursed they were exceedingly few. Close personal attention on the part of individual members of committees has alone secured. this result.

An *interim* balance sheet made up at the end of the year shows the cost of managing the fund to that date. From this it appears that the total expenditure in the central office, including telegrams (the largest item), printing, &c., was rs. 25,315-13-9. The details are as follows :—

	Rs.	a.	p.
Postages	1,024	15	6
Printing (maps included)	3,652	7	0
Establishment	842	8	0
Office furniture, stationery, telegrams, &c. .	10,714	4	6
Charges on specie, remittance and bill stamps .	2,381	10	9
Honorarium and travelling expenses to delegates	5,800	0	0
Total . . .	24,415	13	9
Grants and allotments to date, as per weekly statements	64,47,693	0	0
	64,72,108	13	9
To balance . . 10,32,276 5 7	10,32,276	5	7
Grand total . . 75,04,385 3 4	75,04,385	3	4

Assuming that when all the remittances are received and brought to account the sum will amount to more than 80,00,000 rs., and taking into consideration the expenses of all the local and sub-committees, the executive hope to be able to show working charges of less than one per cent. upon the sum entrusted to them. If this can be accomplished, subscribers will have the satisfaction of knowing that their generous donations have been disbursed with the minimum of attendant expenditure.

As has been already remarked, this is but an *interim* statement. When, happily, the time shall come that no further need for its efforts exists, the general committee will be prepared to render a full account of their stewardship, and trust it will be found that they have wisely disbursed the large sums which were committed to their charge to alleviate the misery of their fellow-subjects in this land.

[The following facts from the honorary secretary, general committee, Friend-in-Need Society, were forwarded, for inclusion in the statement given above :—

As requested by the Friend-in-Need Society special relief committee, I annex certain items of information which you might perhaps deem proper to mention at the public meeting on Monday.

862 persons of the more respectable class of Europeans and East Indians, who felt the pressure of the famine, but could not be expected to go to the feeding houses, were assisted with money doles ranging from 3 to 10 rs., according to circumstances.

Of the pensioners of the society who did not attend the feeding depôts, there were 12 with families who received r. 1-8 each per mensem, and 73 without families on 1 r.

The average number fed *daily* was :—

Adults	1,978
Children	260

These were further assisted pecuniarily—those with families r. 1-8 each, and without families 1 r. per mensem.

Clothing was also distributed at the setting in of the cold season to those receiving food, and to the society's pensioners with their families. The number clothed was :—

Men	757
Women	1,014
Boys	290
Girls	283]

Mr. A. SESHIA SASTRI, C.S.I., proposed the first resolution, which was :—

'That this meeting desires to convey, on behalf of the people of Southern India, an expression of heartfelt gratitude for the sympathy and support so nobly and generously accorded them by the people of Great Britain, her Colonies, and India, in relief of the distress caused by the famine which has overshadowed the land throughout the last eighteen months.'

In moving the resolution, Mr. Seshia Sastri spoke as follows :—

Famines are not new to the world, especially to tropical countries and countries bordering on the tropics, only their occurrence at long intervals renders them unfamiliar to us. Famine and flood, pestilence and plague, storms and storm-waves, have been from earliest times phenomena regarded as signs of Divine wrath, because their appearance is sudden, their effects are terrible, their causes are mysterious, and the course of their destruction swift and irresistible. And it is a strange fact that countries reputed as the granaries of the world have not been spared from famines; for the earliest famine, for which we have the authority of sacred history, as we all may be reminded, was that which occurred in Egypt during the reign of the Pharaohs, and in which Joseph, the wise and discreet officer, played so conspicuous a part, and who, warned beforehand, 'gathered corn as the sand of the sea very much, until he left numbering—for it was without number.' India has been the scene of many famines—some of them, if tradition may be relied on, of 12 years' duration—and not a few have been experienced in our own Presidency. They were, however, local, confined to one or two tracts at a time, where they have left to this day indelible marks of the destruction caused in the shape of whole villages depopulated and now overgrown with jungle, as may be met with notably in the upland taluks of the late Masulipatam and Guntoor districts. Whole colonies of people driven by former famines may be met with in the present day, scattered and settled far away from their homes. Thus a colony of Tamil Brahmins driven from Tanjore have been settled for centuries in the Godavery delta;

several colonies of Telugu Brahmins driven by famines with which their country was visited oftener than others, have settled themselves in Southern Tamil districts. Colonies from Madura have been for centuries settled in Tanjore. Again, several successive waves of famine emigrants from the ancient Pandian Kingdom (Madura and Tinnevelly) may be traced, at this day, settled on the favoured Malabar coast, where famines are unknown; and, in our time, we have had the Orissa famine, the Ganjam famine, and the Bengal famine, none of which, however—thanks to the Government under which we live, and to modern commerce—has displaced and permanently scattered the population from their homes. But so far as could be judged without historic data, and at this distance of time, no former famine appears to have been so wide-spread and to have threatened the simultaneous annihilation of such a large portion of the population as the present one, out of which, let us trust, we are just emerging, under the mercy of God. So fresh must be the occurrences connected with the present famine in the memory of those assembled here, that I must not take up their time with reciting them. The failure of the early rains in 1876 was so serious and the loss of crops so great, that a great scarcity of food, indicated by high prices, was the first feature which presented itself. But, accustomed to high prices, year after year, for a series of years, our minds were unprepared for an approaching famine, and it was not till the utter failure of the north-east monsoon (November 1876) that we realised our dangerous position and stood face to face with a famine which threatened to be extraordinary in magnitude and severity. The lives of a population of 18 millions (180 lakhs) in 11 out of the 20 districts of this Presidency, of three millions in Mysore, and of many millions within the limits of the Bombay Presidency were in jeopardy. It was not easy to tell what food there was in the country. It was consequently impossible to say how much was required from without to supply the deficiency. The local Government, however, doubled and redoubled its efforts in every direction. Relief works were planned and multiplied to enable the able-bodied poor to earn a subsistence. Relief camps were opened at convenient centres for the preservation, by actual feeding, of the lives of those who were too weak, by age or sickness, to work and earn their bread. A system of relief by village money doles was also afterwards resorted to, to save from death the aged and infirm still. left at home. But on the sufficiency and rapidity of the supply of food, from abroad or from available local markets, and on the proximity to the scenes of actual distress to which it was possible to convey that food, depended the safety of millions. This necessity fully recognised, no exertions were spared (and we all know how much we are indebted to the personal exertions of his Grace the Governor in this, among other directions) to expedite and facilitate the supply of food, and the carrying-power of the railway was tried to the utmost possible limit, while the ocean-borne trade proved fully equal to the emergency. The Government of India, on their part, lost no time and spared no pains to help, combine, and concentrate all available carrying-power in the Empire. Some idea of the stupendous character of the operations which taxed the minds of our rulers may be formed by noting a few facts. $1\frac{1}{4}$ million tons of food-grains, valued roughly at $22\frac{1}{2}$ crores of rupees, sufficient at a low calculation to support $7\frac{1}{2}$ millions, 75 lakhs of people, for 12 months, were carried by the railway into the Presidency and Mysore. The State famine expenditure may be taken at four crores, to which one crore for Mysore, and another crore provided by the English and Indian charity, being added, we have a total expenditure of six crores. The support of a million of population cost roughly $2\frac{1}{2}$ crores of rupees. The six crores of money spent must have saved 21 millions of people. The highest number on relief (in September 1877) was a little over two millions (21 lakhs), and five millions of people must have also absolutely perished, even if they had the money, if they had not the food brought to them by the ocean and the railways. Or, in other words, $7\frac{1}{2}$ millions (75 lakhs of people), equivalent to 35 per cent. of the population of the famine district, must have inevitably perished, but for the presence of a mighty commerce, a gigantic carrier in the railway, and a powerful and humane Government which would not count the cost in saving people from death by starvation. At this period of the year, December 1876 to April 1877, no other field for the employment of able-bodied labour was open than public works. The cyclonic rains in April, May, and June 1877, which tempted many to plough and sow, proved delusive —for the results of that cultivation were, as we all know, disastrous —and people were again thrown back on the hands of the State—on public works, and on feeding camps. The failure of another south-west monsoon thus added a sad gloom to the already deplorable aspect of affairs. The money of the Exchequer was well-nigh exhausted, and borrowed money was running out at the rate of 50 lakhs per mensem. But in spite of the unremitting supply of food the condition of the distressed people was growing worse and worse, and as one rainless day succeeded another, and prices were rising with unrelenting steadiness, hope was vanishing and dumb resignation to an inevitable fate was taking its place. The actual condition of the people at this time, and indeed for several months past, was one of sore distress. Its worst features were, the high prices which still kept food inaccessible to many; there was no water to drink, no fodder for the cattle; the cattle indeed had been let loose in hundreds and thousands; the aged and young were succumbing in large numbers to starvation and to disease generated by the famine; the thatch on the roof of the huts had been taken off to feed the cattle. People in thousands, nay hundreds of thousands, abandoned their homes and lands to earn a precarious subsistence on public works, or for a scanty meal in the feeding camps, still wearing the very clothes, now reduced to the last rags, in which they had left their homes, the females laden with baskets on their heads, containing pots and cocoa-nut-shell spoons, their all in the world—and the males, laden with their children, now so starved as to be 'spectres unto their own parents.' Some lived on roots, leaves, on the seed of the grass, on the bark of trees; others on the plantain root and on the plantain stem, and even on the tender stalk of the screw-pine; others again found a meal on the berries of the prickly-pear, on tamarind seeds, on the fruit of the banian and the fig; while others, in the vicinity of forests, lived for weeks on the seed of the bamboo, and it was not rare to find children kept alive on bran! The distress was not confined to the agriculturists. The poor among all other industrial classes, and notably among them the weavers, suffered distress even more severe, because less accustomed to. The curse of famine indeed threatened to 'consume the land. Rain still held off, and affairs became more grave than ever. At this juncture the Viceroy visited some tracts of the famine country. More public works and more agency to work them, more feeding camps and more agency to superintend them, were devised and brought to tell on the alleviation of distress. At about this time (end of August 1877) came symptoms of approaching monsoons, and cast a ray of hope on the gloomy picture. But what were the helpless people to do even if rain came, was the question which vexed the anxious thoughts of many, and among them his Grace the Governor. At the meeting of August 1877, his Grace very truly said, 'When they return to their houses from the relief camps or public works they will have to go to a roofless house, with not a single culinary vessel remaining in it. To provide clothing, even such scanty clothing as this climate necessitates—to enable them to repair their huts—to purchase new implements to replace those sold for bread—here were needs sufficient to justify a call on public charity.' It was consequently resolved to appeal to the charity of England and her Colonies, and of India also. The appeal was made in no faltering voice, or by a voice unfamiliar to the English nation. It was at once responded to, and in a manner without parallel even in a country proverbial for the munificence of its charities. The results have been just placed before us by the honorary secretary. The charity flowed in a continued stream till arrested, when a sum of 82 lakhs of rupees had been reached. The administration of these charity funds was wisely entrusted to a central committee composed of a mixed agency of officials and non-officials, merchants and missionaries, and Christians, Hindoos, and Mussulmans, and presided over by the Honourable Sir William Robinson, a gentleman who has spent a life-time among us, and to whom no corner of our Presidency is unknown, and who is familiar with the condition and wants of every district, and of the people of every portion of it. The central committee in its turn organised local committees of elements similarly composed for each famine district, and they, in their turn, formed sub-local committees, equally and even more representative in character. Individual agencies, consisting of ladies and gentlemen, who volunteered their services, were also largely employed, and by October 1877 all these various agencies, to the number of upwards of 120, were at full work and full of enthusiasm and zeal. The actual detail and *modus operandi* of relief work were wisely (thanks to Mr. Thornhill) left to the discretion of the local committees; and at a sufficiently early date (thanks to Mr. Ballard) a most useful and practical direction was emphatically given for the employment of the larger portion of the fund towards helping the agricultural classes and in forwarding agricultural operations, so necessary to the return of prosperity to the commonwealth, for it has been truly said by a well-known poet :—

> Princes and lords may flourish or may fade,
> A breath can make them as a breath has made,
> But a bold peasantry, their country's pride,
> When once destroyed can never be supplied.

It pleased God at this time (end of August and September) to send us rain, and the transactions of the general committee teem in every page with testimony, from every direction, of the immense good and the variety of good which has been accomplished with the help of their money. , But though I feel that I am unduly taxing the patience of my audience, I cannot refrain from reading a few extracts from reports already in the annals of the committee, explaining the direct effect of relief operations with the English charity. Mr. Webster reports :—'Our attention has been directed to the condition of the better classes of cultivators, those who, in ordinary years, had some small capital and are well-to-do. Many of them are now paupers, who prefer to run the chances of dying by inches at home rather than seek aid on Government relief works—a kind of assistance which they regard with no more favour than a respectable Englishman shows to the workhouse. To people of this class, all Government schemes of relief are and must be practically useless, but the assistance which the famine relief committee has been able to afford has been received most thankfully, as it has not only enabled people to tide over the present time of dearth, but has encouraged them to look forward to an early reaping of crops grown on lands that must have remained waste had there been no relief funds.' Mr. Sheristadar Puttabhiram Pillay's report :—'The rains of September, however, have brought these people back (from relief works and camps) to their fields, and revived the hopes of others who still stuck fast to their homes and fields, contending against all odds of the famine, but they were without means to plough their fields. They struggled hard, mortgaged a portion of their lands, raised a small sum and attempted cultivation. But the means they got were very insufficient; cultivation was therefore indifferent, but yet they could not bring themselves to abandon the young crops for relief works again. Nor had they the means of eking out a subsistence, except the wild-grown greens which the late rains had produced. Their huts were in ruins and afforded them no shelter. Their cloths were all rags ; most of them were next to nakedness. It was while they were in this miserable state that the Mansicn House relief reached them. On the receipt of the relief money, which was always paid in a lump sum, many crowds of ryots went in to purchase seed paddy, seed grain, and seed cumbu. Others set about to patch up their ruined huts, others ploughed their waste fields and sowed, or prepared seeds, beds for rice cultivation under tanks now full with water. The cloths distributed were of the utmost service : the people prized them much. The feeling of gratitude of these poor people for the English charity money that came to their help at this crisis cannot adequately be expressed.' Another agent of the committee, speaking about the distribution of cloths, says that 'the females for want of clothing were ashamed to go out to their usual work on the fields, but when the cloths were distributed, the next day the fields were alive with them.' Relief was peculiarly seasonable and valuable to another section of respectable people, the Gosha women, Mussulman, Mahratta, and Rajpoot. This portion of the duty fell exclusively to my lot and that of my friend, Periasami Mudaliyar, head of the native community of Trichinopoly, who is now here by my side. Living in secluded nooks and corners of a large town, and remote from observation and sympathy, these were slowly passing away, dragging on a miserable existence, and many among whom would surely have fallen victims to starvation but for the aid from English charity which was put into their hands with our own at their own doors. I have but one picture more to present from my part of the country, and that is where relief funds were applied to the relief of a lady of the highest position, who at the age of 88 found this grim famine at her door, with sons and with daughters yet unmarried—grandsons and a staff of old faithful servants who, unwilling to abandon their mistress in adversity, still clung to her. She was in the utmost distress, and the sum of 350 rs. being put into her hands by the deputy collector on behalf of the committee, spoke in these words: 'Please convey my deep sense of their (the English) benevolence, and tell them that I was born the offspring of the ruling nation to be entitled at their hands to this liberal charity:' which is an Oriental expression to convey deepest gratitude. What I have been narrating is but a scanty specimen of the good work which has been accomplished, all as labour of love, by an agency the like of which never worked before in this land. The total good work done has been simply colossal, and the results have been of the happiest kind. This English charity, I again repeat, was peculiarly valuable, peculiarly seasonable, and peculiarly fruitful and happy in its results. European and native gentlemen of the highest position, in the service and out of the service, merchants and sahookars, bishops and missionaries of all denominations, and planters and their agents all over the Hill-ranges, and in many instances, ladies of the highest station in life (all honour to the Honourable Mrs. Carmichael among others) who adopted as their own the orphans, the waifs and strays of the famine, and saw them reared with maternal care and affection, all these vied with each other in the zealous and faithful performance of the task they had so cheerfully imposed on themselves, the task of carrying to the doors of the famine-stricken the noble charity of which the English nation had made them almoners. I have no hesitation in repeating that the opportune and critical moment at which the help arrived—for according to a proverb among us, 'Flood and famine are most treacherous when subsiding'—and the kind manner in which the gift was taken to the afflicted generally, and to certain classes of people in particular, on account of their strong prejudices, to whom public works and feeding camps were, the one a degradation, the other a pollution, gave a hundredfold value to the gift. On behalf of my countrymen generally, and on behalf of the distressed famine-stricken of South India especially, to whom English charity came like sweet water to men dying of thirst, whose drooping spirits, nay, ebbing life, were resuscitated by the timely and kindly help, and enabled them to preserve themselves and their children, to rebuild their huts, to sow their fields, and reap a harvest, when they despaired of living to see another—on behalf of millions of such of my countrymen, and for the good they have experienced, I now express their first prayerful thanks to the all-merciful Providence who is with us in the hour of grief and the hour of joy, and whom it has pleased to order a hopeful change in the season; and their next thankfulness and gratitude to the Empress of India, who headed the charitable movement at home, to the English nation and to the Colonies who gave so cheerfully, so quickly, and so freely; to the Viceroy who headed the contributions in India; and to the Maharajahs of Baroda, Indore, and Travancore, and other princes, nobles, and personages and people of India, who added to their quota of help with equal sympathy and readiness; and personally I feel much honoured by the task which has been entrusted to me, and which I now perform with sincere pleasure, by moving 'That this meeting desires to convey, on behalf of the people of Southern India, an expression of heartfelt gratitude for the sympathy and support so nobly and generously accorded them by the people of Great Britain, her Colonies, and India, in relief of the distress caused by the famine which has overshadowed the land throughout the last ten months.'

Mr. MIRZA FEROZE HUSSAIN KHAÑ BAHADUR seconded the resolution, and, in doing so, delivered an address in Hindustani, of which the following is a translation:—

My Lord Duke,—After first rendering thanks to the Giver of all Good, and bestowing blessings upon the Prophet, I will proceed to say a few words out of gratitude to the friends who have been so good as to ask me to speak on this occasion, though I am painfully aware of my deficiencies as a speaker. On the part of our fellow-countrymen of this Presidency and of all Southern India, I beg to express heartfelt thanks for the noble generosity shown by the inhabitants of Great Britain and the British Colonies, and by the Princes and people of India. For a year and a half past, the people of the Presidencies of Madras and Bombay have been visited with a grievous famine, and in spite of all the efforts of the Government to alleviate the distress, thousands of poor creatures abandoned their homes and fell victims to want and disease, and hundreds and thousands were likewise on the point of perishing; when these generous benefactors, hearing of our distress, subscribed and sent nearly a crore of rupees, which was distributed in food and cloths among the needy, by committees in every station, town, and village throughout the Presidency; and innumerable lives of the servants of God were thus preserved, some from absolute starvation, others from want and misery. Such beneficence has rarely been seen in this world, and everyone will heartily unite with me in applauding the noble generosity of the givers. Let us pray to the true God, saying, O Lord! may their lives be long and happy! may they prosper more and more day by day! Amen. I beg to second the resolution proposed by Mr. Seshia Sastri.

The RAJAH OF VENKATAGHERRY spoke as follows in the Telugu tongue :—

My Lord Duke, Ladies and Gentlemen,—I consider it a high privilege to be allowed to second the resolution which has just been moved, proposing to express our grateful sense of the priceless services rendered by his Grace the Duke of Buckingham and Chandos in the crisis which we may now hope is passing away ; in fact to express that gratitude which has rendered possible our gratitude to good and great England.   But, gentlemen, I am sure that gratitude is not what his Grace has laboured for or expected. His ideal of duty to the people whom it is his destiny to rule and protect is far different. I can fancy his Grace saying at this moment :—' I did not stipulate for gratitude. It is of far more importance to me to know whether I have done my duty, and with what success.' What then ? If in the words of Nelson, used on a very different occasion, England expects every man to do his duty, are we not bound to let England know that a noble son of hers has done his duty well and faithfully, and has secured the success which his labours have so well deserved ? At a time when a humane Government was putting forth all its might, and was almost despairing of success in the alleviation of distress, did he not at once give the danger-signal to the people of England, and invite volunteers to enlist themselves in the great fight which he was fighting against famine and disease ? But for that signal, and for the weight and prestige of his Grace's honoured name, what would have been the fate of the millions of people to whom, as it might almost seem, Providence had for a time refused the means of raising their own sustenance ? His Grace's services then have been simply priceless. Those services might indeed have been in discharge of duty ; but an expression of our appreciation of it is not the less incumbent on us. His Grace has locally represented good and noble England in her catholic charity, in her active benevolence, and in what I may call, her practical Christianity, and achieved a triumph more glorious —because more peaceful—than that won in many a battle-field. Let us then, in the name of Southern India—in the name of misery and destitution itself—thank the hero who has thus so long successfully battled with famine and pestilence, for the almost profuse liberality with which England and her Colonies have come to our succour in our time of need and distress. This liberality has enabled us to tide over an unexampled crisis ; and let us not forget, the people of Southern India will not forget, that this result is due, in no small degree, to the large-hearted sympathy and promptitude of action which has characterised the administration of the Presidency by the illustrious nobleman whom it has been our good fortune to have at the head of the Government during the trying period which it is to be hoped has now passed away. The proposal made by Mr. A. Seshia Sastri, C.S.I. is very laudable, and though I feel myself inferior in ability to speak what I have to say in the presence of his Grace the Duke and the illustrious audience, yet I trust that the few observations I am anxious to make may be acceptable to all present, in the same way as the lovely lisping speech of children is to their parents. It is most material and important that we should express our feelings of gratitude to all those that have cheerfully contributed towards the mitigation of this dire calamity, the terrible famine. But the good that resulted from it would not become prominent unless the horrors of long-past famines are enumerated. I would, therefore, cite a few of them here. The famines that broke out in the years Achaya, Tharana, and Nanadna, were of short duration, lasting but five or six months, when seasonable rains dispelled the horrors, and restored the country to its normal condition. Even in times of such scarcity, rice was sold at 10 to 12 Nellore seers a rupee, while the other grains were comparatively cheap. While circumstances were so placed, no adequate arrangements having been made towards the maintenance and support of the starving poor, many had fallen victims to them ; others again, resigning themselves to fate, forming gangs, committed gang and highway robberies, thereby stripping the rich of their property, burnt houses by setting fire to them, and committed other heinous offences of like nature. Thus were the rich, too, exposed to the dangers of death and ruin. Nor is this all ; they murdered, I hear, indiscriminately, such of the men as had procured their bread by some means or other, tearing open their stomachs and eating the contents thereof, and hence it had been proverbially styled the *Dokka* famine. Others that had five or six children amongst them, being unable to resist the cravings of hunger, ventured so far as to slaughter their children and feed upon them. Hence it has been styled *Pillala* (which means infanticide famine). During this present famine, which has existed for the past eighteen months, rice could not be had even at 5 or 6 Nellore seers a rupee, while all other grains are ruinously high ; and though it rained recently rather partially in certain localities, prices of grain continue to be the same as before. While the matter stands thus, Her Majesty the Queen and Empress of India, who had organised relief works, opened relief camps for the helpless poor, and fed them with a more sumptuous food than they ever had in their own homes even in days of festivity, has been protecting them in every way from death. As the famine has been of long standing, it was doubted, or rather feared, whether they would preserve life any longer. Appeal for public charity was made by his Grace the Duke to England and her Colonies. They all freely and voluntarily came forward with liberal contributions, from the Monarch to the lowest peasant, and sent in large sums. Even in India similar contributions were made, but to a very limited extent. As money poured in, it served nobly to aid the efforts of protecting the poor, by giving the Gosha women many doles ; clothing the naked ; by giving pecuniary aid to repair and rebuild houses, granting advances of money for seed-grain, for purchasing ploughing-cattle, and for procuring the implements of husbandry, to impoverished ryots. In this manner the contributions have been most usefully distributed for these and various other purposes. For these reasons, not only were the poor saved from starvation, but the rich and the opulent also were saved from the ravages they were subjected to on former occasions of scarcity. The fact that famine has ruined the country has alone been recorded,but the munificence of England has warded off the blow that would have prostrated the country. It is therefore a duty incumbent on us to express our sense of deepfelt gratitude to Her Majesty the Empress of India for her enthusiasm and liberality in the protection of the millions that were in distress, to the people of England and her Colonies for their sympathy towards the famine-stricken population of this country, to his Excellency the Viceroy of India, and to his Grace the Duke of Buckingham and Chandos for his very energetic and indefatigable exertions in wisely ministering to the wants of the distressed districts by visiting them, regard having been had to respect every caste and creed. It is our fervent prayer that God the Almighty would pour His blessings on all those who have so nobly and generously contributed to afford protection to the distressed population of Southern India.

The Venerable Archdeacon C. R. DRURY supported the resolution :—

He remarked that he thought it right that the portion of the ecclesiastical department which he had the honour to represent in this diocese during the absence of the Bishop should take a prominent part in these proceedings, inasmuch as the Church of England at home and abroad had shown great sympathy with Southern India in their season of trial, and also contributed liberally to the relief fund. He might also say for the sister church in Ireland that the sum total of her contributors include many sums given at a cost perhaps of the meal which was much needed, and comforts which could hardly be spared by poor people who were readily making a sacrifice to show their sympathy for the suffering and distress which afflicted their fellow subjects abroad. Such gifts were acceptable to God, and either would be, or had been, rewarded by the God of love, who commanded them all, as he (Archdeacon Drury) understood, without distinction of caste or creed, to love and to help one another and to bear one another's burdens. (Applause.) They put off as long as they possibly could asking the people at home, in the Colonies, and other parts of India, for relief, and experience had shown that they did not ask for it a day too soon. How noble a response had their appeal met with! They had received, he understood from his Grace and the gentleman who spoke first to that resolution, money sufficient for their wants. The liberality of Government had been supplemented : the naked had been clothed; others who were in want of seed had seed given them to enable them to lay the foundation of future happiness and comfort by preparing the ground for future crops. In some instances instruments of agriculture had been supplied, and charitable Christian ladies amongst them, to whom he had been glad to hear such a tribute of respect had been shown by Mr. Seshia Sastri, embraced the opportunity afforded of providing a home and protection for many destitute orphan children, and would be able to keep them for a time, perhaps until their relief was no longer required. In short, through the assistance which the committee secured by the liberality of the English people, of residents of the parts of India, including the native princes and notables, everything was being done which could be done in order to mitigate the sufferings of the famine-stricken population. He was glad to call to mind the fact of England, in responding so liberally to their appeal, had only acted in accordance with her usual custom; for she had not confined her liberality merely to fellow-subjects, and he remembered some years ago when a destructive fire destroyed a great portion of the city of Chicago and brought a number of respectable American citizens to great poverty, the English public were among the foremost to send them money to minister to their relief. (Applause.) In saying that, he was not speaking in a vain-glorious or boasting spirit. Almighty God had given to them the means of being liberal, and what was of great importance, he had given them the heart to do so. (Applause.) And he (Archdeacon Drury) took the liberty to say that probably the prosperity of England has been the reward of her generosity and liberality to the afflicted and distressed (Applause), her readiness to come forward to protect the poor and the weak against the tyranny and oppression of the strong. He trusted, and he was sure from what he had heard, that the natives of this country would never forget, as long as memory lasted, the sympathy and good feeling which had been shown towards them all by the English people, and they would also remember, if they had any memorials worth making, his Grace's energetic and benevolent exertions. (Applause.)

Colonel PEARSE, president, Mysore central relief committee, also supported the resolutions, and in doing so addressed the meeting. He read the following resolutions arrived at by the Mysore general relief committee on January 26, 1870 :—

'The Mysore general relief committee desire, on behalf of the sufferers from famine throughout this province, native and European, to express their deep sense of gratitude for the assistance given by the subscribers in the United Kingdom for the relief of the famine in India.

2. ' This committee have already received the large sum of 150,000l. sterling, nearly three-fourths of which have been expended. The assistance has been most timely, and relief has been given in one shape or another to a quarter of a million or more persons, whom it would have been difficult otherwise to relieve. Temporary provision has been made for numbers of destitute orphans ; clothing has been given to thousands of the needy poor ; and aid of the most valuable kind afforded to famine-stricken agriculturists and artisans. Relief has been given to all sufferers without regard to race or creed ; and it is impossible to over-estimate the good that has been done to those who, but for this assistance, must have suffered very greatly.

3. ' Care has been taken to make it widely known that the help thus afforded was purely the charitable gift of English people. It has been distributed almost entirely through the agency of the officers employed on special famine duty, aided by benevolent private individuals. The committee have reason to believe that the funds have been, on the whole, usefully and judiciously spent. From the accounts received from all parts of the province, the committee feel confident that the generous sympathy thus practically evinced towards the people of Mysore in the time of their sore distress by their fellow-subjects in Europe, is very deeply appreciated, and will long be held throughout this province in most grateful remembrance.'

After reading the above, Colonel PEARSE proceeded to observe :—

' I have only very few remarks to offer, and I only wish that some one more eloquent and more capable than myself were present to state the case for the people of Mysore. I have only recently succeeded Mr. J. D. Gordon as president of the Mysore general relief committee, and it is, I think, right that I should advert to the system pursued in the distribution of the funds. Conjointly with other members of our committee I have held that the extension of the system of money and grain doles was an arrangement which, I fear, watched with the closest supervision and most tentatively issued, should only be adhered to in cases of dire distress of the houseless and friendless poor and destitute, there being always the fear of perpetuating pauperism and demoralising our lowest classes by inducing them to idleness instead of sending them back to their ordinary occupations. We have therefore endeavoured to induce relief officers to pay special attention to all other wants, and to endeavour to restore the people to their ordinary occupations, and that is, within ordinary grooves of life to assist those who have lands lying untilled to cultivate them and give them cheap cattle to go on with; also to assist those who lie shivering from cold and fever under detached portions of their old thatching to again place proper roofs over their heads, and to enable others who have lost their implements of trade, their looms and their materials, to start work again; and to distribute clothing to those in need of covering, and thereby restore the poorest classes to that condition of self-respect which the calamity of famine and want has temporarily destroyed. By this system also the ryots have again been enabled to employ the poorer classes in their villages, and contentment and renewed prosperity will be the result, and the dregs of a period of distress not experienced for many generations will, to a great extent, be met and fought against. There are some, I believe, who do not consider this the most correct method of dealing with the funds, but I can only add that many of the most thinking famine officers believe it is a good and true policy and the wisest course, and that if we think thereby to restore to prosperity and contentment a fair percentage of houses reduced to poverty and desolation by the famine, we shall have done much to meet the wishes of the English public who have so largely and liberally contributed to our wants. There is one more point I wish to refer to, and which will be pleasing to English ears to hear. Many intelligent native gentlemen tell me that the fact of this money being a free gift, and which will not be recouped this next harvest or the harvest after, has made a profound impression on the minds of the ryots of Mysore. The fact that it is a huge contribution, sent by those who have not seen or known them, in a true spirit of humanity, to aid them in their hour of misfortune, is such an unthought of and untold boon, that the memory of such timely generosity will form a happy tradition in the minds of those who have benefited by it and who by its aid have again been placed in a position of self-respect, and have been enabled to again earn their daily bread. In conclusion, I have only to offer the acknowledgments of the Mysore famine general relief committee, and those of our fellow-subjects of Mysore whom I now represent, for the unhesitatingly kind and generous spirit in which the president and members of the Madras general committee have met our requisitions for funds, and I wish in the name of all those whom they have benefited to thank them for the consideration shown us and for the liberal manner in which they have shared the fund with us.

The resolution was further supported by the Rev. Dr. Scudder :—

He said he was thankful of the privilege of using his voice, and specially, as an American, in ascribing that honour to England which she so richly deserved for her princely charity. (Applause.) He was proud of his relation to her! She was his mother, and though Americans might be accused of undutifulness and disobedience, yet did they think a mother's love would for that cause be alienated from her children? (Hear, hear.) He thought they might hope that she would give them absolution for all their sins; indeed she had given them many proofs of this. The Archdeacon had just mentioned one illustration of her love for her child in giving her money to relieve the poor and suffering in Chicago. He ventured to say as an American that her glory was their glory, her honour their honour. In many a battle-field she had crowned herself with glory; she had devoted her all for the good of the people; she had done for this country what no other nation he believed would have done. She had given freely and fully of her resources in regard to the famine, and they were there to express their gratitude for the sympathy she had evinced. The word 'sympathy' in such a case was not strong enough—he would rather say the love she had shown for that people in a marvellous manner (applause), responding to their appeal in a way that was the wonder of the world. They ought not on that occasion to forget the obligations they were under to the ladies of the Presidency, whose hearts had been touched by the distress and suffering around them, many of whom had gone into places where there were pestilence and disease, clothing, feeding, and nursing poor orphan children. For this work he said God bless them (applause), and it was for these reasons he said he thought the word sympathy was not strong enough. He wished once more to express his sense of the marvellous good done by the fund.

The resolution was put to the meeting and carried with acclamation.

Surgeon-General GEORGE SMITH, M.D., proposed the second resolution :—

That this meeting desires to tender cordial thanks

To Alderman Sir Thomas White, Lord Mayor, for his initiation of and active interest in the famine relief fund :

To the Lord Provost of Edinburgh, to the Lord Mayor of Dublin, to the Lord Provost of Glasgow, the Mayors of Manchester, Liverpool, and other chief towns of England; to the Mansion House and other committees :

To the committees at Calcutta and others in India :

To the chief municipality and other functionaries in Australasia, New Zealand, and other British colonies :

To the ministers and congregations of the Church of England and religious denominations :

And to *The Times* newspaper and the press generally :

For the earnestness and energy with which they have acted in enlisting sympathy and making available the aid contributed towards the relief of distress.

In proposing the above resolution Dr. SMITH said that he was in the singular position of a speaker whose speech had been forestalled by the points taken up by the previous speakers. The whole of the grounds he had expected to have to go over had been traversed. He offered this explanation in order that any repetition of a fact already noticed might be excused. He then spoke as follows :—

It will be remembered by all who have watched the efforts that have been made for the relief of the sufferers from the disastrous famine in Southern India that a public meeting, called by the sheriff at the requisition of the residents of this city and presided over by your Grace, was held in this hall on August 4 last, at which the prominent facts in connection with the sad condition of large portions of this Presidency were ably and clearly brought to the notice of the general public, and that a resolution was passed recognising the necessity of making an appeal to the public charity of the people of India and of England. At the same time a central committee to undertake the management of the famine relief fund was constituted, and a resolution was taken to appeal by telegraph, and more fully by letter, to the Lord Mayor of London, to the other civil functionaries as noted in the resolution, to the commander of Calcutta and of other towns and stations, and to the editor of the London *Times*, stating the gravity of this crisis, and soliciting that the same may be made known to the British public. I need hardly say how much the success of this and of other appeals depended on the action taken by the Lord Mayor of London. It is true that when proroguing Parliament Her Majesty had referred in a marked manner to the same crisis in India, and it is also true that the Thunderer had struck the key note of human sympathy in an able and sympathetic leading article, the concluding sentence of which I may be allowed to quote :—

' Let not the appeal now at length made to us fall unheeded. Our countrymen at Madras call upon the municipalities at home, and the *cry must be heard*. We have hitherto been too little concerned with the awful trial that has befallen our fellow-subjects ; let us redeem the past by keeping it before our eyes and in our minds *and hearts until all that we can do is done, in order that it may be overcome.*'

Good, brave, manly words these—nevertheless it was necessary that one great public official should take prompt and cordial action in order that generous hearty England might leap response to the call, and feel that there existed a definite and trustworthy channel through which its liberality might with certainty reach the masses of suffering humanity in this Presidency. The Lord Mayor of London, Sir T. White, was the official to whom all eyes were turned, and we well know were not turned in vain. On the day on which the article alluded to appeared in the *Times*, the Lord Mayor at the Mansion House, addressing the chief clerk, read the telegram which he had received from the Madras committee, which he said spoke for itself. He then quoted the paragraph from the leading article of the *Times* which I have already quoted, and then stated that he would be delighted—that was his expression—to receive and transmit to Madras any sums which a generous public might entrust to him, hoping that his appeal would be promptly and liberally responded to. We know in the Lord Mayor's own words what a splendid response the country gave to this appeal. The Mansion House relief committee was appointed and acted with promptitude and energy. The first meeting was held on August 23, and the last of its famine meetings on November 5, when information reached them that the crisis was over and that the closure of the fund might take place. During that short, sharp, brilliant campaign, not to destroy but to save men's lives, a campaign extending over 2½ months, half a million sterling was contributed and promptly remitted to Madras. By the influence of his official position, by his initiation of this famine relief fund, by the personal interest he took in its success, and by the practical help he gave as president and treasurer, Sir Thomas White largely influenced the success of the appeal which had been made to the public. His labours were cordially recognised by the committee over which he presided, and I am convinced that they will receive a similar hearty recognition from this meeting of the public of Madras. And, my Lord Duke, it is no less our duty than our pleasure to recognise most gratefully the generous and ready aid given by the other great civic magistrates noted in the resolution as well as by the Mansion House and other committees at home. Upon them devolved the heavy task of initiating local arrangements and of collecting local subscriptions ; with them it rested to bring the cause home to the hearts of the people and to set on foot the various agencies necessary for this purpose. When all worked so nobly and so well it would be invidious to mete out comparative praise. To all our cordial thanks are due. (Applause.) A glance at the published daily reports of the *Times* and at the subscription lists of provincial papers will show how deep-reaching and how far-extending this appeal was, and how nobly it has been responded to, from the Queen on the throne to the humblest of her subjects, from that huge congeries of cities called London to the smallest hamlet in the land, from the millionaire to the humble labourer who could put but a few pence in the collector's hand. (Applause.) And not money alone was given. The generous heart of the nation was stirred to its inmost depths, and time, and personal effort and, better than all, deep warm sympathy, so deep, so practical, so unselfish, so prompt, has touched a chord of gratitude in Indian hearts which has never been touched before, and we are here this evening to give some feeble expression to the nation's gratitude. And what, Sir, was the response to the appeal from the British colonies? It was prompt, liberal, enthusiastic. Australia heads the list, and well she may. The Mayor of Melbourne took immediate action, a hearty and sympathetic meeting was held, Government gave effectual countenance, and local committees were promptly formed, and the press gave its powerful pen. Enthusiastic meetings were held at Sydney and Adelaide; Brisbane, Wellington, Perth and Hobart Town gave a hearty response to the appeal. Australia, including Tasmania, will probably add 100,000*l.* to the famine relief fund. Well does Australia merit our cordial thanks. (Applause.) To show how deeply the sympathies of our brethren in Australia were moved, it may be mentioned that the prisoners in one of the gaols asked to be put upon half diet for some time, and the value handed over to the fund. (Applause.) The offer was accepted. (Applause.) That sympathy must have been deep and strong which affected so profoundly and so practically a class of the population so little likely to be influenced by the sorrows and sufferings of others. New Zealand, too, has contributed largely, and considering the sparseness of her population the contribution has been proportionately more than that given by the people at home. Help and sympathy have reached us from other colonies, from British Guiana, Jamaica, Mauritius, and elsewhere. From Mauritius has come a donation from the Government, and in addition to the contribution from the residents a further contribution from the Indian emigrants, whose sympathies have been roused by the miseries of their fellow-countrymen in India. A similar contribution has reached the committee from the Indian emigrants in Ceylon. Natal brought as her contribution from them 12,000 rs. We are asked also to tender our cordial thanks to the committee at Calcutta and to others in India. The committees contemplated are the collecting not the distributing committee. The committee at Calcutta has raised for us the handsome sum of about 2 lakhs of rupees. The balance of the Bengal famine fund, 75,000 rs., has been handed over to the committee. Among those in prominent positions who have helped, we mention with gratitude the Maharajahs of Baroda, Travancore, Cochin, Vizianagaram, the Maharajah Holkar, and the Begum of Bhopal. Others have also liberally helped, including contributions from native regiments. The town of Rangoon gave 14,500 rs. The resolution further recognises the valuable efforts made by the ministers and congregations of the Church of England and other religious denominations. Through their active, intelligent, and zealous agency considerable assistance has been given to the fund. The appeal to the clergy was first made by the Lord Mayor, and his results at home have been most satisfactory. On this point I need offer no further remarks. We are called finally to offer our cordial thanks to *The Times* newspaper and to other journals which have, by their advocacy and help, contributed so much to the success of the fund. By the earnestness and energy of their appeals, the home journals and nearly all in this country have effectually roused and effectually sustained the interest of the public in the terrible struggle with want and woe in this Presidency. *The Times* newspaper early recognised the extreme gravity of the crisis, and in its daily issues maintained public sympathy on the one hand and recorded public liberality on the other. The home papers watched the fight, and cheered the labours of the committee with their sympathy, support, and confidence. The illustrated journals, too, deserve special notice. By a correct reproduction of sketches and of photographs of famine scenes they greatly assisted in bringing home to the public some of the terrible scenes of the terrible catastrophe. The hearts of men were moved to their very depths, and liberality was evoked which saved thousands of lives. The photographs from Madras told effectually their own tale of sorrow and of suffering. Thanks having been tendered to all who were deserving of thanks in connection with the relief of the distress caused by the famine, there is yet one point to be considered. The sympathy which had been shown by the people of Great Britain will result in improving the relations existing between the people of Great Britain and the people of this land; and they who aforetime were two peoples, estranged and knowing not each other, will now become one. (Applause.)

Mr. SOMASOONDRUM CHETTY seconded the resolution, and, in doing so, remarked as follows:—

In seconding the resolution just moved by the eloquent speaker who has sat down, I am happy that an opportunity has been afforded me on this public occasion of expressing the gratitude of her Majesty's subjects of this part of India, for the sympathy and support so nobly accorded by the generous people of Great Britain, her Colonies, and India in relief of the wide-spread distress caused by the terrible calamity which has cast such a gloom over Southern India during the last 18 months. I cordially join Surgeon-General Smith in tendering and conveying the warmest and heart-felt thanks of the people of the Madras Presidency to the several agencies and committees named, for the valuable support and aid received at their hands in the trying crisis through which the country has passed. Had it not been for the prompt assistance which has been given to us during this direful calamity, with true sympathy and humanity, by the generous people of England as well as by the committee at Calcutta, including the sum contributed by the Bengal students and the sepoys of many native regiments from their small means, I am unable to say to what dire and distressed condition those people whom the Government system of relief has not reached would have been reduced, and to what extent they would have actually perished. It is due to this timely and spontaneous aid, in conjunction with the widespread relief afforded by Government, that the calamity has been greatly mitigated, and to all the local committees and individuals through whose instrumentality the charitable funds so liberally placed at our disposal have been so well and beneficially distributed. In the name of the people of Southern India we tender our deep-felt gratitude. In conclusion I cannot leave this hall without expressing the warm and deep-felt gratitude which we, the Hindus as a nation, owe to her most Gracious Majesty the Queen of England and Empress of India, for the deep sympathy shown by her towards the people of this country, in a time of sad trial and distress, and for having felt for us a concern such as a mother feels for her child. I convey our ardent hopes and prayers for her Majesty's and England's continued prosperity. May the Almighty allow her gracious banner to fly over all the parts of India, and for ever secure to her the devoted attachment of her Indian subjects to the Government of India, and her Imperial Majesty's representative in this Presidency. To his Grace the Governor the people of this Presidency owe a deep debt of gratitude. To his Grace we cannot be too thankful for the active, powerful, and sympathetic support given by him to the great flow of British benevolence, and the display of British humanity on behalf of suffering India.

In support of the resolution the Rev. J. M. STRACHAN, M.D., spoke briefly. He said there was one point which had not been referred to by the Archdeacon, namely, the help that was afforded by the Church of England and the religious bodies towards this fund. He was informed by the Honorary Secretary that about half, or even more, of the fund was contributed by churches and chapels. He knew very well what the general character of church collections was, and he believed the amount subscribed from this source represented the gifts of millions of our fellow-subjects in Great Britain, many of whom must have given from limited means indeed. He also thought that the Surgeon-General lost sight of a fact which ought not to be lost sight of in Madras. About a fortnight after the formation of the Mansion House Committee an appeal was published from the Lord Bishop of Madras, and he did believe that appeal of their own diocesan had an immense influence on the minds of the people and clergy of England (hear, hear), and that it was the means of raising a very large sum of money and of awakenening a very wide-spread sympathy throughout England. But it must not be supposed that the Church of England only gave help : other religious bodies came forward right nobly. (Hear, hear.) They knew very well that the Jewish Rabbi, and Cardinal Manning, the Cardinal Archbishop, both issued appeals. And he was informed that the Propaganda at Rome actually sent 25,000 francs to the Mansion House. (Applause.) He ventured to say that the venerable church, in all its long and eventful history, never did a more graceful act, or one that more truly and thoroughly entitled it to its name of Catholic. (Applause.) Although many of the persons who had been recipients of England's bounty might have a dim and confused idea about the sources of the charity which had saved them from the most awful kind of death— starvation, yet the educated class of natives knew and believed that the practical sympathy shown by our beloved and most gracious Queen, the Empress of India, by the nobles, the gentry, the mer- chants, the artisans of Great Britain and the Colonies, would do more than sword or diplomacy to secure the local affection and devotion of the people of this Presidency. (Applause.)

This resolution also was carried by acclamation.

The Right Rev. Dr. FENNELLY proposed the following resolution :— 'That a vote of thanks be tendered to his Grace the Duke of Buck- ingham and Chandos for the interest his Grace has taken in the raising and distribution of the famine relief fund, and for presiding on the present occasion.'

Bishop FENNELLY said that it gave him very great pleasure to have to move the resolution. He recollected the meeting at which they were all assembled to supplicate for help, and the noble response given to the appeal was well known and acknowledged. In the history of famines, there had been no famine in this country so wide in its extent, and affecting so large a number of people, as the recent famine which troubled the land. The effects of the famine had been such that it became necessary to appeal for help to Great Britain, and the appeal had met with a ready and liberal response. But they all could not but feel that a great part of the success that had attended the appeal was due to the honoured name of the Duke of Buckingham and Chandos. The appeal for help when sent from Madras was accompanied by a statement which contained at the end of it the honoured name of the Duke. In England the Duke of Buckingham and Chandos was much respected and honoured, and if his name had not accompanied the statement sent with the appeal, the response might not have been as liberal as it had been, however great might be the generosity of the people of England. They all therefore had special reason to be thankful to his Grace the Governor for the interest taken by him in the raising of the famine relief fund. He had no doubt that the name of the Duke would be handed down to posterity for the efforts his Grace had made in alleviating the miseries caused by the famine. He had no doubt that the resolution he proposed would be adopted with acclamation. (Great applause.)

The vote being warmly accorded,

HIS GRACE said :—I rise to express my grateful thanks for the way in which the resolution proposed by Dr. Fennelly has been received, and for the kind and flattering words with which it has been proposed and seconded. My reward for any success that we as yet have attained, for any exertions I may have made, is to look upon those around the country who have been saved (applause), although we cannot but regret the loss which the past year has seen. My reward is to look and to think upon those who have been saved by the zealous, energetic efforts of English officers who have devoted their time, their utmost energies, and health to the task of combating the miseries of those amongst whom they were placed; in seeing the noble response which England made to the appeal from this Hall; and to see the good which it has effected in the country, through the zealous, the warm-hearted exertions of these and natives of all castes and creeds combining with Englishmen and others in one common purpose of devoting that fund so as to produce the utmost possible results of good to the people. (Applause.) A year of anxiety has passed, but the lessons which it is calculated to teach remain. The storm is passed, but the ship has yet to be brought into port, and from the lessons of the past year English Governors and English statesmen, combined with the local knowledge of residents and natives of India, must consider well how such a catastrophe may in the future be guarded against and the attacks of famine most promptly staved off whenever, as is probable, they may recur. To secure this end it is difficult to lay down any rules, but these are questions which must in the future occupy the thoughts of those to whom the government of those countries is entrusted, governing as they do, under the wishes of England and of England's Queen, for the good of the people. My view of the duty of a Government in such a country as this is that the safety and the happiness of the people must be the first object of the Government. (Applause.) By that rule I have endeavoured to guide my conduct through the difficulties we have hitherto had to encounter : by that rule I trust I shall govern my conduct as long as it is my lot to rule over this Presidency. (Applause.) I thank you very sincerely for the vote you have passed, I thank all present here most sincerely and cordially for the exertions that they made in the distributions of the large fund entrusted by England to us. (Applause.)

This concluded the business of the meeting, which had lasted nearly three hours.

APPENDIX F.

DAY NURSERIES.

(*From Mrs. L. S. Cornish, Teynampett, Madras.*)

October 1, 1877.

I have the pleasure to send you, according to promise, the following particulars with regard to the Teynampett Nursery.

This Nursery was opened for the purpose of giving one good meal a day to the children residing in the immediate neighbourhood. On September 1, 22 children attended, on the 15th their numbers had increased to 94, and on the 30th to 203. The average daily attendance for the month has been 97½.

The total cost of feeding the children for the month amounted to rs. 123-2-0. 2,920 rations in all were issued, and the cost per head was 8·1 pies.

The classes relieved are chiefly Pariahs, with perhaps 25 per cent of Mussulmans, Moodellys, and Naicks. All were wretched when first entertained, and showed famine signs, but with a few days' feeding they soon began to improve. The food now given is brown bread made of rolong, and raggi conjee mixed with buttermilk. The ration is 7 oz. of bread and ¾ pint of raggi conjee for the big children, and 5 oz. of bread and ½ a pint of conjee for the small ones. The sickly babies get milk in addition, but this I do not buy; it is given me by Mrs. Kindersley.

I said the food now given. On first starting the Nursery, when the numbers were few, I gave brown bread soaked in boiling water with a little milk, and ½ an oz. of sugar, and ½ a pint of buttermilk, to each child. On the 14th of the month, however, there were so many children that I decided to issue conjee instead. It does not take nearly so long to serve out, and the children like it better.

As to the *poverty* of the children there can be no question, from their condition when taken in. Many are orphans and dependent on their grandmothers, aunts, &c. Many more have lost their fathers, and these are generally in sad plight, for if they are young children it is difficult for the mother to leave them and go out to earn a living. Some have both parents alive, but the father in many cases is out of place or, to use the children's expressive phrase, is ' quite at home.'

The cost of establishment in September was almost nothing. I pay a cook 3 and a peon 2 rs. a month. A poor woman whose children are fed helps in serving out the bread in return for her ration, and that is all. Myself and my butler have done all the rest, and are at the Nursery from 1 to 2 hours every morning.

With regard also to a feeding house I have hitherto been spared the cost of building one, as the members of the Boat Club have kindly let me use their sheds while their boats are up at the Adyar, so that for the month of September nearly all the expenditure has been in the shape of food.

As to casualties we have been fortunate. The only death, so far as I know, has been that of a child who was brought in in the last stage of famine. I gave it a cup of white bread and milk, but an hour or two after the mother came and told me it was dead.

In conclusion I may mention that there is an immense deal of want among the class of out-door servants, as punkah men, grass cutters, watermen, etc. Small cultivators also, and salesmen who deal in petty wares, such as betel, are having a terrible time. Even the families of the better class of servants are feeling the long continuance of high prices. It is melancholy to see the state to which many of the poor little creatures who come to the Teynampett Nursery are reduced, and I think no better way can be found of bestowing charity than feeding these helpless little ones.

February, 1878.

For a single meal the following is given in the Teynampett Nursery :—

Brown bread, from 5 to 7 oz.

Raggi conjee (seasoned with salt or sugar, and containing about 1 oz. of raggi flour for each ration) about $\frac{3}{4}$ of a pint to a pint, including the added buttermilk.

Buttermilk, $\frac{1}{4}$ to $\frac{1}{2}$ pint mixed with the conjee.

At the Barber's Bridge, where two meals a day are given, the bread is from 3 to 4 oz. each meal, and the raggi conjee is given with both meals. In both Nurseries new milk is reserved for the little ones, either pure or mixed with conjee.

For children from 3 to 7 years of age the following quantities are suitable for a single meal :—

Fresh brown bread	4 to 8 oz.
Raggi flour in conjee	1 to 1½ „
Sugar	¼ to ½ „
Salt (enough to season conjee)	
Buttermilk	¼ to ½ pint.

If raggi diet is given, raggi flour sifted, from 3 to 5 oz., boiled into a stiff pudding, and seasoned with salt, buttermilk from ¼ to ½ pint, or a curry of dholl and vegetables alternating with buttermilk. If rice is given, raw rice cleaned and boiled, from . . . .   4 to 6 oz.

Buttermilk ½ pint; salt or sugar as above.

N.B.—Rice when boiled should weigh about 3¼ times the weight of dry raw rice.

A curry of vegetables and dholl may be substituted occasionally for the buttermilk.

The average cost of each meal at the Teynampett Nursery is about 8 pies per head, and here only bread, raggi conjee with sugar or salt, and buttermilk, are given. The fresh milk used is contributed by neighbours who are able to spare of their abundance for the wants of the poor, and the cost is not included. A mere statement of the actual cost of provisions is sufficient to show that a native child cannot be fed on the ' 3 pie' allowance, and where the family wages do not come to more than 5 or 6 rupees a month, it will be obvious that both parents and children cannot be properly fed.

APPENDIX G.
WILD PLANTS AND VEGETABLES USED AS FOOD.

MEMORANDUM.

Government having directed a reprint to be made of the list of the wild plants and vegetables used as food by the people in famine times, with the Telugu synonyms and the additions noted in Proceedings of the Board of Revenue, No. 3,121, dated July 3, 1877, the following revised list is published, as desired by Government.

(Signed)   W. R. CORNISH, F.R.C.S.,
Sanitary Commissioner for Madras.

From Surgeon-Major J. Shortt, M.D., Inspector of Vaccination, Madras Presidency, to the Sanitary Commissioner of Madras, dated May 3, 1877, No. 263.

I have the honour to submit a list of most of the wild plants, their roots, leaves, fruits, or seeds, that are eaten by the poor during seasons of drought and famine. I give both the scientific, Tamil and Telugu names in the list, believing that it may prove of interest just now.

2. I commenced the collection first during a visit to Ganjam, in 1870, and have to thank G. H. Ellis, Esq., and J. G. Thompson, Esq., the then collector and judge of that district, who kindly, at my request, procured for me several specimens for identification. Since that I have been adding to the number, and during a tour to the Bellary, Kurnool, and Cuddapah districts in December 1876, at the onset of the present famine, and in the North Arcot and Salem districts during 1877, I collected further information.

3. The list is alphabetically arranged; many of the leaves and young shoots of those used as greens are much more frequently used as *Calavay Keeray* or mixed greens. This is a favourite mode of using them at all seasons, and they are in great repute even among well-to-do people. Women collect the wild greens both as an amusement and occupation, adding at the same time an additional dish to the family meal. Many European and East Indian families are partial to them, as they are said to be healthy and to have a slight laxative action on the bowels ; that they will frequently send their female servants out to collect them.

4. The tender pith and leaf-bud of the Hedge Aloe is only eaten by

the poor from great pressure of hunger, as it is unwholesome and causes dysentery and diarrhœa.

5. Some of the Arum tribe that are used on these occasions are not only unwholesome but poisonous; to avoid their deleterious effects they are repeatedly boiled ere eating. Of the various fruits, they are eaten ripe as they come into season. The banian, peepul, and country fig furnish food not only to the poor people but to cattle also. The kernel of the mango and the tamarind stone are converted into meal and cooked into porridge or baked into cakes, but as they contain a large proportion of tannin they are not healthy, and are only resorted to during seasons of scarcity. The bamboo seed furnishes a kind of rice, which is generally collected by the poor during the season at all times to keep them in food. In most jungles there is always a succession of bamboo in seed every year. The fruit of the prickly-pear is eaten ripe; sometimes the green fruits are boiled. The tender leaves would furnish good vegetable for curry, but are not often resorted to. As the prickly-pear possesses sub-acid or antiscorbutic properties, it is very beneficial to the health both of man and beast. To Mr. H. S. Thomas, the collector of Tanjore, the credit is due of first suggesting and subsequently demonstrating practically its value as cattle fodder by feeding his own cattle on it and exhibiting the same in public, thus proving its utility, and it has been introduced to public notice by Messrs. Harvey and Sabapathy, of Bellary, since. It has not met with general acceptance in consequence of the trouble and difficulty of freeing the leaves of their sharp spines, but there is a spineless variety—*Apuntia delenii*, or Nopaul,[1] with red flowers—which is met with about Madras. I remember seeing lots of it growing about the village of Karanguli, in the district of Chingleput, some years ago. It would be worth while introducing this cactus into the several districts to form cattle fodder, not only during seasons of scarcity, but at all other times.

The *Guazuma tomentosa*, or Bastard Cedar, was introduced into Southern India from South America very many years ago, to be cultivated for supplying cattle with fodder; it is met with about Madras. The woody seeds are sweet from containing sugar, and they are eaten by the poor during seasons of scarcity, but cattle are partial to both leaves and fruits. This tree also yields good fibre, and its extensive cultivation in the several districts is well worthy of

---

[1] This variety of Opuntia was introduced many years ago by the late Dr. James Anderson to feed the cochineal insect. Dr. Anderson used to supply Her Majesty's ships-of-war in the Madras roads with the green leaves, which in those days were used as an antiscorbutic, after being boiled as an ordinary green vegetable.—W. R. C.

attention with a view to supply fodder for cattle during seasons of scarcity. The Bassia, of which there are two varieties, from the fleshy corolla of which most of the semi-wild tribes distil their arrack; the flowers, being sweet-tasted, are eaten raw, boiled or roasted, and the ripe fruits during the season. The kernels furnish a coarse oil, which is used as food. The palmyra tree is too well known for the various useful products it furnishes. The fusiform root of the germinating stone is boiled and sold in the bazaars during the season, as the palmyra tubers or *Pannei Kulungu*; this is also converted into meal, and the stones of the fruit are carefully collected and put down to germinate for the purpose of securing the roots.

I will not extend these remarks further, as the parts used and the mode in which they are prepared are given opposite each plant.

NOTE.—Since this letter was written I have been to the North Arcot district on a tour of inspection, and at the village of Poloor in that district saw several large clumps of the Nopaul or non-spinous cactus growing in a tope. The tahsildar being absent, I sent for the sheristadar or sub-magistrate, and pointed out the Nopaul to him. I brought with me several specimens of the young plant, and, on receiving a note from Mr. Fernandez, of the Government Office, on the subject, I sent these plants to him to present to the Chief Secretary to Government.

At Vellore, near the toll-gate leading towards the central gaol, I also saw several young plants of the Nopaul growing in a hedge with the common spinous cactus.

In Madras there is a fine specimen of the Nopaul to be seen in a house No. 31, on the High Road, Royapooram, and another in the compound of Trinity Chapel, John Pareira's; both these plants were with flower and fruit when seen by me about two months ago.

A LIST OF PLANTS THE VARIOUS PARTS OF WHICH ARE USED AS FOOD BY THE POOR, DURING SEASONS OF DISTRESS, TO APPEASE THE CRAVINGS OF HUNGER.

Scientific Names	Tamil Names	Telugu Names	Remarks
1. Acalypha Indica	Koopay maynei	Hurita munjari	Grows wild : leaves used as greens.
2. Achyranthes aspera	Nahi ooroovie keeray	Ooteraynie	Do. do.
3. Arna lcenata	Kunpolay keeray	Pindie couda	Grows wild, and cultivated; the leaves eaten.
4. Agati grandiflora	Aghati keeray	Agisi, Bakapushpam	Leaves, flowers, and tender legumes largely consumed by the poor, sold in the bazaars, at one pie the pound; when freely eaten causes diarrhœa.
5. Æschynomene aspera	Sudday keeray	Jilugu benda	Grows wild; the leaflets used as greens.
6. Aloe vulgaris	Kuthalay	Kalabanda	Grows wild, the leaf-bud or cabbage and tender pith eaten. The common food of villagers during the famine.
7. Allenanthera sessilis	Poonanghucunny keeray	Madanaganti, Ponnaganti	Grows wild; leaves used as greens.
8. Amaranthus campestris	Siru keeray	Teseri kura	Grows wild, and cultivated; used as greens.
9. " frumentaceus	Poong keray	Tota kura	Grows wild, and cultivated; leaves used as greens, and the seeds converted into meal.
10. " spinosus	Mooloo keeray	Mulugoranta	Grows wild; leaves eaten as greens.
11. " tenuifolius	Kattoo Siroo keeray	Doggali kura	Grows wild; used as greens.
12. " tristis	Kuppei keeray	Koyyatota kura	Do. do. do.
13. Amorphophallus campanulatus	Kuruna kalungu	Konda muncha kunda	Do. about hills and forests, and the tubers boiled and eaten.
14. Aponogeton monostachyon	Kotee kalungu	Nama	Grows wild, found in tanks, brooks, and nullahs; tubers boiled and eaten.
15. Arum lyratum	Kondai rakis	Konda rakis	The roots are eaten after careful boilings.
16. Asystasia coromandeliana	Midchy keeray	Mukku mungera, Tappeta	Grows wild, used as greens.
17. Atriplex heteranthera	Thoyah keeray	Thoya kura	Do. do.

LIST OF PLANTS, &c.—continued.

Scientific Names	Tamil Names	Telugu Names	Remarks
18. Bambusa arundinacea	Mungil arisee	Veduru	Seeds of the bamboo furnish food (rice) to the poor, and the growing young shoots cooked into curries.
19. Bassia longifolia	Elloopei	Ippa	Grows wild; the deciduous fleshy corolla eaten either raw or roasted, and the fruits when ripe. The seed contains a bland oil used in cooking.
20. ,, latifolia	Caat elloopei	Ippe	Do. do. do.
21. Bergera Kœnigii	Karaway pillay	Kari vepa	Do. is also cultivated; fruits eaten.
22. Boerhavia procumbens	Mookaretti keeray	Ataka mamidi	Grows wild; leaves and tender shoots used as greens.
23. ,, repanda	Mookooty keeray	Maidinika	Do. do. do.
24. Borassus flabelliformis	Pannei	Karatalamu, Tatichettu	Fruits and leaf-bud or the cabbage is eaten, as also the fusiform roots.
25. Bryonia rostrati	Appa kovay	Putribudinga	Grows wild; fruits and leaves eaten.
26. Byttneria herbacea	Aree keeray	Aree kura	Grows wild; leaves used as greens.
27. Calladium esculentum	Saimmay keeray	Chama kura	Grows wild; leaves eaten as greens.
28. Cantheum parvifolia	Carray cheddie	Balusoo kura	Grows wild; leaves and young shoots used as greens.
29. Cardiospermum halicacabum	Moodacottan	Budda kankarakoo, or Nella goolisienda	Do. do. do.
30. Caralluma adscendens	Kullee mooliayan	Karallamu, Taviti chettu	Do. tender shoots used, cooked as vegetable.
31. Carissa corindas	Kalakai	Wakay okachettu	Grows wild; fruits are eaten.
32. ,, diffusa	Chotray kalakai	Kalive chettu	Do. do. do.
33. Cassia sophera	Poonaverie	Pydee tanghadu	Do. leaves used as greens.
34. Cathartiocarpus fistula	Koonnay	Rela	Grows wild; the mucilaginous pulp from the pods eaten.
35. Celocia cristata	Punnee keeray	Erra kodi, Juttu tota kura	Grows wild; leaves and young shoots used as greens.
36. Ciscus quadrangularis	Purundei codie	Nullerootigeh	Do. do. do.
37. Cleome pentaphylla	Valay keeray	Vaminta	Do. leaves used as greens.
38. Cocoinia Indica	Covay kai	Donda, Bimbika	Grows wild; ripe fruits eaten.

				Remarks
39.	Colocasia antiquorum	Shamay kilangu	Chama dumpa	Grows wild, and cultivated; leaves and leaf stalks eaten.
40.	Colocasia nymphaeifolia	Karoonay kilangu	Gadda kanda	Grows wild, and cultivated; the tubers are cooked.
41.	Commelina communis	Kannang keeray	Gangi gadda	Grows wild; leaves and tender shoots used as greens.
42.	Corchas olitorius	Kaat thoothee, or Jews' Mallow	Parinta	Grows wild; leaves and tender shoots used as greens.
43.	Cordia myxia	Vidi maram	Iriki, Nakerachettu	Fruits eaten during the season.
44.	Cucumis momordica	Kaat velleri, Pythum kai	Pedda doskay	Grows wild; fruits eaten.
45.	Cynodon dactylon	Aroogum pillo	Garike	Do. tender leaves and shoots eaten.
46.	Desmanthus natans	Sunday keeray	Niru talvapu	Grows wild; the leaves used as greens.
47.	Dioscorea alata	Yams kalung	Niluva pendalum	Several varieties grow wild; tubers eaten cooked.
48.	Dolichos ensiformis	Kaat Thumbuten kai	Tamma	Grows wild; pods cooked into curries, ripe seeds eaten boiled.
49.	Dracontium polyphyllum	Kaat Kurnay	Adive kanda	Grows wild; tubers eaten cooked.
50.	Eleusine Ægyptiaca	Muttengapilloo	Tamida, Sodee	The seed grains are eaten cooked.
51.	Eriodendron anfructuosum	Elevam	Poor	Found in gardens; seeds roasted and eaten.
52.	Erythroxylon areolatum	Davaahdarum keeray	Devadary kura	The tender leaves are used as greens; grows wild
53.	Euphorbia pilulifera	Amumpatchay ar'see	Bidarie, Nauabeeam	Grows wild; leaves and tender shoots eaten as greens.
54.	Ficus Bengalensis	Alamarum	Marri	Fruits of these and other varieties of the ficus are eaten ripe.
55.	,, glomerata	Attee marum	Maydi	Do. do. do.
56.	,, religiosa	Arasa marum	Ray, Raghie	Do. do. do.
57.	Glinus trianthenioides	Sharunnay keeray	Golijeru	Wild; leaves used as greens.
58.	Gisekia pharmacooides	Nunnelli keeray	Isaka dasari kura	Grows wild; the leaves used as greens.
59.	Guazuma tomentosum	Rudrasum	Rudrakscha chettu	The woody fruits when ripe are eaten.
60.	Gynandropsis pentaphylla	Neivaylla or kadughoo	Vala kura	Grows wild; leaves and young shoots used as greens
61.	Holostemma Rheedi*	Palay keeray	Pala kura	Leaves boiled with salt and chillies, and eaten.

LIST OF PLANTS, &c.—continued.

	Scientific names	Tamil Names	Telugu Names	Remarks
62.	Hoya viridiflora	Cooringee keray	......	Grows wild; leaves used as greens.
63.	Inga dulcis	Coorkapooly	Sima chinta	Ripe fruits eaten.
64.	Ipomœa reptans	Vellay keeray	Tegada	Wild; leaves eaten as greens.
65.	,, reniformis	Perretay do.	Toinnatali	Do. do.
66.	,, sepinaria	Thalee do.	Puriti tige.	Do. do.
67.	Leucas aspera	Thombay keeray	Tummi kura	Grows wild; leaves and tender shoots eaten as greens.
68.	Maba buxifolia	Erimbell'e kai	Pishanna	Grows wild; ripe fruits eaten.
69.	Mangifera Indica	Mankai	Mamedi chettu	Fruits and seeds; latter converted into meal.
70.	Melia azadirachta Indica	Veypa marum	Vapa chettu	The ripe fruits are eaten, as they contain a small quantity of sweet pulp between stone and skin
71.	Mimusops elengi	Moghadum	Poghada	The ripe fruits are eaten.
72.	Mirabilis jalapa *	Undi mandarei	Padracha, Nitcha mulligah	The leaves are used as greens largely at Oossoor in the Salem district.
73.	Morinda citrifolia	Munja pavattay	Molagha, Maddi chettu	Grows wild; green fruits curried, ripe eaten.
74.	,, umbellata	Noona kai	Moolooghoodoo	Grows wild; green fruits curried, ripe eaten.
75.	Nymphea edulis	Shunguneer pushpum	Koteka, Kalharanu	Grows wild in tanks; there are two or three varieties according to the colouring of the flowers. The roots and seeds are eaten cooked.
76.	Œgle marmelous	Vilva marum	Maredoo	Grows wild; the ripe fruits are eaten.
77.	Opuntia vulgaris	Chuppauthumoolloo	Nagamala	Grows wild; the ripe fruits are eaten, the green fruits and tender shoots may be cooked into curries.
78.	Oxalis corniculata	Pooliaray	Pullachinta	Grows wild; leaves and tender shoots cooked as greens.
79.	Pandanus odorata	Thalay	Mogheli	Grows wild: the floral leaves are eaten raw or cooked, and the lower part of the drupes of the ripe fruits are sucked of their pulp.
80.	Phaseolus rostratus	Karalsona	Karalsana, Karu alachanda.	Grows wild; the tuberous roots are cooked and eaten.

	Tamil Name	Telugu Name	Remarks
81. Phœnix sylvestris	Ethum pannay	Ita chettu	Grows wild; leaf-bud or cabbage and ripe fruits eaten.
82. „ farinifera	Ethee	Chiruta-ita	Do. do. do
83. Portulacca oleracea	Paroopoo, or corie keeray	Pedda pail kura, Ganga pavilli kura	Grows wild; leaves and tender shoots are cooked and eaten as greens.
84. „ quadrifida	Passelie keeray	Goddu pavelli, Sun pail kura	Do. do. do.
85. Premna serratifolia	Mooney do.	Ghebboon nellie	Do.
86. „ latifolia	Nella do.	Pedda-nella-kura	do.
87. Prosopsis spicigera	Parumbay	Chamee, or Jammi chettu	do. the seeds from the pods are eaten.
88. Remna latifolia*		Nelli kura	These herbs are gathered and boiled with some salt and chillies and eaten.
89. Rivia hypocrateri formis*	Boodthee keeray	Boddi kura	Do. do.
90. Rothia trifoliata	Nurreypitten keeray	Nucka kura	Grows wild; leaves and legumes used as greens.
91. Salicornia bracheata	Oomarie keeray	Quoiloo, or Koyaloo	Grows wild; leaves and shoots used as greens.
92. „ Indica	Pavala poondoo	Koyya pippali	Used as a pot herb.
93. Salsola Indica	Yella keeray	Yella kura	Wild; leaves used as greens, largely resorted to during famines.
94. Schleichera trijuga	Poomarum, Conjee marum	May Roa Tanglia	Grows wild; ripe fruits are eaten.
95. Schmidelia serrata	Tanalika	Tanalike korra chettu	Grows wild; fruits are eaten.
96. Sesuvium portulacustrum	Vungaravasee		The leaves and tender shoots used as a pot herb; grows wild.
97. Sethia Indica	Tavadrum, Semmanatty	Adivi gerenta, Davadary	Grows wild; leaves and tender shoots eaten as greens. This tree has afforded food to many thousands of people during the famine.
98. Solanum incertum	Munnuthakalee	Kakamachi	Grows wild; leaves and young shoots used as greens, ripe fruits eaten.
99. Solanum jacquini	Cundung katrie	Van kuda, or Nella molunga	Grows wild; fruits are cooked into curries.
100. Solanum torvum	Soonday kai	Choondai kai	Grows wild; fruits used as a vegetable.
101. Spondas mangifera	Mirrey manga	Ambra, or amra journ, Mamedi	Grows wild; leaves used as greens, fruits cooked into curries and pickled.

LIST OF PLANTS, ETC.—*continued.*

Scientific Names	Tamil Names	Telugu Names	Remarks
102. Sterculia foetida	Peenaree marum	Gurapa Badam chettu	Grows wild; the roasted seeds are eaten.
103. Strychnos potatorum	Tettan cottay marum	Toillaghenjaloo, Induga	Grows wild; fruits when ripe are eaten.
104. Sueda Indica	Koyey kaseeray keeray	Kodee kasseery kura	Used as a pot herb; grows wild.
105. Syzygium jambolanum	Navel	Neradi	Grows wild; ripe fruits are eaten.
106. Tamarindus Indica	Poolia marum	Chinta chettu	Leaves, young shoots, fruits, and seeds are eaten, the latter converted into meal.
107. Toddalia aculeata	Moolacarney	Conda cashnida	Grows wild; leaves are used as greens.
108. Trapa bispinosa	Singahara	Kubyakam	Grows wild; seeds are cooked and eaten.
109. Trianthema oboordata	Sharunnay	Ghelijehroo	Do. leaves and tender shoots used as greens.
110. Trianthema obcordata *Var.*	Shavalay keeray	Tella ghelijeghroo	Grows wild; leaves used as greens.
111. Trichianthis cucumera	Popoodel	Chayud potta	Grows wild; fruits curried.
112. Trilobus terristus	Nerrenjee keeray	Palleroo	Do. leaves used as greens.
113. Urtica tuberosa		Pilli dumpa	Grows wild; tuberous roots boiled and eaten.
114. Vellarsia cristata*	Nedel ampel	Alli gadda, Antara tamara	This is a species of water lily found in tanks and wells. The substance found in the plant is cooked or merely boiled and eaten.
115. Xanthochymus pictorius		Jevra memadie	Grows wild; ripe fruits.
116. Ximenia Americana		Oora nechra, Konda nakkera	Do. do.
117. Zizyphus jujuba	Yellanday kai	Reygoo	Ripe fruits.
118. Zeptadenia reticulata†	Palacoody	Kalasa	The leaves and tender shoots used as a vegetable in the Vinucondah taluk, Kistna, at all times.

† This plant was sent to me by the collector of Kistna for identification, with the statement ' that it was eaten by the villagers of Vinucondah taluk as a vegetable, but which they are now using as food.' I have identified it as the Zeptadenia reticulata.

(Signed) J. SHORTT.

NOTE.—Names marked thus * are taken from Mr. H. Yarde's (of the Forest Department) list.

(Signed) J. SHORTT, M.D., Surgeon-Major,

WILD HERBS &c. USED AS FOOD IN THE KALADGI DISTRICT OF THE BOMBAY PRESIDENCY DURING THE FAMINE.

Descriptive Notes by Mr. James MacNabb Campbell, of the Bombay Civil Service, and Remarks thereon by Dr. Wellington Gray, Professor of Botany, Grant Medical College, Bombay.

CLASS I.

EATEN IN ALL SEASONS.

No. 1.

[1] (*S.*) *Bahudugdhi.*	(*M.*) *Jati.*
(*K.*) *Háli.*	(*H.*) *Háli.*

A climbing creeper, with white flowers. A favourite vegetable in all seasons, and said to be perfectly wholesome.

Remark by Dr. W. Gray.—No. 1 appears to be the leaf of an *Asclepiad*, possibly of *Cosmostigma acuminatum*. Its identity is, however, too doubtful to admit of my venturing any remarks as to the properties or uses of the specimen.

No. 2.

(*S.*) *Chágeri.*	(*M.*) *Mábli.*
(*K.*) *Mábli, Nyábali.*	(*H.*) *Nyábali.*

A plant about two feet high, with a white flower and small round fruit. Is used, in ordinary years, both as a vegetable and as a medicine. As a vegetable, the leaves are boiled and mixed with pulse. As a medicine, in cases of fever the juice is poured into the ear. It is not eaten by animals. As a vegetable, if taken in large quantities, this plant is said to cause diarrhœa.

Remark by Dr. Gray.—No. 2 is a leaf of *Gynandropsis pentaphylla*, a plant of the natural order *Capparideæ*; it is a common annual weed, and no doubt possesses, like many other species of the same order, antiscorbutic properties. The leaves are eaten as a vegetable, and bruised when fresh are applied as a counter-irritant in inflammations. The seeds are used as a substitute for mustard. As regards Mr. Campbell's statement, that the vegetable when eaten in large quantities causes diarrhœa, I cannot speak with any degree of certainty.

[1] *S.* stands for Sanscrit, *M.* for Maráthi, *K.* for Kanarese, *H.* for Hindustani.

No. 3.

(*S.*) *Jarjeri.*   (*M.*) *Kurdu.*
(*K.*) *Gorji.*   (*H.*) *Gorji.*

A plant, about six inches high, with a white flower. The leaves are at all times a favourite vegetable. It is not used as a medicine, and is eaten by cattle. Though in common use as a vegetable, this plant is said to be unsafe, except in small quantities, bringing on diarrhœa.

Remark by Dr. Gray.—No. 3 is *Amblogyna polygonoides*, belonging to the natural order *Amarantaceœ*, and a very common weed in cultivated ground. It is much used as a pot herb, and reckoned exceedingly wholesome. So far as I am aware, it does not bring on diarrhœa.

No. 4.

(*S.*) *Kaunti.*   (*M.*) *Negli.*
(*K.*) *Negli.*   (*H.*) *Negli.*

A low-growing plant, with a small yellow flower and round thorny fruit. Is used, in ordinary years, both as a vegetable and as a medicine. As a vegetable, the young leaves are eaten with salt, chillies, and other condiments. As a medicine, the fruit is used as a tonic in cases of fever. The older stems and leaves are gathered as fodder for cattle. As a vegetable, this plant is said to be pleasant to the taste and perfectly wholesome.

Remark by Dr. Gray.—No. 4 is *Polygala chinensis*—natural order *Polygaleœ*. It grows in most parts of the Deccan. Mr. Campbell's remarks as regards its uses are, as far as I know, correct.

No. 5.

(*S.*) *Madhuvrita.*   (*M.*) *Bárik Ghol.*
(*K.*) *Nuchgoli.*   (*H.*) *Nuch Ghol.*

A small plant, with a light-coloured flower. Is, in ordinary years, eaten by people of all classes. As a vegetable, the leaves are boiled and eaten with condiments. It is not used as a medicine, nor as fodder for cattle. As a vegetable it is said to be bitter to the taste, but safe and wholesome.

Remark by Dr. Gray.—No. 5 is *Portulaca quadrifida*, of the natural order *Portulacaceœ*, and a common annual weed in many parts of the Bombay Presidency. It is ordinarily used as a vegetable.

No. 6.

(*S.*) *Madhuvrita.*   (*M.*) *Moti Ghol.*
(*K.*) *Dod Goli.*   (*H.*) *Badi Ghol.*

A low-growing plant, with white flowers, whose young leaves are at all times a favourite vegetable. It is not used as a medicine, nor as fodder for cattle. As a vegetable, through wholesome in moderation, if taken in large quantities this plant is said to cause diarrhœa.

Remark by Dr. Gray.—No. 6 is *Portulaca oleracea*, better known perhaps as Purslane, a widely-distributed plant. It is cultivated in Western India as a pot herb, and possesses antiscorbutic properties.

No. 7.

(*S.*) *Moshiki.*   (*M.*)
(*K.*) *Ilikivi.*   (*H.*) *Chivikikán.*

A creeper, with a green-coloured flower. A favourite vegetable, used at all times, and said to be perfectly wholesome.

Remark by Dr. Gray.—No. 7 is probably *Tylophora mollissima*, of the natural order *Asclepiadeœ*. Its identity is also doubtful.

No. 8.

(*S.*) *Pithari.*   (*M.*) *Pitpapáda.*
(*K.*) *Kalsabasgi.*   (*H.*) *Fatarsoi.*

A low-growing plant, with rose-coloured flowers. The leaf is eaten, in ordinary years, as a vegetable. In medicine, it is used as a remedy for fever. Cattle do not eat it. As a vegetable it is said to be perfectly wholesome.

Remark by Dr. Gray.—No. 8 is a leaf of *Glossocardia boswellia*, a small annual plant of the natural order *Compositœ*, and a rather common weed in dry ground. With regard to its use as a vegetable, I am unable to speak from personal experience. It is said to be employed medicinally in certain diseases of women.

No. 9.

(*S.*) *Tashta.*   (*M.*) *Tákla.*
(*K.*) *Takkarsoni.*   (*H.*) *Tarotu.*

A small bush, growing to about two feet high, with yellow flowers and pods. The young leaves are at all times a favourite vegetable. It is not used as medicine, or as fodder for cattle. The seed yields a blue dye. As a vegetable, it is said to be pleasant to the taste, and wholesome.

Remark by Dr. Gray.—No. 9 is the leaf of a leguminous plant—
Cassia Tora. This is an exceedingly abundant annual in grass lands
throughout the Deccan. Mr. Campbell's remarks on the plant are
correct.

No. 10.

(*S.*) *Shatávari.*   (*M.*)
(*K.*) *Dágadi.*   (*H.*) *Dágadi.*

A creeper, with no marked flower or fruit. The leaves are, in
ordinary seasons, eaten by the poor. It is not used as a medicine, and
is given to milch cows, and to increase their yield of milk. As a
vegetable, this plant is said to be perfectly wholesome.

Remark by Dr. Gray.—No. 10 is *Cocculus villosus*, a slender
climbing plant, found in nearly every part of Western India, and
belonging to the natural order *Menispermaceæ.* A decoction of the
fresh root is given as an alterative in cases of rheumatism and
syphilis. The leaves, rubbed up with water, form a jelly, which is
also taken for the same diseases. I am not aware that the plant is
used simply as a vegetable, but the leaves are eaten as such by persons
who are undergoing a course of the root decoction. Goats and cattle
feed on it.

CLASS II.

EATEN IN TIMES OF FAMINE.

No. 1.

(*L.*) *Aml.*   (*M.*) *Chinch.*
(*K.*) *Hunchi.*   (H.) *A'mli.*

The leaf of the tamarind tree, in ordinary years, is not eaten as a
vegetable, or used as a medicine. Cattle eat it. At present it is used
as a vegetable. But it is said to be unwholesome, and, even when
taken in small quantities, to have a weakening effect.

Remark by Dr. Gray.—No. 1 is a leaf of the tamarind. The
pounded seeds of this tree are commonly eaten in seasons of scarcity,
and were largely consumed by the people during the late famine. It
is highly probable that the leaves produce the effects mentioned by
Mr. Campbell.

No. 2.

(*S.*) *Jillika.*   (*M.*) *Gokaru.*
(*K.*) *Valamuchyaka.*   (*H.*) *Bada Gokaru.*

A low-growing plant, with yellow flowers, not eaten as a vegetable
in ordinary years. As a medicine, it is used in cases of colic ; and its

juice is said to be strong enough to stupify a scorpion. Cattle eat it. The leaves are at present used as a vegetable by the poorer classes. They are said to be unwholesome, and, if taken in large quantities, to cause diarrhœa.

Remark by Dr. Gray.—No. 2 is *Tribulus terrestris*, a small creeping plant of the natural order *Zygophylleæ*. It is abundant in all Deccan pasture lands. As a medicine, it is said to be aperient and diuretic. Except in times of scarcity, it is seldom eaten as a vegetable. Judging from its harsh nature, I should imagine it to be very difficult of digestion.

No. 3.

(*S.*) *Kaunti.*   (*M.*)
(*K.*) *Tondasi.*   (*H.*)

A hill shrub, with no marked flower or fruit. In ordinary years, though not eaten as a vegetable, its juice, mixed with whey, is a common remedy in cases of diarrhœa. Cattle do not feed on it. At present the leaves are eaten by the poorer classes. They are said to have no unwholesome qualities.

Remark by Dr. Gray.—No. 3 is a leaf of *Corchorus trilocularis*, an annual plant of the natural order *Tiliaceæ*, and found in parts of the Deccan. I see no reason why this plant should not be used as a vegetable in ordinary as well as in famine seasons ; it resembles in properties another species, *C. olitorius*, the well-known jute, which is much eaten in Western India as a pot-herb. Medicinally, it is, like the other members of the genus, possessed of demulcent properties.

No. 4.

(*S.*) *Trin Gharmu.*   (*M.*) *Gavat.*
(*K.*) *Hitgoni.*   (*H.*) *Hitgovi.*

A somewhat broad fleshy-leaved grass, growing in clusters; is not, in ordinary years, used either as a vegetable or as a medicine. Cattle feed on it. During the past two months (June and July, 1877), in places where the supply of wild herbs is scanty, this grass has formed a very common article of food. Used in this way, it is said to be unwholesome, causing dropsy and diarrhœa.

Remark by Dr. Gray.—No. 4 is *Commelyna communis*, of the natural order *Commelynaceæ*. It is a spreading weed—not a ' grass,' as Mr. Campbell states—growing abundantly in moist grass lands in the Deccan. Cattle eat it. The dropsy and diarrhœa, said to result from its use as an article of food, may, with greater probability, be attributed to the previous reduced and scorbutic condition of the consumer. The same observation will apply to other unusual articles of diet, which are asserted to produce disease ; these are not resorted to, as a means of sustaining life, till the people are already suffering from the results of chronic starvation and scurvy. The phenomena of such a condition of body are at once laid to the door of the strange diet, to which the people have hitherto been unaccustomed. No doubt, this food is sometimes more or less difficult of digestion, thus giving rise to diarrhœa and other bowel disorders. It cannot be doubted, however, that, in a large majority of cases, disease attributed to an unusual kind of food is, in reality, the result of starvation and the use of inferior kinds of ordinary food.

No. 5.

(S.) Vrindi.   *(M.) Bhui Taravad.*
(K.) Nalavari.   *(H.) Tarota.*

A small creeping plant, with white flowers and fruit. In ordinary seasons its only use is as a cattle medicine in cases of colic. At present the leaves are eaten as a vegetable. It is very bitter to the taste, and is said to be unwholesome.

Remark by Dr. Gray.—No. 5 is the leaf of a species of *Indigofera*, probably *I. trifoliata*, of the natural order *Leguminosæ*. Its identity is doubtful however, and I am consequently unable to offer any decided opinion on Mr. Campbell's remarks. Many species of *Indigofera* are indigenous to Western India. Cattle eat *I. enneaphylia* greedily, and the seeds of *I. glandulosa*, the commonest species of all, are eaten, as pulse, by the people in seasons of scarcity.

General Remarks by Dr. Gray.

I may take this opportunity of mentioning that, besides the plants noted above, there are numerous other indigenous species—herbs, shrubs, and trees—which afford sustenance to the poorer classes during periods of famine. About the end of last rainy season, Mr. Richey, the Collector of Dharwar, forwarded to me the dried fragments of between twenty and thirty kinds of herbaceous plants, which were said to have been used as food by the famine immigrants into his districts. These specimens are, however, so imperfect, and in many cases immature, that I have been unable to determine the botanical names of more than a few. Some are identical with Mr. Campbell's specimens; amongst the others there are several species of *Amarantaceæ*, an order which furnishes a considerable number of the pot-herbs which are ordinarily eaten by the people of this country. I also observe in Mr. Richey's collection *Oxalis corniculata*, a very common creeping plant; the leaf of an *Alæcasiæ*, together with some examples of the natural orders *Leguminosæ, Compositæ,* and *Urticaceæ.*

I trust it will not be thought out of place if I here suggest the advisability of causing a complete collection to be formed of all the indigenous plants which were used as exceptional articles of diet by the lower classes who inhabit the districts affected by the late famine. When the plant is small and of convenient size, the dried specimen should consist of the entire leaf or shrub, with its flower and fruit. If large, a flowering branch, together with some of the fruit and seed, would be sufficient. Each should be accompanied by its native names; its area of distribution should, as far as possible, be ascertained; information should be given as to what districts it is most used in; the parts of the plant which are eaten; the classes who eat it; the effects it is said to produce; and whether it is ever employed medicinally. In fact, the full history of the plant and its uses should be furnished. The complete specimens, carefully gathered and dried, can then be easily identified botanically, and any particulars of scientific interest they may possess added. With their histories detailed as above suggested, the entire collection would form a standard famine herbarium for present or future reference; and the value of such a collection it would be difficult to over-estimate.

GOVERNMENT RELIEF

Perhaps it would not be possible to give English readers a better idea of the extent
following statement, which

FAMINE

Statement showing the Particulars of Expenditure from Famine Advance Account in the District of

Taluks	Relief works	Relief camps	Gratuitous relief	Purchase of grain	Carriage of grain
Collector's Div.—	rs. a. p.	rs. a. p.	rs. a. p.	rs. a. p.	rs. a. p.
Cuddapah Taluk	1,32,605 14 1	3,316 15 10	6,215 6 3	305 0 0	6,026 3 4
Sub-Collector's Division—					
Roachoti Taluk .	1,74,933 7 1½	5,516 0 1	4,901 4 9	1,965 1 6	5,066 14 6
Kadiri „ .	2,72,049 3 2	2,990 10 11	2,087 8 6	11,175 11 0	5,215 13 8
Voilpaud „ .	3,43,977 14 2½	1,157 10 0	2,751 3 4½	1,823 0 8	10,551 13 2
Madanapalli Taluk	3,14,516 9 6	2,714 0 0	12,937 15 10	20,000 0 0	9,056 1 9
Head Assistant Collector's Div.—					
Budwail Taluk .	1,11,133 6 10¼	1,496 8 0	8,395 14 3	—	1,438 12 2
Sidhout „ .	56,756 5 0	1,497 11 1	2,657 2 7	—	1 2 6
Pullampett Taluk	1,42,272 0 2	2,804 0 9	19,079 6 6	—	—
General Dep.-Collector's Div.— .					
Proddatur Taluk	63,591 8 3	3,719 2 0½	5,841 15 0½	1,021 7 10	742 0 4
Jammalamadgu Taluk . . .	1,15,838 14 2	1,464 10 6½	10,639 5 1¼	329 14 9	215 12 0
Temporary Dep.-Collector's Div.—					
Pulivendla Taluk	1,68,842 5 5	1,438 0 1¼	12,890 9 3	—	—
Total . . .	18,96,517 7 11¼	28,115 5 4½	88,397 11 5½	36,620 3 9	38,314 9 5
Huzur . .	20,500 0 0	—	—	80,000 0 0	—
Grand Total	19,17,017 7 11¼	28,115 5 4½	88,397 11 5½	1,16,620 3 9	38,314 9 5

* Loans under Land Improvement Act .
Advance to Weavers . . . .
Balance in hand . . . .

Total . . . . .

CUDDAPAH: *September 28, 1877.*

DPERATIONS.

lo which Government operations for relief have extended, than by publishing the relates to one district only :—

RELIEF.

Cuddapah, called for in Board's Proceedings, No. 766, dated February 21, 1877, to June 15, 1877.

Digging, &c., wells	Cost of materials	Miscellaneous payments	Total	Balance in hand	Grand total
rs. a. p.	rs. a. p.	rs. a. p.	rs. a. p.	rs. a. p.	rs. a. p.
—	1,018 7 0	8,171 11 5	1,57,659 9 11	17,082 0 3	1,74,741 10 2
—	639 11 7	8,000 3 6	2,01,022 11 0½	33,536 11 10	2,34,559 6 10½
—	218 10 6	8,566 9 11	3,02,304 3 8½	1,700 0 0	3,04,004 3 8½
—	403 5 0	2,448 15 0	3,63,113 13 5	8,291 0 0	3,71,404 13 5
—	46 4 0	13,568 9 9	3,72,839 8 10	8,961 12 0	3,11,801 4 10
8,422 0 1	—	6,141 15 0¾	1,37,028 8 5	23,037 14 5½	1,60,066 6 10½
—	—	6,617 14 11	67,530 4 1	5,255 0 9	72,785 4 10
1,352 4 0	3,349 10 6	2,279 15 10	1,71,137 5 9	12,591 8 7	1,83,728 14 4
—	297 3 6	4,377 1 9	79,590 6 9	23,049 9 3	1,02,640 0 0
—	6 9 0	2,819 6 1½	1,31,314 7 8½	13,757 9 7½	1,45,072 1 4
—	264 4 1	3,673 1 3	1,87,108 4 1½	25,717 11 10½	2,12,826 0 0
9,774 4 1	6,244 1 2	66,665 8 6¼	21,70,649 3 9	1,72,980 14 7½	23,43,630 2 4½
—	—	24 0 0	1,00,524 0 0	—	1,00,524 0 0
9,774 4 1	6,244 1 2	66,689 8 6¼	22,71,173 3 9	*1,72,980 14 7½	24,44,154 2 4½

rs. a. p.
1,27,196 2 8
570 10 9
45,214 1 2½

1,72,980 14 7½

(Signed)   M. RAMASAWMY, Deputy Collector.